16 —

Vivian Thomas

G000149515

A
Comprehensive
English Grammar

FOR FOREIGN STUDENTS

C. E. ECKERSLEY, M.A.

AND

J. M. ECKERSLEY, M.A.

LONGMAN

LONGMAN GROUP LIMITED
London

Associated companies, branches and representatives
throughout the world

© C. E. Eckersley and J. M. Eckersley 1960

All rights reserved. No part of this publication amy be reproduced, stored in a retrieval system, or transmitted in any form or by any means, electronic, mechanical, photocopying, recording, or otherwise, without the prior permission of the Copyright owner.

First published 1960
*Ninth impression *1970*

ISBN 0 582 52040 1 Cased edition
ISBN 0 582 52042 8 Paper edition

Printed in Hong Kong by
Dai Nippon Printing Co (International) Ltd

CONTENTS

iii

PREFACE

THIS grammar has been prepared with three objectives in view. First, while covering in an up-to-date manner the ground common to all English grammars, it is designed particularly to meet the needs of the *foreign* student of English. So, for example, the tenses of the verb, the use of prepositions and 'phrasal verbs', the articles, and word order are dealt with in considerable detail; many examples are given of the commonest sentence patterns in English; and there are tables showing the uses of the determinative words —all frequent sources of difficulty to the foreign student.

Secondly, it is intended to be really comprehensive, in that it will, as far as possible, provide an answer to any grammatical problem the student of English is likely to encounter. Brief accounts of the history of the language and of the phonetics and intonation of English have been included also, since these matters—although not strictly 'grammar'—are bound to be of interest and importance to most students of the language.

Lastly, it is meant to be a *practical* grammar, one that is suitable both for work in class and for students working on their own; so it is provided with a very full index and with plenty of exercises.[1]

Although this grammar has not been directed at any particular examination, the needs of examination candidates have been borne in mind, and it should give ample material to prepare students for the English language papers set in any of the usual examinations.

Our thanks are due to Mr. H. W. Acomb, M.A., and to Mr. S. C. White, M.A., for their assistance in the preparation of the exercises and the Key.

C. E. E.
J. M. E.

[1] A Key to the Exercises is published separately.

INTRODUCTION

Most of the earlier grammarians, particularly those of the eighteenth century when the English language was being 'systematized', held the view that one of their functions, perhaps their main function, was to keep the language 'pure', to stamp out errors that were constantly creeping in and to formulate rules that would keep the language on the course they believed it ought to take. The rules were based on Latin syntax, and it was into this Procrustean bed that the grammarians tried to fit the English language, largely disregarding the fact that English was no longer, as it once had been, a highly inflected language. In fact, in the whole of modern English there are really only two major inflections[1] and four or five minor ones[2], for the English language has changed in the 1,500 years that it has been in England from being a synthetic to an analytic one in which inflection has been practically entirely replaced by two other phenomena: (1) Structural words (like *from, in, shall, may, ought, etc.*), and (2) Word Order.

The grammarian of to-day no longer believes that he should attempt the impossible task of 'controlling' the language and directing the course that he thinks it ought to take; he realizes that English is a living language, constantly changing and developing in accordance not with man's laws but with its own genius. Nor does he think that the function of a grammar book is to lay down laws to teach people how they *ought* to speak and write. His task is simply to state how, so far as he can judge, certain people *do* speak and write at the present time. The grammar of a language is the scientific record of the actual phenomena of that language, written and spoken. So, in the present volume we have tried to present the facts of modern English usage so far as we could ascertain them; any

[1] For Number in Nouns and Past Tense in Verbs.
[2] For Genitive of Nouns, Objective forms of Pronouns, Comparison of some Adjectives, 3rd Person Singular in the Simple Present Tense of some Verbs, and a few remnants of the Subjunctive Mood.

'rules' that we have given are merely conclusions drawn from these facts. If at any time a rule does not coincide with the usage, it is the rule that is wrong, and it will be the job of future grammarians to change it.

EXERCISES

I From your own experience in learning English, try to explain how important you consider the study of grammar to be in learning a foreign language.

II Do you consider that the study of grammar is more important or less important in learning English than it is in learning your own native language? Give reasons for your answer.

III The Introduction to this book says, on page one: 'English has changed from a synthetic language to an analytic one'. Compare this with what has happened in your own language and say whether you think this change has made English easier or more difficult for the foreign student to learn.

IV In your opinion, does the abandonment of belief in grammatical rules tend towards a deterioration in the style and quality of a language as it is used in everyday life?

CHAPTER ONE

THE PARTS OF SPEECH

The words that compose the English language—or any other language—can be classified in various ways. Much time and effort has been spent in trying to settle what names should be given to these categories. It seems to us that there is little point in giving anything but the most general definitions of the Parts of Speech, in the first place because it is almost impossible to give a definition which is exact and comprehensive, or with which every grammarian would agree; secondly because it is hardly necessary, since the conception of 'Noun', 'Verb', etc., will almost certainly be familiar to the student in his own language. It seems to us more important that the student should be given examples of the various Parts of Speech and should see, as he will in the pages that follow, exactly how these words behave. We have therefore adhered, in the main, to the traditional,[1] most familiar definitions. Under this system all the words in the English language can be grouped, according to the work they do, into eight classes. These are the *Parts of Speech*.

They are:

I. Words that are the names of things or people or places, e.g.

house, hat, iron, Mary, Russia, London, sweetness, speech, crowd, army.

Words that do this work are called NOUNS.

II. Words that can be used instead of nouns, so that we can refer to people or things without really naming them and being compelled to repeat the names too frequently, e.g.

[1] Professor C. C. Fries, the former Director of the English Language Institute of the University of Michigan and perhaps the most iconoclastic of modern grammarians, writes:

'On the whole, I believe it will be found that most of the traditional terms, though often badly named, correspond to real facts and distinctions in the linguistic material. It may reasonably be doubted whether a serviceable grammar which dispenses entirely with such terms as noun and verb will ever be written. . . . To my mind it is not so much the traditional terms that are unacceptable as the explanations of them which are normally given.'

3

I, you, them, who, that, himself, someone.

Words that do this are called PRONOUNS.

III. Words that qualify a noun by making its meaning clearer, fuller, or more exact. *Examples:*

a *bad* egg, a *blue* dress, the book is *new*.

Words that do this are called ADJECTIVES.

There are a number of words of various types that are sometimes grouped as adjectives, words, for example, like *a(n), the, some, each, no, much*, etc. These are discussed in the section Determinatives. (Chapter Ten.)

IV. Words that express the idea of action or being, that affirm that a person or thing is, does or suffers something. *Examples:*

The boys *played* football.

He *is* hungry.

The enemy *was defeated*.

Words of this kind are called VERBS.

V. Words that we can add to a verb to make its meaning clearer, fuller or more exact. *Examples:*

He ran *quickly*. I saw him *yesterday*.

Words like these are ADVERBS.

VI. Words that are used with nouns or pronouns (generally, but not always, being placed in front of them) and show the relationship between the noun or pronoun and another word, often expressing abstract relationship of case or of time or place. *Examples:*

I sent the parcel *to* him; it went *by* air mail. The smoke went *up* the chimney. The desk was *near* the window.

Words that do work like this are PREPOSITIONS.

VII. Words that are used to join words, phrases or sentences. *Examples:*

Jack *and* Jill; a boy with a dirty face *but* a pleasant smile.

He worked hard *because* he wanted to succeed.

Words like this are CONJUNCTIONS.

VIII. Words that express a sudden feeling or emotion. These words do not enter into the syntactical construction of the sentence. *Examples:*

Hello! Oh! Ah!

Words like these are INTERJECTIONS.

CLASSIFICATION BY FUNCTION

It is most important to remember that words are classified into parts of speech according to their function, that is according to the work that they do and not according to their form. There are in fact a great many words that can be two, three or even more parts of speech according to the work they do. Take for example these sentences.

(1) He came by a very *fast* train.
(2) William ran very *fast*.
(3) They are going to *fast* for three days; during that time they won't eat anything.
(4) At the end of his three day *fast* he will have a very light meal.

In (1) *fast* is an adjective, in (2) it is an adverb, in (3) a verb, and in (4) a noun.

Or note the differing uses of *watch* in:

My father gave me a *watch* for my birthday.

I am going to *watch* a football match.

Rex is a good *watch* dog.

Or of *spring* in:

The *spring* of my watch is broken.

The dog tried to *spring* over the gate.

I love *spring* flowers.

Words like *drink, look, smoke, wash, swim, drive, try* are all generally used as verbs, but, especially in familiar conversation, we put 'have a' before them ('have a drink, look, try, etc.'), and they become nouns. Words like *shoulder, head, finger, eye, elbow, hand*, etc., are generally nouns; but we can '*shoulder* our way', '*head* a football or a procession', '*finger* an object', '*eye* a person', '*elbow* someone else aside' or '*hand* him a cup of tea'. And then these words are all verbs.

EXERCISES

I Use the following words as (*a*) nouns, and (*b*) verbs:
house, iron, crowd, tie, smoke, dress, air, book, step.

II Use the following as (*a*) nouns, and (*b*) verbs, and indicate the change in pronunciation:

> *object, present, record, produce, conflict, conduct, desert, contest, permit.*

Add to the list of such words.

III Substitute pronouns for the nouns and noun phrases underlined in the following sentences, which are impossible or inelegant as they stand:

1. John looked at Mary, but Mary was looking at Mary in the looking-glass.
2. If you don't want the paper, give it to a person who does.
3. The speaker looked his questioner in the eye; then the speaker gave his questioner his answer.
4. Oxford (Oxford is famous for its university) is now becoming industrialized.

IV(*a*) Insert suitable adjectives where the dashes stand:

1. We didn't see each other again for a —— time.
2. In spite of his —— strength he was —— to swim across the —— river, as the current was too ——.
3. The car turned the corner at —— speed.
4. The —— cat lay sleeping in the —— sunshine.
5. The door is —— but the windows are ——.

IV(*b*) Insert suitable adverbs where the dashes stand:

1. It was —— getting dark when we began to climb the —— rising incline.
2. The men were not —— —— awake.
3. He was —— accused of the crime and —— acquitted.
4. I —— have eggs and bacon for breakfast, but —— I take fish.
5. Have you —— been to the Zoo? Yes, I —— go there.

V Name the parts of speech of the words underlined in the following sentences:

1. It's hard work, but I know you can work hard.
2. He's dead keen to get on, but now that his best friend is dead, he is finding life deadly monotonous. Monotony is nearly always deadly.
3. He struck low. Climb high. The flowers look nice. Cut the slices thin.

VI Make sentences using each of the following words as two different parts of speech (not necessarily in the same sentence), and say what parts of speech they are:

August (august); alternate; minute; invalid; absent; frequent.

[*N.B.*—Mark where the stress falls in each example.]

VII Pick out the verbs in this passage and classify them as expressing (i) action, (ii) a state.

John was late. He hurried down to breakfast, said something to his father, which the latter did not seem to understand, glanced at the clock, got even more worried and rushed out of the house. He doubted whether he would ever become manager, for he had been reprimanded too often for not being punctual.

VIII Pick out four prepositions and three conjunctions from the passage in question VII.

IX Replace the dashes by suitable interjections or exclamations:

(*a*) ——, I did not succeed! (*b*) ——, where have you been all this time? (*c*) —— no, I really couldn't! (*d*) —— there's a car coming! (*e*) ——, I *knew* that would happen!

X Arrange the words in the following passage in columns according to the parts of speech which they are:

'It must not be imagined that a walking tour, as some would have us fancy, is merely a better or worse way of seeing the country. There are many ways of seeing landscape quite as good; and none more vivid, in spite of canting dilettantes, than from a railway train. But landscape on a walking tour is quite accessory. He who is indeed of the brotherhood does not voyage in quest of the picturesque, but of certain jolly humours—of the hope and spirit with which the march begins at morning, and the peace and spiritual repletion of the evening's rest. . . .'

Robert Louis Stevenson, *Walking Tours.*

XI Explain, and illustrate in sentences, two senses in which the following words can be used. Name the part of speech of each:

(1) sound. (2) oil. (3) master. (4) clear. (5) speed. (6) water. (7) deal. (8) butter. (9) ring. (10) police.

XII Define the functions of the eight parts of speech and give two examples of each with words not already used in chapter 1.

CHAPTER TWO

THE SIMPLE SENTENCE

SUBJECTS AND OBJECTS

A Simple sentence[1] is one that contains a finite[2] verb (and only one finite verb). It does one of four things:

(1) makes a statement;
(2) asks a question;
(3) gives a command or makes a request;
(4) makes an exclamation.

Examples:

Mr. Brown teaches this class. (*Statement*)
Do you understand me? (*Question*)
Open the door. (*Command*)
Please help me with my work. (*Request*)
How cold it is! (*Exclamation*)

A sentence is composed, usually, of two parts, the SUBJECT and the PREDICATE. Take, for example, the following sentences:

The boy hit the dog. The dog bit the boy.
The girl read the books. The books pleased the girl.

We can divide them like this:

1	2
The boy	hit the dog.
The dog	bit the boy.
The girl	read the books.
The books	pleased the girl.

In the first part there is a person (or thing) that we are talking about. The second part is what we say about this person or thing. Part 1 is the subject, Part 2 is the predicate. The subject of a sentence is the word (or group of words) denoting the person or thing about which something is said.

[1] Sentences and clauses are dealt with fully on pages 318 to 358.
[2] For finite and non-finite verbs see p. 143.

The predicate of a sentence is what is said about the subject. Nouns or pronouns that are in the subject are in the NOMINATIVE case.

Some verbs (Transitive verbs, see p. 154) express an action that passes over from the subject to someone or something else, from the doer of the action to the receiver of the action. Thus, for example, in the first sentence above, the action of hitting passes over from the boy to the dog; in the second sentence the action of biting from the dog to the boy. The receiver of these actions is called the OBJECT. The person or thing expressed by the object stands in a relation to a 'doer' and an action. The noun or pronoun that signifies this is in the OBJECTIVE case.[1] So we could divide the sentences above like this:

SUBJECT	PREDICATE	
	Verb	*Object*
The boy	hit	the dog
The dog	bit	the boy
The girl	read	the books
The books	pleased	the girl

Whether a noun is the subject or object of a sentence is shown not by its form but by its position in the sentence.

There are some verbs that do not take an object, e.g.

The dog *ran* away. The boy *cried*. The girl *laughed*.

Verbs that do not take an object are called INTRANSITIVE Verbs. (See p. 154.)

ENLARGEMENTS

Phrases or words other than an object may accompany both a transitive or an intransitive verb in a sentence. These ENLARGEMENTS of the verb are of various types, e.g.

He walked *slowly*. (MANNER)
The dog jumped *through the window*. (PLACE)
They arrived *on Christmas day*. (TIME)

[1] The concept of case corresponds to a difference of form only in certain pronouns (see p. 98).

I*

My train was late *because of the fog.* (REASON)
My work is *nearly* finished. (DEGREE)
He is saving up *to buy a bicycle.* (PURPOSE)
He worked *like a madman* (MANNER) *in the garden* (PLACE)
on Saturday. (TIME)

Similarly there may be enlargements of the noun or pronoun forming the subject or the object. Thus the sentence:

A bright little boy with rosy cheeks put three metal-topped bottles of milk quietly on my doorstep before seven o'clock.

could be analysed (i.e. broken up into its parts) like this:

SUBJECT		PREDICATE			
Subject word	*Enlargement of Subject*	*Verb*	*Enlargement of Verb*	*Object word*	*Enlargement of Object*
boy	a bright little, with rosy cheeks	put	quietly (*Manner*), on my doorstep (*Place*), before seven o'clock (*Time*)	bottles	three, metal-topped, of milk

THE COMPLEMENT

Many verbs express an idea intelligibly without an object or an extension, e.g.

The sun *shines.* Fishes *swim.* The baby *is walking.* All mortals *die.*

Even verbs that need an object to express their sense fully are intelligible without the object, e.g.

The boy *hit.* The dog *bit.*

The verbs *hit* and *bit* leave us in no doubt about the actions involved.

But this is not the case in such examples as:

Today *is*. The plant *seems*. The man *became*.

Something must be added before these become intelligible, e.g.

Today *is my birthday*.
The plant *seems dead*.
The man *became violently angry*.

The words *my birthday, dead, violently angry* are not objects: the verbs *is, seems, became* are all intransitive verbs. These words or phrases are needed to complete the meaning of the verb; they are called COMPLEMENTS. Verbs like *is*,[1] *seem, become* are verbs of INCOMPLETE PREDICATION. The difference between complement and object can be seen in the following examples:

The little girl smelt *the flowers* (OBJECT). The flowers smell *sweet* (COMPLEMENT). I grow *strawberries* (OBJECT) in my garden. His face grew *pale* (COMPLEMENT) at the news.

A complement may be:

	Example
(1) a noun	Mr. Smith is *a dentist*.
(2) a pronoun	It was *you*.
(3) an adjective	This milk tastes *sour*.
(4) an adverb	The baby is *awake*.
(5) a gerund	The soldier, though wounded, continued *fighting*.
(6) a verb (infinitive)	He seemed *to fall*. He fought *to help* me.
(7) a phrase	The book is *in two parts*.
(8) a clause	That is *what I wanted to know*.
(9) a participle	It is *annoying* to be interrupted.

All the complements mentioned so far have been complements of the subject. These are called SUBJECTIVE COMPLEMENTS. But there are also complements of the object. These are OBJECTIVE COMPLEMENTS; i.e. they occur with verbs[2] that

---

[1] In certain cases *is* and other verbs of incomplete predication can, with a change of meaning, be complete verbs. (See p. 192.)

[2] These are called *Factitive* verbs.

take an object but still need some other word or words to complete the predicate, e.g.

	Object	*Objective Complement*
They made	him	king.
They called	the baby	Timothy.
The jury found	the prisoner	guilty.
The boy set	the bird	free.
His threats filled	her	with terror.
You have made	me	what I am.
His words prove	him (to be)	a fool.
The pain nearly drove	him	mad.
He likes	his desk (to be)	tidy.

The commonest verbs of incomplete predication are:

appear, become, break (he broke loose), *come* (his dreams came true), *continue, fall* (he fell ill), *feel, fly* (the door flew open), *get* (get well), *grow, keep* (keep well), *look, make, prove, remain* (remain calm), *run* (run dry), *seem, smell, sound* (sound silly), *stay* (stay clean), *taste, turn* (the milk turned sour), *wear* (cloth wears thin), *work* (the screw worked loose).

WORD ORDER IN SIMPLE SENTENCES

DECLARATIVE SENTENCES

In declarative sentences, i.e. sentences that make a statement, the usual word order is SUBJECT + VERB, e.g.

1 *Subject*	2 *Verb*	
Mr. Brown	teaches	this class.
George	can speak	English.
You	come	here every day.
They	went	to the theatre.
The children	were playing	in the field.
They	have finished	their work.
The farmer's wife	is feeding	the chickens.

The NEGATIVE of a declarative sentence is expressed mainly in two ways:

(1) By inserting *not* immediately after the verb. This method is used only with the Special Finites (see p. 182). The word order is:

SUBJECT + VERB (Special Finite) + *not*. In informal style, *not* may coalesce with the Special Finite to form one word, e.g.

He is not (isn't) my friend.

George cannot (can't) speak Russian.

He will not (won't) come.

The children are not (aren't) playing in the field.

The farmer's wife is not (isn't) feeding the chickens.

(2) By using *do, does, did*[1] with *not* and the PRESENT INFINITIVE (without *to*).

The word order is:

SUBJECT + *do (does), did* + *not* + INFINITIVE.

This construction is used with all verbs except the Special Finites, e.g.

Mr. Brown does not (doesn't) teach this class.

You do not (don't) come here every day.

They did not (didn't) go to the theatre.

Up to the seventeenth or eighteenth century all verbs could form their own negative merely by adding *not*, e.g.

I *like not* fair terms and a villain's mind. (Shakespeare, *Merchant of Venice*)

I *know not* why I am so sad. (Shakespeare, *Merchant of Venice*)

Let not your hearts be troubled. (*Bible*)

Look not upon the wine when it is red. (*Bible*)

This form may still be found in modern poetry, e.g.

'*Speak not—whisper not;*
Here bloweth thyme and bergamot.'
(Walter de la Mare, The Sunken Garden)

[1] *do (does)* is used for the Present Tense, *did* for the Past Tense.

The auxiliary *do* is not used with another negative or partly negative word such as *never, hardly, scarcely*, e.g.

He *never* speaks English. She *never* came to the party.
He *never* answered my letter. I *hardly* knew him.
He *scarcely* spoke at all.

except for emphasis, e.g. He never *did* like mathematics.

The negative may be expressed too, in literary style, by the verb *fail*, e.g. He *failed* to answer my letter. She *failed* to come to the party.

QUESTIONS

Interrogative sentences can be formed in three main ways:

(1) By inversion of subject and verb, i.e. by the word order VERB + SUBJECT.[1] In modern English this method is used only with Special Finites,[2] e.g.

Is he your friend?
Will they help us?
Can George speak Russian?
Are the children playing in the fields?
Has Henry finished his breakfast yet?

In older English, verbs that were not special finites could also form their interrogative by inversion, e.g.

'How *agrees the devil* with thee about thy soul?' (Shakespeare, *Henry IV*)
'Why *gnaw you* so your nether lip?' (Shakespeare, *Othello*)
'Simon, son of Jonas, *lovest thou* me' (*Bible*)

(2) By using *do* (*does, did*) and the infinitive. This form is used with all verbs except the Special Finites. The word order is: *Do* (*does, did*) + SUBJECT + INFINITIVE, e.g.

Does Mr. Brown teach this class?
Do you come here every day?
Did they go to the theatre?

Questions of types (1) and (2) can be answered by 'Yes' or 'No', and they are said with Rising Tune intonation (see p. 413).

---

[1] For the word order of indirect questions see pages 365–7.
[2] Including the Special Finites used in forming perfect tenses, continuous tenses, etc.

(3) By using 'Question Words': the interrogative pronouns,[1] interrogative adjectives,[2] or interrogative adverbs,[3] *Who? What? Which? When? Why?* etc. In questions of type (3) the question word always begins the question.

If the interrogative pronoun (or interrogative adjective + noun) is the subject of the sentence, there is no inversion, and the word order is: INTERROGATIVE (Subject) + VERB, e.g.

Who is your friend?

Which boy answered the question?

Whose dog bit the postman?

Who wrote *Vanity Fair?*

If the question word is the object or part of the object of the sentence, or if the question word is an interrogative adverb, then, after the opening interrogative, the word order is the same as for questions of types (1) and (2).

Questions of type (3) do not admit of an answer 'Yes' or 'No'. They are said with Falling Tune intonation (see p. 412). *Examples:*

What languages can William speak?

Whose car are you driving?

Which question did you answer?

What did he say?

When are you coming to see us?

Why did you lock the door?

COMMANDS, REQUESTS AND INVITATIONS

In commands[4] there is usually no subject. *Examples:*

Open the door. Come in. Take that dog out. Don't be late. Don't bring that dog in here.

In requests, too, there is often no subject, e.g.

Please lend me your pencil. Pass the sugar, please.

For requests and invitations another construction, in question form, is frequently used. This form is felt to be more polite or less abrupt. It begins with *will, would, would (do) you mind.*

[1] See page 116.   [2] See pages 84, 89, 119-20.   [3] See page 254.
[4] See also page 226.

A subject, normally *you*, is expressed. The word order is: *will* (*would*, etc.) + SUBJECT + INFINITIVE, e.g.

Will you lend me your pencil, please?
Would you come this way, please?
Would you mind passing the sugar, please?
Do you mind not smoking, please?
Won't you come in?
Will you come to tea tomorrow?

For word order in exclamatory sentences see pages 262, 264, 316.

EXERCISES

   I What are the various functions of a Simple Sentence? Give an example of each.

  II Divide the following sentences into subject and predicate in the manner shown on page 9.

     (1) The bird built a nest. (2) The gardener mowed the lawn. (3) The rain has stopped. (4) The sun is shining. (5) The grass is growing. (6) The flowers are opening their petals. (7) Open the door. (8) Who broke the window? (9) The dog barked. (10) Which boy brought that dog?

 III What are the main ways of forming the negative of a sentence? Give three examples of each method.

 IV Make the following sentences negative:

     (1) John is here. (2) Susan can swim very well. (3) The birds are singing this morning. (4) Henry will help me with my work. (5) Mary comes home every week-end. (6) They go to Switzerland every year. (7) He walked to school this morning. (8) Richard writes to Margaret regularly. (9) He wrote to her this week. (10) Mary bakes a cake. (11) Mary and Susan bake a cake. (12) Mary and Susan are baking a cake. (13) The dog chases rabbits. (14) The dogs chase rabbits. (15) The dog is chasing a rabbit. (16) The dogs are chasing a rabbit. (17) That shopkeeper sells good cakes. (18) That shopkeeper has good cakes. (19) Mary speaks English well. (20) Mary can speak English well. (21) Mary is speaking English now. (22) We rode to school on our bicycles. (23) Richard forgave the boy who had taken his pencil. (24) I chose these cakes for tea. (25) The

water froze in the pond last night. (26) He found the lost ball. (27) My roses grew very well this year. (28) The gardener dug up the potatoes. (29) Mr. Brown hung the picture straight. (30) The boy rang the bell. (31) I woke very early this morning. (32) I rose at six o'clock. (33) I got out of bed at six o'clock. (34) The boy ran as fast as he could. (35) John saw that picture at the Cinema. (36) That baker sold us good cakes. (37) The hen laid an egg today. (38) Mary ate her breakfast quickly. (39) You shook the bottle before you took the medicine. (40) Henry tries to understand the lesson. (41) Henry is trying to understand the lesson. (42) The boys try to understand the lesson. (43) The boys were trying to understand the lesson. (44) Mr. Smith lives in that house. (45) Mr. Smith is living in that house now. (46) Mr. Smith was living in that house last year. (47) I cycle to work every day. (48) He went to school this morning. (49) The children sang very well. (50) We sat on these seats yesterday. (51) Tom spoke French when he was ten years old. (52) The cat sprang on the rat. (53) Every boy stood in his place. (54) Henry tore that page out of his book. (55) The sun shone brightly this morning. (56) He told me the secret. (57) The teacher taught us that rule. (58) The class understood the lesson. (59) The ship sank in the great storm. (60) Richard swam across the river. (61) The boys went to the party. (62) The thieves stole all the jewels.

V What are the three main ways of forming the interrogative of a sentence? Give three examples of each method.

VI Make the sentences in Exercise IV interrogative.

VII Write questions to which the following could be answers:

(1) No, I'm Austrian. (2) Yes, he has. (3) No, only for three months. (4) Yes, we go there every year. (5) Yes, I know him very well. (6) No, he has a bad accent. (7) Yes, I went there last May. (8) Yes, I saw her on the ship. (9) She said that she was coming home next week. (10) Because it is such a cold day.

VIII Analyse the following sentences in the manner shown on page 10.

(1) Bright yellow daffodils can be seen in the gardens in spring.

(2) At Wembley last Saturday a hundred thousand spectators saw a most exciting football match.

(3) All the students in my class are working hard this year in order to pass their examination.

IX Pick out the complements in the following sentences.

(1) Nelson was a sailor. (2) The fur feels soft. (3) The room looks clean and tidy. (4) The milk turned sour owing to the thunder. (5) That is true. (6) The work seemed easy but it turned out difficult. (7) He went as white as a sheet. (8) That remark sounds stupid to me. (9) The man grew weaker every day. (10) These shoes have been well worn and they have worn thin. (11) They elected him President. (12) He called the man a thief. (13) He takes his whisky neat. (14) The Committee appointed George captain of the team. (15) Set the people free.

What is the difference between the complements in sentences 1-10 and those in 11-15?

CHAPTER THREE

NOUNS: (1) KINDS

A noun is the name of anything: *man, country, city, Henry, Spain, Paris, happiness, whiteness, crowd, team.* All these are names of people, places or things: all are nouns.

Nouns may be classified logically into two main categories: (1) CONCRETE, (2) ABSTRACT. Concrete nouns are represented by such words as *man, country, Henry, Spain, Paris, crowd, team.* Abstract nouns by such words as *happiness, whiteness, beauty, health.*

Concrete nouns may be sub-divided into two categories.

The names *man, country, county, city* can be applied to any man, any country, any city; they are names that all men, countries, cities share in common. They are called COMMON NOUNS. But *Henry, George Thompson,*[1] *Spain, Yorkshire, Paris* are not names that can be applied to any man, any country, any county, any city. They are names of a particular man, a particular country, a particular county, a particular city. They are called PROPER NOUNS.

Words like *scent, sweetness, whiteness* are not quite like *rose, sugar, snow;* they are names not so much of 'things' as of abstractions. The abstraction may be, as in the examples above, the name of a quality; or it may be the name of a state of being, like *health, poverty, pleasure, youth;* or it may be the name of an activity, like *laughter, arrival, perseverance.*

Nouns that are the names of qualities, states or activities are called ABSTRACT NOUNS.

Finally, there is one other type of noun. This comprises words like *crowd, army, flock, class.* They are names of a group or collection of things, of men, women, sheep, students, etc., regarded as one whole; so we speak of *a* crowd, *an* army, *a* flock, *a* class, i.e. of one thing. These words are COLLECTIVE NOUNS.

A collective noun denotes a group or collection of similar individuals considered as one complete whole.

[1] *George* is the 'Christian' or 'first' name. *Thompson* is the 'surname'. In English the Christian name comes before the surname.

The kinds of nouns may be shown diagrammatically like this:

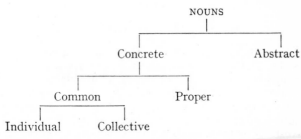

Countable and Uncountable Nouns

An important grammatical distinction may be made between nouns which are countable and nouns which are uncountable.

Nouns like *boys, books, apples, sheep* are 'countable'. Nouns like *bread, glass, sand, steam, air, water, ink* are 'uncountable'; they stand for substances[1] that cannot be counted, they can only be measured. Some of these words, e.g. *glass, paper, stone,* etc., can be 'countable' in one context and, with a different meaning, 'uncountable' in another:

A *glass* (*Countable*) is made of *glass* (*Uncountable*).

You can throw a *stone* (*Countable*) at a wall made of *stone* (*Uncountable*).

I have an evening *paper* (*Countable*). There is *paper* (*Uncountable*) on the wall.

The price of *tin* (*Uncountable*) rose today. The food is packed in *tins* (*Countable*).

The kettle is made of *copper* (*Uncountable*). I gave the boy a few *coppers* (*Countable*).

Common nouns may be countable or uncountable; most abstract nouns, e.g. *help, courage, perseverance, truth,* are uncountable.[2] Only countable nouns have a plural form, and only countable nouns can be preceded in the singular by the

---

[1] Nouns of this kind are sometimes called 'material' nouns.

[2] But some abstract nouns are countable and can be used in the plural, e.g. *ideas, opinions, truths,* etc.

indefinite article (*a, an*). Proper nouns, since they are the
names of a particular person, place or thing, are usually
singular, but they are countable and may at times be plural,
e.g. the *Himalayas*, the *West Indies*, the *Smiths;* or in such a
sentence as, 'There are three Johns (i.e. three boys with the
name *John*) in my class.'

COMPOUND NOUNS

One of the characteristics of English is the capacity it has
for forming compounds, that is, units which, though made up
of two or more parts each of which may be used as a separate
word, are, nevertheless, felt to be single terms. The elements
composing a compound may be almost any part of speech,
e.g. *schoolmaster* (noun + noun), *quick-silver* (adjective +
noun), *whitewash* (adjective + verb), *pickpocket* (verb + noun),
overlook (adverb + verb), *walking-stick* (gerund + noun). The
most important pattern in compound nouns is NOUN + NOUN,
or GERUND + NOUN, and the first element only is stressed, e.g.

*háirpin, shópkeeper, póstcard, néwspaper, súnshine, bóxing-
match, díning-room, wríting-paper,* etc.

The written form of these compound nouns is somewhat
arbitrary; sometimes they are written as one word, e.g. *bláckbird, hoúsewife;* sometimes as two words joined by a hyphen,
e.g. *gás-works, fíre-engine, thúnder-storm, séa-serpent;* or even
occasionally as two separate words, e.g. *póst office.* The GERUND
+ NOUN pattern is always written with a hyphen, e.g. *cýcling-
club, wéighing-machine.*

It is the single stress[1] which differentiates Compound nouns
from 'word groups' (i.e. adjective + noun, or noun used adjectivally + noun). In 'word groups' *both* elements take stress,
e.g. *góld ríng, lády dóctor, ríce púdding, stóne wáll, Lóndon
policeman, Óxford Univérsity.* If the group is longer than two
words the principle is the same, each word has stress, e.g.
Tóttenham Cóurt Róad, Lóndon Pássenger Tránsport Bóard.
This differentiation by stress is important, as it may convey a
difference of meaning. Thus a *bláck bírd* can apply to any bird
(e.g. a crow or a raven) which is black; a *bláckbird* is a bird of a

---

[1] Exceptions to this are the compound nouns *ármcháir* and *héad-
máster.*

particular species (turdus merula). A *hót hoúse* (= a house which is hot) is not the same as a *hóthouse* (= a heated glass building for plants), nor is a *páper basket* (= a basket for paper) the same as a *páper básket* (= a basket made of paper).

The first word, both in word groups and compound nouns is the 'qualifier', and a reversal of positions may bring about a complete change of meaning. Thus a *race-horse* is not the same as a *horse-race*, *lawn-tennis* as a *tennis-lawn*, a *Grammar School* as a *school grammar*, a *flower-garden* as a *garden flower*, an *eye-glass* as a *glass eye*, a *village-green* as a *green village*, *lamp-oil* as an *oil-lamp* or *pipe-tobacco* as a *tobacco-pipe*.

In a number of compound nouns, especially those that have been in the language a long time during which the original meanings of their elements have become obscured, the vowel in one or other, and even occasionally in both, has become shortened or otherwise modified, e.g.

breakfast ['brekfəst] (= break fast); *shepherd* ['ʃepəd] (= sheep herd); *forehead* ['forid] (= fore head); *cupboard* ['kʌbəd] (= cup board); *Sunday* ['sʌndi] (= sun day); *Newton* ['njuːtn] (= new town); *Portsmouth* ['pɔːtsməθ] (= port's mouth); *bonfire* ['bonfaiə] (originally *bone fire*); *postman* ['poustmən] (= post man), etc.

THE GRAMMATICAL FUNCTIONS OF NOUNS

A noun may be used:

(1) As the subject of a sentence, e.g.

The *boy* opened the door.

(2) As the direct object of a verb, e.g.

I saw the *boy*.

(3) As the complement of a verb, e.g.

He is a clever *boy*.

(4) As an indirect object, e.g.

I told the *boy* a story.

(5) In a phrase with a preposition, e.g.

I spoke to the *boy*. The House of *Commons*.

(6) As a prepositional object, e.g.

Give the money to your *brother*.

(7) As the antecedent[1] of a relative pronoun, e.g.

The *ship* that took the Pilgrim Fathers to America was called the 'Mayflower'.

EXERCISES

I Country, tree, peace, Sherlock Holmes, flock, sheep,
· Rubens, square, patience, beauty, Bodmin, rivalry, meeting, city traffic, noisiness, Hyde Park, crowd.

Which of the above words are NOT Common nouns? Which are abstract, which collective?

II 'John, come here! Will you come to the theatre with me?' 'Which theatre?' 'Covent Garden.' 'What's the opera?' 'Tosca.' 'Who wrote it?' 'Puccini.' 'What's the price of the tickets?' 'Twelve and six.' 'Sorry, I haven't the money; I've been betting too much recently. I lost a lot on the Derby.' 'Oh, you didn't back Crepello, then?' 'No, worse luck!'

Pick out and classify the nouns in the above passage.

III Which of the following nouns are 'countables' and which are 'uncountables'?

dog, meat, nuisance, thunder, spoon, fish, cheese, board, party, tree.

IV Form abstract nouns from these words:

proud, beautiful, parent, likely, coward, traitor, infant, sane, courteous, young.

V(*a*) What is the correct collective noun for a number of:

(1) lions. (2) sheep. (3) people at a football match. (4) wolves. (5) elephants. (6) fish. (7) people in church. (8) people listening to a concert. (9) sailors on a ship?

(*b*) Supply the appropriate collective nouns to complete the following expressions:

a —— of stars, a —— of oxen, a —— of cards, a —— of brigands, a —— of trees, a —— of disorderly people, a —— of hounds, a —— of ships, a —— of curios, a —— of books, a —— of aircraft.

VI What qualities (expressed by abstract nouns) do you associate with the following?

Job, Quisling, Shylock, Tartuffe, Uriah Heep, Hercules, Nero, Baron Munchausen, Machiavelli?

[1] The antecedent is the word for which the relative pronoun stands (see p. 324).

VII In each of the following groups of nouns, pick out the one that is different in class from the others. Give the reason for your choice:

(*a*) quietness, country, lake, sun.
(*b*) crew, team, men, crowd.
(*c*) Germany, Rhine, river, Zugspitze, Bavaria.
(*d*) laughter, gaiety, joy, happiness, mirth, humorist.

VIII Identify the nouns in the following passage and name the kind of noun to which each belongs:

'At length, in 1812, Mr. Williams made his début on the stage of Ratcliff Highway, and executed those unparalleled murders which have procured for him such a brilliant and undying reputation. On which murders, by the way, I must observe that in one respect they have had an ill effect, by making the connoisseur in murder very fastidious in his taste and dissatisfied with anything that has been done since in that line.'

De Quincey, 'On the Knocking at the gate in
Macbeth'.

IX In the following examples some common nouns are used as proper nouns and some proper nouns are used as common nouns or adjectives. Point out these words. (1) Church and State do not always agree. (2) He was wearing a tweed ulster. (3) *Hamlet* is a tragedy but *Twelfth Night* is a comedy. (4) Some people prefer China tea to Indian. (5) Paris fashions are famous everywhere.

X Give the collective nouns for:

(1) The group of persons directing the administration of a town. (2) Ships used in time of war (*several words possible*). (3) The 52 cards used in playing Bridge. (4) Father, mother, sons and daughter. (5) The eleven players in a game of football.

XI Form abstract nouns from:
(1) great. (2) succeed. (3) destroy. (4) profound. (5) repel. (6) know. (7) gentle (*two words*). (8) social (*two words*). (9) generous. (10) liberal (*two words*).

XII Which of the following words can be used as countable and also as uncountable nouns? Explain the two senses of each one you find.

(1) sorrow. (2) beauty. (3) wine. (4) tea. (5) brick. (6) pain. (7) wood. (8) paint. (9) timber. (10) food.

XIII Form compound nouns or 'word groups' to express:

(1) A knife for cutting paper. (2) A glass for holding wine. (3) A blade for a safety-razor. (4) A box for holding matches. (5) A desk for writing at. (6) A paper giving news and published in Edinburgh. (7) An instrument for pulling corks out of bottles. (8) A pair of scissors for cutting finger-nails. (9) A driver of taxis in London. (10) A machine for cutting the grass on a lawn. (11) A man whose profession is lending money. (12) A place where cotton cloth is made. (13) A machine for washing clothes. (14) A fish that is golden in colour. (15) A man who gets coal out of the ground. (16) A wall made of bricks. (17) A man who makes a brick wall. (18) A room where you have meals. (19) A room in which you sleep. (20) A room in which you both live and sleep.

In every case mark which words are stressed.

XIV Explain (*a*) the meanings of the following words and expressions as they are given, and then (*b*) their meanings when the two words in each are transposed. In each case illustrate by sentences.

(1) playing-card. (2) grammar school. (3) flower-garden. (4) eyeglass. (5) village-green. (6) house-dog. (7) bicycle pedal. (8) pocket-book. (9) oil-lamp. (10) bus station. (11) tobacco-pipe. (12) lawn-tennis.

CHAPTER FOUR

NOUNS: (2) NUMBER

There are two grammatical numbers in English, (*a*) SINGULAR to denote one, (*b*) PLURAL to denote more than one.

Only countable nouns can be used in the plural.

FORMATION OF THE PLURAL

The plural of almost all nouns is formed by means of a sibilant suffix. This suffix is written as *-s* or *-es*. It is pronounced as [s] when added to a word ending in any voiceless consonant except the 'hissing' sounds [s], [ʃ], [tʃ], e.g.

book — books [buk — buks]
cat — cats [kat — kats]

It is pronounced [z] when added to a word ending in any voiced sound except the consonants [z], [ʒ], [dʒ], e.g.

dog — dogs [dog — dogz]
bird — birds [bə:d — bə:dz]
day — days [dei — deiz]

It is pronounced [iz] when added to a word ending in the sounds [s], [ʃ], [tʃ], [z], [ʒ], [dʒ], e.g.

horse [ho:s] — horses ['ho:siz]; rose [rouz] — roses ['rouziz]
judge [dʒʌdʒ] — judges ['dʒʌdʒiz]; ash [aʃ] — ashes ['aʃiz].

NOTE: The *s* of *house* [haus] is voiced in the plural ['hauziz]. The unvoiced -th in *bath* [ba:θ], *mouth* [mauθ], *oath* [ouθ], *path* [pa:θ], *sheath* [ʃi:θ], *truth* [tru:θ] and *youth* [ju:θ] is voiced in the plural: [ba:ðz], [mauðz], [ouðz], [pa:ðz], [ʃi:ðz], [tru:ðz] and [ju:ðz].

In writing, this sibilant suffix is spelt *-s*, with the following exceptions, in which it is written *-es*.

(1) Words that end in the letters, *-s*, *-sh*, *-ch*, *-x*, *-z:*

glass — glasses, brush — brushes
church — churches, box — boxes.

(2) Most words that end in -*o:*

negro — negroes, potato — potatoes
hero — heroes, volcano — volcanoes.

But there are some exceptions to this. Thus, though words that have been in the language for a long time tend to use the -*es* form,

(*a*) Those words that are still felt to be 'foreign' take the -*s* form. The principal ones are:

pianos, photos, dynamos, magnetos, kilos, mementos, solos.

(*b*) All nouns ending in -*o* preceded by a vowel take only the -*s* form, e.g.

cuckoos, cameos, bamboos, portfolios, curios, studios, radios.

The following changes occur in the formation of the plural:

(1) Words ending in -*y* preceded by a consonant letter change the -*y* to -*ies:*

lady, ladies; story, stories; army, armies; fly, flies.

Words ending in -*y* preceded by a vowel letter simply add -*s:*[1]
valley, valleys; donkey, donkeys; boy, boys; key, keys.

(2) The ending -*f* or -*fe* in most nouns is changed to -*ves,* with a corresponding change of pronunciation of [f] to [v], e.g.
leaf, leaves; wife, wives; thief, thieves; loaf, loaves; half, halves.

But there are many words ending in -*f* or -*fe* that simply add *s* to form their plural:

roofs, gulfs, cliffs, reefs, proofs, chiefs, hoofs, turfs, safes, dwarfs, griefs, beliefs.

Some words have both forms:

scarfs, scarves; wharfs, wharves; staffs, staves; hoofs, hooves.

Irregular Plurals

(1) There are eight nouns, the 'mutation'[2] plurals, which form their plural by a change of vowel: *man, men* (and

---

[1] But there is a technical term in banking, finance, etc., that is spelt *monies,* and not, as one might expect, *moneys.*
[2] Mutation (change of vowel) was caused by the presence of an *i* that once stood after the final consonant of the stem. Thus the Primitive Germanic plural of *fot* (foot) was *foti,* later *fet* and then *feet.*

compounds of *man*, e.g. *gentleman, gentlemen*);[1] *tooth, teeth; foot, feet; mouse, mice; woman, women; goose, geese; louse, lice; dormouse, dormice*. The plural of *mongoose* is *mongooses; dormouse* is a compound of *mouse* but *mongoose* is not a compound of *goose*.

(2) Some words have the same form for singular and plural:

sheep, swine, deer, fish (but also *fishes*).

To these could be added the names of other animals, especially when used in a hunting context. This applies to game, birds and fish, e.g.

to hunt *elephant, antelope*, etc.; to shoot wild *duck, grouse*, to catch *salmon, trout*.

We have, too, the unchanged plural in some words showing number and measurement of weight:

two *dozen* (abbreviation: *doz.*) eggs; three *hundred* pounds; four *thousand* people; two *gross* of pencils; three *score* years; two *stone* of potatoes; four *hundred*weight (abbreviation: *cwt.*) of coal; 10,000 *candle*-power; 20 *horse*-power; forty *head* of cattle; two *yoke* of oxen. So 2,300,501 is 'two *million*, three *hundred* thousand, five *hundred* and one'.

But these words (except *gross*) take -*s* when they have no numeral in front of them, e.g. *dozens* of eggs; *hundreds* of pounds; *scores* of times; *hundredweights* of coal. Sometimes either form is possible: 'He weighs twelve *stones*' and 'He weighs twelve *stone*', 'He is six *feet* tall' and 'He is six *foot* tall'.

The words *barracks, species, series, means, works* (and compounds like *gas-works, iron-works*, etc.) are the same in singular or plural.

So, too, are some proper nouns that end in a 'hissing' sound:

Swiss, Chinese, Japanese, Portuguese, Viennese.

(3) Three words form their plural in -*en*. They are:

child — children; ox — oxen; brother — brethren.

The usual plural of *brother* is, of course, *brothers*. *Brethren*, which was the usual plural until the seventeenth century, is now used with the meaning 'members of the same society or religious order'.

---

[1] But *Romans, Normans, Germans*, because these words are not connected with the independent word *man*.

Historical Reason for these forms

In Anglo-Saxon there were five possible endings to denote plural: *-as, -an, -u, -a* and *-o*. In addition, there were some 'neuter' nouns that had the same form for the singular and plural, and that is why, in modern English, the singular and plural of a few words, e.g. *sheep* and *deer*, are the same. By about 1400 these five endings had, with one or two exceptions, been reduced to two: *-es* and *-s* (both developed from *-as*). The word *oxen* is one of these exceptions; it still keeps the Anglo-Saxon *-an* (later *-en*) ending for the plural. There used to be, almost to modern times, quite a number of plurals ending in *-en: shoen* (later *shoon*) for *shoes* is used by Shakespeare. Chaucer's Prioress had *'eyen* (= eyes) grey as glass', and there were *housen* (= houses), *hosen* (= hose), *peasen* (= peas). *Children, brethren* are really double plurals.[1] The Old English plural for Anglo-Saxon *cild* (= child) was *cildru;* for *brothor* it was *brothru.* In Middle English, *childru* became *childer* (a form that is still heard in dialect) and *brothru* became *brether.* Then to what were already plural words an extra plural ending *-en* was added making, *childeren, bretheren,* which developed to *children, brethren.*

FOREIGN PLURALS

Mention will be made later of the large number of foreign words that have been absorbed into the language.[2] Sometimes, especially in the technical language of science, these have not been thoroughly 'naturalized' and they keep their foreign plural forms. The largest number by far of these foreign plurals are of Latin or Greek origin, for example:

Latin: axis — axes; bacillus — bacilli; medium — media; stratum — strata; bacterium — bacteria; locus — loci; radius — radii; corrigendum — corrigenda; addendum — addenda; erratum — errata; larva — larvae; nebula — nebulae.

Greek: analysis — analyses; basis — bases; crisis — crises; hypothesis — hypotheses; thesis — theses; phenomenon — phenomena; criterion — criteria; oasis — oases.

[1] So is *kine.* The plural of Old English *cu* (= cow) was a 'mutation' pleral *cy.* To this was added another plural form *-en.* Then *cyen* became *kine.*　　　　[2] Chapter 30.

The longer the words have been in the language, the more they tend to conform to the English plural in -s. Some words are at the half-way stage with two plurals, the original foreign one and the English one. So you will find:

appendix — appendixes, appendices; formula — formulae, formulas; terminus — termini, terminuses; fungus — fungi, funguses; retina — retinae, retinas; cactus — cacti, cactuses; focus — foci, focuses; aquarium — aquaria, aquariums; curriculum — curricula, curriculums; maximum — maxima, maximums; memorandum — memoranda, memorandums; minimum — minima, minimums; sanatorium — sanatoria, sanatoriums; vortex — vortices, vortexes; automaton — automata, automatons.

Most words taken in fairly recent times from French or Italian have their original and also their English plural. Practically all the older words conform to the English pattern.

Recent words with two forms are:

bureau — bureaux, bureaus; tableau — tableaux, tableaus; portmanteau — portmanteaux, portmanteaus; adieu — adieux, adieus; trousseau — trousseaux, trousseaus; bandit — banditti, bandits; libretto — libretti, librettos; soprano — soprani, sopranos; virtuoso — virtuosi, virtuosos.

In some cases the two plurals have different meanings (see also page 38):

Singular		*Plural*
index	{ indexes	(= tables of contents).
	indices	(= algebraical signs).
genius	{ geniuses	(= persons of unusually great mental powers).
	genii	(= good or evil spirits).
die	{ dies	(= metal stamps for making money).
	dice	(= small cubes of bone or wood used in games of chance).
formula	{ formulas	(= forms of words).
	formulae	(= mathematical terms).

Singular	*Plural*

medium $\begin{cases} \text{mediums} & (= \text{people claiming communication} \\ & \text{with spirits}). \\ \text{media} & (= \text{means, agencies}). \end{cases}$

There are also one or two native English words that have two plurals with different meanings (see also page 38):

brother $\begin{cases} \text{brothers} \\ \text{brethren}^1 \end{cases}$

cloth $\begin{cases} \text{cloths (different pieces or kinds of cloth).} \\ \text{clothes (articles of dress).} \end{cases}$

penny $\begin{cases} \text{pennies (individual coins).} \\ \text{pence (collective value).} \end{cases}$

But the word *sixpence* (meaning the small silver coin) forms a plural *sixpences*, e.g. 'Can you give me two sixpences for a shilling?'

Many foreign words have now become completely naturalized and always take the English plural, such as:

bonuses, choruses, circuses, isthmuses, omnibuses,[2] *prospectuses, areas, arenas, encyclopædias, eras, ideas, panaceas, peninsulas, sonatas, solos, umbrellas, villas, albums, asylums, chrysanthemums, museums, irises, demons.*

CONCORD

(1) A singular subject takes a singular verb, a plural subject takes a plural verb, e.g.

The *boy is* here. The *boys are* here.

(2) Difficulties arise sometimes in the case of Collective Nouns in the singular. A collective noun was defined as a noun denoting a group or collection of similar individuals considered as one complete whole. It is therefore naturally regarded as being singular and as such takes a singular verb.

The football team *is* playing well.

The Government *has* decided to pass the bill.

That family *is* a very happy one.

---

[1] See page 28.
[2] *omnibus* is a Latin dative plural = 'for all'. The word is usually shortened to *bus* (plural *buses*).

But, when the parts or members that compose the thing denoted by the collective noun are thought of individually, a plural verb may be used:

> The football team *are* having baths and *are* then coming back here for tea.
>
> The Government *have* discussed the matter for a long time but they have shown no signs of reaching agreement.
>
> The family *are* very pleased about the news of William's success.

The nouns *people, police, public, clergy, cattle* are always used with a plural verb, e.g.

> The *people* of Norway *are* called Norwegians.
>
> The *police are* making enquiries about the murder.
>
> The *public are* requested not to leave litter in these woods.

People is often used as the plural of *person;* it also means *nation,* e.g. The French *people,* the *peoples* of Europe.

(3) Two or more subjects connected by *and* take a plural verb, e.g.

> The boy and his dog *are* here.

But if the two subjects joined by *and* are considered as one thing, a singular verb is used, e.g.

> Brown bread and butter *is* usually eaten with smoked salmon.
>
> Whisky and soda *is* his favourite drink.
>
> His courage *and* endurance *was* tried to the utmost.
>
> The stitching *and* binding of books *is* done on this machine.
>
> The *secretary and accountant* of the Company *was* present (One man doing both jobs.)

But:

> The secretary and (the) accountant of the Company *were* present. (Two men.)

So, too, in such sentences as:

> Ten years *is* a long time.
>
> Five thousand pounds *is* a lot of money.

where the subject, though plural in form, is really singular in meaning (ten years = *a period* of time); £5,000 = *a sum* of money) or sentences such as:

'Modern Painters' *is* one of Ruskin's best known books.

(4) If the second noun is merely part of a phrase qualifying the first singular noun, the verb is singular, e.g.

The boy with his dog *is* here.

Mr. Smith, accompanied by his wife and three children, *has* just arrived.

(5) Singular subjects joined by *or* or *neither . . . nor* take a singular verb, e.g.

A cigar *or* a cigarette *is* very enjoyable.

Neither George *nor* Henry *has* come yet.

But by the 'rule of proximity', if one subject is singular and another one is plural, the verb generally agrees with the nearest subject, e.g.

Either the teacher or the students *are* to blame for the bad results.

Neither he nor they *are* wholly right.

(6) The distributives[1] take a singular verb and a singular possessive adjective,[2] e.g.

Every boy in the class *is* present.

Each of the boys *has* gained a prize.

Neither answer *is* correct.

Everybody *is* doing *his* best.

But this rule about using a singular possessive adjective with distributive adjectives like *everyone, each*, etc., is, especially in conversation, frequently disregarded owing to the fact that there is not in English a possessive adjective that can stand for both masculine and feminine, singular and plural nouns. Consequently the plural *their* is frequently used, e.g.

Everyone was talking at the top of *their* voices.

When *each* person comes in *they* must show *their* ticket.

None may take a singular verb or a plural one, e.g.

'None but the brave *deserves* the fair.' (Dryden)

None of us *is* perfect.

None of the children in his class *are* bored with the lesson.

I have checked your answers and none of them *are* correct.

---

[1] See pages 89, 126–8.   [2] See page 84.

The word *number* sometimes takes a singular verb, sometimes a plural one, e.g.

The *number* of students in the class *is* small.

But:

A number of students *were* waiting for the lesson to begin.

(7) The verb agrees with the pronoun *it* in identifying or emphatic sentences, e.g.

'Who broke the window?' '*It was* Henry and William.'
It is they who are wrong.

(8) The relative pronoun takes the same number and person as its antecedent, e.g.

This is one of the best books that *have* ever been written on the subject.

(9) If the 'formal subject' *there* is used, the verb agrees with the real subject, e.g.

There is a cherry tree in my garden.
There are cherry trees in my garden.

EXERCISES

I Rewrite the following sentences, putting as many words as possible into the plural, and making any other necessary alterations.

(1) A witch used to be burnt. (2) A match is taken from a box or torn from a 'book'. (3) The leaf which the bird was carrying fell on to the roof of the house. (4) The monkey jumped from rock to rock up above, watching the movement of the man in the valley below. (5) The defeated army had not even time to bury the body of its hero. (6) The chief of the tribe had his own means of catching a salmon. (7) The cheese could not be sold, as a mouse had left a tooth-mark on it. (8) Which is the greater curse in the Middle East, the fly or the louse? (9) While the negro was voicing his belief, the mulatto kept banging on the floor with his staff. (10) This crisis comes in a long series.

II Give the plurals of the following nouns:

negro, wish, studio, daily, convoy, reef, wharf, dormouse, echo, inch, mongoose, dwarf, calf, bough, fox, yoke.

III Express the following in words instead of figures and expand the contractions to their full forms:

(*a*) 250. (*b*) 2,300. (*c*) 3,430,654. (*d*) 144 (*three forms possible*). (*e*) 150 cwt.

IV Give the plurals of:

bacillus, axis, radius, hypothesis, crisis, oasis, phenomenon, fungus, cactus.

V Explain the meanings of the singular and plural forms of the following words:

air, premise, brace, compass, fruit, spectacle, damage, wit, pain, powder, colour, body, spirit.

VI Make a list of as many nouns as you know which have the same form in singular and plural.

PLURALS AND COMPOUND NOUNS

Old compound nouns usually form their plural as if they were simple nouns, i.e. the final element is made plural:

schoolroom — schoolrooms; armchair — armchairs; horseman — horsemen; housewife — housewives; washerwoman — washerwomen; tooth-brush — tooth-brushes.

This is generally the case even when the elements of the compound are not themselves nouns:

handful — handfuls; breakdown — breakdowns; drawback — drawbacks; outbreak — outbreaks; forget-me-not — forget-me-nots;

or even if the compound consists of two separate words:

ticket collector — ticket collectors; boy friend — boy friends; watch repairer — watch repairers; girl guide — girl guides; boy scout — boy scouts; motor show — motor shows.

In the following, both elements are made plural:

man servant — men servants; gentleman farmer — gentlemen farmers; woman servant — women servants;[1] men students/ teachers/doctors, etc., and *women students/teachers/doctors; Lord-justice — lords justices; Knight-Templar — Knights-Templars.*

In syntactical compounds, especially where the first component is a noun qualified by a prepositional phrase, adverb or adjective, it is the noun which takes the plural form:

[1] But the plural of *maid servant* is *maid servants.*

father-in-law — fathers-in-law;[1]   commander-in-chief — commanders-in-chief; man-of-war — men-of-war; looker-on —lookers-on; passer-by—passers-by; justice-of-the-peace—justices-of-the-peace; governor-general—governors-general; court-martial — courts-martial; poet laureate — poets laureate.

But, especially in popular speech, there is a tendency to say:

mother-in-laws, court-martials, attorney-generals, commander-in-chiefs, poet laureates; and always *will-o'-the-wisps, good-for-nothings, ne'er-do-wells.*

FORMS OF ADDRESS

The following forms are used:

SINGULAR	PLURAL
For a man, married or unmarried Mr. Brown	Messrs. Brown; the Messrs. Brown; the two Mr. Browns; Mr. John (Brown) and Mr. Henry Brown. The form *Messrs.* (standing for *Messieurs*, which is never written in full in English) is used only in business language, e.g. Messrs. Brown and Smith Ltd.
For an unmarried woman Miss Brown	The Misses Brown; the Miss Browns; the two Miss Browns; Miss Margaret (Brown) and Miss Lilian Brown.
For a married woman Mrs. Brown	The two Mrs. Brown; the two Mrs. Browns.

[1] And similarly: *mothers-in-law, sons-in-law,* etc.

NOUNS WITH NO PLURAL FORM

Many nouns are never used in the plural, e.g. most abstract and many material nouns (see p. 20).

NOUNS WITH NO SINGULAR FORM

Some nouns are never used in the singular, e.g. the names of:

ARTICLES OF DRESS: *trousers, breeches, knickers, pants, pyjamas, shorts, drawers, clothes.*

TOOLS AND INSTRUMENTS CONSISTING OF TWO PARTS: *scissors, shears, pliers, pincers, spectacles, glasses* (= spectacles), *tongs, bellows.* The word 'pair' is generally used with these terms, e.g. 'a pair of trousers', etc.

NAMES OF DISEASES OR ILLNESSES: *mumps, measles.*

NAMES OF SOME GAMES: *billiards, cards, bowls, dominoes, draughts.*

MISCELLANEOUS OTHER WORDS: *alms, riches, eaves, scales* (for weighing), *contents* (of a book, etc.), *goings-on, gentry, dregs, oats, credentials, tidings, soap-suds, winnings, sweepings, surroundings, ashes* (from the fire, but cigarette *ash*). Though the nouns *whisker, shaving, saving, filing* can be used, the plural form *whiskers, shavings, savings, filings* is much more common.

A plural verb is used with the above words. So we say:

My trousers *are* being cleaned. Riches *do* not always bring happiness. Oats *are* grown in Scotland. Cards *are* played every evening etc.

But if these words are used attributively in compound nouns they are usually made singular, e.g. my *trouser* leg; *oat* cakes; a *card* table.

Some nouns have a plural form but are followed by a singular verb: *news, innings, gallows, works, physics, phonetics,* and as a rule so are all other sciences or subjects ending in *-ics,* but this usage is not fixed. Singular or plural can often be used, e.g.

Politics *have* (*has*) always interested me.
Mathematics *is* (*are*) well taught at that school.

The news *is* good. The first innings *is* finished. An ironworks *is* being built.

PLURALS WITH DIFFERENT MEANINGS

The plurals of some nouns have two or more meanings,[1] one similar to the singular meaning, the other different from it.

colours	=	(1) hues.
		(2) regimental flags.
compasses	=	(1) instruments for navigation.
		(2) instruments for drawing circles.
customs	=	(1) habits.
		(2) taxes on imported goods.
draughts	=	(1) a game.
		(2) currents of air.
dominoes	=	(1) a game.
		(2) kinds of masks.
effects	=	(1) results.
		(2) goods, personal property.
forces	=	(1) powers ('the *forces* of nature').
		(2) organized bodies of men ('armed *forces*', 'police *forces*').
glasses	=	(1) vessels for drinking from.
		(2) spectacles; binoculars.
grounds	=	(1) land (usually enclosed) round a house.
		(2) reasons ('*grounds* for complaint').
		(3) dregs ('coffee *grounds*').
letters	=	(1) signs of the alphabet.
		(2) epistles.
		(3) learning ('a man of *letters*').
manners	=	(1) ways, customs.
		(2) behaviour.
minutes	=	(1) spaces of time.
		(2) secretary's record of proceedings at a meeting.

[1] See also pages 30 and 31.

pains　　= (1) sufferings.
　　　　　　(2) care, trouble ('to take *pains* with something').

premises　= (1) things assumed as true as basis for an argument.
　　　　　　(2) buildings.

quarters　= (1) fourth parts.
　　　　　　(2) lodgings.

returns　= (1) recurrences ('many happy *returns*').
　　　　　　(2) statistical details ('*returns* of income for tax purposes').

spectacles = (1) sights; things seen.
　　　　　　(2) glasses to aid sight.

spirits　= (1) souls.
　　　　　　(2) alcoholic liquors.
　　　　　　(3) mental or moral attitude ('in high *spirits*').

An interesting peculiarity is the occasional use of the plural form to intensify the meaning expressed by the singular or to suggest great quantity or extent, e.g.

the *sands* of the desert; the *snows* and *frosts* of the Antarctic; the *waters* of the lake; the *heavens* above our heads; a walk through the *woods*; swayed between *hopes* and *fears*.

EXERCISES

I Which of the alternatives in the following sentences are correct? Give reasons.

(1) The committee was/were of the opinion that the matter should be dealt with at once.

(2) The crowd behaved itself/themselves admirably.

(3) The congregation is/are not numerous tonight, but it/they seems/seem to be listening very attentively to the sermon.

(4) The staff was/were opposed to any change.

(5) The orchestra is/are playing tomorrow evening.

(6) The whole herd rushed headlong to its/their destruction.

II What is the plural form of the following nouns?

Onlooker; looker-on; tiger-lily; woman teacher; moth-ball; major-general; madam; manservant; manhole; man-at-arms.

III What is wrong with the following sentences, and why? (1) I have come to perfect my knowledges of English. (2) Can you give me any informations or advices on this matter? (3) The news are good this evening. (4) I opened the letter and it contained an important information. (5) I went to my doctor for an advice about my health. (6) I have several jackets, but only one trousers. (7) My pyjama is at the laundry.

IV Each of these words can have two different meanings. Illustrate this in sentences.

spirits; letters; customs; forces; grounds; minutes.

V What are the plural forms of the following:?

gentleman, lady-in-waiting, stepson, watchman, trade-union.

VI How would you describe:

(1) Two men named Smith. (2) The two daughters of Mr. Jones. (3) The wives of the two men in (1)?

VII Give one word for the following:

(1) The table on which the games of (*a*) billiards, and (*b*) cards are played. (2) One half of a pair of trousers. (3) The place where the game of bowls is played. (4) The board on which the game of draughts is played. (5) An instrument for weighing groceries, etc.

VIII Complete the following sentences with *is, are, was, were* as appropriate:

(1) The clergy —— generally dressed in black. (2) Greens —— a wholesome spring vegetable. (3) Wheat —— used to make flour. (4) The first innings of the Test match —— nearly disastrous for the English team. (5) The *Politics* of Aristotle —— studied at Oxford.

IX Comment fully on the meaning and number of the following words, explaining differences of meaning between singular and plural forms where both exist:

salts, alms, paper, quarter, spectacles, draught, effects, return, manner, glass, work, pain.

CHAPTER FIVE

NOUNS: (3) GENDER

The concept of gender has no grammatical function in modern English. It is possible, however, to group words into three categories according to whether they can be replaced by the pronouns 'he', 'she' or 'it' respectively. In all but a few cases these categories correspond to the ideas of 'male', 'female' and 'inanimate'. Animals are usually referred to by the pronoun *it*, but may also be spoken of as 'he' or 'she' according to their sex. Thus we have these categories:

MASCULINE GENDER for all words representing males, e.g.

boy, king, uncle, prince.

FEMININE GENDER for all words representing females, e.g.

girl, queen, aunt, princess.

NEUTER GENDER for inanimate objects, e.g.

book, house, pencil, table.

Words which may designate either males or females are sometimes said to be of COMMON GENDER, e.g. *cousin, friend, child,* etc.

MASCULINE AND FEMININE FORMS

I. Generally, when there is no wish to make a distinction of sex, the masculine form is used. In other cases, however, a separate form will be used for the female. This word may:

(1) be formed from the masculine by adding *-ess* (sometimes with other slight changes):

Masculine	Feminine	Masculine	Feminine
poet	poetess	priest	priestess
author	authoress	shepherd	shepherdess
god	goddess	Viscount	Viscountess
heir	heiress	actor	actress
host	hostess	waiter	waitress
Jew	Jewess	emperor	empress

Masculine	Feminine	Masculine	Feminine
giant	giantess	negro	negress
Prince	Princess	tiger	tigress
Baron	Baroness	murderer	murderess
Count	Countess	Duke	Duchess
manager	manageress	Marquis (*or*	
lion	lioness	Marquess)[1]	Marchioness
master	mistress	conductor	conductress

The only cases in which the masculine is formed from the feminine seem to be *bridegroom*[2] (from *bride*) and *widower* (from *widow*).

(2) be a different word:

Masculine	Feminine	Masculine	Feminine
boy	girl	bullock	heifer
man	woman	brother	sister
sir	madam	gentleman ⎫	
King	Queen	lord ⎬ lady	
Earl	Countess	son	daughter
father	mother	uncle	aunt
husband	wife	nephew	niece
bachelor	spinster	monk ⎫	
horse	mare	friar ⎬ nun	
(stallion)		tutor	governess
bull	cow	wizard	witch
cock	hen	drake	duck
buck	doe	gander	goose
colt	filly	dog	bitch
stag	hind	ram	ewe
boar	sow	fox	vixen

II. In words of COMMON GENDER, the distinction of sex may be shown by forming a compound word of which one element denotes the sex, e.g.

[1] Though this ends in *-ess* it is not a feminine noun.
[2] This was originally *brydguma* (Old English: guma = a man). This word became obsolete in Middle English times and was replaced by *-groom*.

Masculine	Feminine	Masculine	Feminine
manservant — maidservant		man friend — woman friend	
boy cousin — girl cousin		landlord — landlady	
boy friend — girl friend		he-bear — she-bear	
cock sparrow — hen sparrow		he-wolf — she-wolf	
peacock — peahen		he-goat ⎱ __ ⎰ she-goat	
tomcat — tabby cat		billy-goat ⎰ ⎱ nanny-goat	

III. There are a number of 'foreign feminines'. The most common is *heroine* (masculine *hero*). Other examples of foreign feminines are:

Masculine	Feminine	Masculine	Feminine
executor	executrix	prosecutor	prosecutrix
testator	testatrix	beau	belle
Czar	Czarina	Sultan	Sultana
(Tsar)	(Tsarina)		

IV. With regard to words of common gender, it is interesting to note that occasionally for living beings we have three words, one masculine, one feminine and one common gender, e.g.

Masculine	Feminine	Common
father	mother	parent
boy ⎱ son ⎰	girl ⎱ daughter ⎰	child
man	woman	person
king	queen	monarch, sovereign, ruler
schoolmaster	schoolmistress	teacher
stallion	mare	horse
ram	ewe	sheep
boar	sow	pig
cock	hen	bird, fowl

EXERCISES

I What are the feminine forms of the following words?
bachelor; sir; monk; cock; widower; executor; fox; wizard; ambassador; marquis.

II Fill in the blanks:

(1) Josephine was a celebrated —— of the French. (2) A woman becomes a —— on her wedding-day and a —— thereafter. (3) When a woman becomes engaged her fiancé refers to her as his ——. (4) Florence Nightingale was the —— of the Crimean War. (5) Sarah Bernhardt was a famous ——. (6) The former Mrs. Simpson is now the —— of Windsor. (7) The little piglets were suckled by the ——. (8) Sauce for the g—— is sauce for the g——(*Proverb*). (9) Barbara Hutton became —— to the Woolworth millions. (10) Sappho was a lyric ——.

III In how many ways can the feminine of English nouns be formed?

Give two examples of each.

IV What are the genders of the following nouns?

table, draper, ship, baby, sovereign, professor, puppy, chorus, representative, doctor, tomboy.

V A wedding usually brings together members of several families; it also causes certain changes in relationships. About twenty words can be used to describe those concerned. How many can you find?

VI Give five nouns of common gender.

VII Give three nouns with masculine *and* feminine forms that you can use about:

religion, nobility, restaurants, farm animals, law.

VIII Give the alternative forms, masculine or feminine, of: tomcat, widow, wolf, emperor, bride, marquis.

CHAPTER SIX

NOUNS: (4) CASE

Grammatical case is the relation in which one noun or pronoun stands to some other word in the sentence, or the form of the noun or pronoun which shows that relation.

In Old English, nouns had five cases, Nominative, Vocative, Accusative, Genitive and Dative, each generally distinguished by 'case endings'.

In modern English there is only one case ending for nouns, the POSSESSIVE (or GENITIVE). There is no distinction in form between nouns that are in the nominative case and nouns that are in the objective case, though there is this distinction with some pronouns. (See p. 98.)

THE POSSESSIVE (GENITIVE) CASE

I. The possessive form of the noun (sometimes called the 'Saxon Genitive') is formed as follows:

(1) For singular nouns, by adding -'s:[1]

The boy's book (i.e. the book of the boy).

Tom's house (i.e. the house of Tom).

Keats's poems (i.e. the poems of Keats).

With some names, chiefly classical ones, ending in -s, we use only the apostrophe:

Hercules' labours; Phoebus' horses; St. Agnes' Eve; Moses' laws; Sophocles' plays.

So also in: for *goodness*' sake, for *conscience*' sake,

(2) For plural nouns ending in -s by adding apostrophe only:

The boys' house (i.e. the house of the boys).

The soldiers' horses (i.e. the horses of the soldiers).

(3) For plural nouns not ending in -s (a very limited number) by adding 's, e.g.

---

[1] The usual ending for the Old English genitive singular was -es. When, later, the -e was omitted, its absence was shown by an apostrophe (').

The *men's* room (i.e. the room of the men).

The *women's* Society (i.e. the Society of the women).

The *children's* voices (i.e. the voices of the children).

The 's can have three pronunciations:

[s] with words ending in voiceless consonants (except [s], [ʃ], [tʃ]) e.g. *Smith's, cat's, Philip's.*

[z] with words ending in vowel sounds or voiced consonants (except [z], [ʒ] and [dʒ]) e.g. *boy's, lady's, Bob's.*

[iz] with words ending in [s], [ʒ], [z], [ʃ], [dʒ], [tʃ] e.g. *horse's, judge's, James's, witch's.*

II. When the 'possessor' is represented by a number of words, the possessive ending is used with the last one only, e.g.

Crosse & Blackwell's jam; Bryant & May's matches; Jones, the butcher's, shop; my father-in-law's house; The Prince of Wales's feathers; my father and mother's friends.

III. The possessive, or genitive case shows possession, using the word 'possession' in its widest sense. Thus the possessive form 'John's father' does not mean that John 'possesses' his father, nor does 'Shakespeare's death' mean that Shakespeare 'possessed' death. The Genitive form is used to indicate not only possession in the strict sense of the word but something, signified by another noun, which appertains to the person.

IV. The possessive form is used chiefly with the names of human beings and some animals, e.g. *John's friend; Mrs. Brown's car; the cat's tail; a spider's web.* With inanimate things we use the 'of' construction. Thus we say:

'the window of the room', not 'the room's window'.

and similarly:

The colours of the flowers; the noise of the traffic; the walls of the house; the foot of the mountain.

There are some exceptions to this rule:

(*a*) In the case of nouns denoting measurement, time or space, or quantity, as :

a *week's* holiday; two *days'* wages; a *year's* absence; an *hour's* time; *today's* post; *yesterday's* news; a *stone's* throw; a *hair's* breadth; a *shilling's* worth.

(*b*) In a number of traditional idiomatic expressions:

at his *wits'* end; out of *harm's* way; to your *heart's* content; in my *mind's* eye; to get one's *money's* worth.

Subjective and Objective Genitive

V. When a possessive word qualifies a noun that has something of verbal force (i.e. that denotes an action), the relation of this noun to the possessive word may be that of (*a*) a verb to a subject, or (*b*) a verb to an object. Thus:

'Thompson's murder' may imply (*a*) that Thompson committed the murder, or (*b*) that Thompson was murdered.

'The King's praise' may imply (*a*) that the King praised someone ('He was pleased by the King's praise'), or (*b*) that someone praised the King ('He is always singing the King's praise').

Similarly with the 'of' construction when the noun has a 'verbal association':

'The love of his wife' may imply (*a*) that he loved his wife ('He did that for love of his wife'), or (*b*) that his wife loved him ('He was happy in the love of his wife').

'The punishment of the teacher' may imply (*a*) that the teacher gave punishment, or (*b*) that the teacher received punishment.

In the examples (*a*), the genitive case indicates the subject or doer of the action. They are SUBJECTIVE GENITIVE. In the examples (*b*) it indicates the *object* or receiver of the action. They are examples of the OBJECTIVE GENITIVE.

Elliptical Use of the Genitive

VI. The genitive is frequently used 'elliptically', i.e. without a headword when referring to a business, building, etc.

I must go to the *butcher's* this morning. (butcher's = butcher's *shop*.)

I bought this at *Harridge's* (*shop*).

We visited St. *Paul's* (*Cathedral*).

He was educated at *Merchant Taylors'* (*School*).

We are having dinner at my *aunt's* (*house*) tonight.

The headword is sometimes omitted to avoid repetition:

She put her arm through her *brother's* (*arm*).
I have read some of Shaw's plays, but none of *Shakespeare's*.
William's is the only homework that is never badly done.
'Whose book is this?' 'It's *John's*.'

VII. The 'of' construction cannot be used with 'classifying genitives', i.e. genitives that are completely adjectival, e.g.

He is a *ship's* carpenter. (NOT: 'the carpenter of a ship'.)
She is a *lady's* maid.
He has a *doctor's* degree.
It was a *summer's* day.

VIII. With proper nouns the genitive is perhaps commoner than the *of* construction; the latter is used mainly for balance. So we say:

'Henry's work' but 'the work of Henry and John'; 'Scott's *Waverley*' but 'The collected novels of Scott'.

We should also use the *of* construction in order to avoid putting an *'s* to a long phrase, e.g.

Richard Cromwell was the son of Oliver Cromwell, the Protector of England. (NOT: 'Oliver Cromwell the Protector of England's son'.)

This is the car of the man we met. (NOT: 'the man we met's car'.)

THE DOUBLE POSSESSIVE

IX. An idiomatic construction of the language is the use of the *'s* form and *of* together:

He is a friend of *Henry's*. We saw a play of *Shaw's*.[1]

This construction is very similar in meaning to 'one of Henry's friends'; 'one of Shaw's plays'.

A difference is that *a friend of Henry's, a play of Shaw's,* could be said if Henry had only one friend or if Shaw had written only one play. 'One of Henry's friends', 'one of Shaw's plays', could not be said if this were the case.

This construction is of importance since it enables us to make a difference in meaning between:

[1] See also p. 109.

A portrait of Rembrandt (= one portraying him).
and

A portrait of Rembrandt's (= one painted by him or belonging to him).

or between:

a criticism of Shaw (= opinion about Shaw).
and

a criticism of Shaw's (= opinions by Shaw).

EXERCISES

I Express by using the possessive form:

The car of my father. The car of my parents. The
property of my son-in-law. The toys of the children.
The reign of William the Conqueror. The plays of
Sophocles.

II Express by means of idioms containing a possessive
case:

(1) In one year from now. (2) I got good value for the
money I spent. (3) I live very near here. (4) I bought
potatoes to the value of a shilling. (5) I have enough
work here to last me for a week. (6) He very narrowly
missed colliding with another car.

III Combine by means of a double possessive:
play — Shakespeare; friend — John; fugue — Bach;
hobby — Cecil; work — Hugo.

IV Combine the following in *two* ways to result in different
meanings. In each case explain the difference.

A photograph — Cecil Beaton. A judgment — this
famous historian. A condemnation — Judge Jeffreys.
An opinion — my father.

V Introduce possessive cases into each of the following
sentences, where possible, making any necessary
changes in wording.

(1) That house belongs to my sisters. (2) The refectory
of the brethren has a fine vaulted ceiling. (3) Those
careless visitors left the gate of the field open. (4) This
tie was good value for ten shillings. (5) An unexpected
turn of the wheel of Fortune made him a rich man.
(6) November 1st, the day of All Saints, is called

'——' in England. (7) He borrowed a book belonging to me last week. (8) The Cathedral of St. Giles is the principal church in Edinburgh. (9) There is a shop belonging to Freeman, Hardy and Willis in almost every English town. (10) We set out on our journey on a cold morning in winter. (11) After climbing for two hours we were glad to take a rest for a few minutes. (12) Here are the football results for today. (13) They have worked well all day today. (14) A drive of 500 miles in a small car is very tiring. (15) As we flew south the peaks of the Alps were gleaming in the sunlight.

VI How do you interpret the meaning of the possessive form in the following sentences?

(1) The President's proclamation was welcomed by the people. (2) The President's assassination caused a political crisis. (3) Peter's photograph in the exhibition was much praised. (4) John's wedding presents were magnificent. (5) The general opinion of the critic is not very favourable.

VII Introduce a genitive form in the following where possible, changing words as may be necessary.

(1) Blenheim Palace is the residence of the Dukes of Marlborough. (2) To live abroad is the desire of his heart. (3) The shop of Blackwell, the bookseller, is in Broad Street. (4) We had tea at the restaurant of Fortnum & Mason. (5) The crest of the Prince of Wales is three feathers.

VIII Describe the forms of genitive used in the following sentences:

(1) Those shoes are my brother's. (2) The soldiers' horses were superbly harnessed. (3) Shakespeare's birth took place at Stratford-on-Avon. (4) St. John's is a well-known College in Oxford. (5) That officer holds a master's certificate.

IX A fond mother asked a distinguished musician to come and hear her daughter play the piano, which he agreed to do. When the girl had finished playing, the following conversation took place:

MOTHER: Do tell me what you think of my daughter's execution.

DISTINGUISHED MUSICIAN: Madam, I think it would be an excellent idea!

Comment on this

CHAPTER SEVEN

THE ARTICLES

The words *a* (*an*), and *the* are generally called 'articles'; *a* (*an*) is the INDEFINITE ARTICLE, *the* the DEFINITE ARTICLE. The definite article is invariable for gender and number. The indefinite article is invariable for gender; it is not used with plural nouns.

A has the pronunciation [ə] weak form, [ei] strong form.

An has the pronunciation [ən] weak form; [æn] strong form. The weak forms are almost always used in normal speech.

a is used before a word beginning with a consonant sound; *an* before a word beginning with a vowel sound. *Examples:*

a day, a boy, a train, an apple, an open book, an angry child, an hour, an honest man, an honourable act, an heir.

An is used sometimes even before a normally aspirated *h* when the stress does not fall on the first syllable of the word, e.g. *an hotel, an historical* novel.

We say *a European, a University, a useful* book, *a one-eyed* man because the first sound in each of these words is not a vowel sound but a consonant one.

The has three pronunciations:

(1) [ðə] when followed by a consonant sound, e.g.

the boy [ðə boi]; the cat [ðə kat]; the university [ðə juːniˈvəːsiti].

(2) [ði] when followed by a vowel sound:

the apple [ði ˈapl]; the ear [ði iə]; the heiress [ði ˈeəris].

(3) [ðiː] when specially emphasized. In print it would appear in italics, e.g.

I was told you were Mr. Crosby; are you *the* Mr. Crosby? [ˈðiː ˈmistə ˈkrozbi]

He was one of the first persons, if not *the* first person to drive a car.

'I am never at a loss for *a* word; Pitt is never at a loss for *the* word.'[1]

---

[1] Said by Charles James Fox (1749–1806), a great orator, about his rival William Pitt (1759–1806), an even greater orator.

History of the Articles

Historically, the 'articles' are really adjectives. *The* was originally a form of *that*, a demonstrative adjective. You can see its nature as a demonstrative with the meaning *that* in such sentences as:

I was not there at *the* time (i.e. at that particular time). I told him I was busy at *the* moment. That car cost £2,500 and was cheap at *the* price. He is an engineer, or something of *the* kind. Lend you money? I shall do nothing of *the* kind.

In Old English *an* was a numeral adjective. A stressed form became modern English *one;* an unstressed form became *an*. *An* was used before consonant sounds as well as before vowel sounds until about 1300 and before sounded *h* until 1700 or later. At about the fifteenth century *a, an* were often written joined to the noun. Owing to a later wrong division we get *an apron* (original *a napron*, cf. French *nappe*), *an adder* (original *a nadder*), *an orange* (original *a norange*), *a newt* (formerly *an ewt*).

THE INDEFINITE ARTICLE

The indefinite article is used only before singular countable nouns.[1]

The plural of *a book, a year, a child*, is:

books (or *some books*), *years* (*some years*), *children* (*some children*).

The indefinite article is used:

(1) With the meaning *one*,[2] *any, it doesn't matter which*, e.g.

I have *a* sister and two brothers. The animals came in two at *a* time. '*A* stitch in time saves nine' (*Proverb*). *A* triangle has three sides. Please pass me *a* fork.

(2) In certain expressions of measurement:

He drove the car at ninety miles *an* hour. This material is 12s. 6d. *a* yard. Butter is 4s. *a* pound. We have lessons three times *a* week. He earns £1,000 *a* year.

---

[1] See also Determinatives, Chapter 10.
[2] *One* is used when the numeral is emphasized.

(3) Before *dozen, hundred, thousand, million.*

There are *a* dozen eggs here. *A* hundred sheep were in the field.

(Note that when these words are in the subject, they take a plural verb.)

(4) Before singular predicative[1] nouns denoting a profession, trade, religion, class, etc. (In some languages the article would not be used here.)

George wants to be *an* engineer. Mary's father is *an* officer in the Navy. You ought not to call him *a* fool. The King made him *a* lord. He was *a* Muslim not *a* Christian. Is he *a* Conservative or *a* Socialist?

But if the noun denotes a title or office that can only be held by one person at a time, the indefinite article is not used, e.g.

They made him King (NOT: '*a* King'). Mr. Priestley was Professor of English at Oxbridge University (NOT: '*a* Professor of English'). As Chairman of the Society, I call on Mr. X to speak. Nelson became Captain of the *Victory* in 1800.

It is not used after the verb *turn* in the meaning *become*, e.g.

He was a Conservative but he *turned Socialist.* He used to be a teacher till he *turned writer.*

nor after the nouns *rank* or *title*, e.g.

He gained the rank of Colonel. He was given the title of Duke.

(5) It is used also to refer to a person known only as a name, e.g.

A Mr. Johnson called to see you when you were out.

(The *a* gives the meaning 'I have no idea who he is, but he said his name was Mr. Johnson'.)

(6) With the meaning *same* in proverbs and certain fixed expressions:

Birds of *a* feather flock together (a feather = the same kind). They were much of *a* size (= of the same size).

[1] Predicative nouns are nouns forming the complement of verbs such as *to be, make,* etc., see pages 11, 12.

(7) Before a noun in apposition when the thing or person is assumed to be unfamiliar, e.g.

Blake, *an* English poet; Lowton, *a* small town in Lancashire; 'Lycidas', *a* poem by Milton.

(8) In exclamatory sentences[1] introduced by 'What', where the noun is singular and countable:

What *a* foolish thing to do! What *a* pretty girl! What *a* day!

The Indefinite Article is not used with uncountable nouns:

What weather we are having! *What* good milk this is!
What care he's taken with this!

(but notice 'What *a* pity', though *pity* is generally an uncountable noun.)

(9) In a number of phrases, e.g.

It's *a* pity that . . .; I want to keep this *a* secret; as *a* rule; to be in *a* hurry; to be in *a* temper; all of *a* sudden; it's *a* shame to do that; to take *an* interest in; to take *a* pride in; to take *a* dislike to; to make *a* fool of oneself; to be in *a* position to; to have *a* headache/*a* pain/*a* cold/*a* cough (but to have toothache, earache, rheumatism, influenza); to have *a* mind to; to have *a* fancy for; to have *a* chance/opportunity/ to; at *a* discount/premium; on *an* average; *a* short time ago.

Notice also the constructions, *such a; quite a; many a; rather a*, e.g.

I have had *such a* busy day. There were *quite a* lot of people there. *Many a* ship has been wrecked there. He is *rather a* fool.

and the construction *so* + ADJECTIVE + *a*, e.g.

We have not had *so good a* day as this for a long time.

EXERCISES

I Put 'a' or 'an' in front of the following words or phrases:

university; one-sided affair; honest deal; history of England; historical survey; ewe; unintentional mistake; unilateral agreement; bottle; ink-bottle; hotel.

[1] See page 316.

II Read the following aloud:

(1) The cat. (2) The owl. (3) The heir. (4) The host.
(5) The United States. (6) The one and only. (7) That's
not the Mr. Knight I used to know. (8) 'That's Mr.
William Morris'. 'What, *the* Mr. William Morris?' (9) The
day we met was a wonderful day; but the day we get
married will be *the* day. (10) He gets paid by the hour,
not by the week.

III Put into the singular:

men, women and children; roofs; cherries; wives; feet;
hundreds of times; Europeans, Africans, Americans,
Asians and *Australians; potatoes and other vegetables;*
hippopotami in rivers; intelligent students.

IV Insert the indefinite article in the blank spaces *where*
necessary. Otherwise leave the space blank:

(1) —— geometry set contains —— ruler —— pair of
compasses, —— protractor and —— pair of dividers.
(2) His father was —— lawyer and earned £3,000 ——
year. (3) Go and buy —— half —— pound of sugar.
(4) One tenth of —— thousand is —— hundred, and
—— thousand thousands are —— million. (5) What
—— nuisance! I left —— meat on the table and the
dog has eaten it. (6) For breakfast we have —— porridge, —— bacon and eggs, or sometimes —— fish,
and we end up with —— toast and —— marmalade or
—— apple. (7) He became —— member of Parliament
as —— Conservative, but later turned —— Socialist
and became —— Member for Salton. (8) What ——
humorous man your friend is, and what —— fun he is!
(9) Byrd, —— Elizabethan musician, wrote many
motets.

V Explain the senses in which the indefinite articles are
used in the following sentences:

(1) 'Shall we give her *a* book for Christmas?' 'Oh, she
already has *a* book.' (2) We shall be late if we don't
take *a* taxi. (3) Some modern planes can fly at over *a*
thousand miles *an* hour. (4) *A* score of people is twenty
people. (5) My brother is studying to be *a* doctor.

VI Supply the indefinite articles *where required* in the
following:

(1) He used to be —— missionary in Africa but now he
is —— Rector of this parish. (2) '—— man's —— man
for all that.' (3) As —— Leader of the Opposition he
receives an official salary. (4) He was so ravenously

hungry that he ate three sandwiches at —— mouthful.
(5) 'Much of —— muchness' means that there is little
difference between two things. (6) Where there's ——
will there's —— way. (7) What —— weather we are
having and what —— abominable climate this is!
(8) *King Lear*, ——play by Shakespeare, is among the
greatest of all tragedies. (9) I have —— corn on my foot
but it's less painful than —— toothache. (10) We
haven't —— hope of catching the train now.

VII Express the following by sentences containing an
indefinite article:

(1) The animals went in *two by two*. (2) One pound of
meat costs about three shillings and sixpence. (3) In one
year a teacher has holidays three times. (4) Someone called Mr. Rolfe rang up and asked for you.
(5) I have seen him *many times* out with his dog. (6) My
stomach aches. (7) People of similar tastes enjoy one
another's company. (8) The play we saw wasn't much
good. (9) He asked me *not to mention the matter to
anyone else*. (10) He *behaved very foolishly*. (11) I got
these goods *more cheaply* by buying a large quantity.
(12) They *generally* go to the seaside but this year they
changed their plans *without warning* anyone. (13) He
was given the opportunity of travelling round the world,
lucky fellow! (14) That book was written *when my
grandfather was young*.

THE DEFINITE ARTICLE

The definite article can be used before singular or plural
nouns whether countable or uncountable.

The definite article is used:

(1) Before a noun that is to be particularized by a defining
relative clause,[1] e.g.

This is *the* book that I promised to lend you.

(2) With the meaning: 'the only one', e.g.

The sun rises in *the* east and sets in *the* west. *The* Bible, *the*
Lord (= God).

(3) With the meaning: 'The one we have just spoken about',
e.g.

---

[1] For defining and non-defining clauses, see pages 324–6.

Once upon a time there was *a* little boy who lived in *a* cottage. *The* cottage was in the country and *the* boy had lived there all his life.

The indefinite article *a* here introduces a new thing or person; the definite article, *the* denotes a thing or person already mentioned.

(4) Before a noun which is followed by a defining prepositional phrase, e.g.

the battle of Trafalgar; *the* Palace of Westminster; *the* house with green shutters; *the* road to London; *the* letter from America; *the* fourteenth of April.[1]

(5) Before ordinals in titles, e.g.

Queen Elizabeth II (Queen Elizabeth *the* Second).

(6) Before a common noun followed by a proper noun which identifies it, e.g.

the planet Mercury; *the* poet Byron; *the* play 'King Lear'.

Nouns expressing trades or professions often follow the proper noun; they are preceded by *the*, e.g.

Jackson, *the* butcher; Brown, *the* General Manager; Lizzie, *the* cook.

Similarly with nouns in apposition:

Rome, *the* capital of Italy.

(7) Before the name of a country that is a union of smaller entities, e.g.

The United Kingdom; *the* U.S.S.R.

or one that is plural in form, e.g.

The Netherlands; *the* United States.

and in cases where a common noun which usually accompanied the geographical name has been dropped, e.g.

The Sahara (desert); *the* Crimea (peninsula).

(8) Before groups of Islands, e.g.

The West Indies, *the* Hebrides, *the* Bahamas.

---

[1] Note that in writing the date we omit *the* and *of*, but in reading that date we generally put them in, e.g., May 15th (*The* fifteenth *of* May); 25th July (*The* twenty-fifth *of* July or July *the* twenty-fifth).

C

(9) Before the names of rivers, chains of mountains and oceans, e.g.

The Thames, *the* Danube, *the* Atlantic, *the* Alps, *the* Andes.

(10) Before the names of ships, trains and aeroplanes, e.g.

The Queen Mary, *the* Flying Scotsman, *the* Comet.

(11) Before the names of hotels, shops, institutions, etc., where the name is an impersonal one, e.g.

The Ritz Hotel, *the* Army and Navy Stores, *the* Midland Bank, *the* Odeon Cinema.

(12) Before a singular countable noun to make a generalization about a species, e.g.

The horse is being replaced by *the* tractor.

(13) Before the names of musical instruments used in a general sense:

Mrs. Priestley plays *the* piano; Mr. Priestley is learning *the* violin.

(14) Before superlatives used attributively, e.g.

This is *the* oldest building in Canterbury.

sometimes before superlatives used adverbially, e.g.

I like Shakespeare but it is modern drama that interests me *the* most.

People who have those seats in the theatre will pay *the* least.

and before superlatives used as nouns, e.g.

This is *the best* I can do.

The most he can get is a fine of £5.

(15) Before adjectives used as nouns denoting a whole class:[1]

The rich (= rich people) should help *the* poor (= poor people).

The *French* cook better than the *English*.

The definite article is not used:

(1) Before abstract nouns used in a general sense, e.g.

Life is very hard for some people. (NOT: 'the life'.)

We will have freedom or death. (NOT: 'the freedom', etc.)

---

[1] See also page 65.

But we use *the* before abstract nouns that are limited or qualified, e.g.

The life we live here is hard.
The freedom of the seas. . . .
The work that we do. . . .

(2) Before names of materials used in a general sense, e.g.

Butter is made from cream. (NOT: *'the* butter' . . . *'the* cream'.)
Wheat is grown in Canada.

(3) Before plural nouns used in a general sense, e.g.

Books are my best friends.

BUT:

The books that are on the table are mine.

In the second sentence we are referring not to books in general but to some particular books.

(4) Before names of meals used in a general sense, e.g.

Come to dinner/lunch/tea with me.

but:

Are you coming to *the* dinner that we are having in London next week?

(5) Before most proper nouns, e.g.

I walked in Hyde Park. (NOT: *'the* Hyde Park'.) Do you know Regent Street? Lucille comes from France.

(6) Before *Lake, Cape, Mount:*

Lake Superior, Loch (= Scottish 'Lake') Lomond. Cape Wrath, Cape Cod, Mount Everest, Mount Vesuvius.

except when these words are followed by *of*, e.g.

the Lake of Lucerne; *the* Cape of Good Hope; *the* Mount of Olives.

(7) Before titles followed by a proper noun, e.g.

King George; Doctor Livingstone; Professor Russell; Lord Byron; President Lincoln.

(8) With the names of languages, e.g. She speaks Spanish.

(9) With words like *school, church, prison*, when the idea expressed concerns the use made of the building, e.g.

> He has gone to school (to learn).
> They are in church just now (to worship).

but:

> He has gone to *the* school (just to see the place).
> They are in *the* church just now (merely looking round).

(10) Before the names of seasons and festivals, e.g.

> Winter is the best time for reading.
> We are going there in spring/at Easter/on Boxing Day.

(11) With words like *cook, nurse, teacher* when they have the meaning 'our cook/teacher', e.g.

> Cook has made mince-pies for Christmas.
> Teacher was very pleased with my work.

Here they have the function of names, so the omission of the article is natural.

(12) Sometimes before predicative superlatives, e.g.

> The sea is *deepest* about twenty miles from the coast.
> He is *happiest* when he is working.
> Your help was *most valuable*.

(See also Adjectives p. 76.)

(13) In various stock phrases:

> He showed great bravery *in face of* danger. *In place of* meat we are having fish. We are *in sight of* land. Arrange the books *in order of* size. He is *beyond reach of* danger now. The car was damaged *beyond hope of* repair. They set off *under cover of* darkness. *In case of* fire ring the bell. He did it *by way of* helping me. As soon as I *set foot on* the island he wanted to *shake hands with me*. She is going to *keep house for*. . . . The ship has *set sail*. This will easily *catch fire*. We came *by land/by sea/by air*. To go *on board ship*. . . . To stay *at home*. . . . To be *out of doors*. The men work *by day* but not *by night*. He is *in debt/in trouble*. *At daybreak/sunset*. He did the work *for love*, not *for money*. The ship is *at anchor*.

IDIOMATIC USE OF *the*

There is an idiomatic use of *the* with the comparative of adjectives.[1]

The harder you work, *the* more you will be paid.

The more he gets, *the* more he wants.

The sooner that work is finished, *the* better.

I hope a lot of people come to the party; *the* more, *the* merrier.

EXERCISES

I Which one of these words, *used in a general sense*, must be preceded by the definite article? Why?

milk, butter, cheese, eggs, cows, cow.

II Insert the definite article *where necessary:*

(1) —— boy over there is —— worst in the class at French. (2) —— Magna Carta was signed by —— King John in —— year 1215. (3) —— Armistice came on —— eleventh day of —— November 1918. (4) —— Armistice Day is now observed on —— nearest Sunday to —— eleventh of —— November. (5) —— Treaty of Versailles laid down —— harsh terms. (6) —— supervisor inspects all —— work. (7) All —— work and no —— play makes —— Jack a dull boy. (8) My brother is a sportsman; he plays —— tennis, —— football, —— cricket and —— hockey: my sister is a musician; she plays —— harp, —— piano and —— violin. (9) Brown, —— chemist, sells —— pills. (10) Have you had —— tea yet? Yes, I had it out, and my friend paid —— bill. (11) ——monkeys are intelligent animals. Yes, but they are not —— most intelligent of all —— animals. (12) He is a student of —— architecture; an important part of his studies is —— History of Architecture. (13) —— world opinion is against —— aggression. (14) In —— opinion of —— Captain Brown —— shortest way to —— Japan would be through —— Panama Canal. (15) —— information on this matter is lacking, or at least —— information we are all wanting. (16) Which do you prefer, —— Lake Geneva or —— Lake of Constance? (17) What is —— difference between —— middle age and —— Middle Ages? (18) —— pen is mightier than —— sword. (19)

[1] See 'Adjectives', page 77.

—— Prince Philip is —— Duke of Edinburgh. (20) —— Duke of Windsor was once —— King of England. (21) —— Queen is —— queen of —— England and also of other countries in —— Commonwealth. (22) Which language do you speak better, —— German or —— French? (23) —— French language is better known here than —— Russian. (24) I go to —— school every day except —— Sundays; then I go to —— church. (25) —— life is hard, especially —— life of an altruist. (26) We read —— papers every day to improve our English vocabulary. (27) —— irregular verbs in —— French language are very difficult. (28) They always give —— postman a present at —— Christmas time. (29) —— eldest son of —— Edward —— Third was called —— Black Prince. (30) ——burglars were sent to —— gaol for —— six months. (31) I prefer —— going by —— sea to going in —— train. (32) —— Domestic Science College teaches —— girls how to keep —— house. (33) Avoid —— short cuts. —— longest way round is often —— shortest way home. (34) Many boys leave —— school at eighteen to begin —— military service. (35) —— Oxford Street is one of —— busiest streets in —— London.

III Use each of these words in two sentences, once *with* and once *without* a definite article:
  teacher; both¹; all¹; princess; rich; life; cream; dinner; church; glass; iron; tin.

IV Explain the sense in which the definite article is employed in these three sentences:
  (1) That's the man you are looking for. (2) The Lord Chancellor is the principal law officer of the Government. (3) I met two foreigners yesterday. The one was here to study English but the other had come to England for a holiday.

V Change these sentences into the plural:
  (1) The telephone is almost a necessity in the modern world. (2) The book he bought at the auction proved to be a first edition. (3) This boy is going to school tomorrow for the first time but his brother has been in the sixth form at the Grammar School for some time. (4) 'The daring young man on the flying trapeze' (*title of popular song*). (5) The ape is the animal nearest to man in appearance.

¹ These words are sometimes *followed*, though never preceded by 'the' (see also pages 83, 125, 128).

VI Supply articles where you think they are required:

(1) This house is for sale; in fact they have just put up for sale notice in window. (2) 1914 marks end of epoch. (3) Now that he wears long trousers Johnny looks very much grown-up. (4) He is charming and so is his wife, but their daughter is most charming. (5) When I was fourteen I was sent away to boarding school. School hall was very ancient but did not provide room for all boys attending school.

VII Explain why the definite article is used or omitted in the following :

(1) *Faith* is the finest of human qualities, but *the faiths* of *the West* differ widely from those of *the East.* (2) *Milk* is sold by the pint but *sugar* is sold by weight. (3) *The* Lord Mayor's Banquet always takes place in *Guildhall.* (4) *The* more we are together, *the* merrier we shall be. (5) *Cider* is made from the juice of *apples.* (6) *The* Easter holidays were very pleasant but at *Whitsuntide* we had only two days' break. (7) *The* Channel Islands are a favourite resort of tourists. (8) As soon as you hear *the result* of your examination, do send word. (9) *Patience* is a virtue. (10) Many English inns are called *the* King George the Fourth.

CHAPTER EIGHT

ADJECTIVES

The traditional definition of an adjective is 'a word used to describe or give more information about a noun',[1] or, rather more fully, 'a word that qualifies a noun, adds to its meaning but limits its application'. An example will make this latter definition clearer. The noun 'house' can be used to signify any house. 'The *big* house' tells more about the house but limits the application (it rules out all *small* houses). 'The *big new* house' tells still more, but narrows the field still further. The description 'The *big, new, white* house' applies to only a very few houses; it gives the fullest picture, and the most limited application.

THE ATTRIBUTIVE AND PREDICATIVE USE OF ADJECTIVES

Adjectives can be used in two ways: (1) attributively, (2) predicatively.

Adjectives are used attributively when they qualify a noun. e.g.

Henry is an *honest, hardworking* boy.

Mr. Brown has just bought a *new, powerful* and very *expensive* car.

Adjectives are used predicatively when they form the predicate with the verb *to be* or other verbs of incomplete predication. So in the sentence:

'That is a *new* house'

the adjective *new* is used attributively. In the sentence:

---

[1] The objection could be made that in using such a definition we are confusing a *noun* (which is a *word*) with a *thing*. Thus if we say that in the phrase 'a big house' *big* is an adjective describing the noun *house* we have fallen into an error in definition. It is the *thing* 'house' that is big and not the *noun* 'house'. This is true, of course. Nouns are words, and words are merely symbols for things. It is the thing meant by the noun that is described. Whenever, therefore, for the sake of brevity, we speak of adjectives describing 'nouns' this distinction should be kept in mind.

'That house is *new*.'

the adjective *new* is used predicatively.

Other examples of the predicative use of adjectives after verbs of incomplete predication are:

Richard is very *tired*. The dog was *hungry*. I thought him very *intelligent*. That boiler makes the water *hot*. His efforts proved *useless*. Tom has fallen *asleep*. Mary dyed her hair *brown*.

Note, that in interrogative sentences, formed by inversion of subject and verb, the predicative adjective comes after the subject, e.g.

Is the house *new?* Was the car *expensive?* Isn't Miss Jackson *pretty?* Aren't these peaches *delicious?*

Most adjectives can be used attributively or predicatively; but some, especially those that begin with *a*-, can only be used predicatively, e.g.

asleep, afraid, awake, alone, aware, alive, afloat, ashamed, content, exempt, unable.

A few, e.g. *former, latter, inner, outer* can only be used attributively.

Adjectives, whether predicative or attributive, are invariable for number, gender, person or case.

ADJECTIVES FUNCTIONING AS NOUNS

As has been already pointed out (p. 5), many English words can belong to more than one part of speech, and the deliberate use of a word that is normally one part of speech to do the work of a different part of speech is a characteristic feature of English. Thus, words that are usually adjectives may function as nouns. In this case they are always preceded by the definite article and, if they refer to people, are plural in meaning and take a plural verb, e.g.

The *blind* are taught trades at St. Dunstan's to fit them for work in the world.

Nurses are required to look after the *sick* and *wounded*, the *old* and *infirm*.

Fortune favours the *brave*.

Similarly, we can speak of *the English*, *the Irish*, *the French*, *the Dutch*, etc., but the plural noun must be used in: *the Germans*, *the Italians*, *the Americans*, *the Indians*, etc.

Occasionally the adjective is used as a noun and takes the definite article and a singular verb. In these cases it stands not for people but for an abstract quality, e.g.

The *good* in him outweighs the *bad*.

He thought that the aim of philosophy was to discover the *good*, the *beautiful* and the *true*.

'the *long* and *short* of it is . . .'; 'for *better* or *worse*'.

NOUNS FUNCTIONING AS ADJECTIVES

Words that are generally nouns can act as adjectives, e.g.

a *stone* wall, a *leather* belt, a *gold* watch, a *silver* wedding, a *Turkey* carpet, the *University* football match, *spring* onions, a *corner* seat (in a railway carriage), a *garden* table, *rubber* gloves, a *cotton* frock, *lawn* tennis, a *London* policeman, a *Shakespeare* play, *rice* pudding, the *Loch Ness* monster.

These groups are distinguished from compound nouns (see p. 21) by the stress pattern. They have a stress on each word, e.g. *stóne wáll* as compared with *mílk-bottle*.

Some of the 'material' nouns have another form which is distinctly adjectival, e.g. *wood — wooden; silver — silvery; gold — golden; flax — flaxen; brass — brazen*. There is a tendency to use the adjectival form for a figurative meaning, e.g. *golden* corn/hair/sunset; *silvery* hair; a *silken* voice; *flaxen* curls; *brazen* impudence. Sometimes the *-en* ending has the meaning 'made of'. Compare 'a *wool* merchant' and '*woollen* socks'; 'a *wood* fire' and 'a *wooden* box'.

THE FORMATION OF ADJECTIVES FROM NOUNS

In addition to the simple procedure just mentioned of using the same form with different grammatical values (the function being understood from the context) there is another method of forming adjectives from other parts of speech. That is by the use of a suffix. The principal suffixes used are *-y*, *-ly*, *-ful*, *-less*, *-en*, *-ous*, *-able*, *-some*, *-ic*, *-ed*, *-like*, *-al*, *-an*, *-ian*, *-ical*, *-ish*, e.g.

Noun	Adjective	Noun	Adjective
storm	stormy	good nature	good natured
friend	friendly	child	childlike[1]
harm	harmful	god	godlike[2]
care	careless	brute	brutal
wood	wooden	education	educational
danger	dangerous	America	American
fame	famous	republic	republican
honour	honourable	Shakespeare	Shakespearian[3]
trouble	troublesome	Edward	Edwardian[3]
quarrel	quarrelsome	history	historic(al)
Iceland	Icelandic	economy	economic(al)
atom	atomic	Turk	Turkish
talent	talented	girl	girlish

PARTICIPLES USED ADJECTIVALLY

Many participles,[4] both present and past, have all the characteristics of adjectives, thus, they can be used attributively or predicatively; they can be modified by adverbs like *very, too, quite*; they form their comparative[5] by adding *more*, and their superlative[5] by adding *most*, e.g.

He told a very *amusing* story. That book has made a *lasting* impression on my mind. Henry is a *more promising* pupil than Richard, but John is the *most promising* of them all. He is a *never-failing* help in time of trouble. My flight from London to Paris in a small 'plane was a *terrifying* experience.

These participles with purely adjectival characteristics are sometimes called PARTICIPIALS. Though they have exactly the

---

[1] The adjective *childlike* has a favourable implication, e.g. 'innocent'. The adjective *childish* has often the implication 'foolish', 'futile', etc.
[2] *godlike* = like a god; majestic. *Godly* = devoted to God; pious.
[3] Pronounced [ʃeiks'piəriən] [ed'wɔːdiən]. All similar formations are stressed in this way.
[4] For Participles see pages 236–242.
[5] For Comparatives and Superlatives see pages 70–77.

same form as participles forming part of a verb, their function is not the same.

Note the difference in function between:

The hour's delay was most *annoying*. (Adjective) and:

Is the smoke *annoying* you? (Participle helping to form the Continuous tense.)

A *singing* bird in a cage fills me with anger (*Adjective*). The bird was *singing* on the tree (*Participle*). He told an *amusing* story (*Adjective*). Henry was in the nursery *amusing* the children (*Participle*).

Similarly with Past Participles:

There were a lot of *broken* bottles on the road (*Adjective*). The glass was *broken* by the girl's carelessness (Participle helping to form Passive Voice). A *confused* mob stormed the Government buildings (*Adjective*). You have *confused* the meanings of the two words. (Participle helping to form Present Perfect Tense). The *tired* child fell asleep in her mother's arms (*Adjective*). That long walk has *tired* me (*Participle*).

THE FORMATION OF THE NEGATIVE OF ADJECTIVES AND ADVERBS

The negative of adjectives (and adverbs) is frequently formed by the use of prefixes or suffixes, e.g.

un-: unhappy, unfortunate(ly), unpleasant(ly); *in-:* inaccurate, inartistic, inattentive; *im-:* impossible, imperfect, immodest; *ir-:* irresponsible, irregular, irresolute; *il-:* illegal, illiterate, illegitimate; *dis-:* disagreeable, disrespectful, dishonest; *-less* (to the stem of adjectives, especially adjectives ending in *-ful*)*:* helpless, hopeless, useless, valueless.

EXERCISES

I Supply suitable attributive adjectives for these nouns:
tyrant; sunset; crossing; pianist; fox; hermit; prayer; suitor; disaster; legend.

II Supply suitable predicative adjectives:

(1) His unsuccessful life had left him ———. (2) James was very ——— of his son's success. (3) After his friends had remonstrated with him about his idleness he became much more ———. (4) His argument proved most ———. (5) Charles seemed ——— to be off at the earliest possible moment, and to be growing more and more ——— of delay. (6) We should be ——— if you would send us samples. (7) The publishers are ——— the success of the book will be ——— and ———.

III Form sentences, using the following words, (*a*) as participles, and (*b*) as participial adjectives:

inspired; learned;[1] *aged;*[1] *blessed;*[1] *sweeping; guiding; manufactured; finished; annoying.*

IV Re-write the following passage so that the adjectives used attributively become predicative and vice versa: The Browns are a lazy family but they are very kind-hearted despite the fact that they live in distressing poverty, so we must feel grateful to them and encourage them to be more industrious.

V Name the function of the words in italics in the following sentences:

(1) He is *writing* a book, but the *finished* text will not be ready for some months. (2) His work showed a *decided* improvement as soon as he had really *decided* to study hard. (3) They were just *finishing* the race as we reached the *starting* point. (4) When I have *retired* from work I shall live a very *retired* life. (5) The diamonds were *twinkling* in the glare of the lights like *twinkling* stars.

VI What, in your opinion, would be the ideal definition of an adjective to use in a textbook of grammar? Support your answer by examples.

VII Which of the following adjectives can be used (*a*) only predicatively, (*b*) only attributively, (*c*) either predicatively or attributively? List them under the three headings mentioned above and then construct sentences to illustrate their use:

dyed, astonished, former, unwell, disturbed, major, lonely, agog, happy, dutiful.

---

[1] *N.B.* These words, when used as adjectives, are pronounced as dissyllables ['lɔːnid; 'eidʒid; 'blesid], though, in the case of 'blessed', only when used attributively.

CHAPTER NINE

COMPARISON OF ADJECTIVES

When one thing is compared or contrasted with another (or others) in respect of a certain attribute, we use an inflection called COMPARISON. Comparison can express *equality, superiority* or *inferiority;* that is to say it can state whether two people or things possess some quality in the same degree (*equality*) or in different degrees (*superiority* or *inferiority*). It can also express *supremacy* of one person or thing in respect of an attribute.

There are three degrees of Comparison: POSITIVE DEGREE, COMPARATIVE DEGREE, SUPERLATIVE DEGREE. *Examples:*

Positive	Comparative	Superlative
old	older	oldest
hot	hotter	hottest
careful	more careful	most careful

Equality is expressed by the Positive Degree, e.g.

Harry is *as old as* William. It is just *as hot* today *as* it was yesterday. Mary is *as careful as* Margaret.

Superiority is expressed by the Comparative Degree, e.g.

George is *older than* William. It is *hotter* today *than* it was yesterday. Elizabeth is *more careful than* Margaret.

Inferiority is expressed by using '*less . . . than*'.

Margaret is *less* careful *than* Elizabeth.

It is *less* hot today *than* it was yesterday.

but this construction is rarely used; it would be far more usual to say:

Margaret is *not so* (*as*) careful *as* Elizabeth.

It is *not so* (*as*) hot today *as* it was yesterday.

It isn't *so* (*as*) hot today *as* it was yesterday.

In affirmative sentences the construction *as . . . as* is always used; in negative sentences *so . . . as* is the normal form, but *as . . . as* is frequently found.

Supremacy is expressed by the Superlative Degree, e.g.

That was the *happiest* day of his life.

He is the *oldest* man in the village.

I think 'Hamlet' is the *most sublime* of Shakespeare's plays.

The superlative degree often expresses the same thing as the comparative but from a different point of view. Thus:

'Richard is the *tallest* of the three brothers and is the *oldest* boy in the school' is really the same as: 'Richard is *taller* than his two brothers and is *older than* any other boy in the school.'

The POSITIVE DEGREE is the simple form of the adjective, e.g.

clear, happy, good.

FORMATION OF DEGREE OF COMPARISON

THE COMPARATIVE DEGREE is formed:

(1) By adding *-er* to the positive, e.g.

Positive	*Comparative*
clear	clearer
sweet	sweeter
soft	softer

(2) By using *more* with the positive, e.g.

Positive	*Comparative*
beautiful	more beautiful
interesting	more interesting
splendid	more splendid

THE SUPERLATIVE DEGREE is formed:

(1) By adding *-est* to the positive, e.g.

Positive	*Superlative*
clear	clearest
sweet	sweetest
soft	softest

(2) By using *most* with the positive, e.g.

Positive	*Superlative*
beautiful	most beautiful
interesting	most interesting
splendid	most splendid

Method (1) used:

(*a*) With monosyllabic adjectives (except *right, wrong, real*).

(*b*) With disyllabic adjectives that end in a vowel sound[1] or syllabic -*l*, e.g. *pretty — prettier — prettiest; simple — simpler — simplest; narrow — narrower — narrowest;* or that have the stress on the last syllable, e.g. *polite — politer — politest*.

(*c*) With certain frequently-used disyllabic adjectives that have their stress on the first syllable: *quiet — quieter — quietest; pleasant — pleasanter — pleasantest; handsome — handsomer — handsomest; common — commoner — commonest; narrow — narrower — narrowest*.

Method (2) is used:

(*a*) With most disyllabic adjectives with the accent on the first syllable, e.g. *hopeful — more/most hopeful; porous — more/most porous; fertile — more/most fertile*.

(*b*) With all adjectives of more than two syllables: *beautiful — more/most beautiful; extravagant — more/most extravagant*.

This method of comparison is used with adjectives like *afraid, alive,* etc. (see p. 65) that are only used predicatively.

There are a number of IRREGULAR COMPARISONS:

Positive	*Comparative*	*Superlative*
good (well)	better	best
bad (ill)	worse	worst
little	less (lesser)	least
near	nearer	nearest (next)
much (many)[2]	more	most
far	farther (further)	farthest (furthest)
late	later (latter)	latest (last)
old	older (elder)	oldest (eldest)
(out)	outer (utter)	outmost (utmost)
		outermost (uttermost)
(up)	upper	uppermost
(in)	inner	inmost, innermost
(fore)	former	foremost, first

---

[1] Including -*er* [ə] see p. 405.

[2] *much* is used with uncountable singular nouns, *many* with countable plural ones. (See also pages 93–5.)

Certain orthographic and phonetic points should be noted:

1. Words ending in -*y* preceded by a consonant letter, change this to *i* in comparative and superlative, e.g. *happy — happier — happiest*. This does not happen if the *y* is preceded by a vowel, e.g. *grey — greyer — greyest; gay — gayer — gayest*.

2. The final consonant letter of the word is doubled in the case of words of *one* syllable[1] containing *one* vowel letter followed by *one* consonant letter: *big — bigger — biggest; thin — thinner — thinnest*. (But notice that there is no doubling in, for example, *thick — thicker — thickest* because it ends in *two* consonant letters.)

3. A final mute -*e* disappears: *ripe — riper — ripest; fine — finer — finest*.

4. An *r* which was not sounded in the positive, is sounded in the comparative and superlative: *near — nearer — nearest*.

5. The sound [g] is added after [ŋ] in *strong — stronger — strongest*, and in *long* and *young*.

6. Syllabic [l] becomes non-syllabic, e.g. *able — abler — ablest; simple — simpler — simplest*.

THAN

To express superiority or inferiority, *than* with a comparative is used, e.g.

George is taller *than* Henry.

This car is less expensive *than* that one.

Than is also used after *rather*[2] and *sooner*, e.g.

He would *rather* (*sooner*) play *than* work.

It is also used, but less frequently, after *other* and *another*, e.g.

The result was quite *other than* we had expected.

This was quite *another* result *than* we expected.

---

[1] The rule applies to adjectives of more than one syllable if the accent is on the last syllable.

[2] *rather* is, historically, a comparative. The positive form was *rathe*, which is now obsolete. It meant 'early' and was used, with this meaning by Milton, 'The *rathe* primrose that forsaken dies' (Lycidas) and by Tennyson, 'Men of *rathe* and riper years'.

The more usual construction would be:

The result was quite different from what we expected. (*Different than* is sometimes heard but is better avoided.)

The comparative without *than* may be used:

(*a*) With a noun or *one*, e.g.

I want a *better* job.   Give me a *larger* piece of paper. Bring me a *smaller* one. 'In the spring a *livelier* iris changes on the burnished dove.' (Tennyson, *Locksley Hall*).

(*b*) In a predicative construction, e.g.

He is *better* now. It is *warmer* this morning. The apples will get *redder* in the autumn.

(*c*) After a noun or pronoun in such construction as:

They have made the house *bigger*. You must keep your work *cleaner*. He wants the work done *better*.

In these cases the comparison is implied though not expressed.

(*d*) After the following comparatives which are only used attributively:

inner, outer, upper, former, latter, utter, elder.

(*e*) After *senior, junior, superior, inferior, anterior, posterior.*

When used in comparisons these are followed by *to*.

This is *superior to* that. I am *junior to* him.

NOTES ON THE COMPARISON OF ADJECTIVES

1. *Major* and *minor* are used attributively and not predicatively, e.g.

The *major* part of his work. This is a *minor* point.

2. The forms *good* (*well*), *bad* (*ill*), *little, much, far* are not really corresponding forms to the superlative and comparative. They have a semantic connection but are from different roots.

Well is generally an adverb (see p. 271). It is a predicative adjective in such expressions as: I am very *well*; He looks/feels *well*.

Ill is an adjective in such expressions as to be/feel/look/fall *ill*; and in *ill* health/news/luck (but *bad* would be more usual).

3. The comparatives *outer, upper, inner* and the corresponding superlatives are derived from adverbs; i.e. the positive forms are adverbs, the comparative and superlative forms are adjectives.

The words *utter, utmost, uttermost* are, historically, comparatives and superlatives of *out,* but their modern meaning has little connection with *out.*

4. *Lesser* is archaic or poetic and is used only in a few phrases:

'to choose the *lesser* of two evils'; Cibber is one of the *lesser* poets of the eighteenth century; the *lesser* spotted woodpecker, etc., 'the *lesser* light to rule the night' (Genesis i. 16).

5. *Nearest*[1] refers to distance; *next* to order, e.g.

Where is the *nearest* Post-Office?
The *next* station is Oxford Circus.

6. *Farther* generally refers to distance, e.g.

I cannot walk any *farther.*

Manchester is *farther* from London than Oxford is.

Further, though it can replace *farther* in all contexts, has the specialized meaning of 'additional', e.g.

I will give you *further* details later.

I shall need *further* help with this.

Farthest and *furthest* are interchangeable.

7. *Older* and *oldest* can be used of people or things:

Henry is *older than* David.
That is the *oldest* house in the city.

Elder and *eldest* can be used of persons only, and only for members of the same family. Moreover, they can only be used attributively, e.g.

My *elder* brother is three years *older* than I. Henry is David's *elder* brother. Mary is my *eldest* sister.

---

[1] *near* is actually a comparative form of *nigh* (A.S. *neah*). Compare *neighbour* (A.S. *neahgebur,* literally *nigh boor*—'near husbandman'). *nigh* is now practically obsolete, except in the compound 'well nigh'.

Elders can, however, be used as a noun meaning 'those of an earlier generation' (implying, 'and so, wiser than we are'), e.g.

You should respect your *elders* and betters.

In one phrase 'an *elder* statesman', i.e. a statesman deserving respect for his age and wisdom, *elder* is used as an adjective.

8. *Less* is used with uncountable nouns, *fewer* with countable ones, e.g.

He has spent *less* time on his work than he ought to have done.

There are *fewer* boys than girls in my class.

9. *Latter* means the second of two and is contrasted with 'former', e.g. He studied French and German; the *former* language he speaks very well, but the *latter* one only imperfectly.

Latest means 'the most recent', 'the last up to the present', e.g. Have you read John Scribbler's *latest* book? It was written in three weeks and published two days ago.

Last has the meaning 'final', e.g. *The Tempest* was probably the *last* play that Shakespeare wrote.

It also has the meaning 'previous', e.g. I think this recent book is better than his *last* one. Compare also:

last week/year/month/night, etc.

10. Notice that before an attributive adjective in the superlative degree, *the* should be used, e.g. This is *the* best advice I can give you.

11. *most* + an adjective may express the presence of a quality in a very high degree, but without thought of a direct comparison:

What you have said is *most interesting*.

When this construction is used attributively, the indefinite article or no article is used, e.g.

She is *a most beautiful* girl. That was *a most extraordinary* thing to say. He wrote me *a most interesting* letter. These are *most delicious* cakes.

If the superlative without *most* is used, then the definite article precedes the superlative, e.g.

He showed *the* greatest (*the* utmost) patience.

12. When two persons or things are compared the comparative is generally used:

To choose the *lesser* of two evils. The *greater* part of the work. The *latter* half of the twentieth century. She is the *older* and the *more beautiful* of the two sisters. BUT:

She is the *oldest* and the *most beautiful* of the three sisters.

However, in conversational English the superlative is often used. Even in 'literary' English many writers have disobeyed this 'rule', e.g.

'She was the *youngest* of the *two* daughters' (Jane Austen).

IDIOMATIC CONSTRUCTIONS

There are a number of interesting idiomatic constructions with the comparative and the superlative.

The sooner this is done, *the better. The more the merrier. The harder* he tried, *the less* progress he seemed to make.

If you take a holiday now you will be *all the better* for it. He told a lie about it, and that makes his fault *all the worse*.

Every day you are getting *better and better*. He ran *faster and faster*. His voice got *weaker and weaker*. The storm became *more and more* violent.

If he will help us, *so much the better*. If he doesn't work, *so much the worse* for him. He is rather *the worse* for drink.

You will be *no worse* for having had the experience. You are *none the worse* for the experience; in fact, you are *all the better*.

I *had better*[1] go now before it is too late. He *would rather* play than work.

If the *worst comes to the worst* we can always walk home. He made a living *as best* he could.

ADJECTIVES NOT ADMITTING OF COMPARISON

There are some adjectives that, on account of their meaning, do not really admit of comparison at all, e.g.

perfect, unique, matchless, full, empty, square, round, circular, triangular, wooden, monthly, daily, etc.

[1] Meaning, 'It would be better if I went now. . . .'

But comparative and superlative forms of some of these words, e.g. 'perfect', 'full', are used because we are not considering them in their literal sense, e.g.

'This is a *more perfect* specimen than that one' (we really mean: 'This is nearer to perfection than that').

My glass is *fuller* than yours.

He says he has given me *full* details, but I want him to give me *fuller* particulars.

EXERCISES

I Give, with two examples of each, the methods used in forming comparatives and superlatives of adjectives and say to what class of adjective each method is applied.

II (*a*) Form a comparison of equality, a comparison of superiority and a comparison of inferiority from each of the following skeleton sentences:

(1) George —— industrious —— his brother. (2) The window —— narrow —— the door. (3) This car —— fast —— that one. (4) William's work —— good —— John's work.

(*b*) Rewrite these sentences so that they express the same meaning, but use comparatives of superiority instead of comparatives of inferiority:

(1) A pig is less intelligent than a horse. (2) The Thames is less long than the Severn. (3) Marlowe is less well known than Shakespeare. (4) A lake is usually less rough than a sea. (5) After that heavy rain the grass is less brown than it was a week ago. (6) Joan seems less afraid of wasps than of spiders.

III Give the comparative and superlative degrees corresponding to the following positive degrees:

long; bitter; convenient; evil; beautiful; sly; cruel; severe; constant; pleasant; afraid; wicked; good.

IV Fill in the blank spaces with an adjective in the correct degree:

(1) Mary is 5 ft. 6 in.; Joan is 5 ft. 8 in. Which is the —— of the two? (2) John is eighteen years old, Arthur is nineteen and James is twenty-one. John is the —— and James is the ——. (3) What was your worst subject at school? Mathematics was my —— and

French my ——. (4) I have £5, Mr. Jones has £10 and
Miss Evans has £25. Have I the most? No, Miss
Evans has the —— and you have the ——. (5) Who
has ——, Mr. Jones or I? You have; Mr. Jones has
——. (6) Is it —— from London to New York? Yes,
about 3,000 miles, but San Francisco is much ——
from London. (7) Do you drink a lot of wine? No, on
the contrary, I drink very ——. (8) Where is the ——
bus stop? (9) It is very —— to learn German well, but
even —— to learn Russian, while Chinese is said to
be the —— language in the world. (10) A bicycle tyre
consists of an —— cover and an —— tube. (11) The
question of how —— to preserve peace is the one that
is —— in men's minds. (12) He is one of the ——
politicians of the day.

V   The adjective in brackets at the beginning of each
of the following sentences is compared irregularly.
Insert in the blank spaces its appropriate form.

(1) (good *or* well) 'I say, you *do* look brown and ——.'
'Yes, I've just returned from the —— holiday
I've ever had.'

(2) (good *or* well) 'I say, that stew looks ——.' 'Yes,
it smells —— too, don't you think? Let's try
some and see if it tastes as —— as it smells.'

(3) (bad *or* ill) 'Gorgonzola cheese smells —— but
tastes delicious.' 'I agree, but it always makes me
——. I had some on board while crossing the
Channel, with the —— possible results. It was very
rough, and after the mishap some person with an
evil mind accused me of being the —— for drink!'

(4) (little) 'Of the two evils, let us choose the ——.'
'I don't think it matters in the —— which
alternative you accept; there is —— to choose
between them.'

(5) (little) Noble birth is of —— account than solid
worth.

(6) (near) Of the two versions I think yours is ——
the truth.

(7) (near) 'Can you direct me to the —— post-office?'
'Yes, it is just over the road, —— door to that
baker's.'

(8) (much, many) 'Do the French eat —— bread?'
'Yes, —— than we do.' 'Do they eat —— ——?'
'Oh yes; —— people have remarked about it to me.'

(9) (far) 'How —— is it from here to London?' 'Twenty miles by train; by road it is ——.'

(10) (far) The good pupil at school should by rights go —— in life than the bad one. Alas, it is not always so. Indeed, a cynic would say that the most unscrupulous go —— in life.

(11) (late, latter) Jones and Brown are two important members of the community; the former is the village postman and the —— the police constable.

(12) (late) Have you seen the —— edition of this dictionary? It has over a thousand pages, the —— one being numbered 1,075.

(13) (old) My wife has three brothers, all —— than she. The ——, George, is a bishop.

(14) (out) Please take the —— care of this bracelet.

(15) (out) Don't talk such —— nonsense.

(16) (out) Journeys into —— space will soon be possible.

(17) (up) Keep a stiff —— lip in adversity.

(18) (in) The only real happiness comes from —— peace.

VI Correct the following sentences:

(1) The cheetah runs faster than all animals. (2) Of all other animals the cheetah runs the fastest. (3) I lent you two books the other day. If you have read them, tell me which you find the most interesting. (4) No sooner had he settled down to read when the telephone bell rang. (5) Mary is elder than her cousin. (6) He paid less for his new house as for his old one. (7) London is a bigger city as Paris. (8) English customs are very different than continental. (9) John is senior than his cousin George. (10) That subject in the syllabus is minor. (11) French wine is superior than Californian. (12) He isn't so good at English than he likes to think. (13) My first impressions of England were quite different than I had expected.

VII List any adjectives you know which cannot be compared.

VIII Write sentences to illustrate the different senses which the following words can express, and explain the exact meaning of each sentence:

farther, further; latter, later; last, latest; nearest, next; less, lesser; foremost, first; uppermost.

IX Comment on the words in italics in the following sentences, correcting them where necessary and justifying your correction.

(1) This is the *eldest* church in the town. (2) Henry is my *oldest* brother and William is my *eldest* friend. (3) My cousin Harry is *elder* than I. (4) He has been so long in politics that he is considered as an *older* statesman. (5) She has three sisters of whom Jane is the *younger*. (6) I was able to get *farther* information about trains at the railway-station. (7) It is generally wise to choose the *lesser* of two evils. (8) His sister, who is his *next* relation, can be described as his *nearest* of kin.

X Supply the idiomatic expression containing comparatives or superlatives necessary to complete the following sentences. Each dash represents one word.

(1) —— haste —— speed. (2) He looks —— —— —— for his accident. (3) If he won't take advantage of his opportunities, —— —— —— —— for him. (4) He continued his studies —— —— —— —— after leaving school early. (5) —— —— I see of him, —— —— I like him. (*several possibilities*) (6) With regular practice he became —— —— —— at English. (7) How is the invalid today? He is much the same, —— —— and —— ——. (8) You have to get up early tomorrow, so you —— —— go to bed now. (9) The noise of the aircraft became —— —— —— until it died away completely. (10) If you can come for four lessons a week instead of two, —— —— —— ——

THE POSITION OF ADJECTIVES

1. Where adjectives are used attributively they generally come *before* the noun they qualify, e.g. a *brown* horse; a *hot* day; a *new* car. But there are occasions, especially in literary English, when they come *after* the noun that they qualify. These are:

(*a*) when accompanied by a phrase expressing measurement, e.g.

a river two hundred miles *long;* a road fifty feet *wide;* a man eighty-five years *old;* a building ten-storeys *high.*

(*b*) when more adjectives than one are used with the noun, e.g.

He is a writer both *witty* and *wise*.[1]

The hymnal we use is 'Hymns *Ancient and Modern*'.

He climbed the mountain by a route *uncharted, steep* and *dangerous*.[1]

He had a face *thin* and *worn*, but *eager* and *resolute*.[1]

(*c*) when the adjective is followed by a prepositional phrase, e.g.

He is a man *greedy* for money.

Alfred was a King *anxious* for his people's welfare.

All these are matters *worthy* of attention.

(*d*) in a few fixed expressions (mainly from French) such as: the Theatre *Royal*, the Poet *Laureate*, the heir *apparent*, from time *immemorial*, court *martial*, all the people *present*, by all means *possible*, letters *patent*, proof *positive*, the Postmaster *General*, Knight *errant*.

The words *next* and *last* may follow, though they generally precede, e.g. *last* Friday or Friday *last; next* Monday, Monday *next*.

(*e*) when used with *something* (*-one*), etc., *anything, everything, nothing*, e.g.

I'll tell you *something* very *important*.

That's *nothing new*.

He'll provide *everything necessary*.

There is *someone hurt*, I think.

(*f*) Adjectives preceded by *the* may also follow a proper noun, e.g.

Alfred the *Great*, William the *Silent*, Ivan the *Terrible*.

(*g*) Participles that are predominantly verbal in meaning follow the noun, e.g.

I have answered all the letters *received*.

After the accident the policeman took the names of the people *involved*.

We went through a door *opening* on to the garden.

---

[1] These are perhaps condensed relative clauses, 'who is . . .', 'which was . . .'.

A penny *saved* is a penny *gained*. (*Proverb*)
The words *mentioned* below. . . .

But participles that are predominantly adjectival in meaning precede the noun, e.g. a *broken* bottle; a *painted* table; a *crying* child.

2. *All* and *both* precede a noun, a possessive adjective, a demonstrative adjective (or pronoun) and the definite article,[1] e.g.

All (*both*) his friends are gone. *All* (*both*) these statements should be quite clear. *All* (*both*) the boys have gone home.

But they follow a personal pronoun, e.g.

When they saw the policeman they *all* (*both*) ran away.
We *all* (*both*) hope you will be successful.

3. *Half* and *double* precede the noun when they are used in a descriptive sense, e.g.

He drank a *half* bottle of wine. He drank *half* a bottle of wine.
He is my *half*-brother. He gave *half-a-crown* for a *half-crown* book.
The stockings were sold at *half* price. (= half the original price).
He drank a *double* whisky. I want a *double* room.

But *half*, *double* (and *twice*) are often followed by the definite article or a possessive adjective:

I bought the stockings at *half the* (*that*) price (= half the price you mentioned).
That will cost *half* (*double*, *twice*) *the* money.
Half his time he does no work.
That would cost *double* (*twice*) *his* capital.

4. When an adjective is qualified by *rather* or *quite* these words sometimes follow and sometimes precede the indefinite article without any difference of meaning.

He played *quite* a good game. He played a *quite* good game.
That is *rather* a valuable picture. This is a *rather* valuable picture.

[1] See tables pp. 91–93.

5. *Enough* normally comes before the noun but can come after it with no difference of meaning, e.g.

We haven't *enough* time. We haven't time *enough*.

It can be used with singular nouns or plural ones, e.g.

We have done *enough* work for today.
There are *enough* chairs to seat everybody.

POSSESSIVE ADJECTIVES

The possessive adjectives[1] with their corresponding personal pronouns are:

Personal Pronoun	Possessive Adjective	Personal Pronoun	Possessive Adjective
I	my	we	our
thou[2]	thy[2]	you	your
he	his	they	their
she	her	one	one's
it	its		

The possessive adjectives change according to the gender and number of the possessor, and not, as in some other languages, according to the person or thing possessed, e.g.

The *boy* has lost *his* dog.
The *girl* has lost *her* dog.
The *boys* have lost *their* dog.
We have lost *our* dog.

The possessive adjective is used in English where often the definite article would be used in some other languages, e.g.

I have had *my* hair cut. He hurt *his* foot.
She has changed *her* mind.

---

[1] Some grammarians call these possessive pronouns, considering them as genitive forms of the personal pronoun. We prefer to call them possessive adjectives, and the forms *mine, yours,* etc. (see p. 108) possessive pronouns.   [2] *thou* and *thy* are archaic or poetical.

But there are certain idiomatic phrases in English where the definite article is used instead of the possessive adjective, e.g.

I have a cold in *the* head. She was shot in *the* leg. He got red in *the* face. She took me by *the* hand. The ball struck him in *the* back.

Occasionally *own* is used with the possessive adjectives, usually to express or imply a contrast, e.g.

I have bought *my own* book, I don't need yours. Do *your own* dirty work; don't ask me to do it for you. Here's a book called 'Every man *his own* lawyer'.

(See also Chapter Ten, *Determinatives*.)

OTHER TYPES OF ADJECTIVES

INTERROGATIVE, DISTRIBUTIVE and INDEFINITE adjectives may generally function also as pronouns. They are dealt with in Chapter Eleven (*Pronouns*); see also Chapter Ten.

EXERCISES

I (*a*) Form the negative of the following adjectives by adding or changing a prefix or a suffix:
happy; pleasant; attentive; perfect; regular; legal; honest; useful; careful; pure; patient; ordinary; hopeful; safe; human; fruitful; respectful; religious; valuable; merciful.

(*b*) Insert an adjective into each blank space to make a traditional idiomatic comparison:
as —— as iron; as —— as gold; as —— as lead; as —— as a ghost; as —— as a March hare; as —— as a lord; as —— as a judge; as —— as a new pin; as —— as a hunter; as —— as a cartload of monkeys; as —— as a door-nail; as —— as a daisy.

II Complete these sentences by means of a possessive adjective or definite article:

(1) I live in the country; —— house stands alone near a stream. (2) 'Love —— neighbour as thyself.' (3) John has a car but —— sister hasn't. (4) Joan has a bicycle, but —— brother has a motor cycle. (5) They have sold —— house. (6) This is a slow train; —— engine is out

of date. (7) We have passed —— examination. (8) She has failed —— examination. (9) He was stabbed in —— back by a cowardly assailant. (10) They were blue in —— face with cold. (11) You can't trust him; he never keeps —— promises. (12) ——wife and I celebrate —— silver wedding next month. (13) Do come, and bring —— friend with you. (14) Farmers like —— crops to be gathered in as soon as possible in autumn. (15) You must allow this matter to take —— proper time.

III (a) Use the following participles as adjectives immediately preceding a noun :

withered; broken; whistling; spoken; torn; folding; humming; written; chosen; wanted.

(b) Use these as adjectives immediately following a noun.

listed; lined; sprinkled; made; involving; flavoured; studded; written; sung; running.

IV Compose sentences with 'quite', 'rather', 'half', 'double'. Use all these words once with the article (definite or indefinite) before them, and once with it after them.

V (a) Make sentences using the following adjectives as nouns singular or plural:

European; wicked; Japanese; individual; heathen.

(b) Use the following nouns as adjectives:

leather; gold; London; rice; meat; cotton; Beethoven; University; Brussels; garden.

VI (a) Form adjectives from the following nouns and use each of the adjectives in a sentence.

beauty; rain; ghost; winter; geometry; lady; day; man; Titan; woman; art; love; Paris; reason; lead; botany; spite; crime; spirit; ability; hero; malice; Elizabeth; child (two forms).

(b) Give the nouns corresponding to the following adjectives:

proud; ironical; horrible; dreadful; temperate; secure; full; candid; hungry; grand.

VII Introduce the word 'own' into each of the following sentences:

(1) I can surely do as I please with my money. (2) You must do your work and not copy from your neighbour.

(3) She has no servant and so she has to do all her housework. (4) Each guest must bring his supply of drinks with him. (5) They don't pay any rent because they live in their house.

VIII Invent five sentences in each of which there is an adjective (other than any in Ex. V) used as a noun and three sentences in each of which there is a proper noun (other than any in Ex. V) used as an adjective.

IX Complete the following sentences with adjectives formed from the nouns in brackets.

(1) In old age the hair often becomes (silver). (2) The colour of ripe corn is (gold). (3) In Scandinavia one often sees people whose hair is (flax). (4) I was appalled at his (brass) impudence. (5) The sword of Damocles was suspended by a (silk) thread.

X In English, adjectives used attributively usually come before the nouns they qualify. Construct five sentences illustrating exceptions to this rule and for each sentence explain why the exception is made.

XI Complete the following sentences by inserting the words given in brackets in their correct positions.

(a) A loaf is better than no bread. (half)
(b) I have two sisters of whom are older than I. (both)
(c) At the sales things can often be bought at price. (half)
(d) How many roads are there to Rome? (leading)
(e) As a result of his accident he is suffering from a leg. (fractured)

XII Complete the following sentences by inserting in each a word chosen from the following; all the words can be used. What do you notice that is rather unusual about the adjectives used with these words?

something, someone, somebody, nothing, nobody, everything, everybody, anything, anyone, anybody.

(1) There is —— strange in his behaviour today. (2) Is there —— specially interesting in the paper this morning? (3) No there's —— startling. (4) There is —— very outstanding in English in my class. (5) —— valuable was taken by the burglars. (6) ——well-known in the theatre attended that first night. (7) I'm sure —— cleverer than he will get the prize. (8) Was there —— specially well dressed at the dance last night? (9) —— interested in the subject is invited to attend the

lecture. (10) There must be —— clever enough to solve this problem.

XIII Insert 'rather' or 'quite' in the correct position in these sentences.

(1) He can do difficult exercises correctly. (2) This is a valuable violin though it is certainly not a Stradivarius. (3) They are not very generous people ; in fact they are mean. (4) He was not clever enough to pass his exam, though he worked very hard. (5) She is an unhealthy-looking girl. I don't think she gets enough exercise. (*Use both words in this sentence.*)

CHAPTER TEN

DETERMINATIVES

It is convenient to group under the term 'Determinatives' certain classes of words the usage of which is discussed more fully elsewhere. These are:

ARTICLES: *a(n); the.*

ADJECTIVES OF QUANTITY: *one, two, three,* etc. (all the cardinal numbers); *all, some, several, any, much, many, (a) few, (a) little, no, enough,* etc.

DISTRIBUTIVE ADJECTIVES: *each, every, both, neither, either.*

INTERROGATIVE ADJECTIVES: *which, what, whose.*

DEMONSTRATIVE ADJECTIVES: *this, that, these, those.*

POSSESSIVE ADJECTIVES: *my, your, his, her, its, their, our.*

NOUNS AND NOUN-PHRASES IN THE POSSESSIVE CASE: e.g. *John's, the man's, an old lady's.*

Many of these words may stand alone as pronouns, or may qualify nouns. When they qualify nouns, they differ from qualificative adjectives (*big, blue, intelligent,* etc.) in two important respects:

1. *Word Order:* They are always placed *before* any qualifying adjectives: *the* red book, *this* old chair, *my* new brown hat.

2. *Distribution.* One of the appropriate determinatives must always be used before a singular countable noun (see p. 20). An appropriate determinative may be used before uncountable nouns and plural countable nouns, but is not always needed in these cases. Except for the combinations shown below, only one determinative can be used before a noun.

Determinatives are used before (*a*) singular countable nouns, (*b*) plural countable nouns, (*c*) uncountable nouns, as shown in the following tables.

D

TABLE A. SINGULAR COUNTABLE NOUNS

NOTE: Any word may be used with any other word in an adjoining column from which it is not separated by a horizontal line. The words in parentheses can be either used or omitted.

DETERMINATIVES		*Example of* (*adjective +*) *noun*
(many)	a(n) another	
the that this some any no which what	(one)	book egg new hat red bicycle word
my her his its your our their whose John's the man's an old lady's, etc.	(one) (every)[1]	
every each either neither one		

[1] The combinations with *every* are rare.

TABLE B. PLURAL COUNTABLE NOUNS
(see note at Table A)

DETERMINATIVES				(*Adjective +*) noun
		(*No determinative*)		

		all
		no
		any
		what
		which
			(two[2]
			three
			four, etc.)
				good books
				old hats
				large white
				   cups
				sharp pencils
				houses
				cats
				important
				   letters
				clever students
				friends

(all) (how)	(all) (both) (all of) (both of) (enough of) (one of) (two, three, etc. of) (which of) (more of) (fewer of) (many of) (a lot of) (plenty of) (some of) (none of) (any of)	the my your his her its our their whose John's the old lady's his father's these those	(few) (many) (two,[2] three, etc.)	
	(how)	(a few) (a lot) (many) (no)[1] (some)[1] (plenty)[1]	fewer more	

[1] Used only with *more*.   [2] Not used with *all*.

TABLE B (*continued*)

DETERMINATIVES		(*Adjective +*) *noun*
(any) (several) (two, three, etc.) (far)	fewer more	good books old hats large white cups
several enough both some two, three, etc. (how) many (a) few a lot of plenty of		sharp pencils houses cats important letters clever students friends

TABLE C. UNCOUNTABLE NOUNS
(see note at Table A)

DETERMINATIVES	*Examples of* (*adj. +*) *noun*
(*No determinative*)	
all any what which enough no some (how) much a lot of plenty of (a) little	milk time money cleverness hard work cold water

TABLE C (*continued*)

DETERMINATIVES			*Examples of (adj. +) noun*
(no) (a little) (a lot) (much) (some)[1] (plenty)[1] (any) (far)	more less		milk time money cleverness hard work cold water
(how)	(all) (of) (enough of) (much of) (more of) (less of) (a lot of) (plenty of) (some of) (any of) (more of)	the that this my your his its our their whose John's the old lady's	

[1] Not used with *less*.

NOTES ON SOME DETERMINATIVES

MUCH, MANY

much is used with uncountable (singular) nouns, e.g.

You haven't *much* time if you want to catch that train.

He hasn't very *much* money.

many is used with plural countable nouns, e.g.

You haven't *many* minutes to spare if you want to catch that train.

How *many* cigarettes a day do you smoke?

The only occasion when *many* is used with a singular noun is in the phrase *many a*, e.g.

Many a ship has (= many ships have) been wrecked on those rocks.
Many a man would be glad of your job.
I've been there *many a time*.

Much and *many* are most frequently used in negative or interrogative sentences, *much* with singular uncountable nouns, *many* with plural nouns.

I haven't *much* time. Did you have *much* rain on your holidays? There's not *much* sugar in the sugar bowl.
Do you know *many* people in London? There are not *many* mistakes in your exercise.

In colloquial use in affirmative statements they are frequently replaced by *a lot of, lots of, a large quantity of, plenty of, a good deal of*, e.g.

He will have *a lot of* time to spare when he has finished the book he is working on.
She knows *lots of* people in London.
He has done *a good deal* of research on that subject.

Note that with *a lot of* and *plenty of* the verb is singular with uncountable nouns, plural with countable ones, e.g.

There is *plenty of* sugar in the sugar bowl.
There are *plenty of* chairs for everyone.

Much and *many* are usually preferred even in affirmative constructions:

(a) in Indirect Questions introduced by *whether* or *if:*

I doubt whether there'll be *much* time for seeing the sights of London; your train leaves at six o'clock.
I wonder if *many* people will be at the party.

(b) when preceded by *so, too, as, how*, e.g.

He has *so much* money and I have so little.
There are *too many* mistakes in your exercise.
He has drunk *too much* wine and ought not to drive his car home.

You can have *as much* wine (as *many* bottles of wine) as you want.

I know how *much* money (how *many* pounds) that ring cost.

(c) when they qualify the subject of the sentence, e.g.

Many Englishmen like to spend their spare time working in their gardens.

'*Many* hands make light work.' (*Proverb*)

Much time would be saved if you planned your work properly.

(d) in the case of *much*, when it stands alone, i.e. with no noun, e.g.

Much depends on what answer the Prime Minister gives to that question.

I would give *much* to know what he is thinking now.

Much of what he says is true.

Much as[1] I should like to come, I'm afraid I must refuse.

(e) in the case of *much*, when it is followed by an abstract noun, especially when the noun is preceded by an adjective, e.g.

The book is the fruit of *much* patient research.

FEW, LITTLE

Few (contrasted with *many*) is used with plural countable nouns; *little* (as a determinative and contrasted with *much*) is used with singular uncountable nouns. Both *few* and *little* have a negative implication.

Few has the meaning 'not many', e.g.

The *few* friends that he had are all dead.

Few people would agree with you.

Little has the meaning, 'not much', and the emphasis is on the scantiness, e.g.

The *little* money that he has will hardly keep him in food.

The shipwrecked sailors had no food and *little* water.

A few and *a little* have a positive implication. They mean 'some, though not many (much)', e.g.

[1] *much* here is concessive (see p. 341–2).

He has *a few* friends who call to see him quite frequently.

A few people would agree with you.

He has *a little* money and can live quite comfortably on it.

The shipwrecked sailors had *a little* water.

EXERCISES

I Use expressions chosen from the following list to complete these sentences: *few, a few, little, a little, the little.*

(1) 'Is there any tea left in the pot?' 'Yes, ——.'

(2) 'Do you smoke at all?' 'Yes, but very ——.'

(3) 'Do you smoke at all?' 'Yes ——.'

(4) Our driver had had —— drinks and wasn't fit to take the wheel.

(5) Having had —— opportunities to practise, I did not play the piece as well as I might have done.

(6) Having had —— opportunities to practise, I played the piece reasonably well.

(7) He is a lonely man, he has —— friends.

(8) I have only —— coal in my cellar because the coal man has not come.

(9) We must save —— money we have left for our journey home.

(10) He always has —— in reserve for emergencies.

(11) Can you come to our house this evening? I am inviting —— friends for coffee.

II In what cases are *much* or *many* used affirmatively? Illustrate each part of your answer by constructing one sentence employing *much* and another employing *many*.

CHAPTER ELEVEN

PRONOUNS

A pronoun is a word used instead of a noun.
Pronouns may be classified into the following kinds:

(1) Personal   (2) Possessive   (3) Demonstrative
(4) Reflexive   (5) Interrogative   (6) Indefinite
(7) Relative   (8) Distributive

Pronouns may show number, person, gender and case. The table of personal pronouns will illustrate this.

I. PERSONAL PRONOUNS

	SINGULAR *Nominative*	*Objective*	PLURAL *Nominative*	*Objective*
1ST PERSON	I	me	we	us
2ND PERSON	thou	thee	you (ye)	you (ye)
3RD PERSON				
(*Masculine*)	he	him		
(*Feminine*)	she	her	they	them
(*Neuter*)	it	it		
(*Indefinite*)	one	one		

PERSON IN PRONOUNS

Speech naturally presupposes two persons: a person who speaks (the *First Person*) and a person spoken to (the *Second Person*). So *I*, *we*, are pronouns of the First Person; *you* (*thou*, *thee*, *ye*) are pronouns of the Second Person. Beyond these two persons there is the whole world of people and things that may be spoken about. For all these we use the pronouns of the Third Person, *he*, *she*, *it*, *one*, *they*.

D*

CASE IN PRONOUNS

In addition to the possessive case, already discussed in Chapter Six, there are two other cases in modern English, the *Nominative Case* and the *Objective*[1] *Case*.

The form of nouns in English is the same, no matter whether they are in the nominative case or in the objective case. The case of nouns is shown not by inflection but by word order. But some pronouns *are* inflected to show case. The sentences on page 9, if instead of the nouns *boy, dog, girl, books* we use pronouns, will read:

SUBJECT	PREDICATE	
	Verb	*Object*
He	hit	*it*
It	bit	*him*
She	read	*them*
They	pleased	*her*

There is one other occasion when the objective form of the pronoun is used: this is when a pronoun is governed by a preposition, e.g.

I spoke to *him*.

I had a letter from *her*.

The pronouns *him* and *her* are in the objective case, governed respectively by the prepositions *to* and *from*.

The only pronouns, in fact the only *words* in English, that have different forms for nominative and objective case are six in all:

[1] Some grammarians use the terms *Accusative Case* and *Dative Case* instead of the general term *Objective Case*. The distinction is a purely theoretical one for there is no difference in form in any noun or pronoun in English to mark one from the other. These grammarians use the term 'Accusative' when the noun is: (*a*) the direct object of a verb; (*b*) governed by a preposition. They use the term *Dative* when the noun or pronoun is the *Indirect Object* of a verb, e.g. I gave *the boy* a shilling.

Nominative	Objective	Nominative	Objective
I	me	we	us
he	him	they	them
she	her	who	whom

In 'literary' or in formal English, when the pronoun comes after the verb *to be* the nominative form of the pronoun is used, e.g.

I (*we, he, she*, etc.) did this.

It was *I* (*he, she, we*, etc.) who did this.

In informal, colloquial English the objective form is frequently used:

That's *her* (*him, us*, etc.). It's all right; it's only *me*.

But in sentences where the pronoun is felt to be the subject of a verb, e.g. 'It was *he* who told me about it', 'It was *I* who did it', the nominative form would always be used.

Notes on the Personal Pronouns

FIRST PERSON

I is always written with a capital letter, but *me, we* and *us* are not.

We (*us*) is not the plural of *I* in the same way as *boys* is the plural of *boy*. *We* means not 'two or more *I*'s' but 'I and you' or 'I and he' or 'I and all these other people'.

It is a convention for a newspaper editor or writer of leading articles in a newspaper, perhaps from modesty and a desire not to sound egotistical or perhaps because he feels that he is speaking not only for himself but for the whole board of management of the paper, to use the plural *we* ('the Editorial *we*') when giving his opinions, e.g.

'*We* believe that the Government has made a profound mistake in imposing this tax.'

In the same way, formal Royal Proclamations use the 'Royal *we*', i.e.

'*We*, George III, King of England . . . .

In very colloquial English, *us* is sometimes used for *me*, especially after an imperative, e.g. Let's have a look (meaning let *me* have a look). Tell *us* (= tell *me*) what he said.

SECOND PERSON

Thou, thee, ye are archaic and are rarely used in modern English except in poetry.

THIRD PERSON

He, him can be used instead of masculine nouns; *she, her* instead of feminine nouns; *it* instead of neuter nouns. All the others, except *they* and *them*, are used instead of masculine or feminine nouns. *They, them* are used instead of masculine, feminine or neuter nouns.

She (*her*) is sometimes used for inanimate objects, especially ships, motor-cars, locomotives, aircraft, etc., to express affection or familiarity. Countries, and even cities, especially in rather formal or rhetorical speech, are sometimes made feminine:

OWNER OF CAR AT PETROL STATION: 'Fill *her* up, George.'
That's the Queen's yacht, *Britannia; she's* a beautiful ship.
England has done what *she* promised to do.
'Oxford taught me as much Latin and Greek as *she* could.' (Said by John Ruskin.)

A baby can be referred to as *it*—but preferably not in the hearing of its fond parents.

IT

1. The pronoun *it* is generally applied to things and not to people; but *it* is often used to identify an unknown person. Then, once this has been done, *he* (*she*) would be used, e.g.

Someone was moving stealthily about the room; *it* was a burglar. As we watched, *he* went to the safe and tried to open it.

2. *It* is used as a 'formal' subject with verbs concerning weather conditions, e.g.

It is raining/snowing/freezing. *It* is very warm/cold/wet. *It* was a *bitterly* cold night and at ten o'clock *it* began to blow a gale.

and also with expressions of time and measurement:

> *It* is half past two.
> *It* is fifteen miles to London.
> '*It's* a long way to Tipperary.'

and with other impersonal statements, e.g.

> *It* says here that Shakespeare's plays were written by Bacon.

3. *It* is used as a formal subject or object, in other constructions, the real subject or object usually following as an infinitive or a subordinate clause, e.g.

> *It* is easy enough *to talk.* *It* was quite plain *that he didn't want to come.* I took *it* for granted *that you would stay with us.* I find *it* difficult *to believe that.*

It may, in sentences beginning: 'It is' or 'It was . . .' precede the real subject and a relative clause, e.g.

> *It* was the training that he had as a young man that made him such a good engineer.

This construction can be used to give special emphasis to the real subject, e.g.

> *It* was his mother, not his father, who said that.

4. *It* is used idiomatically in other sentences or phrases (usually colloquial or slang) where it seems to have very little specific meaning, e.g.

> When the thieves saw the policeman coming, they ran for *it*.
> If the teacher sees you doing that, you'll catch *it*.
> Hang *it* all, we can't wait all day for him.
> If you go camping you'll have to rough *it*.
> When I see him, I'll have *it* out with him.
> I'll let him have *it*, hot and strong.
> You are fairly going *it;* you've eaten nearly the whole box of chocolates.
> We'll make a day of *it*.

5. *It* can stand for a whole sentence, e.g.

> You have saved my life; I shall never forget *it*. He is trying to win a scholarship to Oxford: he won't find *it* easy.

But this construction (*it* standing for a preceding sentence) is not generally used with the verbs *know, remember, try, tell, forget*, e.g.

'We are having a holiday tomorrow.' 'Yes, I know,' (NOT: I know *it*.)
'You won't forget to write, will you?' 'No, I won't forget.' (NOT: I won't forget *it*.)

So

1. *So* is similarly used to stand for an affirmative statement, especially after certain verbs (*say, think, hope, believe, suppose, expect, hear, tell, imagine, fear, be afraid*). The word *so* is used more or less with this function of *it*, that is to stand for an affirmative statement, e.g.

'Will George pass his examination?' 'I think *so*.'
'Was this cathedral built in the fourteenth century?' 'I believe *so*/I have heard *so*/I was told *so*.'
'Is he very ill?' 'I'm afraid *so*.' (For this construction and its negative, see p. 401.)
He'll pay me the money next month; at least I hope *so*.
Why do you say *so*? I told you *so*.
You thought Henry stole the money; well, *so* he did.
'You told me I should go to Oxford to learn English.' 'And *so* you shall.'
We have information that the enemy will attack tonight. And if *so* what are we going to do?

The negative of this construction can be expressed by two forms:

(i) I think/believe/suppose/expect/hope/hear/am afraid/*not;* if *not* . . .

(ii) I don't think/believe/suppose/expect/*so*.

Notice that the second construction is not used with *hear, hope, am afraid*.

2. *So* is used with *do* to refer to a preceding verb:

I told him to come and see me the next day, and he did *so*.
If you want me to help them I will do *so*.

3. *So* is used also to represent an adjective or noun with the verb *to be, to remain, to seem, to make:*

> He has been very helpful to me in the past and I hope he will be *so* (= helpful) in the future.
>
> The country round my house has been unchanged for twenty years; may it long remain *so* (= unchanged).
>
> 'There is nothing either good or bad but thinking makes it *so*.' (= good or bad)—(Shakespeare, *Hamlet*.)
>
> He has been a teacher here for five years and I hope he will be *so* (= a teacher here) for many more years.

4. Note the use of *so* to mean *also* in such sentences as:

> My husband likes French cooking and *so* do I.
>
> Peter is working hard for his examination, and *so* is James. (See also p. 185.)

ONE

One is, of course, a numeral (e.g. There was only *one* boy there, not two), and, like all the numerals, can be used as a pronoun, e.g.

> *One* cannot do the work of *twenty*.
>
> *One* of your brothers came to see me today.

The plural of *one* with this usage is *some*, e.g.

> *Singular:* Take *one* of these chocolates.
>
> *Plural:* Take *some* of these chocolates.

The other uses of *one* as a pronoun are as follows:

1. It is used to stand for 'people' or 'I or any person in my position'. It can be a subject or an object; it has the Possessive form *one's* and the Reflexive *oneself*. It is followed by a third person singular verb. *Examples:*

> *One* can only do *one's* best.
>
> *One* can't be too careful in matters like this.
>
> The South Pole Expedition film gives *one* a good idea of the hardships the men endured.
>
> I don't think *one* should overwork *oneself*.

It is generally felt that this use of *one* too often in a sentence is stylistically clumsy, e.g.

> When *one* is given *one's* choice of courses of action, any of which would be to *one's* disadvantage, *one* often has a difficulty in deciding what *one* ought to do.

The attempt to avoid this awkwardness may, unless care is taken, lead to such incorrect sentences as:

> When *one* is given *his* choice of courses of action, any of which would be to *his* disadvantage, *they* often have difficulty in deciding what *they* ought to do.

Preferable forms would be:

(a) When someone is given his choice of courses of action, any of which would be to his disadvantage, he often has difficulty in deciding what he ought to do.

(b) When you are given your choice of courses of action, any of which would be to your disadvantage, you often have difficulty in deciding what you ought to do.

2. It may have a general indefinite meaning of 'a person', e.g.

> You are the first *one* who has ever explained this clearly.
> He is not *one* to be easily frightened.
> '. . . Then must you speak
> Of *one* who loved not wisely but too well.' (Shakespeare)

One AS PRONOUN OR ADJECTIVE

3. *One* is used with something of its meaning as a numeral when contrasted with *other* or *another*, e.g.

> There are two choices open to you. You must take either the *one* or the *other*. (Pronoun)
> The two twins are so much alike that I can't tell the *one* from the *other*. (Pronoun)
> *One* evening we went to the theatre, *another* evening we went dancing. (Adjective)

4. In the following cases it has lost its numerical meaning and is used to express some vague time:

> He always hopes that *one* day he will win a prize. (Adjective)
> *One* of these days I'll go and see him. (Pronoun)
> I must have met him at *one* time or another. (Adjective)

5. Occasionally it has the meaning 'only', 'single'. With this meaning *one* is always an adjective, e.g.

The *one* man who could have saved the situation was dead.
No *one* woman could run a big house like that single-handed.
'The *one* thing that could make Charles I dangerous—was a
violent death.' (Macaulay)

THE PROP-WORD *One*

6. It is very frequently what is sometimes called a *Prop-Word*. In some constructions adjectives (including the definite
article) cannot stand alone and need the prop-word *one* to
support them. This prop-word refers to some previous noun.
If the prop-word *one* were not used, the noun would have to be
repeated, and for stylistic reasons we want to avoid this.
It is only countable nouns that *one* can replace in this way.

Examples:

Brown's old car is a good *one;* it's much better than our
new *one*.

There was an old man and a young *one* there.

I like a strong cup of tea better than a weak *one*.

The plural of *one* with this usage is *ones*, e.g.

I prefer red roses to white *ones* (*one* used in the plural).

There was a mother bird in the nest and there were four
young *ones*.

One can be a prop-word with the definite article, e.g.

'Which girl is Joan Robinson?' 'The *one* in the green dress.'
'Which biscuits do you like best?' 'The *ones* with chocolate
on them.'

One is not generally used with *own*, e.g.

I can't write properly with your pen; I'd rather use my own.
(NOT: my own *one*.)

Ones is never used after a cardinal numeral, e.g.

You have three books; I have only two. (NOT: two *ones*.)

OTHER IDIOMATIC USES OF 'ONE'

He can go or he can stay; *it's all one* to me (= it makes no
difference).

He was a man that was liked by *one and all* (= everybody).

EXERCISES

I For which nouns do the pronouns in the following passage stand?

Mr. and Mrs. Brown were talking about their neighbours, Mr. and Mrs. Smith, and their new house.

'He must be making a good income to be able to live in a house like that,' said he, 'to say nothing of the car they have. It's a Rolls.'

'Oh, I don't think he makes much money,' she replied, 'but I fancy she has a private income.'

'I wonder whether they paid for it themselves or whether her parents gave it to her,' he said.

She answered, 'Yes, they bought it after a lucky week with football pools. But as for the car, I can't speak definitely about that, though I think it is hers rather than his.'

'I know which of the two I would sooner have,' was his comment.

II Complete each of the following sentences with the correct form of the personal pronoun, choosing one of the two in brackets:

(1) This parcel is for George and —— (I, me). (2) Is that Mary over there? Yes, that's —— (her, she). (3) —— Scots are always making jokes about ourselves (we, us). (4) My wife and —— have not been well recently (I, me). (5) My uncle and aunt love animals. Between —— (they, them) they own four dogs and two cats. One cat was a present from my wife and —— (I, me).

III Complete the following passage by means of personal pronouns:

'This coming week-end my brother and —— intend to do a little motoring. Between —— —— have bought a new Austin. ——'s a lively little car.'
'—— lucky people! I've always wanted a car like that. Still, —— suppose —— must remember the Commandment, "—— shalt not covet[1] ".'

'—— are very welcome to come with ——. —— will ring my brother up and tell —— there will be three of ——. Jessie and Doris have decided to spend the week-end together away from their men-folk, so —— shall be leaving —— behind.'

[1] To covet = to desire something that belongs to another person.

'——'s unusual to hear of women who can keep away from a new car!'

'Yes, indeed. Your mother enjoys a drive, doesn't ——? Would —— care to bring —— along?'

'That's very kind of ——, but —— is celebrating a birthday party on Saturday with her brother, and —— always visit each other on their respective birthdays. Dear ——, —— must be off! Thank —— for the offer of a ride. —— am looking forward to ——.'

IV (a) Express these statements in another way, by means of the pronoun 'it', altering the wording completely where necessary. In some cases a verb in brackets is given to help you.

(1) John, not James, rang up. (2) The temperature is below zero. (3) The afternoon was bright and sunny. (4) The journey to Brighton from London takes only one hour by train. (5) Some parts of *King Lear* are extremely difficult to understand. (6) (call) We won't do any more work today. (7) (pig) They were used to living primitively and disregarding table manners. (8) (lord) This cockerel obviously considered himself superior to the other inmates of the hen-house and acted accordingly. (9) That he will fail is clear to everyone but himself.

(b) Try to discover other expressions like 'rough it', 'go it', etc. consisting of verb and 'it', and use them in sentences.

V Express these passive sentences in a different way, by using the pronouns 'one', 'we', 'you', or 'they':

(1) It is said he is a very rich man. (2) I am a Londoner, my dear Wolfgang, and English is spoken there, of course. (3) What language is spoken in Moscow? Russian, of course. (4) If a person takes any given action, the consequences must be borne. (5) Such questions may not be asked.

VI When can a feminine pronoun be used to represent an inanimate thing? Use each example you can find in a sentence.

VII Construct sentences illustrating the use of 'it':

(1) as a formal subject. (2) with expressions of time and distance. (3) as a slang expression. (4) as a provisional subject. (5) standing for a whole sentence.

VIII Write down all the colloquial expressions you know in which the pronoun 'it' can be used in an indefinite sense and explain the meaning of the expressions.

IX (*a*) Give an affirmative answer to each of the following questions using the construction with *so*.

(1) Have we time to finish this game before going to bed? (2) The Severn is England's longest river, isn't it? (3) Will it be fine tomorrow? (4) Will our examination results come soon? (5) Is his salary £20,000 a year?

(*b*) Supply a negative reply to each of the following using the verbs in brackets. If two forms are possible give both.

(1) Did they catch their train yesterday? (be afraid) (2) Shall we risk going out without umbrellas? (think) (3) Very well, I won't forget to send you a card from Paris. (hope) (4) Do you think Mary will be successful? (think) (5) A visa is no longer required to enter France, is it? (believe)

X Complete the following sentences with 'one' or 'you' as you think best.

(1) —— told another and so the news got around. (2) —— can't make a silk purse out of a sow's ear. (3) Did you see that shooting star? It is the third —— I have seen tonight. (4) Have you heard this ——? It's a very funny ——. (5) —— can always try to do a little better than —— best.

II. POSSESSIVE PRONOUNS

Possessive adjectives are discussed on pages 84–5. They can be used only before a noun or the prop-word *one*. The possessive pronoun, however, may stand alone. Here is a list of the possessive adjectives and the corresponding possessive pronouns:

Possessive Adjective	*Possessive Pronoun*
That is *my* book.	That book is *mine*.
That is *your* book.	That book is *yours*.
That is *his* book.	That book is *his*.
That is *her* book.	That book is *hers*.
That is *our* book.	That book is *ours*.
That is *their* book.	That book is *theirs*.

History has *its* lessons and fiction has *its*.

Other examples:

> *Ours* is the only garden in the lane that has oak trees in it.
> Their house is older than *yours*.
> He took the bone from his dog and gave it to *hers*.
> I lend my books gladly to my friends and to *yours*.
> Today we went in our car; tomorrow we are going in *theirs*.
> 'Who steals my purse steals trash; 'tis something, nothing;
> 'Twas *mine*, 'tis *his*, and has been slave to thousands.'
> (Shakespeare, *Othello*)

The possessive pronoun *its* is very rarely used, but it could be used in such a sentence as:

> The cherry tree gives its share of colour to the garden, and the lilac tree gives *its*.

The possessive pronouns are used in such phrases as:

> My best wishes to you and *yours* (= your family) from me and *mine* (= my family).

and in the conventional ending to letters:

> *Yours* sincerely/truly/faithfully.

THE 'DOUBLE POSSESSIVE'

There is another pattern used with the possessive pronouns. i.e. *of* + possessive pronoun, e.g.

> He is a friend of *mine*. (NOT: 'a friend of me')
> It was no fault of *yours* that we mistook the way.
> I gave him some plants of *mine* in exchange for some of *his*.

For a similar construction used with a noun in the possessive case, see page 48.

III. DEMONSTRATIVE PRONOUNS

We have noted the demonstrative adjectives, *this*, *that* and their plural, *these*, *those* used with nouns, e.g.

> I want *this* car, not *that* car.

If these words are used without the noun, they are demonstrative pronouns, e.g.

'*This* is what I want you to do.' 'Well, *that's* exactly what I did.' Why are you telling me all *this? That's* an excellent idea. *This* is where I live. *This* is my brother; and *these* are my two sisters. Are *those* your sisters? I believe you, but there are *those* who wouldn't. My seat was next to *that* of the Mayor. Compare Chopin's waltzes with *those* of today.

These pronouns, besides taking the place of a noun, suggest the idea of a *position* with regard to the speaker, *this* (*these*) being nearer in space or time, *that* (*those*) being more distant, e.g.

There is this seat here, near me, or there is that one in the fourth row. Which will you have, *this* or *that?*

That is what I thought last year, *this* is what I think now.

The former and *the latter* may also be regarded as demonstrative pronouns. (See also p. 76.)

The orchestra played two Beethoven Symphonies, the Third and the Fifth; the *former* was played magnificently; the *latter* was not so well done.

SUCH

Such is a demonstrative pronoun or a demonstrative adjective. It is an adjective in sentences like:

I have had *such* a busy morning.
You shouldn't say *such* things.

Note that when the indefinite article is used with *such*, the article comes after, not before, *such*.

I never saw *such* wonderful stained glass as that at Chartres.
They are *such* clever people.
Don't be in *such* a hurry.
It's difficult to work indoors on *such* a lovely day.

It is a pronoun in:

John is the captain of the team, and, as *such*, must decide who is to bat first.
His carelessness is *such* as to make it unlikely that he will pass the examination.
Such is life!

Such as has the meaning 'for example', e.g.

They export a lot of fruit, *such as* oranges, lemons, etc.

Such as, with some part of the verb *to be*, is sometimes used with a depreciatory, contemptuous or apologetic implication, e.g.

He gave me his help, *such as* it was (meaning 'but it wasn't of much use').

I expect his friends, *such as* they are, will be at the party.

My services, *such as* they are, are entirely at your disposal.

EXERCISES

I Substitute possessive pronouns for the words in italics. In (5) use a different verb too.

(1) His marks are higher than *the ones I gained*. (2) John's sister has an even better post than *the one he holds*. (3) You have some fine strawberries. *The ones in our garden* are not so good. (4) Which cards shall we use? *Those you possess* or *those they have brought*. (5) The coat she is wearing *does not belong to her*.

II Replace the words in italics by possessive or demonstrative pronouns.

(1) I like this hat better than *the hat over there*. (2) *The dog you see here* is the dog that saved my wife and daughter. (3) *My mother's illness* was the reason for my not coming. (4) John is older than James. *John* is eighteen and *James* sixteen. (5) Cuthbert is a Guards officer, and as *Guards Officer* he has to maintain a certain standard of living.

III Correct the following, giving reasons for your corrections:

(1) I am going out with my wife and a friend of her. (2) This parcel is from a friend of my father. (3) Did you take that book of me? (4) It's strange the baby won't eat it's food. I see you have no difficulty with your's. (5) It's them who caused all the trouble. (6) One should not do such things if you wish to keep your dignity.

IV Supply the appropriate demonstrative pronouns in the following sentences, giving alternative forms where possible.

(1) —— are more expensive than —— but they are worth the extra money. (2) —— is the best way to learn English. (3) Here is £5, but —— is all I can do for you. (4) The University of Durham is the oldest in England after —— of Oxford and Cambridge. (5) 'Figaro' and the 'Barber' contain the same characters but —— is by Mozart and —— by Rossini.

V Identify the possessive and demonstrative pronouns in the following passage:

His father and mine have offices in the same building. Ours is on the first floor, but theirs is on the fourth. That is the building, over there, and the windows just above the main door are those of my father's office but you cannot see his because they are at the back. There are two entrances, this which is for visitors and that at the side for goods, but those who know the building often enter by either.

VI Complete the following sentences with possessive or demonstrative pronouns.

(1) '—— were the days' is a popular B.B.C. programme. (2) What with —— and ——, I have been very busy all day. (3) One idea of equality is that 'What's —— is —— and what's —— is my own'. (4) 'Here's to you and —— and me and ——' is a good toast. (5) That careless driver has had an accident; —— is what I expected to happen.

VII Construct sentences using the following words as (*a*) pronouns, (*b*) adjectives: *his, those, former, that, such.*

VIII Say whether 'such' in the following sentences is used as adjective or pronoun.

(1) Such men are dangerous. (2) His courage is such that he does not know the meaning of fear. (3) Many sports, such as climbing, skiing and sailing, can be practised in Switzerland. (4) George is such a thoughtful person; he is always helping people. (5) Industrial areas are generally dirty, and of such, alas, there are many in England.

IV. REFLEXIVE AND EMPHASIZING PRONOUNS

The '*self* pronouns' are formed by adding -*self* (plural -*selves*) to the possessive adjectives of the first and second person, and to the objective case form of the personal pronouns of the third person. The forms are:

	Singular	*Plural*
1st person	myself	ourselves
2nd person	yourself (thyself)	yourselves
3rd person	himself herself itself oneself	themselves ———

These pronouns have two functions. They can be

    (*a*) Reflexive.   (*b*) Emphasizing.

A REFLEXIVE PRONOUN indicates that the action expressed by the verb passes from the subject back again to the subject and not to any other person or thing. In other words the person denoted by the subject and the person denoted by the object are identical. *Examples:*

I am teaching *myself* Latin.

He shaves *himself* every morning.

The visitors helped *themselves* to the cakes.

She saw *herself* in the looking-glass.

One should try to see *oneself* as others see one.

It's a pity we can't see *ourselves* as others see us.

There is so much noise I can hardly hear *myself* speak.

Make *yourselves* at home.

'The climate makes the English so dirty that they have to be perpetually washing *themselves*.'

                     (Shaw, *Arms and the Man*)

The reflexive pronoun may have either a strong stress or a weak stress. It has the strong stress when a contrast is stated or implied, e.g.

She thinks only about *herself*, never of other people.

Little Albert said, 'I don't need nurse to wash me; I can wash *myself*, now.'

In the following sentence the reflexive pronouns have a weak stress:

> Little Albert is only four, but he can feed *himself*, wash *himself* and dress *himself*.

The reflexive pronoun can be:

(*a*) a direct object as in most of the examples above.

(*b*) an indirect object, e.g.

> You have given *yourselves* a great deal of work. I told *myself* there was nothing to be afraid of. He cooked *himself* a good meal. She bought *herself* a new hat.

(*c*) part of the predicate of the verb *to be*, in which case it always has a strong stress:

> If he has a holiday at the seaside he will soon be *himself*.
> Ah, that's better. You are *yourself* again.

(*d*) used after a preposition, e.g.

> She looked at *herself* in the looking-glass. What have you to say for *yourself?* I want a little time to *myself*. She loves me for *myself*, not for my money. He ought to be ashamed of *himself*. Speak for *yourself*. This is strictly between *ourselves*. George is very pleased with *himself*. He works for *himself*, not for an employer.

But if there is no doubt about the identity of the person denoted by the pronoun, the simple, not the reflexive form of the pronoun is used after a preposition, e.g.

> He took food for the day with *him*. She shut the door behind *her*. We have the whole day before *us*. He put the thought from *him*. They stood on the cliff looking about *them*.

The reflexive pronoun is sometimes used instead of the ordinary personal pronoun for added clearness of meaning, e.g.

> She suspected that they recognized her sister but not *herself*.

and sometimes because, perhaps, the '-self' form is vaguely felt to be more polite—or perhaps because the speaker is not quite sure whether the correct pronoun should be *I* or *me*, e.g.

> My wife and *myself* were invited to the party.
> There was an invitation to my wife and *myself*.

The *-self* pronoun, especially *myself,* is occasionally used where the ordinary personal pronoun would also be possible:

My brother is as old as *myself.*

That argument is repugnant to a lawyer like *myself.*

No one realizes that more than *myself.*

'Coleridge and *myself* walked back to Nether Stowey that evening' (*Hazlitt*).

Whether the enemy defeats us or not depends upon *ourselves.*

Did anyone see him besides *yourself?*

The *-self* pronoun in the last two examples seems to be emphasizing (i.e. = 'depends upon us ourselves' — 'besides you yourself').

VERBS USED REFLEXIVELY

A few verbs are practically always used reflexively:

I *pride myself* on always having a tidy garden.

He *availed*[1] *himself* of the opportunity to speak to her.

All the students *absented* [æb'sentid] *themselves* from the class.

Some are reflexive in certain senses, e.g.

I hope the children will *behave themselves.*

They *acquitted themselves* well.

I hope you will *enjoy yourself* at the party.

He *applied himself* to the task of organizing the finances of the Company.

The verbs *acquit, enjoy, behave* and *apply* can be used non-reflexively:

The judge *acquitted* the prisoner.

I *enjoyed* the concert very much.

He *applied* a hot poultice to the sore foot.

The children *behaved* very well.

Occasionally the reflexive pronoun is used in a reciprocal sense:

They were busy arguing among *themselves* (= with each other).

[1] But in the well-known poem of Clough there is the line: 'Say not the struggle nought *availeth*', where the verb is not used reflexively.

THE EMPHASIZING '-SELF' PRONOUNS have exactly the same form as the reflexive pronouns but their function is different. They are always strongly stressed and they are used for the sake of emphasis; generally to point out a contrast such as:

You *yourself* (i.e. 'you and not anyone else') told me the story.

The emphasizing pronoun can go, as in the sentence above, after the word for which it stands, but it is usually placed at the end of the sentence, e.g.

I saw him do it *myself*.

The Duke piloted the plane *himself*.

Never leave to others what you ought to do *yourself*.

In these and similar sentences the person denoted by the subject and the person denoted by the object are not identical. The emphasizing pronouns (but not the reflexive ones) could be omitted without destroying the sense of the sentence.

Sometimes emphasizing pronouns have the meaning 'alone' or 'without help', in which case they generally have *by* with them:

This is a machine that works *by itself*.

The little girl travelled from London to New York *by herself*.

All can be used with this construction as an intensifying word:

Don't you feel lonely living here *all by yourself?*

The meaning 'without help' can be suggested without *by*, e.g.

You can't do all the work *yourself* in a garden as big as this.

He tried to move the piano into the other room *himself*, but couldn't manage it.

Finally, we may note examples like:

Shakespeare *himself* (= even Shakespeare) never wrote a better line than that.

It was a portrait that Reynolds *himself* (= no less a painter than Reynolds) might have painted.

V. Interrogative Pronouns

The Interrogative Pronouns are *who* (*whom, whose*), *which, what*. They are used in forming questions and they always precede the verb, e.g.

Who broke that window?
Which do you prefer, dry sherry or sweet sherry?
What have you written?
Whose are these gloves?
Who(m) did you see?

The interrogative pronouns are invariable for gender and number. So the answer to the question '*Who* broke the window?' may be: 'Henry' (*Masculine, Singular*) or: 'Henry and Frederick' (*Masculine, Plural*) or: 'Mary' (*Feminine, Singular*) or: 'Mary and Elizabeth' (*Feminine, Plural*) or: 'Henry and Mary' (*Masculine, Feminine*). If we say: 'Here are some apples; *which* would you like?' we may be offering one or more than one. If we wish to make the number of *which* clear, the interrogative adjective with *one* or *ones* must be used, e.g.

'Here are some apples; *which one* would you like?' (*Singular*)
'Here are some apples; *which ones* would you like?' (*Plural*)

Note that the interrogative can introduce a direct question or an indirect one:

'*What* happened after that?' (*Direct*)
He asked me *what* had happened after that. (*Indirect*)
'*Who* is going to the party?' (*Direct*)
He asked me *who* was going to the party. (*Indirect*)

WHO

Who is used only for persons. It may be singular or plural and may be used to stand for a masculine noun or a feminine one, e.g.

'*Who* spilt the ink?' 'Henry did.'
'*Who* can answer that question?' 'Mary can.'

Who is the nominative form; the objective form is *whom*, e.g.

'*Who(m)* did you see?' 'I saw George.'
'To *whom* did you give the letter?' (*Who(m)* did you give the letter to?)

(*Whom* is the 'literary' form and is preferred in writing. In conversation it is generally replaced by *who* unless it immediately follows a preposition.)

Note the difference in construction between the use of *him* and *who(m)* as indirect objects. With *who(m)* the preposition is always necessary, with *him* it may be omitted. 'To whom did they give the prize?' or 'Who(m) did they give the prize to?' 'They gave him the prize.'

The possessive form is *whose*, e.g.

Whose are these gloves and *whose* is this umbrella?

WHAT

What is generally used for things. It may be singular or plural, subject or object, and it has no possessive form.
Examples:

What is this? *What* are those strange objects?
What is his name/address/telephone number?

The distinction between *who* (for persons) and *what* (for things) can be seen clearly in the sentences:

'*Who* broke the window?' and: '*What* broke the window?'
'*Whom* did you see?' and: '*What* did you see?'

What can stand for an activity, in which case the answer will be usually a verb in the *-ing* form, e.g.

'*What* are you doing?' 'I'm cleaning the car.'
'*What's* that thing for?' 'It's for punching holes in paper.'

but the answer may contain another form of the verb, e.g.

'*What* have you done?' 'I've knocked the vase off the table.'

What is used also to ask for a person's profession, etc., e.g.

'*What* is that man talking to your father?' 'He's a lawyer/a gardener/a Member of Parliament.'

Note the difference between this and: '*Who* is that man talking to your father?' To such a question the answer would be: 'He is Mr. ——.'

Both forms are seen in:

I don't know *who* or *what* he is; and I don't care.

Note, too, the construction: *What . . . like?* e.g.

'*What* is he like?' To which the answer might be:
'He's tall, dark and handsome.'

or:

'*What's* he *like* as a pianist?' 'Oh, he's not very good.'

or:

'*What's* his work *like*?' 'It's quite good.'

WHICH

Which is used for things and persons, singular or plural, subject or object. It has no possessive case.

WHAT AND WHICH

What is used when we make a selection from a more or less unlimited number; *which* is used to present a choice from a limited number. The choice with *which* is usually made more explicit by 'which of', e.g.

Which of you boys can't do this exercise?

Which will you have, tea or coffee?

'*What* are you taking in your examination?' 'I'm taking English, French, and German.'

'*Which* of them is your best subject?' 'English.'

'*What* would you like to study in next year's literature course?' 'A Shakespeare play.'

'Very good; *which* would you like?'

WHO AND WHICH

There is a different implication in each of these two sentences:

(a) *Who* would like to come for a game of football?

(b) *Which* of you would like to come for a game of football?

In (a) the speaker is prepared to take all who wish to come; in (b) he is only prepared to take a certain number.

INTERROGATIVES

The interrogative adjectives corresponding to the interrogative pronouns are *whose, what, which*. Like all adjectives they are invariable. They can be used for persons (masculine or feminine) or for things. They can be part of the subject or of the object and can be followed by a singular verb or a plural one. *Examples:*

WHOSE

Whose car is that? *Whose* little boy (*whose* little girl) are you? *Whose* house did you like?

WHAT

What places did you see? *What* class does Professor Grey take? *What* assistants has he? *What* man or *what* woman could have done more? *What* work have you done?

In questions that ask about the nature of a thing or person we generally use, '*What* kind of?' '*What* sort of?' e.g.

What kind of chocolates do you like best?
What sort of a girl is she?

WHICH

Which boy (girl) has (*which* boys/girls/have) answered correctly all the questions?
Which eye was injured, his right or his left?
Which apples did you grow yourself?

The remark about the interrogative pronouns *what* and *which* (page 119) applies also to the corresponding interrogative adjectives, e.g.

'*What* subjects are you taking in your examination?'
'English, French and German.'
'*What* play would you like to study next term?'
'*Which* subject is your best one?' 'English.'
'*What* play would you like to study next term?' 'One of Shaw's.' 'Very good; *which* play would you like?'

Emphatic Forms

Ever is added to *what* or *who* or *which* usually to express more emphatically a feeling of surprise, anger, indignation, etc.:

Who ever can be calling at this time of night?
Who ever heard of such a silly idea?

What ever were you thinking of to suggest such a plan?

'He gets up at five o'clock every morning.' *'What ever* for?'

The word *ever* here has a meaning like 'on earth', 'in the world'.

IDIOMATIC EXPRESSIONS

Some idiomatic expressions with *who, which, what* (not necessarily as interrogatives) are:

What about a cigarette/something to eat, etc? (= would you like; shall we have . . .)

Oh! There's Mr. *What's-his-name.*⎫ said when you cannot
It's a *what-do-you-call-it.* ⎭ remember the name.

What with high prices, high taxation and low wages he's very badly off.

It was so dark I couldn't tell *who was who.*

The two twins are so alike I can't tell *which is which* (or *who is who*).

I don't know anyone at this party; you must tell me *who's who.*

You'll find his name in *Who's Who* (= a reference book of contemporary biography).

He's a clever fellow; he knows *what's what* (= what is good, useful, profitable, etc. from what is not).

EXERCISES

I Identify the 'self' pronouns in the following sentences as reflexive or emphasizing.

(1) The Archbishop himself preached the sermon. (2) I made this myself but it was you yourself who gave me the idea. (3) Make yourself at home and help yourself to anything you fancy. (4) If you want a job well done, do it yourself. (5) Brown doesn't seem very well these days. No, he has not been himself for some time. (6) The thieves quarrelled among themselves about the division of the booty. (7) He's a conceited young man and thinks too highly of himself. (8) Your success in life depends very largely on yourself. (9) The Minister himself signed the letter.

E

II Make a list of English verbs which are always used reflexively and construct one sentence for each verb illustrating its use.

III (*a*) Make sentences, using each of these verbs twice, once intransitively and once reflexively:

wash; shave; dress; move; behave; stop.

(*b*) Form sentences, using these verbs first non-reflexively and transitively and then reflexively:

fancy; apply; acquit; enjoy; prove; settle; acknowledge; make; strain; call; consider.

IV Fill in the blanks with pronouns ending in -*self* or -*selves*. Say whether they are emphatic or reflexive; and, in the case of reflexive pronouns, whether they are direct or indirect objects:

(1) I shall do the job ——. (2) The Headmaster —— will take this particular lesson. (3) She stood admiring —— in front of the mirror. (4) Why don't you go ——? (5) They think —— clever. (6) Look after ——. (7) We gave —— a lot of trouble. (8) The Duke, piloting the plane ——, took off amidst loud cheers. (9) The Duke took —— off in high dudgeon. (10) It's time you got —— a new coat.

V In the following sentences state which -*self* pronouns are strongly stressed and which are not:

(1) No one was there except myself. (2) George stopped himself just in time. (3) George's wife went on, but he himself stopped and stared. (4) The fault lies in ourselves, not in our stars. (5) He worked himself to death. (6) He shaves himself; he trusts no barber. (7) He shaves himself at night to save time in the morning. (8) The Queen herself is not at liberty to do that. (9) Mother is not feeling herself today, but I don't think she will do herself any good by worrying.

VI Complete the following sentences with phrases consisting of the preposition 'by' together with an emphatic pronoun, *or* with an emphatic pronoun alone —whichever makes the better sense.

(1) Poor Timothy looks so lonely, sitting all —— in the corner. (2) Were you quite —— when you undertook this work? It is clear that you don't like the job. (3) Were you quite —— in the church? Didn't anyone come in to listen to you playing? (4) Did James do this work —— or did his sister help him?

VII Construct sentences to illustrate the use of emphasizing pronouns in the sense of 'alone', 'even' and 'also'. Where possible, give two forms—with and without the preposition 'by'.

VIII Define the *-self* pronouns in the following:

(1) He is himself a good player, but his son is even better when he is really himself. (2) She made that dress herself while she was living by herself. (3) What would you yourself do in such circumstances? (4) Especially if you had caused those circumstances yourself. (5) The heirs quarrelled among themselves about the terms of the will.

IX Supply the interrogative words necessary from among the words *who, whom, whose, which, what,* to complete the following sentences:

(1) —— are you studying at school? (2) —— is the quickest way from here to the Bank? (3) —— is the horse that won the race? (4) —— did you meet at the party last night? (5) —— do you find easier to learn, English or German?

X Ask questions to which the following statements are answers (the key words in each answer are in italics. Only interrogative pronouns or interrogative adjectives to be used.)

(1) It was *Peter* that gave the news. (2) It was *Peter* they chose. (3) *That* is Peter; the other boy is his brother. (4) It's a book on *natural history* that I'm reading. (5) I'm studying *Modern Languages*. (6) At *Oxford* (University). (7) Those gloves belong *to me*. (8) This parcel is from *my aunt*. (9) *Henry and Mary* are getting married tomorrow. (10) Henry and Mary are *getting married* tomorrow. (11) That's *Mr. Saunders*. (12) That's *a letter-box*. (13) That's *the postman*. (14) Charles is *a postman*. (15) I'll take *the yellow one*. (16) It's *Henry and Mary's wedding* that's taking place tomorrow. (17) He's *short and tubby, has a sandy moustache, a waddle and a foul temper*. (18) I like '*thrillers*' best.

XI Express idiomatically by use of 'what', 'who', or 'which' the words in italics:

(1) *Shall we have* a game of darts? (2) Let's look in the the paper to find out *the films and plays we might see* in London. (3) My father knows *a good thing when he*

sees one. (4) Do you know *which rôles you are respectively playing?* (5) One of these table napkins is yours,
the other is mine; I *can not distinguish yours from
mine.*

XII Complete the following sentences with interrogative
pronouns or with idiomatic expressions using interrogative pronouns.

(1) —— —— made you trust him with all that money?
(2) I'm absolutely parched. —— —— a pint of beer?
(3) I can't remember what you call it. It's a —— ——
——. You know what I mean, don't you? (4) Those
girls are so much alike that it's hard to tell —— ——
——. (5) '——'s ——' is a reference book containing
the names of important people. (6) —— —— the noise
of traffic outside and of typewriters in the office, I can
hardly hear myself speak. (7) —— can possibly be
knocking as late as this?

VI. INDEFINITE PRONOUNS

This is a group containing the pronouns:
some (*-thing, -body, -one*[1]), *any* (*-thing, -body, -one*): *all, one,
none, no* (*-thing, -body, -one*), *every* (*-thing, -body, -one*), *other,
another, much, less,* (*a*) *few,* (*a*) *little, enough, each, either,
neither.*

Many of these words can also be used adjectivally as Determinatives (see Chapter 10), e.g.

Have you *any* matches? (*Adjective*). Ask John if he has *any*
(*Pronoun*). I wish I had *some* red roses (*Adjective*). I must
try to grow *some* next year (*Pronoun*). The notice said: '*All*
boys must be in school by 9 o'clock' (*Adjective*). But *all* were
not there at nine o'clock (*Pronoun*). We *all* like Mr. Thompson very much (*Pronoun*). He told me a lot of *other* things
that I can't remember now (*Adjective*). Which one are you
going to choose, that one or the *other?* (*Pronoun*). At the
party *each* child was given an orange and a bag of sweets
(*Adjective*). *Each* of them was also given a present from the
Christmas tree (*Pronoun*).

[1] There is no difference in meaning or usage between *nobody — no one;
somebody —someone; anybody — anyone; everybody — everyone.*

NOTES ON SOME OF THE INDEFINITE PRONOUNS AND ADJECTIVES

Either means 'one or the other of two'; *neither* means 'not this and not the other'; it is a rejection of both of two. Both *either* and *neither* can be distributive adjectives or distributive pronouns. Both are singular in number, e.g.

Either of these machines *is* suitable for the work you want done.

Neither of my friends has come yet.

There is a train at 11.30 and one at 12.5: *either* train will get you to Oxford in time for the meeting (*Adjective*). If you don't want *either* of those, there is another one at 10.30 (*Pronoun*).

I have travelled by the 11.30 train and the 12.5 and *neither* train had a restaurant car (*Adjective*).

I am very surprised that *neither* of them had a restaurant car. (*Pronoun*)

Either can occasionally mean "one *and* the other of two," e.g.

He came down the road with a girl on *either* arm.

'On *either* side the river, lie

Long fields of barley and of rye.'—(Tennyson)

ALL

All can be used as pronoun or as adjective in the singular or the plural. It is used in the singular:

(1) as a pronoun with the meaning of *everything*, e.g.

When he saw his troops retreat, the General cried, '*All* is lost.'

'*All's* well that ends well.' '*All* is not gold that glitters.'

(2) as an adjective with the meaning, 'the whole of':

All the money is spent. *All* the world has heard of his name. He worked hard *all* the time he was here. He spent *all* last week in London.

It is used in the plural as an adjective or as a pronoun, e.g.

All the pupils were present. (*Adjective*) *All* are welcome.

(*Pronoun*) I don't like to speak before *all* these people.
(*Adjective*) He has written six novels and *all* of them are good. (*Pronoun*)

When the subject is a noun, *all* can precede it or follow it, e.g.

All the students agreed that the concert was good.
The students *all* agreed that the concert was good.

If the Subject is a pronoun, *all* generally follows it, e.g.

They *all* (but not '*all* they') agreed that the concert was good.

ALL and EVERY

All often has the meaning of *every*. The constructions are:
all + plural verb; *every* + singular verb, e.g.

That's the sort of job that $\begin{cases} all \text{ boys like doing.} \\ every \text{ boy likes doing.} \end{cases}$

The explosion broke $\begin{cases} all \text{ the windows} \\ every \text{ window} \end{cases}$ in the street.

All the people were cheering loudly. *Everybody* was cheering loudly.

The distinction between *all* and *every* is that in a sentence like, 'All the boys were present', we consider the boys in a mass; in the sentence, 'Every boy was present', we are thinking of the many individual boys that make up the mass.

In addition to being a pronoun and an adjective, *all* is used adverbially in such expressions as:

His face was *all* covered with blood. If you can finish the work by Wednesday instead of Thursday, that will be *all* the better. Did you catch your train *all* right? If it is *all* the same to you, I'd rather go by car than by train.

EACH, EVERY, (-ONE, -BODY)

Each and *every* also express totality and are usually called DISTRIBUTIVES. *Each* can be a pronoun or a determinative adjective. *Every* can only be an adjective; its pronominal forms are *everyone, everybody, everything*. *Each* can be used when the total number referred to is two or more; *every* can be used only when the total number exceeds two.

EACH as a pronoun:

Each must do his best. They *each* signed the paper. Mr. Brown came to the school with a bag of apples, and gave the boys two *each*. *Each* of the boys has done his work.

EACH as an adjective:

Each man must do his best. *Each* person signed the paper. He gave *each* boy two apples. Before choosing a pen, she looked at *each* one in turn.

EVERY as an adjective:

Every man must do his best. *Every* person signed the paper. He gave *every* boy two apples. *Every* one of the boys has done his work. '*Every* cloud has a silver lining.' (*Proverb*)

Pronominal Forms of *every*

Everyone knows that Rome is the capital of Italy. He told *everyone* that he was a lord. *Everybody* was disappointed that you could not come. *Everything* he says is true. *Everything* in the house was destroyed by fire.

Notice that *each, every, everyone, everybody, everything* take a SINGULAR verb.

Observe the difference between 'everyone' ['evriwʌn], which can be used only for persons, and 'every one' ['evri 'wʌn], which can be used also to speak of things, e.g. She has kept *every one* of my letters.

EACH and EVERY

There are some differences in meaning and usage between *each* and *every* as adjectives.

The feeling of 'distribution' is stronger in *each* than in *every*. *Every* tends to gather the separate items into a whole; *each* focuses attention on them individually and so tends to disperse the unity. This can be seen if we consider the sentences:

I visited him *every* day while he was in hospital.

and: I visited him *each* day while he was in hospital.

Note, too, the following idiomatic uses of *every:*

> The cheaper paper is *every* bit as good as the dearer one.
> . . . '*every* inch a king' (Shakespeare, *King Lear*). He is *every* inch a gentleman. You have *every* right to be angry. There is *every* reason to think he is speaking the truth.

In none of these could *each* replace *every*. Nor could *each* be used in such phrases as:

> '*every* other day'. '*every* two days'. '*every* now and then'.

Note the two meanings of the phrase 'every other day', the difference being indicated by a difference of intonation and stress, e.g.

> (*a*) 'I go there every other day' [evri ʌðə 'dei] means I go on alternate days (e.g. on Monday, Wednesday, Friday, Sunday).

> (*b*) 'We have a lesson on Monday, but on *every other day* [evri 'ʌðə dei] there are no lessons', means 'there are no lessons on all the other days'.

BOTH

Both, like *all*, as a pronoun or as an adjective, indicates totality, but is applied to only two persons or things. It is used only before plural nouns, and takes a plural verb.

Both can be a pronoun or a determinative adjective.[1]

Both as a pronoun:

> I have two brothers; they are *both* engineers.
> I don't know which book is the better; I shall read *both*.
> 'Which of the two girls is he in love with?' '*Both!*'

Both as an adjective:

> *Both* his legs were broken in the accident. There are houses on *both* sides of the street. *Both* (the) men were found guilty.

Both is used adverbially in such a sentence as:

> The book is *both* useful and amusing.

---

[1] For the position of *both* as a determinative, see p. 83.

SOME[1] (-THING, -BODY, -ONE)

Some has the following uses:

1. As an adjective or a pronoun it is used before, or to refer to, uncountable nouns and plural nouns, to express an indefinite quantity or number. As an adjective, the weak form [səm] is generally used; as a pronoun, the strong form [sʌm]. *Examples:*

(*Adjective*) He wants *some* money. I have spilt *some* ink on the table. There are *some* cows in the field.

(*Pronoun*) I hadn't any cigarettes, so I went out to buy *some*. If you have no money I will lend you *some*.

2. As an adjective or a pronoun it is used before, or to refer to, uncountable nouns and plural nouns to suggest contrast. Both adjective and pronoun are pronounced [sʌm]. *Examples:*

(*Adjective*) *Some* people hate cats; others dislike dogs. I enjoy *some* music, but much of it bores me.

(*Pronoun*) *Some* of us agree with that statement; *some* disagree. Not all your answers were correct; *some* were, *some* were not. '*Some* are born great, *some* achieve greatness and *some* have greatness thrust upon them'. (Shakespeare)

3. As an adjective only it is used before singular countable nouns with the meaning 'a particular, but unidentified person, or thing' (often with derogatory meaning). With this meaning it is always pronounced [sʌm]. *Examples:*

Some fool had left the lawn-mower on the garden path, and in the dark I fell over it. He arrived with *some* old book that he had picked up at a second-hand book-shop.

Something and *some* [sʌm] (the latter before a numeral) have the meaning 'approximately', e.g.

I'll whistle the tune for you; it goes *something* like this.

It happened *some* twenty years ago.

It will take *some* three or four thousand pounds to rebuild the house.

---

[1] For the use of *some* as a Determinative, see pages 90–3.

ANY (-THING, -BODY, -ONE)

1. *Any*, used emphatically, has the general meaning, 'it doesn't matter who, which or what', e.g.

Come *any* day you like. Get me some cigarettes, please; *any* kind will do. *Any* student can answer the question. He is a man who will do *anything* for money. You must give an excuse for not going; *any* excuse will do. I have *any* number of (= a great many) small plants in my garden; I will give you as many as you want.

2. *Any* used unemphatically has the same meaning as *some* (1. above); but see below.

3. *Any* can be used with a singular countable or uncountable noun or a plural one, e.g.

Any sane person would have acted as you did.
Haven't you *any* work to do?
Are there *any* cows in the field?

4. *Any* is used adverbially in such sentences as:

I am sorry to say he isn't *any* better.
I couldn't come *any* sooner.
In spite of your careful explanation, I don't think he is *any* the wiser.

SOME and ANY

Note the difference in meaning between the sentences:

Richard is older than *some* of the other boys in his class (= he is not the youngest, but he is not the oldest).
Richard is older than *any* of the other boys in his class (= he is the oldest).
That firm does more business than *some* of its competitors (= a number of, but not all).
That firm does more business than *any* of its competitors (= all).

A general rough, and ready, distinction between *some* and *any* is that *some* is used in affirmative sentences, *any* in interrogative and negative sentences, e.g.

I am looking for *some* matches (Affirmative).
Have you *any* matches? (Interrogative).
I haven't *any* matches (Negative).
There is *someone* in the room (Affirmative).
Is there *anyone* in the room? (Interrogative).
There isn't *anyone* in the room (Negative).
There's *something* I want to ask you (Affirmative).
Is there *anything* you want to ask me? (Interrogative).
There isn't *anything* I want to ask you (Negative).

A negative meaning may be conveyed by words like *never, without, seldom*, etc., in which case *any* is used, e.g.

He *never* had *any* luck.
He worked hard but *without any* success.

An interrogative meaning is sometimes conveyed by a conditional clause, in which case also *any* is used, e.g.

If there are *any* good apples in the shop, bring me two pounds.

Moreover, *some* as well as *any* can be used in interrogative sentences; it depends on the reply expected. If the reply expected is 'Yes', we tend to use *some* in the question, e.g.

'Didn't you put *some* matches in your pocket?' has the meaning: 'I'm almost sure I saw you put some matches in your pocket.' Or: 'You put some matches in your pocket, didn't you?'

The question: 'Are you expecting *someone* this afternoon?' expects the answer 'Yes'. If the answer 'No' were expected, the question would be: 'Are you expecting *anyone* this afternoon?'

similarly:

'Is *someone* coming this afternoon?' (implication: 'I see that preparations are being made.')
'Have you lost *something*?' ('You seem to be searching.')

The same conditions apply to the adverbs *somewhere, anywhere:*

'Have you seen him before *somewhere*?' ('You seem to recognize him.')

Again, if the question is really a request, an invitation, or a command in the form of a question, *some* is used, e.g.

Will you ask *someone* to carry this bag for me, please?
May I give you *some* more tea?
Won't you try *some* of this cake?
Could you let me have *some* money, father?

NO, NOTHING, NOBODY, NO ONE, NONE

The determinative *no* is only used attributively and has the meaning 'not any', e.g.

There is *no* (there isn't any) salt on the table, and *no* (there aren't any) glasses
'*No* smoking allowed.'

No has the meaning 'not a' in such sentences as:

He is *no* hero.

Nothing can be replaced by *not*[1] *anything; nobody* (or *no one*) by *not*[1] *anybody* (*-one*), except when they are the subject of the sentence.

There was *nothing* (*wasn't anything*) in the shop that I wanted to buy.
Can *no one* (*Can't anyone*) answer the question?
There's *nobody* (There *isn't anybody*) in the room.

Nobody and *no one* are used of persons; *none* is used of persons and things, e.g.

No one came to the class. There was *nobody* in the room.
I wanted some more coffee but there was *none* left.

None is a pronoun and is equivalent to 'not one' or 'not any', e.g.

None of his pupils failed their examination.
'How many fish did you catch?' '*None.*'
'*None* so blind as those who will not see.' (*Proverb*)

Nobody, nothing and *no one* are singular in number and are used with a singular verb.

None is used with a singular or with a plural verb, e.g.

None of us *is* perfect; we all make mistakes.
'There *are none* so deaf as those who will not hear.' (*Proverb*)

---

[1] *not* will generally be in the contracted form and attached to the appropriate Special Finite. This construction is the usual one in conversation.

The singular verb with *none* is considered by some grammarians to be the more correct.

None, nothing, nobody, no one are frequently used in 'short answers', e.g.

'How many of the exercises did you get right?'

'*None.*'

Generally speaking, the difference between *nothing* and *none* is that in 'short answers' 'nothing' might be the reply to a question beginning 'What?' or 'Who?' whereas 'none' might be the reply to one beginning 'How many?' or 'How much?' The same distinction applies to *nobody* and *none*, e.g.

'*What* is on the table?' '*Nothing.*'

'*How many* books are on the table?' '*None.*'

'*Who* is in the dining-room?' '*Nobody (no one).*'

'*How many* people are in the dining-room?' '*None.*'

'*How much* petrol is there in the car?' '*None!*'

No, something, nothing can also be used adverbially, e.g.

He is *no* better and is still very ill.

It is *no* faster to go there by train than by car.

No sooner had I let the cat out of the room than she wanted to come in again.

He is *something* like what his father was at that age.

Your work is *nothing* (isn't anything) like so good as Henry's.

It is a peculiarity of *no* that it can be used, as in the above three examples, with the comparative form of an adjective but not with the positive (except with *different* and certain idiomatic senses of *good*) or with superlative forms.

OTHER, ANOTHER

Other may be an adjective or a pronoun. As an adjective it is invariable; as a pronoun it is countable and has the plural form *others*. When it is used with the indefinite article (*an*), they are written as one word *another*.

The other (singular) means 'the second of two', e.g.

He held a sword in one hand and a pistol in the *other*.

One of my brothers is named Richard, the *other* is named Frederick.

When we got to that roundabout we ought to have taken the *other* road.

The other(s) means the remaining (ones), e.g.

We got home by 6 o'clock, but the *others* didn't get back until about 8 o'clock.

The *other* guests that we had expected didn't come.

Other(s) may simply mean 'different', 'additional', 'remaining', e.g.

There are *other* ways of doing this exercise.

I have no *other* friend but you.

Some like milk chocolate, *others* prefer plain chocolate.

Another means:

(1) 'an additional one', e.g.

Joe is terribly greedy; his hostess offered him *another* cake but he took one cake, then *another* and *another*. Mr. Brown already has two cars, and now he has bought *another*.

(2) 'a different one', e.g.

The point of this pencil is broken; can you lend me *another*, please?

On one day he will say one thing and on *another* day something quite different.

EACH OTHER, ONE ANOTHER

Each other and *one another* are used after transitive verbs to express reciprocity, i.e. that the feeling or action is mutual. Some grammarians make the distinction that with *each other* there are two people concerned, e.g.

The two sisters love *each* other.

while with *one another* there are more people concerned, e.g.

Little children, love *one another*.

This usage, however, is frequently not observed.

Note the position of the prepositions when used with *each other* and *one another*.

They gave presents *to* each other.

They are very fond *of* one another.

EXERCISES

I Fill in the blanks with suitable indefinite pronouns, distributive pronouns or adjectives.

(1) 'Is there —— ink in the pot?' 'No, ——.'

(2) Will you have —— more tea? There's plenty in the pot.

(3) You don't want —— more cake, do you? I want to save —— for tomorrow.

(4) 'Are you doing —— tonight?' 'No, ——.'

(5) Can —— tell me the right time?

(6) Tell me —— you know, and —— will be well.

(7) We —— know how hard you have worked. —— shares your joy at your success.

(8) —— are agreed that the government has taken a bold decision.

(9) 'Who is in the corridor?' '——.'

(10) 'How —— does that cost?' 'Very ——, only a few shillings.'

(11) Look at my hands; —— is on the table and the —— on my knee.

(12) Now they are —— under the table!

(13) I have only two eyes; —— are good, but if I had six, I should need them —— to supervise those children properly.

(14) 'Which arm have I raised?' 'The left ——.'

(15) 'Which of my hands is in my pocket?' '——; they are —— on the table.'

(16) 'Which —— do you want?' '—— will do.'

(17) There will be a prize for —— of you.

(18) —— sat for the examination, but —— passed it.

(19) One man's meat is —— 's poison.

(20) —— must look after himself.

(21) 'Who is going to the lecture?' 'N——.'

(22) 'How —— went last week?' 'N——!'

(23) 'Have you —— money?' 'Yes, —— but not ——.'

II Use these words as adjectives and as pronouns:

each; all; either; some; another; other (adjective only); others (pronoun only).

III State the part of speech of the words in italics:

(1) Don't leave *all* your books on the floor. (2) *Every* dog has his day. (3) *Every one* of the eggs was cracked.

(4) *Everyone* in that house is mad. (5) *Every* penny counts; *each* should try to contribute at least *one*. (6) *Each* penny on the table was given by a different person. (7) Please *all* join in. (8) *All* the gentlemen were in evening dress. (9) He was kind *both* to his equals and to his inferiors. (10) He was kind to *both* his father and his mother. (11) He was kind to *both* his sisters. (12) He was *both* kind and generous. (13) This may please *some*, but not *all*.

IV Insert 'each' or 'every' in the blanks, whichever is more suitable.

(1) I take a lesson —— other day. (2) This method is —— bit as good as the other. (3) On —— occasion he has been late. (4) He seizes —— opportunity to get away from the house. (5) —— time you do that you will be punished. (6) He shouted her name twice, —— time banging his fist on the table.

V Correct or improve the following sentences:

(1) Which pullover will you have, the green or the blue? (2) My brother has three children and my sister two ones. (3) We see us twice a week. (4) Mary has any friends but her sister has nothing. (5) None of the two boys is suitable for this post. (6) Both of these boys is unsuitable for this post. (7) One of the laws of Christianity is: 'Love yourselves.'

VI Complete the following sentences with indefinite pronouns or adjectives:

(1) I wanted —— of those nice red apples but the greengrocer hadn't ——. (2) Will you have —— sugar in your tea? Yes, a —— please. (3) These shoes are almost worn out. I must buy —— new ——. (4) He is a most obliging man; —— is too much trouble for him. (5) I want two seats for tonight's concert. Have you ——? (6) We began our holiday with plenty of money, but now we have hardly —— to get home with. (7) No members were absent from the meeting; —— were present. (8) —— of those present agreed with the chairman. (9) There is little money in my pocket and —— in my banking account. (10) —— has taken my umbrella.

VII Construct sentences to illustrate the uses of '*all*' as a pronoun and explain the sense in which it is used in each sentence.

VIII What are the words opposite in meaning to the following:

someone, none, anybody, neither, each, everything, little, something, nothing, many.

If alternative forms are possible mention them.

IX Which number (singular or plural) may be used with the following pronouns or adjectives? Make sentences to illustrate their use:

neither, every, both, nobody, none, another, all, some, any.

X Are the words in italics in the following sentences adjectives or pronouns?

(1) Have you *any* pennies in your pocket? I need *some* for the telephone. (2) *Every* child born in England must be vaccinated. (3) *Each* of the first three runners received a prize. (4) I don't like *either* of these. Can you show me *some* others? (5) *Some* people are born clever, but *many* find study very difficult.

XI Rewrite the following sentences so that the same sense is expressed with the words in italics used as pronouns.

(1) Almost *all* boys like sport. (2) *Each* guest received a present. (3) I think the *other* books are more interesting than these. (4) *Either* road will take you to the railway station. (5) *Neither* hotel had any rooms vacant.

XII Complete the following sentences and justify your choice of the words you use. If more than one word can be used, explain in what senses.

(1) Do you think the postman has brought —— letters today? (2) That bicycle must have cost —— about £25. (3) —— succeeded, —— failed, but —— had worked hard. (4) Has —— lost this purse? Yes, —— has, but —— can discover who. (5) —— his arms were broken in the accident. (6) If you haven't this make of razor-blade, —— will do. (7) —— was delighted with the cruise. (8) What work is he doing? He never does ——. (9) There is a penny in one of my hands. Is it in this —— or the ——? (10) —— knows the trouble I've taken over this exercise.

XIII Comment on the use of the words in italics in the following sentences:

(1) These imported apples are sweeter than *some* I have tasted but they are inferior to *any* grown at home. (2) How much money have you in your pocket? I have hardly *any*. (3) Letters, if *any*, should be forwarded at once. (4) Didn't you hope to hear *something* of your family's plans today? (5) Will you send *someone* to repair my wireless set?

VII. Relative Pronouns

The Relative Pronouns are *who* (nominative), *whom* (objective), *whose* (possessive), *which, that, what* and occasionally *as* and *but*. They have the same forms for singular or plural, masculine or feminine.

The relative pronouns *who* and *which* are pronounced with a weaker stress than the interrogative pronouns *who, which*.

The following account gives general principles for the use of relative pronouns. The choice of a relative pronoun will also be determined according to whether the adjective clause in which it appears is defining or non-defining. (For adjective clauses, defining and non-defining, see pp. 324–7.)

WHO, WHOM, WHOSE

Who, whom, whose are used of persons, e.g.

The man *who* spoke was my brother.

He is one of the men *whom* I feel I can trust.

He is a man *whose* word is as good as his bond.

Which as a relative pronoun is used only of things or animals, e.g.

The current, *which* is very rapid, makes the river dangerous.

The dog *which* was lost has been found.

But if the animal is named, it is thought of as a 'person' and the pronoun *who* would be used, e.g.

Our dog Jock, *who* had been lost for two days, was found and brought home by a policeman.

With collective nouns denoting persons, *which* is used if the noun is regarded as singular, *who(m)* if it is regarded as plural, e.g.

The London team, *which* played so well last season, has done badly this season. The team, *who* are just getting their tickets, will meet on the platform at 2.30.

Which is used when the antecedent is a whole sentence, e.g.

He invited us to dinner, *which* was very kind of him.

THAT

That is invariable (i.e. it may be nominative or objective case, singular or plural number) and is used for persons or things. When used as a relative pronoun *that* is always pronounced with the weak form [ðət]. *Examples:*

Shakespeare is the greatest poet *that* England has ever had.
The plays *that* he wrote have been performed in almost every country in the world.
They live in a house *that* was built in 1600.
Have you everything *that* you need?

That (not *who* or *which*) is used:

(1) after an adjective in the superlative (including *first* and *last*) and after most indefinite pronouns, e.g.

Yesterday was one of the *coldest* days *that* I have ever known.
His book is the *best that* has ever been written on that subject, and yet you say this is the *first* time *that* you have heard of it.
He never says *anything that* is worth listening to.
'*All that* glitters is not gold.'
There's not *much that* can be done.

(2) after the openings 'It is . . .', 'It was . . .', etc., and the corresponding interrogative forms:

'It's an ill wind *that* blows nobody good.' (*Proverb*)
It is the teacher *that* is important, not the kind of school he teaches in.
What was it *that* he wanted?
In which play of Shakespeare's is it *that* Viola appears?
Was it you *that* broke the window?

(3) when the antecedent is both a person and a thing, e.g.

He talked brilliantly of the men and the books *that* interested him.

That cannot be used in non-defining clauses (see p. 326) and it cannot be preceded by a preposition, as *which* or *whom* can; the preposition must be at the end of the clause. Compare the sentences:

Here is the car *about which* I told you.

Here is the car *that* I told you *about*.

That can be used as a relative pronoun after the word *same*:

She wore the *same* dress *that* she wore at Mary's wedding.

but the usual relative pronoun after *same*, and the one that is always used after *such*, is *as:*

I shall be surprised if he does this in the *same* way *as* I do.

She wears the *same* kind of clothes *as* her sister usually does.

I never heard *such* stories *as* he tells.

'We are *such* stuff *as* dreams are made on.' (Shakespeare, *The Tempest.*)

WHAT

What is used when the antecedent is not expressed. It is a relative pronoun and an antecedent in one word, e.g.

Tell me *what* you want to know.

Here, *what* has the general meaning of 'the things (*antecedent*) which (*relative pronoun*)'.

What is also used when the antecedent is a sentence which follows *what:*

He is an interesting speaker, and, *what* is more important, he knows his subject thoroughly.

Whichever, whatever, whoever are compound relative pronouns, e.g.

You can have *whatever* you want.

Take *whichever* you like.

She can marry *whoever* she chooses.

CONCORD IN RELATIVE PRONOUNS

The relative pronoun agrees with its antecedent in number and person but not necessarily in case.

Care should be taken with such sentences as:

He waved his hand to Brown, *whom* he saw buying cigarettes in the shop. (*Correct*) AND:

He waved his hand to Brown, *who*, he saw, was buying cigarettes in the shop. (*Correct*)

In the first sentence *whom* is the object of *saw*. In the second sentence *who* is the subject of the verb 'was buying'.

Another pitfall is the number of the verb in relative clauses when *one* is used in the principal clause:

All the following sentences are correct:

This is one of the most difficult questions that *have* been asked.

That is one of the books that *were* given to us for study.

Richard is one of the boys who always *do* good work for me.

The antecedent in each case is not *one* but *questions, books, boys,* respectively.

The relative pronoun should be as close as possible to its antecedent. This will avoid such absurdities as:

After the wedding the bride and bridegroom left in a car for London which had been given as a present by the bride's father.

EXERCISES

I Combine the following pairs of sentences by means of relative pronouns (the words in italics in each sentence are to be replaced by the pronoun).

(1) The gentleman is my uncle. You met *him* yesterday. (2) The gentleman is my uncle. *He* impressed you when you met him. (3) The gentleman over there is my uncle. *He* is ninety years old. (4) The gentleman over there is my uncle. You would do well to humour *him*. (5) The gentleman over there is my uncle. *His* face must be familiar to you. (6) The gentleman over there is my uncle. I know you have a great respect for *him*. (7) The gentleman is my uncle. You were introduced to *him* yesterday. (8) In an effort to improve discipline, boys are to be 'dissuaded' from running along the corridors. *This* is a step in the right direction. (9) The cow has disappointed us this year. *It* gave so much milk last year. (10) Our cat, Peter, didn't eat his fish this morning. *He* is usually fond of his food.

II Express differently, using a relative pronoun. (Indications to help you are sometimes given in brackets.)

(1) This is an excellent film: I like it better than any other I have seen. (Use a superlative.)

(2) Someone is ringing you up tonight. Who?

(3) You said something. What?

(4) Did *you* tell me that, or was it someone else. (Was it ——?)

(5) What you say matters less than how you say it. (It is not ——.)

III Supply the words missing from the following sentences:

(1) The crowd, —— was very angry, shouted down the speaker. (2) The spectators, —— were very numerous, could not all find seats. (3) The audience, —— —— most enthusiastic, applauded the soloist. (4) Our visitors, —— we were very pleased to see, stayed until midnight. (5) He is one of the kindest men —— I have ever met. (6) Everything —— he says shows him to be an intolerant man. (7) There was little —— could be done for the injured man. (8) He systematically overworked, —— gradually ruined his health. (9) They spoke appreciatively of the teachers and the teaching —— had helped them. (10) The Tower of London, —— the Crown Jewels are kept, stands on the left bank of the Thames.

IV State with examples the rules governing the agreement of relative pronouns with their antecedents.

V Comment on and, if necessary, correct the following sentences:

(1) That is one of the City churches that was destroyed by bombing. (2) He is one of the boys who always does well at school. (3) He took off his hat to the lady whom he passed in the street. (4) He waved to his cousin whom, he noticed, was coming to meet him. (5) He is a brilliant soloist and, which is unusual, he is also a sound orchestral player.

CHAPTER TWELVE

VERBS

Though it is possible to have a sentence without a verb (if our definition of a sentence is wide enough),[1] it is true that, in the great majority of sentences, the verb is the word that plays the most important part. It is primarily the 'action' word in a sentence, the term 'action' embracing not only the meaning 'doing an action' but also 'having an action done to a person or thing'; nor must it exclude the *absence* of action, the idea of 'being in a state of rest'. This conception is expressed, more or less in the traditional definitions of a verb:

'A verb is a word for saying something about some person or thing.'

'. . . the part of speech by which we are able to say what a person or animal or thing is' (e.g. 'Jock *is* a dog') or does (e.g. 'He *walks* and *runs*') or what is done to that person or animal or thing (e.g. 'He *is brushed* and *combed* every day').

'. . . the part of speech that predicates, assists in predication, asks a question and expresses a command.'

Verbs have certain features that are not shared by other parts of speech; they have forms that indicate the time of an action (present, past or future); they can indicate the duration, completeness or incompleteness of an action; they can show whether a person or thing is doing or receiving an action, and can even express, in certain cases, the emotional attitude of the speaker toward the action. On the other hand they do not indicate gender, comparison or case.

FINITES AND NON-FINITES

The verb forms that can form the predicate by themselves are FINITE verbs; the ones that cannot are NON-FINITE verbs. The non-finites are the infinitives (e.g. *to speak, to write, to be, to have spoken, to have written, to have been*), the present participles and gerunds (e.g. *speaking, writing, being*) and the past participles (e.g. *spoken, written, been*). All other parts of the verb are finites.

Most English verbs have four inflectional forms, e.g. *walk — walks — walked — walking*. Some have five, e.g. *give — gives*

[1] See page 318

143

— *gave* — *given* — *giving*. No verb has more than five except *be* (*be, am, are, is, was, were, been, being*). Some have only three, e.g. *put* — *puts* — *putting;* *can* has only two, *can* — *could;* and *must* has no other forms. There are three fundamental forms (the 'principal parts'); they are the infinitive (or Present Simple tense), the simple past tense, and the past participle. From these the other forms of the verb can be made. The past participle is used with various parts of the verb *to be* to form the passive voice, and with the verb *have* to form the perfect tenses.

REGULAR AND IRREGULAR VERBS

All English verbs belong to one of two conjugations; they are either REGULAR verbs or IRREGULAR[1] verbs. Regular verbs are those that form their past tense and past participle by adding *-ed* to the present tense. This ending is pronounced [t] if the root of the verb ends in a voiceless consonant sound other than [t] (e.g. *ask* — *asked* [aːskt]; *finish* — *finished* ['finiʃt]; it is pronounced [id] if it ends with [t] or [d] (e.g. *expect* — *expected* [ks'pektid]; *intend* — *intended* [in'tendid]; it is pronounced [d] if the root of the verb ends in a vowel sound or a voiced consonant sound other than [d] e.g., *answer* — *answered* ['aːnsəd]; *open* — *opened* ['oupənd].

Irregular verbs form their past tense and past participle generally by a change of vowel, e.g. *give* — *gave* — *given; fly* — *flew* — *flown; eat* — *ate* — *eaten*.

Some spelling changes should be noted in the formation of past tense, present participle (and gerund):

(*a*) Verbs ending in *e* add *d* only for their past tense, e.g. dance — danc*ed*; love — lov*ed*. This *e* is omitted before *-ing* in the present participle and gerund, e.g. *dancing, loving*, etc.

---

[1] No new verb has adopted the Irregular conjugation since English came to England. The Regular conjugation has become the invariable method of forming the Simple Past and Past Participle whenever new verbs are called into existence. 'Historical' grammarians divide verbs into the categories 'Weak' and 'Strong', which correspond in the main to the categories 'Regular' and 'Irregular' given here, but there are some verbs which are, etymologically, 'Weak' but are not 'Regular' in so much as they have vowel changes in forming their Past Tense and Past Participle (e.g. *buy* — *bought; seek* — *sought; feed* — *fed; hide* — *hid* — *hidden*). As this is a purely historical point and of no practical value to the foreign learner we have classified verbs not as 'Weak' and 'Strong' but as 'Regular' and 'Irregular'.

(b) Verbs that end in *-ie* change this to *-y* before *-ing;* so *to die* has the present participle *dying.*

(c) Verbs that end in *y* preceded by a consonant change the *y* to *i* before *-ed*, e.g. marry — marr*i*ed; try — tr*i*ed.

(d) The final consonant letter is doubled before *-ed* and *-ing* if the consonant is single, is preceded by a single vowel letter, and if the verb is monosyllabic or stressed on the last syllable, e.g. *fit — fitted; control — controlled; stop — stopped.* Verbs ending in *-l* double the final consonant even when the last syllable is not stressed, e.g. *travel — travelled; marvel — marvelled;* also: *kidnap — kidnapped; worship — worshipped.*

(e) The form from *to singe* (= to burn slightly) is *singeing;* compare this with *singing* (from the verb *to sing*).

IRREGULAR VERBS

The following are the principal parts of the irregular verbs arranged according to their methods of forming past tense and past participle. Where two forms are given, one marked *, it is the latter that is used adjectivally.

Present Tense	*Past Tense*	*Past Participle*
	[a]	[ʌ]
begin	began	begun
drink	drank	drunk, drunken*[1]
ring	rang	rung
run	ran	run
shrink	shrank	shrunk, shrunken*[2]
sing	sang	sung
sink	sank	sunk, sunken*[3]
spring	sprang	sprung
stink	stank	stunk
swim	swam	swum

NOTES AND EXAMPLES

1. The *drunken* man had *drunk* a lot of wine. He was *drunk*.
2. The cloth had *shrunk* after being washed. The *shrunken* cheeks of the man showed how ill he was.

3. The ship has *sunk* with all hands on board. In his grounds there is a *sunken* rose garden.

Present Tense	Past Tense	Past Participle
	[ʌ]	[ʌ]
cling	clung	clung
dig	dug	dug
fling	flung	flung
hang	hung, hanged	hung, hanged[1]
sling	slung	slung
slink	slunk	slunk
spin	spun	spun
stick	stuck	stuck
strike	struck	struck, stricken*[2]
sting	stung	stung
swing	swung	swung
win	won	won
wring	wrung	wrung
	[ou]	[ou]
break	broke	broken
choose	chose	chosen
freeze	froze	frozen
steal	stole	stolen
speak	spoke	spoken
wake	woke	woke, woken
weave	wove, weaved[3]	woven, weaved
	[ɔː]	[ɔː]
bear	bore	borne, born[4]
swear	swore	sworn
tear	tore	torn
wear	wore	worn

NOTES AND EXAMPLES

1. *hanged* refers to death by hanging, e.g. The man *hanged* himself. The murderer was *hanged*.

2. *stricken* is used in certain phrases, e.g. 'conscience-*stricken*', 'poverty-*stricken*', 'terror-*stricken*', '*stricken* with disease'; but '*struck* by lightning', 'thunder*struck*'.

3. *weaved* is used with the figurative meaning 'thread (a way) through', e.g. He *weaved* his way through the crowd.

4. *born.* The form *born* is used with the verb *to be* in such sentences as 'Shakespeare *was born* in Stratford'. It is always passive. In all other cases *borne* is used, e.g. He has *borne* the pain bravely. The boat was *borne* out to sea by a strong tide. She has *borne* three children.

Present Tense	*Past Tense*	*Past Participle*
	[e]	[e]
bereave	bereaved, bereft	bereaved, bereft[1]
bleed	bled	bled
breed	bred	bred
creep	crept	crept
dream	dreamed, dreamt	dreamed, dreamt[2]
feed	fed	fed
feel	felt	felt
flee	fled	fled
keep	kept	kept
kneel	knelt	knelt
lead	led	led
leap	leapt [lept]	leapt
leave	left	left
mean	meant [ment]	meant
meet	met	met
read	read [red]	read
sleep	slept	slept
smell	smelt, smelled	smelt, smelled
speed	sped, speeded[3]	sped, speeded
spell	spelled, spelt	spelled, spelt
sweep	swept	swept
weep	wept	wept
	[u:]	[o:]
draw	drew	drawn
overdraw	overdrew	overdrawn
withdraw	withdrew	withdrawn

Present Tense	Past Tense	Past Participle
	[u:]	[ou]
blow	blew	blown
grow	grew	grown
know	knew	known
throw	threw	thrown
fly	flew	flown

NOTES AND EXAMPLES

1. *bereaved* = 'having lost someone by death'.
   bereft = 'deprived of', e.g. I was so surprised that, for the moment I was *bereft* of speech.
2. *dreamed* is preferred in poetry or emotional prose. *Dreamt* is pronounced [dremt].
3. *speeded* is used with the meaning 'went at a great speed', e.g. The car *speeded* along the road at 80 miles an hour. With 'up' it has the meaning 'made faster', e.g. Production has been *speeded up* by the introduction of new machinery.

Present Tense	Past Tense	Past Participle
	[ɔ:]	[ɔ:]
beseech	besought	besought
bring	brought	brought
buy	bought	bought
fight	fought	fought
· seek	sought	sought
think	thought	thought
catch	caught	caught
teach	taught	taught
	[ou]	[i]
drive	drove	driven
ride	rode	ridden
(a)rise	(a)rose	(a)risen
shrive	shrove	shriven
smite	smote	smitten
stride	strode	stridden
strive	strove	striven
thrive	throve, thrived	thriven, thrived
write	wrote	written

Present Tense	Past Tense	Past Participle
	(no change)	
bet	bet, betted	bet
burst	burst	burst
cast	cast	cast
broadcast	broadcast, broadcasted	broadcast, broadcasted
cost	cost	cost
cut	cut	cut
hit	hit	hit
hurt	hurt	hurt
let	let	let
put	put	put
rid	rid	rid
set	set	set
shed	shed	shed
shut	shut	shut
slit	slit	slit
split	split	split
spread	spread	spread
thrust	thrust	thrust
[-end]	[-ent]	[-ent]
bend	bent	bent[1]
lend	lent	lent
rend	rent	rent
send	sent	sent
spend	spent	spent
[ai]	[au]	[au]
bind	bound	bound
find	found	found
grind	ground	ground
wind [waind]	wound [waund]	wound [waund]

NOTES AND EXAMPLES

1. The usual past participle is *bent*, e.g. See how the wind has *bent* that tree. The adjectival use, too, is generally *bent*,

e.g. a *bent* pin; a *bent* old man. But *bended* is used in the phrase '*bended* knees', e.g. He went down on his *bended* knees before the Emperor.

Present Tense	Past Tense	Past Participle
[e]	[ou]	[ou]
sell	sold	sold
tell	told	told
[ai]	[i]	[i]
bite	bit	bitten[1]
chide	chid	chidden
hide	hid	hidden
[ei]	[u]	[ei]
forsake	forsook	forsaken
shake	shook	shaken
take	took	taken
mistake	mistook	mistaken
partake	partook	partaken
[i]	[ei]	[i]
bid[2]	bade, bid	bidden, bid
forbid	forbade	forbidden
forgive	forgave	forgiven
give	gave	given
[i]	[a]	[a]
sit	sat	sat
spit	spat	spat
	[-d]	[-n]
hew	hewed	hewn
mow	mowed	mown
sew	sewed	sewn
show	showed	shown
sow	sowed	sown
saw	sawed	sawn
strew	strewed	strewn

Notes and Examples

1. *bitten* is the usual form. But the proverbial phrase is 'the biter *bit*'.

2. *bid.* There are really two verbs here. *Bid, bade, bidden* is used in such sentences as, He *bade* us goodbye. I was *bidden* to the wedding. I *bade* him go, with the meaning *say, invite, command,* etc. (But a customary phrase is: Do as you are *bid.*) The forms *bid, bid, bid* are used with the meaning 'to make an offer at a sale or auction', e.g. the auctioneer might say, 'You, sir, *bid* £50 for this picture, but this lady *has bid* £60'.

bade, forbade have alternative pronunciation [bæd] [fə'bæd].

(*Miscellaneous*)

Present Tense	*Past Tense*	*Past Participle*
abide	abode	abode
(be), am, is	was	been
beat	beat	beaten
build	built	built
burn	burned, burnt	burned, burnt*
clothe	clothed, clad[1]	clothed, clad
come	came	come
becóme	became	become
overcome	overcame	overcome
do	did	done
outdo	outdid	outdone
dwell	dwelt	dwelt
eat	ate	eaten
fall	fell	fallen
forget	forgot	forgotten
get	got	got[2]
go	went	gone
undergo	underwent	undergone
have	had	had
hear	heard [hə:d]	heard
overhear	overheard	overheard

Present Tense	Past Tense	Past Participle
hold	held	held
behold	beheld	beheld, beholden[3]
withhold	withheld	withheld
knit	knitted, knit	knitted, knit*[4]
lay	laid	laid
mislay	mislaid	mislaid
learn	learned, learnt	learned,[5] learnt
lie	lay	lain
light	lit, lighted[6]	lit, lighted*
load	loaded	loaded, laden [7]
lose	lost	lost
make	made	made
melt	melted	melted, molten*[8]
pay	paid	paid
rot	rotted	rotted, rotten*[9]
say	said [sed]	said
see	saw	seen
shave	shaved	shaved, shaven*[10]
shear	sheared	sheared, shorn*[11]
shine	shone	shone
shoe	shod	shod
shoot	shot	shot
slide	slid	slid
spill	spilled, spilt	spilled, spilt*[12]
spoil	spoiled	spoiled, spoilt*
stand	stood	stood
understand	understood	understood
withstand	withstood	withstood
swell	swelled	swollen, swelled[13]
tread	trod	trodden, trod[14]
work	worked	worked, wrought[15]

NOTES AND EXAMPLES

1. *Clad* is more usual in the passive, e.g. The poor man was *clad* in rags.

2. The customary American usage for the past participle is *gotten*. This form is found in English in the phrase 'ill-*gotten* gains'.

3. *beholden* has a quite different meaning from *beheld*. It means 'obliged to', 'indebted to', e.g. I am not asking for a favour; I don't wish to be *beholden* to him for anything.

4. *Knit* has the meaning 'joined together', e.g. 'a *well-knit* story', 'a *well-knit* body'.

5. *learned* is used as an adjective to mean 'of great learning', e.g. 'a *learned* man'. It is then pronounced ['lə:nid].

6. *Lighted* is used (1) when it is adjectival, e.g. a *lighted* lamp (2) when the meaning is 'to provide light', e.g. The moon *lighted* us on our way.

7. *laden* is only used adjectivally meaning 'burdened (with)', e.g. He came in *laden* with parcels.

8. *molten* is only used adjectivally, e.g. The mould was filled with *molten* metal. The word is restricted to substances that are normally hard; so we can speak of *molten* iron, lead, steel, etc., but not of 'molten snow' or 'molten butter'. In these cases *melted* would be used.

9. *rotten* is only used adjectivally, e.g. The wood had *rotted* away. The trunk of the tree was quite *rotten*. There were some *rotten* apples on the floor.

10. I have *shaved* twice today. He is clean *shaven* (i.e. he hasn't whiskers or a moustache).

11. The farmer has *sheared* his sheep. 'God tempers the wind to the *shorn* lamb' (*Proverb*). But *shorn* is used as a participle with the meaning 'deprived of', e.g. Wolsey was *shorn* of his wealth and honours by Henry VIII.

12. For example: 'It's no use crying over *spilt* milk' (*Proverb*).

13. *swelled* is used in the colloquial expression 'He is suffering from *swelled* head' (= He is very conceited). *Swelled* is also used when the meaning is 'increased', e.g. The small river had *swelled* to a roaring torrent with the heavy rains. My class has *swelled* from 10 students to 30.

14. *trod* is used as a past participle with the meaning 'walked on', e.g. 'Many people have *trod* this ancient road'; and as an adjective in such phrases as 'a well-*trod* path'.

F

15. *wrought* is seldom used in modern English except in such phrases as 'a *wrought* iron gate', and (as a verb in the past tense) '*wrought* havoc', e.g. The frost *wrought* havoc with the fruit blossom.

Transitive and Intransitive Verbs

An action expressed by a verb may pass over from a subject to an object. For example, in the sentence: 'I hit the ball', the action of 'hitting' is not confined to the doer only, but goes over from *I* to *the ball*. When the action expressed by the verb goes from a subject to an object, that verb is called a TRANSITIVE verb.

In the sentences: The sun rose. The child cried. A leaf fell, the actions do not go beyond the persons or objects performing them. These verbs, as used in these sentences, have no objects. They are INTRANSITIVE verbs.

The only object that an intransitive verb can have is a COGNATE OBJECT, i.e. an object already implied more or less in the verb itself, e.g.

He lived a happy *life*. He died a sad *death*. The girl laughed a merry *laugh*. She slept a peaceful *sleep* and dreamed a happy *dream*. He sighed a *sigh*.

Quite often the same verb may be used transitively or intransitively, e.g.

Intransitive	*Transitive*
The bell *rings*.	The waiter *rings* the bell.
The window *broke* with the frost.	The burglar *broke* the window.
The door *opened*.	Tom *opened* the door.
Things have *changed* since I saw you.	I will go and *change* my clothes.
Time *passes* slowly when you are alone.	Will you *pass* the salt, please?
My watch has *stopped*.	The driver *stopped* the car and got out.

Intransitive	*Transitive*
The class *begins* at 9 o'clock.	He *began* his speech with a humorous story.
The fire *lit* quickly.	I have *lit* the fire.

Causative Use of Verbs

With some verbs the transitive use is the CAUSATIVE function of the verb.

The boy *ran* well.	She *ran* the car into the garage (= she caused it to run).
Coffee *grows* in Brazil.	They *grow* coffee (= cause it to grow) in Brazil.
Water *boils* at 100°C.	She *boiled* the water for tea.
The piece of wood *floated* on the water.	He *floated* his boat on the lake.

Sometimes a different form of the verb is used to mark the difference between the transitive and the intransitive form, e.g.

Intransitive	
The tree *fell* (verb *to fall*).	The woodmen *felled* the tree (verb *to fell*).
The book *lay* on the table (verb *to lie*)	The Mayor will *lay* the foundation stone (verb *to lay*).
The sun *rises* in the east (verb *to rise*).	The firm have *raised* his salary (verb *to raise*).
They all *sat* down (verb *to sit*).	The innkeeper *set* food and drink before the travellers (verb *to set*).

EXERCISES

I Give examples, naming the forms used, of one English verb having four inflectional forms, one of a verb having five such forms, and *all* such forms of the verb 'to be'.

II What are the principal parts of the following verbs: *hang, wake, melt, strike, rot, knit, bid, bend, lie, light?*

If any of them have special forms used in special senses, give those forms and construct sentences illustrating their use.

III Explain fully, giving examples, the terms 'finite' and 'non-finite'.

IV Show by examples, one using a regular verb and the other using an irregular verb, how the other forms of a verb can be made from the three fundamental forms (principal parts).

V Explain the difference between regular and irregular verbs in English and indicate how a regular verb can be identified.

VI Construct five sentences employing verbs which can be transitive or intransitive.

VII State the rules for the pronunciation of the past tenses and past participles of regular verbs and give examples to illustrate your answer.

VIII Give a list of all the verbs you know of which the three principal parts are the same.

IX Correct the following where necessary :

burned toast, a *learnt* man, a *sheared* sheep, *spilled* milk, a *spoiled* child.

X Construct for each of the following verbs two sentences in one of which the verb is used transitively and in the other intransitively:

sing, move, walk, taste, change.

CHAPTER THIRTEEN

VERBS: (2) TENSE

A clear distinction should be made between 'tense' and 'time'. The notion of time—of present time, past time, future time—is universal, and is independent of any particular language, or of language at all.

Tense, on the other hand, is a linguistic device, varying from language to language. It means the verb-form or forms used to express certain time relations. Thus, one form, e.g. *I speak* indicates present time,[1] another form, *I spoke* indicates past time,[1] still another form *I shall speak* indicates the future time.[1]

There are in English only two 'Simple' tenses, i.e. tense forms that consist of one word. They are the Simple Present Tense, e.g. *walk,* and the Simple Past Tense, e.g. *walked.* In the earliest form of Old English these two forms alone had to serve for the expression of all the various ideas of present, past and future that are now expressed by the elaborate system of tenses that has since grown up.

The other tenses are 'Compound' ones, i.e. they consist of two of more verb forms, for example:

He *is teaching* his class at present.

We *have finished* our work.

Verbs (like *be, have*) which help to form tenses, moods, etc., are called AUXILIARY verbs.

It is very important to note two points:

(1) A Present Tense does not necessarily express an action taking place in the present time, nor does a Past Tense necessarily express an action taking place in the past time. In the sentence:

We feed our cat on fish.

The verb *feed* is in the Present Tense. But that sentence does not mean that the action of feeding takes place only in the present. We have fed her for some years in the past, and shall,

---

[1] This is a generalization that is only partly true. The matter is explained more fully in the next few pages.

we hope, feed her for some years in the future. Thus the *Present* Tense can express actions taking place in the present, the past or the future.

Here are two other sentences:

If I *trusted* him I would lend him the money.

It is time I *went* home.

In both these sentences the verbs have a Past Tense form, but 'if I trusted him' implies 'if I trusted him NOW', i.e. it expresses a *present* time. And though *went* is a Past Tense form, the time of 'going home' cannot be the past; it must surely be the future.

(2) Time is not the only concept expressed by the tense of a verb. Tense may also indicate the completeness or incompleteness of an action[1]—whether it is or was still continuing (expressed by a Continuous Tense), whether it took place within a time that began in the past but extends to and includes the present (expressed by a Perfect Tense), and so on.

On the opposite page are the tense forms (Active) of the verb *to speak*.

I. THE SIMPLE TENSES

THE SIMPLE PRESENT TENSE

The Simple Present Tense is used:

(*a*) For a habitual, permanent or repeated action, e.g.

I *come* to the class every day.

She *speaks* French.

He always *sleeps* with his windows open.

He *smokes* too much.

(*b*) For a general statement, or a proverb, where no particular time is thought of, e.g.

The earth *moves* round the sun.

Actions *speak* louder than words.

The river Tweed *separates* England and Scotland.

His family *come* from Wales.

Shakespeare *says:* 'Neither a borrower nor a lender be.'

---

[1] 'Action' here, and in similar contexts, should be understood to include both 'activity' and 'state of being'.

	Simple	*Continuous*	*Perfect*	*Perfect Continuous*
PRESENT	I speak you speak he speaks we speak they speak	I am speaking you are speaking he is speaking we are speaking they are speaking	I have spoken you have spoken he has spoken we have spoken they have spoken	I have been speaking you have been speaking he has been speaking we have been speaking they have been speaking
PAST	I spoke you spoke he spoke we spoke they spoke	I was speaking you were speaking he was speaking we were speaking they were speaking	I had spoken you had spoken he had spoken we had spoken they had spoken	I had been speaking you had been speaking he had been speaking we had been speaking they had been speaking
FUTURE	I shall speak you will speak he will speak we shall speak they will speak	I shall be speaking you will be speaking he will be speaking we shall be speaking they will be speaking	I shall have spoken you will have spoken he will have spoken we shall have spoken they will have spoken	I shall have been speaking you will have been speaking he will have been speaking we shall have been speaking they will have been speaking

(*c*) In subordinate clauses of Time or Condition expressing a future action, e.g.

When you *see* (NOT: 'will see') Jack tomorrow, remember me to him.

Unless he *sends* the money before Friday, I shall consult my lawyer.

Don't write until I *tell* you.

If you *go* to the party you will meet Elizabeth.

(*d*) Sometimes in giving the summary of a story, e.g.

'Bassanio *wants* to go to Belmont to woo Portia. He *asks* his friend Antonio, the merchant of Venice, to lend him money. Antonio *says* that he *hasn't* any at the moment until his ships *come* to port; but Shylock *offers* to lend him 3,000 ducats.'

This could, of course, be told in the Simple Past Tense, but the Simple Present is felt to be rather more dramatic.

(*e*) Sometimes to express a future action about which a decision has already been taken, e.g.

He *sets* sail tomorrow for New York, and *comes* back next month.

My train *leaves* at 6.30.

The Thompsons *arrive* at 7 o'clock this evening.

We *attack* at dawn.

The verbs used like this are frequently ones expressing coming or going.

(*f*) In exclamatory sentences:

Here *comes* the bride! There *goes* our train! Here they *are*!

THE SIMPLE PAST TENSE

The Simple Past (or Preterite) Tense is used:

(*a*) to express an action wholly completed at some point, or during some period, in the past, e.g.

Peter *arrived* at our house yesterday.

We *lived* at Bournemouth for six years.

I *went* to the cinema last night.

The Simple Past Tense is usual with words or phrases that are time indicators, e.g. *yesterday, last week, in* 1956, or when the sentence is a question about time, e.g.

When *did* you go there? What time *was* it when you arrived?

(*b*) in some conditional sentences, and sentences expressing a supposition, e.g.

If Henry *worked* he would pass the examination.
If I *were* in your place I should accept his offer.
He acts as if he *wanted* to make trouble.
I wish I *had* a garden like yours.
Fred wishes he *spoke* French as well as you do.
Suppose I *asked* you what you would like for a birthday present.
It's (high) time I *went.*
I'd rather you *told* me the truth.
It isn't as if we *knew* the people well.
It would be better if you *went* there yourself.

Note that in all these sentences the Past Tense form indicates frequently both present time and future time. The Past Tense form in these cases is not used to indicate time at all but rather suppositions implying non-fulfilment or desirability, and would be more correctly described as the Past Subjunctive.[1] It indicates that the subordinate clause does not express a fact. This is known as the MODAL PRETERITE. This modal preterite is also used in the principal clause but only with the preterites of *can, may* and *will* (i.e. *could, might, would*):

He *could* tell you a story that would make your hair stand on end.
You *might* give the fellow a chance; he's doing his best; he *might* turn out a success.
I *would* ask you to think carefully before you speak.

THE FUTURE TENSE

The Future Tense is formed by using the auxiliaries *will* and *shall.* The original meaning of *will* was 'to resolve'; it denoted

[1] See pages 226, 228, 350.

volition. The original meaning of *shall* was 'to be under a necessity'; it expressed obligation, compulsion, necessity or constraint. The verbs still retain some remnants of these meanings.

One of the main causes of the difficulty with *shall* and *will* is that we use two verbs to express three things, viz. volition, obligation and futurity. Moreover, the distinction between these three conceptions cannot always be clear-cut; futurity may be tinged with volition, and volition is almost certain to take effect in the future rather than at the present moment.

'Pure' Future

To express merely futurity uncoloured by anyone's inclinations or intentions, the normal usage is *shall* for the first person singular and plural and *will* for all other persons.[1]

I shall	we shall
you will	you will
he, she, it will	they will

In conversation *will* is generally shortened to '*ll*, e.g. *He'll*, *You'll*, etc., and the negative *will not* to *won't*. The Interrogative is made by inversion, e.g. *Shall* I? *Will* they?

Examples of the 'pure' future:

I *shall* be twenty-one on Thursday.

If we take the 11 o'clock train we *shall* be in Oxford at 12.30.

I think it *will* rain tomorrow.

Next year Christmas Day *will* be on a Tuesday.

You'll get wet if you go out without an umbrella.

When *shall* I see you again?

When *will* you be in London again?

It looks as if Henry *won't* be in time for his train.

In England[2] the first person interrogative is almost always *Shall I?* though there are one or two exceptions, e.g.

[1] In U.S.A., and to some degree in Scotland and Ireland *will* is used for all three persons.

[2] The usage is not the same in Scotland, Ireland and U.S.A.

'You'll never pass the examination.' '*Won't* I?' (meaning:
'I am determined to pass it.' or: 'Don't you think so?')

'My brother can't come to play tennis with you this evening.
Will I do instead?' (i.e. 'Am I an adequate substitute?')

Shall I? (*shall we?*) often has the meaning 'Would you like
me (us) to ——?' e.g.

Shall I open the window?

Shall I get you a cup of tea?

Shall we all go to the theatre tonight?

Shall we begin work now? Let's begin now, *shall we?*

Will you? often has the meaning 'Are you willing to' or 'Would
you like to', e.g.

'*Will you* help me to carry this heavy bag, please?'

'*Will you* have another cup of tea?'

If the subject of *shall* is *I* (*we*) joined with a noun or pronoun
in the second or third person, we use *will* and not *shall*. Thus:

'We *shall* go on the four o'clock train.'

but:

You and I (Mary and I) *will* go on the four o'clock train.

Other uses of 'shall' and 'will'

It often happens that in addition to futurity, some other
feeling, e.g. willingness, determination, promise, command,
etc., colours the pure futurity. In that case the usage may be
different from that shown in the table on page 162. Note, first,
the usage with *shall*.

SHALL

Shall with the first person may express determination or
resolution,[1] e.g.

I *shall* do what I like. I *shall* go there if I want to.

'We *shall* defend our island, whatever the cost may be. We
shall fight on the beaches, we *shall* fight on the landing-
grounds, we *shall* fight in the fields and in the streets, we
shall fight in the hills; we *shall* never surrender.'—(From a
speech by Winston Churchill, June 1940.)

[1] *Will* also is used for this purpose (see p. 165).

The second person *you shall*[1] and third person *he, she, it, they shall* denote determination or promise or threat on the part of the speaker, e.g.

> If you work hard you *shall* have a holiday on Saturday. (*Promise*)
>
> You *shall* have the money as soon as I get it. (*Promise*)
>
> If you children won't do as I tell you, you *shan't* go to the party. (*Threat*)
>
> He *shall* suffer for this; he *shall* pay you what he owes you. (*Threat* and *Determination*)
>
> These people want to buy my house, but they *shan't* have it. (*Determination*)
>
> The enemy *shall* not pass. (*Determination*)

The form with *shall* occurs in literature in oratorical, prophetic utterance. The speaker wants to express things that he believes are bound to happen: God, Destiny, Fate has so willed it. Examples occur in, for example, the Bible:

> 'They *shall* beat their swords into ploughshares and their spears into pruning-hooks; nation *shall* not lift up sword against nation, neither *shall* they learn war any more . . . for the earth *shall* be full of the knowledge of the Lord, as the waters cover the sea.'

So, too, Mark Antony, prophesying over the body of the murdered Caesar, says in Shakespeare's *Julius Caesar:*

> 'A curse *shall* light upon the limbs of men;
> Domestic fury and fierce civil strife
> *Shall* cumber all the parts of Italy;
> Blood and destruction *shall* be so in use,
> And dreadful objects so familiar,
> That mothers *shall* but smile when they behold
> Their infants quartered with the hands of war.'

---

[1] The second Person singular 'thou shalt' is an archaic form used only in poetry or older prose, e.g. Thou *shalt* not kill. Thou *shalt* love thy neighbour as thyself.

> 'That thou *shalt* see the difference of our spirits
> I pardon thee thy life before thou ask it.'
>
> (Shakespeare, *Merchant of Venice*).

Shall is also used after such constructions as: 'I intend that . . .', 'It has been decided that . . .', e.g.

I intend that this school *shall* be the best in the country.
It has been decided that he *shall* be given the job.
'We here highly resolve that this nation under God, *shall* have a new birth of freedom, and that government of the people by the people, for the people, *shall* not perish from the earth.' (Abraham Lincoln, *Gettysburg Address*, 1863.)

WILL

Will is used to express willingness, promise or determination, and it is with this meaning that *will* with the first person is most commonly used. *Examples:*

All right; I *will* pay you at the rate you ask. (*Willingness*)
I *won't* forget little Margaret's birthday. I *will* send her a present. (*Promise*)
I *will* make this radio work even if I have to stay up all night. (*Determination*)
'*Will* you take this woman to be your lawful wedded wife?'
'I *will*.' (*Willingness. Promise*)

In the examples where *shall* was used in the second or third person to express determination or resolution, note that the determination is in the mind of the speaker.

'He *shall* pay you what he owes you,' meaning, 'I (the speaker) will make him do it.'

But the determination may be in the mind not of the speaker but of the subject of the sentence. In that case *will*, not *shall*, is used. The *will* is strongly stressed, and consequently the contracted forms *I'll*, *he'll*, etc., are not used.

We have noted, in the examples above, this usage in the first person, but it occurs also with the second and third person, e.g.

George *will* go out without his overcoat although it is a bitterly cold day.

The sentence: 'George *shall* go without his coat' means: 'I (the speaker) am determined to make George go out without his coat.' The sentence: 'George *will* go without his coat' means that the speaker's will is of no avail; it is the will of George, the subject of the sentence, that wins the struggle.

Further examples of this usage:

Oh, Richard, why *will* you always do the opposite of what I tell you?

Boys *will* be boys.

That silly dog *will* chase motor-cars.

I've tried to get my cat to eat that tinned meat, but she *won't* even look at it.

Peaches *won't* ripen outside in the north of England.

(In this last sentence we give the human attribute of a will to an inanimate object.)

The tendency to use *will* in the second and third persons is so strong that even where it is the volition of the speaker and not of the subject of the sentence, there are cases where we use *will*, e.g.

You *will* go at once and pick up all the paper you have scattered on the floor.

All members of the team *will* be at the station at 2.15 sharp.

No one *will* leave the examination room before 12 o'clock.

We seem to use this form where no resistance to the command, or refusal to obey it, is anticipated.

Will is also used to express possibility or assumption, e.g.

That man with the umbrella *will* be the Prime Minister.

There are other ways of expressing futurity, e.g. by the use of the Present Continuous Tense (see p. 169) the Simple Present Tense (see p. 160) and by *going to*.

GOING TO

The construction (*to be*) *going to* is used to express:
(1) Intention:

I *am going to* write to Margaret this evening.

Mr. Brown says he *is going to* buy a new car next year.

When *are they going to* pay you the money they owe you?

I know what you are *going to* say.

(2) Strong probability:

I think it *is going to* rain (i.e. I think it is very probable that it will rain).

I am afraid that the repairs to our house *are going to* cost a lot of money.

(3) The speaker's certainty:

Look out! That milk is *going to* boil over.

My wife's *going to* have a baby.

He's *going to* regret the day he ever wrote that letter.

The *going to* construction cannot be used for pure futurity, i.e. futurity not depending on any person's will or intention. You cannot say:

I *am going* to be 15 years old in May; or:

Today is the 19th of October; tomorrow *is going* to be the 20th.

Going to is not often used when the futurity is contingent on a condition, because then the intention of the person is no longer important, e.g.

If you ever go to France you *will* like (not: are *going* to like) the food there.

EXERCISES

I There are twelve tense forms in the active voice of English verbs. Construct twelve sentences each employing one of these forms. Use any person, singular or plural.

II Complete the following sentences with 'shall' or 'will' and explain, in each case, why you have chosen one or the other, and which type of future each exemplifies:

(1) They —— not pass. (2) I think he —— soon arrive now. (3) You —— have a rise in pay next month if business is good. (4) All members —— sign the book on joining the club. (5) We —— leave London on Friday if all goes well. (6) John and I —— share the driving as it is a long journey. (7) He —— not go out till the doctor gives him permission. (8) Oranges —— not grow out-of-doors in England. (9) We —— never get to the station in time for the train. (10) Will you help me with this exercise? Certainly I ——.

III Show, by constructing one sentence for each type of usage, the senses in which (*a*) the Simple Present, and (*b*) the Simple Past tenses are used in English.

IV In whose mind is the determination expressed in the following sentences? Which auxiliary—'shall' *or* 'will'—should be used to complete them?

(1) He —— never marry my daughter (2) He has made up his mind that he —— succeed this time. (3) Tell him that I —— never speak to him again. (4) He —— make good the damage caused by his carelessness. (5) He —— take unnecessary risks when he is driving.

V In which of the following sentences can the 'going to' construction correctly replace the future tense used.

(1) If you go to England you will notice many differences from your own country. (2) Will you be able to find your way about in London when you arrive? (3) He will take his final examination next summer. (4) I expect I shall feel very much a stranger during my first few weeks in England. (5) If the crossing is rough I expect I shall be ill. (6) A good holiday by the sea will do you good. (7) It will not rain as long as this wind keeps up. (8) This train will take me to Birmingham without stopping. (9) You won't learn a foreign language perfectly unless you live in the country where it is spoken. (10) I shall be twenty-five next August.

II. THE CONTINUOUS TENSES[1]

THE PRESENT CONTINUOUS TENSE

This tense is formed by using the Simple Present Tense of the verb *to be* + a present participle, e.g. *I am writing, you are writing, he is writing*, etc. It is used:

(*a*) For an action which began in the past and will terminate in the future, but which at the moment of speaking is incomplete and is still continuing, e.g.

The sun *is shining*, the bees *are humming*, the birds *are singing*, the fruit *is ripening*. Summer is here. What *are* you *doing?* I *am resting* in a deck-chair.

[1] The continuous tenses are sometimes called *Progressive Tenses*.

This feeling of immediate present is often emphasized by using *just*, e.g.

The children are *just* having breakfast.

The action may not necessarily be literally 'continuous' at the time of speaking, e.g.

PARENT (to SCHOOLMASTER): '*Is* my son *working* hard this term?'

SCHOOLMASTER: 'Oh, yes, *he's trying* his best now.'

The boy may not be working at that particular moment but in the 'general present' he is trying and working.

(*b*) To express futurity, especially with verbs of movement like *go, come, leave,* etc., e.g.

We *are going* to Paris on Friday; we *are leaving* from London Airport.

John *is coming* here next week and *is staying* here until August.

What *are* you *doing* next Saturday?

William, I have put the visitors in your room, so you *are sleeping* in the small bedroom tonight.

Verbs not used in the Continuous Tense

1. Certain verbs ('Verbs of Perception', e.g. *see, hear, feel, taste, smell*) are not generally used in the Continuous Tenses. When one of these verbs is used to express an activity or a state that is still continuing, the Simple Present Tense, not the Present Continuous Tense, is used,[1] e.g.

I don't *see* anything there (NOT: 'I am not seeing'). I *see* (= understand) what you mean. Do you *hear* that noise? I *smell* something burning. I *feel* a sharp pain in my chest, Do you *taste* (NOT: Are you tasting) the sherry in this pudding?

Some of these verbs, however, may be used in the Continuous Tense form, when they have special meanings, e.g.

I *am seeing* (= meeting, visiting) Margaret tomorrow.

They *are seeing* their cousin *off* (= saying goodbye to) at the station.

[1] See also *can*, p. 198, 239.

I *am not hearing* as well as I used to (= my sense of hearing is not so good as it used to be).

Henry *was feeling* (= groping) his way along the face of the cliff.

2. There are a number of other verbs which denote, not actions but states of mind, feelings or relationships. These verbs are not generally used in the Continuous Tenses. The Simple Present Tense used in the following examples could not be replaced by a Present Continuous Tense:

Betty *loves* swimming, but *hates* diving.

John *knows* your brother.

Henry *understands* Spanish.

I *remember* what you told me.

I *recognize* you now; you are Margaret's brother.

I *believe* you are telling the truth.

The poor dog *seems/looks/appears* ill.

This box *contains/holds* tins of fruit.

That house *belongs* to me.

We *own/possess* a house in Oxford.

What you are saying *matters* a lot to me.

That hat *suits/fits* you very well.

This applies to most verbs that introduce noun clauses, e.g.

I think that . . . I suppose that . . .

Present Continuous and Simple Present Tense

As was stated before, the Continuous Tense is used for an action that is continuing but that is expected to end sooner or later. If the action is, by its nature, permanent or lasting for a long time, the Simple Present is used. The following pairs of sentences will illustrate this point:

Where *does* Henry work? (= in his *permanent* job). Where *is* he *working* at present? (= he has made a number of changes; what is his, more or less, *temporary* job?)

Westminster Bridge *crosses* the Thames near the Houses of Parliament. (*Permanent*) Our bus *is* now *crossing* the Thames at Westminster Bridge. (*Temporary*)

We *start* work at nine o'clock (*usual arrangement*), but for this week only we *are starting* at 8.30. (*Temporary arrangement*)

In this last sentence, though the action may be a repeated one, we want to imply that it is not a regular or permanent one.

The 'Adverbs of Frequency'[1] are generally used with the Simple Present Tense since this tense expresses repeated action. But *always* and words of similar meaning can be used with the Continuous Tense when repeated action—especially some action that is causing annoyance or irritation—is indicated, e.g.

Richard *is always trying* to borrow money from me.

You *are continually finding* fault with me.

Alice is an annoying guest; she *is constantly complaining* that the house is cold.

'*I'm for ever blowing* bubbles.' (Music Hall song.)

Note that the meaning in these sentences is not really 'always' but rather 'very often'.

THE PAST CONTINUOUS TENSE

This is formed by using *was* (*were*) and the present participle. It is used to express an action that was going on during a certain time in the past, e.g.

As I *was running* to the station I met the Browns. They *were driving* home.

I *was playing* tennis all this afternoon. What *were* you *doing?*

(1) It is often used to indicate that an action was going on (like a 'background') at a time when something else, more important and more dramatic (the 'foreground' action) happened. The new action is expressed by the Simple Past Tense, e.g.

As I *was walking* along Piccadilly ('background' action), a car *mounted* the pavement ('foreground' action) and crashed into a shop.

While the man *was looking* at the picture, the thief *stole* his watch.

[1] See pages 188 and 252.

If, however, you want to state that two actions were going on at the same time in the past and it is the concurrence of both rather than the striking interest of one that is being indicated, then the Past Continuous is used in both parts of the sentence, e.g.

The thieves took precautions against surprise; while one *was working* on the safe, the other *was keeping watch* for policemen.

(2) This tense occurs in reported speech,[1] e.g.

He said that he *was working* all day on Saturday.
She said that Alice *was* always *complaining* that the house was cold.

(3) It is used with some conditional sentences[2] (after *if*) and with suppositions[3] (after *I wish*, etc.), e.g.

If your foreign visitors *were staying* longer they would soon perfect their English.
They wouldn't have spent all that money on the house unless they *were thinking* of living there themselves.
They wish they *were coming* to England again this year.

(4) There is one further point to be noted. Compare the following answers to the question, 'Did you hear about Henry's new job?':

(*a*) Yes, my wife *was telling* me about it this morning.
(*b*) Yes, my wife *told* me about it this morning.

The Past Continuous Tense in (*a*) suggests: 'I have heard a little about it, but I should like to hear more.'
The Simple Past Tense in (*b*) suggests: 'I know, more or less, all about it; I don't need any further information.'

THE FUTURE CONTINUOUS TENSE

The Future Continuous Tense is formed by using the Simple Future Tense of *be* + present participle. It is used to express a future activity, beginning before and finishing after some given time in the future, e.g.

What *will you be doing* this time tomorrow?
This time tomorrow I *shall be flying* to Spain.

---

[1] See pages 361–72.   [2] See pages 343, 347-51.   [3] See pages 178, 228.

My friend *will be waiting* for me at Madrid airport. I hope the plane will arrive on time. If it is late *he will be wondering* what has happened.

It is also used to indicate future plans that have already been decided on, e.g.

The Robinsons *will be staying* with us again this year.

The Future Continuous is sometimes used instead of the Simple Future when the speaker wishes to give the impression of casualness, that the action will happen by chance and not by his design.

I *shall be meeting* her this evening and will give her your message.

Will you be going to London next week? If so, perhaps you could buy something for me.

('Will you go . . .?' might be interpreted as a request.)

EXERCISES

I Complete these sentences with the Present Continuous form of the verbs given in brackets, changing the word order where necessary.

(1) I —— a holiday today (take). (2) He —— his best to win the prize this term (do). (3) They —— from Paris next 'Monday and —— in Rome on Wednesday (start, arrive). (4) What play are you —— at the theatre on Saturday? (see) (5) The house is full, so you —— next door (sleep). (6) I —— on him tomorrow (call). (7) Where we —— this evening? (go). (8) My partner —— to see me tomorrow on business (come). (9) How you —— after your first week in London? (feel). (10) We —— as hard as possible to increase our turnover (try).

II In the following sentences turn the verbs in italics into the Past Continuous tense and rewrite the sentences using that form.

(1) She always *worked* while they *amused* themselves, so naturally she passed her examination. (2) If you *stayed* longer you would soon make a lot of friends. (3) If you *dug* the garden and Mary *played* tennis all morning, who cooked the dinner? (4) What *did you say* about your latest girl friend? (5) It rained as they *prepared* for the picnic.

III Turn the verbs in italics in these sentences into the Future Continuous tense:

(1) The orchestra *will give* six concerts during the winter. (2) My friend *will meet* my train when it arrives at Victoria Station. (3) A week today I *shall cross* the Atlantic Ocean. (4) I *shall* often *think* of you when you have left England. (5) We must go home now or Mother *will feel* anxious about us.

III. THE PERFECT TENSES

The three tenses, Simple Present, Simple Past and the Future, are concerned mainly with the aspect of *time* of an action. But in the Perfect Tenses our interest is primarily not in the time of the action but in the fact of its occurrence and in its result. Thus in the sentences

Henry *has been* to Paris three times.

I *have mown* the lawn.

Mary *has bought* a new dress.

the attention is directed not on the time in the past when these actions were done but simply on the fact that Henry's visits have taken place, that the grass is cut and that Mary now has a new dress. If we wanted to direct attention to the time of those actions we should use a Past Tense and, generally, an adverbial that indicated definite past time, e.g.

Henry *went* to Paris in 1956, 1957 and 1958.

I *mowed* the lawn this afternoon.

Mary *bought* a new dress on Friday.

THE PRESENT PERFECT TENSE

The Present Perfect Tense is made by using the Present Tense of the verb *to have* and a past participle. The interrogative, as with all Perfect Tenses, is formed by inversion of *have* and the subject; the negative by the addition of *not*, e.g.

Affirmative: George *has eaten* all the sweets.

Interrogative: Has George *eaten* all the sweets?

Negative: George *has not (hasn't) eaten* all the sweets.

The Present Perfect Tense, though it indicates an action that took place in the past, is associated with the *present* idea of NOW, e.g.

I *have* never *met* your sister. (Up to NOW.)

I *have studied* all the documents in this case. (So NOW I am fully informed on the matter.)

We *have bought* our yearly stock of coal. (So NOW our cellar is full; NOW we are all right for the winter.)

The Present Perfect Tense is used:

(1) For an action just concluded when the resulting state is still present, e.g.

I *have lost* my pen; I am unable to do my exercises.

He *has unlocked* the door; there is nothing to prevent you from going out.

This watch was working all right a moment ago but now it *has stopped*.

With activities completed in the immediate past, *just* is often used, e.g.

The post has *just* come.

Note that though *just* is an adverbial of the present, *just now* (= a little time ago) is an adverbial of the past and the verb used with it will be a Past Tense, e.g.

The post *came* just now.

(2) For duration of an action or of absence of an action begun in the past and continuing to the present (and possibly to the future),[1] e.g.

I *have not visited* him for ten years.

I *have taught* this class for ten years (and am still teaching it).

Compare this with:

I *taught* this class for ten years (but no longer teach it).

(3) When the time of the action is indefinite, e.g.

I *have seen* this film before.

Compare this with:

I *saw* it last January when it was first shown in London.

where the time is definite.

[1] But note that to express affirmative duration until the present, the Present Perfect Continuous tense is normally used (except with *to be*); see page 179.

Note the difference in meaning suggested by the following two sentences:

PRESENT PERFECT: Have you *seen* Sir Laurence Olivier's production of *Titus Andronicus?* (The production is still running.)

PAST TENSE: *Did* you *see* Sir Laurence Olivier's production of *Titus Andronicus?* (The production is no longer running.)

There are some words or phrases or constructions that are usually associated with the Present Perfect Tense. Thus, the verb in sentences modified by phrases or clauses beginning with *since* is almost always in the Present Perfect, e.g.

He *has been* here *since* two o'clock/yesterday/Tuesday/1952, etc.

They *have* not *visited* us *since* Henry went to America.

This tense is usual with *already:*

I have *already* explained that.

with the Adverbs of Frequency: (see pages 188, 252)

He has *often/never/always*, etc. done that.

Have you *ever* heard of such a thing?

and with the words: *now, today, this week/month/year*, etc., *up to now, up to the present, so far, not yet, lately.*

The Present Perfect is used with *ever* and *never* if they have the meaning 'at any time *up to now*'. With other meanings almost any tense can be used.

But the exclamatory sentence '*Did* you ever *hear* of such a thing!' has the Past Tense.

The Present Perfect tense is not used with:

ago (I *received* your letter two days *ago*), *then, at that time, yesterday, last week/month/year*, etc., *in* 1950, *at Christmas*, etc.; with words and phrases like this the Past Tense should be used.

This morning, this afternoon, this evening can be used with a Present Perfect or a Past Tense depending on the time the statement is made, e.g.

I *have written* two letters this morning (said during the morning).

I *wrote* two letters this morning (said in the afternoon or evening).

THE PAST PERFECT (PLUPERFECT) TENSE

This tense is formed by *had* + a past participle. It is used:

(1) To speak of an action concluded before a certain time in the past or before the time of the occurrence of another action (denoted by the Simple Past Tense) and yet continuing into it, e.g.

Lucille *had learned* English before she came to England.

When we got to the field the football match *had* already *started*.

I didn't go to the cinema because I *had* already *seen* the film.

Just as the Present Perfect is used when the resultant state is still 'now', so the Past Perfect Tense would be used to refer, at a subsequent time, to this prior action. So the examples on page 175 would, in the Past Perfect Tense, read:

I had lost my pen and I was unable to do the exercises.

He had unlocked the door; there was nothing to prevent you from going out.

(2) To express duration up to a certain time in the past, e.g.

By the time I left the school I *had taught* that class for ten years.

(3) In indirect speech[1] to express an idea that, in direct speech, had been in the Present Perfect Tense, e.g.

Direct: He said, 'I have written her a letter.'

Indirect: He said that he *had written* her a letter.

Direct: Mary said, 'John has just set out for the office.'

Indirect: Mary said that John *had* just *set out* for the office.

Or in the Simple Past Tense:

Direct: A great battle was fought on this spot in 1815.

Indirect: The guide told us that a great battle *had been fought* on that spot in 1815.

(4) To express a past condition or supposition with an implied negative,[2] e.g.

If I *had known* that you wanted the book, I would have sent it. (Implied negative 'but I didn't know'.)

---

[1] See pages 361–72.   [2] See page 350.

If he *had worked* steadily he would have passed the examination (. . . but he didn't work steadily).

If only I *had known* that you wanted to meet him! (. . . but I didn't know).

(5) with such verbs as *wish, hope, expect,* etc., to express a past wish, hope, etc. that was not realized, e.g.

He *wishes* now that he *had taken* your advice.

We *had expected* you to stay at least a week.

I *had hoped/intended/meant/*to take a good holiday this year but I wasn't able to get away.

(6) with 'as if', e.g.

He described the scene as vividly as if he *had been* there.

Some of the conjunctions with which the Past Perfect tense is often associated are: *before, when, after, once, as soon as, until,* e.g.

He came round to our house *before* I *had finished* my breakfast.

*When/After/*the cheering *had died* down, the Prime Minister began his speech.

*Once/As soon as/*approval of the plans *had been given,* the work went ahead rapidly.

It was not *until* I *had read* your letter that I understood the true state of affairs.

THE FUTURE PERFECT TENSE

This tense is formed by the Future Tense of *have* + a past participle. It is used to indicate:

(1) an action that will be completed before a certain time or another action in the future. The state it brings about will still exist at that time or at the time of that action. So the Future Perfect bears the same relation to a future moment as the Present Perfect bears to a present moment and the Past Perfect to a past moment. This tense is often associated with the preposition *by* and the construction 'by the time (that)'. *Examples:*

It is now 6.30 p.m.; *I shall have finished* my work by 8 o'clock.

The taxi *will have arrived* by the time you finish dressing.

In another year or so, *you will have forgotten* all about him.

(2) duration up to a time in the future, e.g.

When I leave the school next week I *shall have taught* this class for ten years.

On December 18th *we shall have been married* for 25 years.

Note that in time clauses beginning *when*, etc., the Future Perfect is *not* used; the correct tense is the Present Perfect, e.g.

I will repair your bicycle when I *have finished* (NOT: 'shall have finished') this job.

By the time you *have read* (NOT: 'shall have read') that book, you will know all the answers.

I will come with you; but wait until I *have written* (NOT: 'shall have written') this letter.

(3) possibility or assumption, e.g.

You *will have heard*, I expect, that Elizabeth is going to be married.

It's five o'clock; *they will have arrived* home by now.

THE PRESENT PERFECT CONTINUOUS

This tense is formed by the Present Perfect of the verb *to be* and the present participle. It is used to express the duration of an action up to the present. The tense suggests that the action is still continuing at the moment of speaking. The action may continue into the future, e.g.

I *have been teaching* this class for two years (and am still teaching it).

He *has been learning* English for six months.

The boys *have been watching* television since seven o'clock. (. . . and are still watching now and will probably go on watching for some time).

This tense, and the other Perfect Continuous tenses, are particularly associated with the words *for* and *since* (see pp. 176 and 299).

THE PAST PERFECT CONTINUOUS TENSE

This is formed by *had been* + present participle and is used:
(1) To express the duration of an action up to a certain time in the past, e.g.

When I got to the meeting the lecturer *had* already *been speaking* for half an hour.

The telephone *had been ringing* for three minutes before it was answered.

(2) To express the Present Perfect Continuous in reported speech, e.g.

I asked her what she *had been doing* since she arrived in England.

She told me that she *had been studying* English literature.

THE FUTURE PERFECT CONTINUOUS TENSE

This tense is formed by the Future Tense of *have* + *been* + a present participle, and is used to express the duration of an action up to a certain time in the future. *Examples:*

On April 2nd, 1960, we *shall have been living* in this house exactly thirty years.

In another month's time, Henry *will have been working* in the Weavewell Woollen Company's office for five years.

EXERCISES

I Rewrite the following sentences using the Present Perfect tense of the verbs and omitting or changing words rendered incorrect or unnecessary by the change of tense:

(1) I saw him twice last week. (2) Did you go to London after our last meeting? (3) Do you go to Paris often? (4) He began to study English when he was sixteen. (5) We first lived in this house in 1949.

II Explain, with an example of each, how the Present Perfect, Past Perfect and Future Perfect tenses are formed.

III Construct sentences to illustrate the following:

(a) Adverbs specially associated with the Present Perfect tense.

   (*b*) Two ways of using the expression 'this afternoon', one employing the Present Perfect and one the Simple Past tense.

IV Explain the differences of meaning expressed by the tense of the verb in the following pairs of sentences:
   (1) (*a*) I have subscribed to this magazine for several years.
       (*b*) I took out a subscription to this magazine last January.
   (2) (*a*) Have you read many books by Dickens?
       (*b*) Did you read the leading article in *The Times* yesterday?

 V Insert the correct form of the verb *to read* (Simple Past tense or Present Perfect tense) in each of the following sentences, and give a reason for your choice.
   (1) I ———— this book.
   (2) I ———— this book last week.
   (3) I ———— this book since you were here.
   (4) I ———— this book often.
   (5) I ———— this book this morning.

VI List the various uses of the Past Perfect tense and construct sentences to exemplify each of them. How is the tense formed?

VII Correct the following sentences where necessary, and give reasons for your corrections.

   (1) As soon as I shall have mastered the English language I shall begin to study Spanish. (2) Next February we have been married for ten years. (3) Don't come to see me again before I shall have told you to do so. (4) We have learnt English since we are twelve years old. (5) I asked them what they have been doing since our last meeting. (6) In a few days we shall have worked for the firm for twelve months. (7) You hear the news of her engagement, I expect. (8) It was not till after your letter has arrived that I knew of your promotion. (9) They told the story as if it has happened to them. (10) They did not write to us since they left England.

VIII Construct sentences illustrating the use of the Present Perfect Continuous, the Past Perfect Continuous and the Future Perfect Continuous tenses.

CHAPTER FOURTEEN

VERBS: (3) THE SPECIAL FINITES (i)

There are certain verbs that demand special attention. These are sometimes called the 'auxiliary' verbs because they 'help' other verbs to form interrogative, negative and emphatic forms of speech and to form tenses, mood and voice. There are twelve[1] of them in all, viz. *be, have, can, do, shall, will, may, must, need, ought, dare, used* (*to*).

The term 'auxiliaries' for all these verbs is not quite correct as some of them, e.g. *be, have, do*, are sometimes the only verb in the sentence, e.g. 'Keats *was* a poet'. 'They *have* a large house.' 'He *did* the work well.' A better term is Special Finites or Anomalous Finites.

They have certain characteristics which they, and they only, possess and which distinguish them from all other verbs. The following are their special features:

(I) FORMATION OF THE NEGATIVE

The negative[2] of these verbs is formed by placing *not* immediately after them, e.g.

Affirmative	*Negative*
He is here.	He is *not* here.
They can speak English.	They can*not* speak English.
They would help us.	They would *not* help us.

The word *not* is generally, in conversation, contracted and fused with the verb, e.g. He *isn't* here. They *can't* speak English. They *wouldn't* help us. They *didn't* answer.

The special finites are the only verbs that take the contracted form of *not*.

---

[1] Or twenty-four if we reckon twelve other derived forms (excluding the imperative) for tense, number and person, viz. *am, is, are, was, were; has, had; does, did; should; would; could; might.*

[2] Except for the Imperative. Only three of these verbs have an imperative form (*be, have, do*). The negative imperative is formed with *do* and *not*, e.g. *Do not* (*Don't*) *be* stupid. *Don't have* too much to eat. *Don't do* that.

(2) FORMATION OF THE INTERROGATIVE

The interrogative of special finites is made by inversion, i.e. by putting the verb before its subject:

Affirmative	*Interrogative*
He can speak English.	*Can he* speak English?
She will come to the party.	*Will she* come to the party?
I ought to answer the letter.	*Ought I* to answer the letter?

All other verbs use *do* (*does, did*) and the infinitive, e.g.

He speaks English.	*Does he speak* English?
She came to the party.	*Did she come* to the party?
He answered the letter.	*Did he answer* the letter?

(3) QUESTION PHRASES

The special finites alone have the ability to form 'Question Phrases'. We frequently, especially in conversation, add one of these phrases to a statement, thereby turning it into a question, e.g.

It's a fine day, *isn't it?* You knew him quite well, *didn't you?*

1. To an affirmative statement a negative Question Phrase is added:

Mr. Brown is a doctor, *isn't he?*
You can speak Spanish, *can't you?*
Your friends will come, *won't they?*

2. To a negative statement an affirmative Question Phrase is added, e.g.

Mr. Smith isn't a doctor, *is he?*
You can't speak Spanish, *can you?*
Your friends won't come, *will they?*
That job is hardly suitable for Peter, *is it?*[1]

Note that the subject of the Question Phrase must be a pronoun (or *there*), e.g.

There's no one in the house, *is there?*

[1] The words *hardly, seldom, scarcely,* etc., make the equivalents of negative statements.

3. If the verb in the statement is a special finite, a form of that verb is used in the Question Phrase, e.g.

> They *were* there, *weren't they?*
> He *ought* to know the answer, *oughtn't he?*
> You *haven't* answered the letter, *have you?*
> The work *has been* done, *hasn't it?*

(Note that if there are two auxiliaries in the verb, only the first one is used in the question phrase.)

4. If the verb in the statement is not a special finite, *do (does, did, don't, doesn't)* is used in the Question Phrase, e.g.

> He *speaks* Spanish, *doesn't* he?
> They *came* to the party, *didn't* they?
> He *didn't* help them, *did* he?
> She *doesn't* teach French, *does* she?

Note that there are two meanings to some of these phrases according to the tone of voice used.

(i) If information or confirmation of an opinion is wanted, the Question Phrase is said with a rising intonation, e.g.

> It's raining, ↗ isn't it? (*Rising Intonation*) (See pages 413–15.)
> Your name's Brown, ↗ isn't it? (*Rising Intonation*)

(The speaker is not quite sure whether it is raining or not, whether the man's name is or is not Brown. The answer might be, 'No, the rain has stopped now'. 'No, it's Smith.')

(ii) But when the sentence is the expression of an opinion or a statement of which no contradiction is expected, the Question Phrase is said with a falling intonation, e.g.

> It's a terrible day, ↘ isn't it? (*Falling Intonation*)

(It is a cold, foggy day, and you know it. The answer, 'NO' would somewhat nonplus the questioner and would be considered rather impolite.)

> You are Brown, ↘ aren't you? (*Falling Intonation*)

(You are practically sure he is; you had met him before or been told about him.)

In both forms the only verbs that can be used in Question Phrases are the Special Finites.

(4) SHORT ANSWERS

The special finites are used for 'Short Answers' to avoid repetition of the verb, e.g.

Question: 'Can you speak Russian?'
Full Answer: 'Yes, I can speak Russian.' 'No, I can't speak Russian.'
Short Answer: 'Yes, *I can.*' 'No, *I can't.*'

These Short Answers may be of several types:

(*a*) *'Yes' or 'No' answer,* e.g.
'Will he help us?' 'Yes, *he will.*' 'No, *he won't.*'
'Could he come to the party?' 'Yes, *he could.*' 'No, *he couldn't.*'
'Dare you go there alone?' 'Yes, *I dare.*' 'No, *I daren't.*'
'Do you speak Spanish?' 'Yes, *I do.*' 'No, *I don't.*'
'Did you hear me?' 'Yes, *I did.*' 'No, *I didn't.*'

(*b*) *Answer to a question introduced by an interrogative,* e.g.
'Who was here first, Henry or Richard?' *'Henry was.'*
'Who can answer the question?' *'I can.'*
'Who doesn't understand this?' *'I don't.' 'My friend doesn't.'*

(*c*) *Short Answers expressing agreement,* e.g.

'I think John is working well.' 'Yes, *he is.*'
'Mary has done well in her examination.' 'Yes, *she has.*'
'He'll pay the money, won't he?' 'Yes, *he will.*'

(*d*) *Short Answers expressing disagreement,* e.g.
'It will take hours to do this work.' 'No, *it won't.*'
'That car must have cost a lot of money.' 'Oh, no, *it didn't.*'
'He will pay the money.' 'Of course *he won't.*'
'Richard works hard.' 'I'm afraid *he doesn't.*'

(*e*) *Additions and responses to sentences.*
(i) with *so,* meaning 'also':
'I have written a letter to Jean.' *'So have I.'*
'John has given the right answer.' 'And *so has Mary.*'
'Pedro can speak English well and *so can Olaf.*'
John will help and *so will Margaret.*
Henry must come and *so must Charles.*

Lucille speaks French and *so does Anna.*

Alice answered the question well and *so did Jane.*

'I was born free as Caesar, *so were you.'* (Shakespeare, *Julius Caesar*)

(ii) The negative construction parallel to (i):

'John hasn't given the right answer, *neither (nor) has Mary.'*

'Pedro can't speak Russian. *Neither (nor) can Olaf.'*

'Alice didn't answer the questions, *neither (nor) did Jane.'*

(iii) with *so,* expressing surprised agreement:

'It's the 15th today, and you've dated your letter the 14th.' *'So I have.'*

'That's William coming in at the gate.' *'So it is.'*

Note the inversion of subject and verb in (i) and (ii), but not in (iii).

Finally, there is a construction that combines the Short Answer and the Question Phrase. It is used when we want to express surprised, and truculent, disapproval. The tone of voice indicates the feeling. Here are some examples:

'I've left my book at home.'	'Oh, you have, have you?'
'I can't pay you the money I owe you.'	'Oh, you can't, can't you?'
'I won't be spoken to like this.'	'Oh, you won't, won't you?'
'I don't like you.'	'Oh, you don't, don't you?'
'Richard tore up his book.'	'Oh, he did, did he?'
'Olga hates English coffee.'	'Oh, she does, does she?'

The only verbs that can be used for Short Answers of any of these types are the special finites.

(5) ELLIPTICAL SENTENCES

This construction avoids repetition of the verb, etc., in such sentences as:

He doesn't often come to the class, and when he *does* (= does come) he is generally late.

He speaks Spanish better than Henry *can* (= can speak it), better than Henry ever *will* (= will speak it).

I go for a swim every day. *Do you?* (= go for a swim every day)

I can't understand a word he says. *Can you?* (= Can you understand a word he says?)

The only verbs that can be used for these elliptical sentences are the special finites.

(6) THE EMPHATIC FORM

The Emphatic form of the verb is expressed by using one of the special finites. There is a strong stress on the special finite for affirmative emphasis, a strong stress on the *not* (*never*) immediately following the special finite for negative emphasis, e.g.

Affirmative Emphasis

My sister *will* be pleased to see you.

We *have* enjoyed our visit.

You *can* sing beautifully.

I *should* like a holiday in Switzerland.

I *do* enjoy good music.

Negative Emphasis

I did *not* take your book.

They will *never* agree to that.

You ought *not* to do that.

Sometimes we want to be emphatic to assert an affirmative when the listener seems to assume a negative, e.g.

'Why don't you work hard?'   'But I *do* work hard.'

'Why didn't she give him the book?'   'But she *did* give him the book.'

'Why won't they keep their promise?'   'But they *will* keep their promise.'

'Why haven't you tidied your room?'   'But I *have* tidied my room.'

The only verbs that can take this stress for affirmative emphasis are the special finites. If an ordinary verb is emphasized it is the *meaning* of the verb that is being stressed, not its affirmative nature. If, for example, instead of saying: 'But she *did* give him the book', you said: 'But she *gave* him the book' your sentence would now suggest:

She didn't *lend* him the book, or *sell* him the book, nor did he *steal* it; she *gave* it to him.

(7) POSITION OF ADVERBS

With the special finites certain mid-position adverbs, chiefly the 'adverbs of frequency' (*always, often, sometimes,* etc.), have a different position from the position they have with other verbs. For this, see page 265.

(8) THIRD PERSON SINGULAR

One final peculiarity:

The third person singular of the Present Tense in all verbs except the special finites has a characteristic regular ending in -*s* added to the first person singular, e.g.

he speaks, writes, reads, sings, etc.

Compare the corresponding forms of the special finites:

he can, shall, will, may, must, is, has, does, need,[1] ought, dare,[1] used to.

EXERCISES

I Write a list of all the forms you know in which special finites used with 'not' are spoken, and sometimes written, in contracted form. Give both full form and contracted form in each case.

II Give examples of Special Finites helping: (*a*) to form a negative, (*b*) an interrogative, (*c*) a tense.

III Complete the following sentences with Question Phrases:

(1) It's a fine day ——? (2) You are studying English ——? (3) He is a handsome man ——? (4) She is very well-dressed ——? (5) Lucille has a new car ——? (6) My watch is right ——? (7) You were in England last year ——? (8) He can speak English ——? (9) You could understand me ——? (10) They must do the work ——? (11) You don't mind waiting ——?

---

[1] When the forms *needs* and *dares* are used, these verbs are not functioning as special finites (see pp. 209, 212).

(12) You will write to me ——? (13) She can come tomorrow ——? (14) He gives a lesson every day ——? (15) You read modern writers ——? (16) Shaw wrote *St. Joan* ——? (17) They gave her a clock ——? (18) You went to the theatre ——? (19) I wrote to you ——? (20) He speaks English ——? (21) You are not coming to the class tomorrow ——? (22) You haven't finished your work yet ——? (23) The students are not all Turkish ——? (24) He can't play football well ——? (25) He isn't a good player ——? (26) He doesn't play very well ——? (27) He didn't play very well ——? (28) He couldn't play very well ——? (29) He hasn't played very well ——? (30) That wasn't your brother who spoke to me ——? (31) You didn't have any letters this morning ——? (32) I oughtn't to ask the driver for a ticket ——? (33) She won't play tennis tomorrow ——? (34) You won't forget to send a Christmas present ——? (35) You didn't forget to send a Christmas present ——? (36) You haven't forgotten to send a Christmas present ——? (37) They don't come here every day ——? (38) They didn't come here yesterday ——?

IV Make the following sentences (*a*) negative, (*b*) interrogative, (*c*) interrogative by adding question phrases expecting the answer, 'Yes', (*d*) interrogative by adding question phrases expecting the answer, 'No'. (e.g. It is raining. (*a*) It isn't raining.

　　　　　　　　　(*b*) Is it raining?
　　　　　　　　　(*c*) It is raining, isn't it?
　　　　　　　　　(*d*) It isn't raining, is it?)

(1) These verbs are difficult. (2) My aunt is awake. (3) You saw George in London. (4) He ought to change his doctor. (5) The students can speak Italian. (6) Mary spoke Italian well. (7) The policeman will arrest the thief. (8) He had only an apple and some chocolate for lunch. (9) George plays tennis well. (10) He has a new tennis racket. (11) We shall arrange a party for our friends. (12) You can go now. (13) The boys could swim across the Thames. (14) They did it easily. (15) Your friend was wrong. (16) You should polish your shoes every morning. (17) He found a better job. (18) He went for a swim. (19) You can find your way in the moonlight. (20) It will be warm on the beach. (21) He ought to grow a beard. (22) You have quite finished.

V Give the full answer and then the short answer, (a) affirmative, (b) negative, to the following:

(1) Can he speak Russian? (2) Will they come to dinner tomorrow? (3) Ought I to answer the letter? (4) Did he find the money he lost? (5) Do you go to the pictures often? (6) Did you hear what he said? (7) Have you spoken to him about it? (8) Shall I see you tomorrow? (9) Will you be at the party tomorrow? (10) Didn't they finish the work? (11) Can you dine with me this evening? (12) Could you come and see us tomorrow? (13) Who likes the flavour of garlic? (14) Can I get across London in fifteen minutes? (15) Are they coming with us this evening?

VI Give Short Answers to the following expressing AGREEMENT:

(1) Henry is a very lucky fellow. (2) He'll come again tomorrow, won't he? (3) Lucille speaks English well. (4) William answered that question correctly. (5) Don't you think he ought to pay the money? (6) You said that before. So —— ——. (7) It's begun to rain. So —— ——. (8) That window's open. So —— ——.

VII Give Short Answers to the following expressing DISAGREEMENT:

(1) It will be two hours before you get there. (2) That house was surely built before 1940. (3) They built that house before 1940. (4) He'll return the book he borrowed. (5) Your car runs well. (6) Why didn't you tell me so? But —— —— .(7) Why are you angry with me? But —— ——. (8) Lord Northwood has a lot of money. Oh, no, —— ——.

VIII Construct sentences containing the following special finites used to avoid repetition of the verb in Short Answers:

will, can, do, am (are, was), have, must, could.

IX (a) To what remarks could the following expressions be appropriate answers and what feeling do you think is expressed by each?

(1) Oh, I mustn't, mustn't I? (2) Oh, she wouldn't, wouldn't she ? (3) Oh, you will, will you? (4) Oh, they did, did they? (5) Oh, it was, was it?

(b) Make responses expressing surprise or anger to the following.

(1) I don't like this exercise. (2) Richard hasn't done his homework. (3) You mustn't open that box. (4) I'm very fond of chocolate. (5) I'd rather have chocolates than cake. (6) I hate sausages. (7) We've three dogs in our house. (8) The students want a holiday tomorrow. (9) I thought you would give us one. (10) I told him what you said.

X Invent questions to which the following sentences are the answers:

(1) But I *did* post your letter. (2) But I *can* walk faster. (3) But they *did* telephone this morning. (4) But he *has* finished his exercise. (5) But the dinner *is* ready punctually.

XI Say the following sentences, stressing one of the verbs in each to make the sentences emphatic:

(1) Margaret can play the violin well. (2) Andrew is a big boy for his age. (3) I shall be glad to be home again. (4) We were sorry you had to go so early. (5) You will try to come again, won't you? (6) I must get this work done before Friday.

XII Write the following sentences in the emphatic form by introducing a Special Finite into each one:

(1) Richard likes cake. (2) He enjoyed the ones he ate at the party. (3) I like the cakes that your mother bakes. (4) We had a good swim this afternoon. (5) You bought a lot of chocolate. (6) Andrew runs fast. (7) The wind blew hard when we were at sea. (8) You brought a lot of clothes with you. (9) Henry came here quickly. (10) Henry comes here quickly. (11) Richard drank a lot of lemonade. (12) They took a long time to come here. (13) Those shoes I bought wore well. (14) He promised he would write and he wrote. (15) It froze hard last night. (16) You told me to see the picture at the cinema and I saw it. (17) He asked me to teach him French and I taught him. (18) You did these exercises well.

XIII Disagree with the assumptions in the following sentences:

(1) Why don't you come by bus? (2) Why hasn't he written to his brother? (3) Why won't he sign the paper? (4) Why isn't he willing to come here? (5) Why aren't you going to the dance?

XIV Explain the difference between:

'But I *did write* to him', and 'But I *wrote* to him'.

THE SPECIAL FINITES (ii)

TO BE

The parts of this verb are: *am, is, are, was, were, being, been.*
The Present Tense has the contracted (weak) forms:

I'm [aim], he's [hiːz], she's [ʃiːz], it's [its], we're [wiə],
you're [juə], they're [ðeə].

The contracted negative has two forms, except for the first
person singular:

I	2
I'm not	——
he's (she's, it's) not	he (she, it) isn't
we're not	we aren't
you're not	you aren't
they're not	they aren't

The shortened interrogative negative is *aren't you, isn't he,*
etc., and for the first person *aren't I?* (or *a'n't I*)[1], e.g.

I'm right, *aren't I?*

(1) The verb *to be* is used, as an auxiliary verb, with the
present participle to form the Continuous Tenses, e.g.

'He *is* walking'. 'She *was* speaking', and it is used with the past
participle to form the passive voice, e.g.

He *was* asked to sign his name.

You *are* invited to the birthday party.

(2) The verb *to be* is a verb of INCOMPLETE PREDICATION, i.e.
it requires something else (called the Complement) to complete
its meaning in such sentences as:

Your dinner *is* ready.

In four minutes it *will be* nine o'clock.

His father *was* a famous man.

(3) It is a full verb, when it has the general meaning of 'to
exist' in such expressions as:

[1] In Scotland and Ireland *amn't I?* ['æmənt ai].

Whatever *is* is right.

'I think; therefore I *am*.'

There *are* people who try to help others.

The memory of what *has been* and never more *shall be*.

> 'Can such things *be*
> And overcome us like a summer's cloud
> Without our special wonder?'[1]

(4) A part of the verb *to be* followed by an infinitive with *to* is used to express an arrangement, e.g.

I *am* to have tea with Betty this afternoon.

The wedding *is* to take place on Saturday.

If we *are* to be at the station by nine o'clock we must go now.

This construction implies futurity or, as in the following example, Future in the Past:

My sister and her husband *were* to come and see us this week-end, but they couldn't come. She *is* to let me know if they can come next week.

(5) The same construction expresses also what is equivalent to a command, e.g.

You *are* to see the headmaster in his room at 4 o'clock.

You *are* not to leave the building without permission.

(See also p. 209.)

(6) The construction 'If I (he, she, it) *were* . . .' is one of the few remaining subjunctive inflections in modern English.[2]

(7) Some of the Special Finites are used with *do*,[3] but the verb *to be* is never used with *do* except in the imperative. With the negative imperative, *do* must be used (unless it is replaced by *never* = do not ever), e.g.

Don't be late tomorrow.

Never be cruel or unjust.

Do may be used with the affirmative imperative and usually implies more emotion of some kind, e.g.

Do be careful when you cross the road; there is always a lot of traffic at that spot. (*Apprehension*)

---

[1] Macbeth on seeing the ghost of Banquo.
[2] See page 228.   [3] E.g. *have, need, dare* (see pp. 195, 209, 213).

Do be as nice to him as you can; he's terribly shy. (*Begging* rather than *Commanding*)

The usual imperative form is simply '*Be* . . . '.

(8) The verb *be* is not used in the Perfect Continuous tenses.

TO HAVE

The parts are *have, has, had, having*.

1. *Have* (*had*) is used to form the Perfect Tenses, e.g.

I *have* answered your question. *Has he* finished his dinner? They *hadn't* heard that story before. I ought *to have spoken* but I didn't.

When it is used like this as an Auxiliary verb it is always a special finite.

2. *Have* may also be a 'full' verb, i.e. used as the only verb in the sentence. In conversation and, less frequently, in more formal style, *got* is often added, e.g.

Mr. Brown *has* (got) a dog named Fido.

They *have* (got) a new car.

I'*ve* (got) a bad cold.

3. When it is used as a full verb it sometimes, but not always, behaves like a special finite, for example forming its interrogative by inversion and its negative simply by adding *not*. It behaves like a special finite when it is denoting possession (using the word 'possession' in its widest sense), e.g.

How many brothers and sisters *have you* (got)?

A triangle *has* three sides.

You *haven't* (got) much room here.

He *hasn't* a lot of time to spare.

We *haven't* much money, but we do see life.

Has your sister (got) blue eyes or brown eyes?[1]

---

[1] American usage is different. Americans would not treat *have* as a special finite in these negative or interrogative sentences. They would say:

> How many brothers and sisters *do you have?*
> You *don't have* much room here.
> He *doesn't have* a lot of time to spare.
> *Does* your sister *have* blue eyes or brown eyes?
> We *don't have* much money but we do see life.

4. It does not behave like a special finite when it has meanings other than 'possession', e.g.

Did you *have* (= receive) a letter from home this morning?
I *didn't have* (= eat) any breakfast this morning.
Did you *have* (= drink) tea or coffee for breakfast?
I *don't have* (= find, experience) much difficulty with English grammar.
Did you *have* (= experience, enjoy) a good time at the dance last night?

In these sentences *got* could not be used with *have*.

Note these three sentences (all correct).

Have you a headache? (*Special Finite*)
Yes, but I *hadn't* one when I came here. (*Special Finite*)
Do you often *have* headaches? (*not Special Finite*)
You *don't* often have headaches, *do* you? (*not Special Finite*)

The general principle is that *have* is treated as a special finite: (a) when the 'possession' is a permanent thing, e.g. blue eyes, the three sides of a triangle, etc.
(b) when we are speaking of one particular occasion, e.g. *Have you* a headache *now?* But when the 'possession' is a recurring or habitual thing, e.g. '*Do* you often *have* a headache?' then *have* is not treated as a special finite, e.g.

Have you anyone staying with you at present?
Do you often *have* visitors staying with you?

In the past tense, however, the Interrogative form 'Did you have . . .' is often preferred where the above rule would demand 'Had you . . .'

THE CAUSATIVE USE OF 'HAVE'

5. A construction containing *have* + a past participle is used to show that, without doing something ourselves, we cause it to be done, e.g.

We have just *had* our house painted (= caused our house to be painted).
I *have* just had my hair cut; why don't you *have* yours done?
Why didn't you *have* that suit cleaned?
Did you take the car to the garage to *have* it overhauled?

Why don't you *have* these knives sharpened? They won't cut.
The trousers of this suit are too long; I must *have* them shortened.

Why didn't you *have* your luggage sent on in advance?

6. There is a similar construction, where, instead of *causing* something, you *suffer* something, e.g.

I *had* my pocket picked (i.e. something stolen from it) this morning.

You won't *have* your house burgled easily if you keep a good dog.

Ralph *had* his licence endorsed for careless driving.

In most of these examples the causative *have* could be replaced by *get*, e.g.

Why didn't you *get* that suit cleaned?

Why don't you *get* your hair cut?

HAVE TO (= MUST)[1]

7. *Have* (*got*) *to* is used to express compulsion, obligation or necessity, e.g.

You *have to* (you've got to) work hard nowadays to make a living.

My car wouldn't start this morning and I *had to* walk to the office.

We *had to* (we'd got to) answer all the questions in the examination.

The negative of *have to*, with the meaning 'there is no necessity' is expressed by *have not to*, *haven't got to* or *do not* (*don't*) *have to*, e.g.

They *haven't got* to go to school every day.

They *don't have* to go to school every day.

I *haven't got* to go to the dentist this afternoon.

I *don't have* to go to the dentist this afternoon.

There is perhaps a tendency to use the *do* construction for habitual actions and the *haven't* (*got*) construction for one particular occasion, but this is by no means always observed.

[1] See also *must* (p. 208).

The construction *have not to* is not generally used to express a prohibition.

For *had better*, *had rather*, see pages 71, 228, 231, 395.

CAN

The verb *can* is defective; it has neither infinitive, past participle, *-ing* forms, nor imperative. Its only other form is its past tense *could*. The missing forms are supplied by the appropriate form of *to be able*, e.g.

I *shall be able* to do the work. (*Future*)

I *have been able* to do the work. (*Present Perfect*)

I hope *to be able* to do the work. (*Infinitive*)

1. *Can* and *could* are always special finites. They are used to express ability, power, capacity, e.g.

John *can* speak French well.

Can you swim?

Mary *could* play the piano well when she was quite young.

2. In colloquial speech *can* is used to replace the more formal *may* to express permission; the negative *cannot* (*can't*) is used to express prohibition, e.g.

In London buses you *can* smoke on the upper deck, but you *can't* smoke downstairs.

You *can* have my seat, I am going now.

Father said we *could* go to the concert.

3. *Can* is also used to express a possibility:

You *can* attend an Advanced Class or an Intermediate Class, but you *can't* attend both as they take place at the same time.

4. *Can* is used in questions and exclamations to express the idea, 'Is it possible . . .?' e.g.

Can it be true?

Can he really believe that he can deceive us so easily?

It surely *can't* be four o'clock already!

Could anyone be such a fool as to believe that!

5. *Can* is also used to express what may be possible, or what a thing or person is occasionally or generally capable of (usually, but not always, something unpleasant), e.g.

Driving on these roads *can* be a very nerve-racking business.

Our house is on the top of a hill, and in winter the winds *can* be pretty cold.

But for a particular occasion rather than for a general condition, *may* would be used, e.g.

Driving on this frosty road *may* be dangerous today, so go carefully.

Can suggests previous experience, *may* merely uncertainty.

He is a bad-tempered fellow, but he *can* be quite charming when he wishes.

6. *Cannot* (*can't*) is also used to express a virtual impossibility,[1] e.g.

George *can't* have (= it's practically impossible that he has) missed the way. I explained the route carefully and drew him a map.

7. With 'verbs of perception' (see pp. 169, 239) the Continuous tense is not used; the use of *can* gives an appropriate equivalent to the Continuous tense, e.g.

Listen! I think I *can hear* (not: *am hearing*) the sound of the sea.

I *can smell* (not: *am smelling*) something burning in the kitchen.

COULD

1. *Could*, besides being the Past tense, is also the conditional of *can*, e.g.

If you tried, you *could* do that work.

Could you finish the exercise if you had more time?

Even if he had been there he *couldn't* have helped you.

2. *Could* is not always equivalent to *was able*. If the reference is to something that can be done because of knowledge or skill, either *could* or *was able* may be used, e.g.

I *could* (*was able to*) swim when I was only six years old.

Richard hurt his foot, and *couldn't* (*wasn't able to*) play football.

The door was locked, and I *couldn't* (*wasn't able to*) open it.

---

[1] See also *must* (p. 208).

But if the implication is achievement, that is if the meaning is 'managed to', 'succeeded in doing', then, *was able* and not *could* would normally be used, e.g.

Because he worked hard he *was able* (= managed) to pass his examination.

I finished my work early and so *was able* (= managed) to go to the concert this afternoon.

'Something went wrong with my car when I was coming here.' '*Were you able to drive* (= did you succeed in driving) it home or had you to take it to a garage?'

But with the negative, either *could* or *be able* is possible.

'I wonder why Jane hasn't come yet?' 'Perhaps she *was not able to* (*couldn't*) *get* (= didn't succeed in getting) away from the office.'

3. Both *can* and *could* are used to make rather informal requests, e.g.

Can you change a ten-shilling note for me, please?
Could you tell me the right time, please?

In this case, *could* is felt to be rather more polite than *can*.

4. *Could* is also used to express a rather gentle doubt, e.g.

Yes, his story *could* be true, but I hardly think it is.
Well, I *could* do the job today, but I'd rather put it off until Friday.

SUMMARY OF THE TENSES OF *Can* (*to be able*)

Present Infinitive	to be able	*Past Perfect*	I had been able
Past Infinitive	to have been able	*Future Perfect*	I shall have been able
Simple Present	I can (I am able)	*Conditional* (*Present*)	I could (I should be able)
Simple Past	I could (I was able)		
Present Perfect	I have been able	*Conditional* (*Past*)	I could have (I should have been able)

EXERCISES

I Invent a series of sentences each one of which illustrates one of the uses of the verb 'to be'.

II Explain the term 'verb of incomplete predication', and illustrate your answer by examples.

III (*a*) Describe the function—full verb or Special Finite—of the verb 'have' in each of the following sentences:

(1) I have no doubt that he is right in his opinion.
(2) How many marks have you got for this exercise?
(3) We haven't time to come to see you this week.
(4) When do they have lunch? (5) Has your fiancée met my sister?

(*b*) Make these sentences interrogative:

(1) Her brother has curly hair. (2) A triangle has three sides. (3) He had eggs and bacon for breakfast this morning. (4) He had a letter by the evening post. (5) They have a lesson every day. (6) He has a lot of money. (7) They have a lot of trouble with their car. (8) Margaret had an enjoyable time at the dance. (9) Susan has a bad cold. (10) She often has colds in winter.

(*c*) Make these sentences negative:

(1) I have a dark blue suit. (2) A triangle has four sides. (3) He had coffee for breakfast this morning. (4) I had some letters by the morning post. (*Be careful with 'some'.*) (5) They have lunch before twelve o'clock. (6) We have a lesson every day. (7) Mr. Brown has a lot of money. (8) We had a very comfortable journey to Scotland. (9) That country has a very good climate. (10) I have some cigarettes in my cigarette-case.

(*d*) After doing these exercises quote the rule by which you can decide when 'have' is being used as a Special Finite.

IV Rewrite these sentences using some part of *have* or *get* with a past participle, e.g.

The tailor made a new suit for me last week.

I *had* a new suit *made* for me last week.

(1) Someone cleaned my shoes for me. (2) Painters painted my house last week. (3) One of my teeth was taken out this morning. (4) Someone must chop this wood for us. (5) We must ask someone to mend the car.

(6) Someone picked Henry's pocket at the football match. (7) It's time your hair was cut. (8) William broke his leg playing football. (9) This knife won't cut; we must ask someone to sharpen it. (10) His house was burgled while he was away on holiday.

V Change the construction of the following sentences in such a way that the verb employed is *have* in its causative form. After each sentence give an alternative form, where possible, using *get* in place of *have*.

(1) Tom's clothes are all made by a London tailor. (2) I told the builder to put a bay window in my study. (3) Our car needs thoroughly overhauling. (4) My watch was stolen yesterday. (5) Their piano was tuned the other day. (6) Why don't you arrange for your newspapers to be delivered regularly? (7) My dinner jacket is a little too small for me; I must tell the tailor to alter it. (8) His tonsils were removed when he was a boy.

VI Construct four sentences illustrating the use of *have to* to express compulsion, obligation, necessity and a regular habit. Use the shortened form and give the alternative form of *got to* in each case.

VII Complete the following sentences by inserting *can* or *may* as you think is correct.

(1) Motoring in London —— be a great trial of patience. (2) You —— choose either subject in the examination but you —— not take both. (3) He —— know a lot about musical theory but he —— not play the piano well. (4) ——I give you a hand with that heavy trunk? (5) —— you cash this cheque for me, please?

VIII Supply *could* or *was (were) able to* to complete the following. When is it possible to use only *was (were) able?*

(1) Because he had saved money all his life he —— retire early. (2) Despite the period of depression Henry —— make a profit. (3) —— (you) get him on the telephone? (4) I —— see very well when I was young but my sight has grown weaker. (5) They —— catch their train because John drove them to the station. (6) I —— drive a car when I was sixteen. (7) The night was clear and we —— see the stars. (8) After a lot of hard work I —— pass the examination two years ago. (9) The aeroplane was damaged but the pilot —— bring it safely to land. (10) I —— finish the work by

ten o'clock. (11) When I was a boy I —— write with my left hand as easily as with my right hand. (12) —— (you) do things with your left hand as easily as with your right hand? (13) After hard fighting the soldiers —— drive the enemy out of the town. (14) The firemen —— put the fire out before it destroyed the house. (15) After I had studied the lesson I —— do the exercise correctly.

IX Invent sentences to illustrate the use of 'can' or 'could' in the following senses:

(*a*) possibility. (*b*) capability. (*c*) conditional. (*d*) polite request. (*e*) doubt.

X Say the following in the Future tense, adding the words in brackets.

(1) I can speak English (after I have had some lessons).
(2) I can play football (when my foot is better).
(3) Herbert can play football (when his foot is better).
(4) Pierre can speak English better (after he has had more lessons). (5) We can do this exercise (now that we have had it explained). (6) The students can do this exercise (now that they have had it explained).
(7) Jane can cook well (when she has had more practice). (8) Robert can't do this work (until he tries harder). (9) I can read a lot of books (when my holidays come). (10) You can see the house (when you get to the top of this hill).

DO

The parts are *do, does, did, doing, done.*

Do can be a full verb or a special finite. It is a full verb in such sentences as:

He *does* his work well. He *did* good work yesterday. What *were* you *doing* this morning? The holiday *did* me good. What *does* he *do* for a living? He *doesn't do* anything.

When *do* is a full verb it forms its interrogative and negative with the special finite *do*, as is shown in the last two examples.

As a special finite *do* is used:

(1) To form the negative and interrogative of all verbs except special finites;[1]

---

[1] But see 'Special Finites', formation of Interrogative, and sections on *have, need, dare*—pages 195, 209, 213.

(2) For Question Phrases with all the verbs that are not special finites, e.g.

You understand me, *don't* you?
You didn't come here by bus, *did* you?

(3) To make the emphatic form of verbs, e.g.

I haven't much money but I *do* see life.
He *does* look well.
You *did* give me a fright.

(4) To avoid repetition of a verb, especially in Short Answers, e.g.

'Do you understand that?' 'Yes, I *do*.' 'No, I *don't*.'
I like swimming, so *does* Peggy.
Richard doesn't like hard work, neither *does* Fred.
Those wishing to go may *do* so now.
'May I help myself to a cake?' '*Do*, by all means.'
They said Henry wouldn't pass his examination, but he *did*.

(These last two examples illustrate the emphatic use of *do* in addition to its function of avoiding the repetition of a verb.)

(5) Occasionally with the imperative of verbs, e.g.

Do come and see us soon. *Do* have some more of this pudding. *Do* stop that noise.

When *do* is used, the imperative is an urgent request rather than a command.
Do not (*don't*) is always used to make the negative imperative, e.g.

Do not (*Don't*) do that.
Don't go till I tell you.

SHOULD, WOULD

Shall and *will* are defective verbs and have neither infinitives, participles, gerunds nor imperative. Their uses are dealt with in the sections on the Future Tenses and the Conditional. The past tense of *shall* is *should* and of *will* is *would*. The distinctions given on the differences in usage between *shall* and *will* (p. 161

to 166) apply when these verbs are put into the past tense
for indirect speech. e.g.

	Past Form
	I said that
I shall write	I should write
I will write	I would write
He will write	He would write
He shall write	He should write
They will write	they would write
They shall write	they should write

But note that in indirect speech[1] a pronoun in the first person
is generally changed into a pronoun in the third person, in
which case *shall* in the direct speech becomes *would* in the
indirect speech, etc.

> DIRECT: Henry said, 'I *shall* write to her.'
> INDIRECT: Henry said that he *would* write to her.

But not usually in the first Person Interrogative, e.g.

> DIRECT: *Shall* I get you a taxi?
> INDIRECT: He asked whether he *should* get her a taxi.

Would may indicate habitual action in the past, e.g.

> Every day he *would* get up at six o'clock and light the fire
> (see also p. 215).

Besides being the Past tense of *shall* in reported speech, *should*
is also used:

1. With a meaning similar to *ought to*[2], e.g.

> You *should* do what the teacher tells you. 'People who live
> in glass houses *should* not throw stones.' (*Proverb*)
> Why *should* I pay him?
> What's happened to the money? How *should* I know?
> If John's train is up to time, he *should* be here any minute
> now.

2. On occasions where *must* might seem too peremptory, e.g.

> Members who want tickets for the dance *should* apply before
> September 1st to the Secretary.

3. To form a substitute for the Present Subjunctive (see p. 227).

[1] See page 363.   [2] See section on *ought*—page 211.

MAY, MIGHT

May is a defective verb, its only part being *might*, used as its Past tense in indirect speech. For other parts, some verb like *allow*, *permit*, etc., has to be used, e.g.

I *shall be allowed* to go to the party.

It is always a special finite.

May (*might*) is used to express:

(1) PERMISSION (asked or given or refused), e.g.

You *may* go now.

'*May* I take this book?' 'No, you *may* not.'

May I go to the party? She asked if she *might* go to the party; I told her that of course she *might*. (*Negative:* I told her she *might* not.)

If I *may* say so, I think you have treated him very badly.

There is a feeling that in making a request, *might* is rather more deferential and courteous than *may*, e.g.

Might I see you for a few minutes, please?

(2) PROHIBITION (usually in official notices) with *not*, e.g.

Dogs *may* not be taken into these carriages.

People *may* not pick flowers in this park.

(3) POSSIBILITY, e.g.

The news *may* be true, of course.

He admitted that the news *might* be true.

You *may* deserve success, but you cannot command it.

'You *may* lead a horse to the water but you can't make it drink.' (*Proverb*)

(Note that in this use the negative of *may* is *cannot* (*can't*), not *may not*.)

Might as well as *may* is used to express a present or a future possibility. The use of *might* in this case suggests rather more reserve or doubt on the part of the speaker than *may* would, e.g.

'Joe *might* pass his examination.' 'Yes, and pigs *might* fly.'
I'm not very hopeful about the plan, but it *might* be worth trying.

(4) *May* is used with the Perfect Infinitive to express DOUBT at the present time about a possibility in the past, e.g.

'Henry is late.' 'Yes, he *may* have been detained at the office or he *may* have missed his usual train.'

Their house *may* have been sold, but I have not been told about it.

If *might* is used with this construction there is often an implied negative, e.g.

John *might have lent* you the money if you had asked him (. . . but you didn't ask him).

You shouldn't have run across the road without looking round, you *might have been knocked* down by a car (. . . but as it happened you were not).

(5) *May* (*might*) is used in exclamatory sentences to indicate a WISH, e.g.

May all your dreams come true!

May you have a very happy holiday!

He hoped that we *might* have a very happy holiday.[1]

'And *may* there be no moaning of the bar
When I put out to sea.' (Tennyson, *Crossing the Bar*)

'And, when he next doth ride abroad,
May I be there to see!' (Cowper, *John Gilpin*)

In these examples *may* is a subjunctive equivalent (see p. 227).

(6) *May* and *might* are used in 'that' clauses following verbs like *trust* and *hope*, e.g.

I hope that he *may* get the job he wants.

I trust (hope) that you *may* find this plan to your satisfaction.

He trusted (hoped) that we *might* find the plan to our satisfaction.

(7) *May* and *might* are used in adverb clauses[2] of PURPOSE, e.g.

Lift little Harry up so that he *may* see the procession.

William is working late tonight so that he *may* be able to go to the cricket match tomorrow.

---

[1] Notice that *might* must be used in indirect speech introduced by a verb in the Past tense.　　[2] For Adverb Clauses see pages 337–44.

He saved all the money he could so that his son *might* have a good education.

She was studying English so that she *might* read English books.

In such sentences *can* (*could*) is frequently used instead of *may* (*might*).

(8) *May* and *might* are also used in clauses of concession,[1] e.g.

He *may* be poor but (= though he is poor) he is honest.

It *may* be June but it's bitterly cold.

Try as he *may*, he will not pass the examination.

Try as he *might*, he could not persuade his friends to go.

(9) *Might* (but not *may*) is sometimes used to make a sentence expressing petulant reproach, e.g.

You *might* try to be a little more helpful (= 'Please try to . . .' 'I wish you would be . . .')

You *might* listen when I am talking to you.

You *might have helped* me with my work (. . . but you didn't).

He *might* at least have answered my letter (. . . but he didn't).

MUST

Must is a defective verb having only the one form. It is always a special finite.

1. In one of its meanings, *must* has an imperative quality suggesting a command or an obligation. The negative *must not* (*mustn't*) expresses a prohibition, an obligation *not* to do something, e.g.

You *must* wipe your feet before coming into the house.

The pupils were told that they *must* write more neatly.

In England traffic *must* keep to the left.

You *mustn't* walk on the grass.

Cars *mustn't* be parked in front of this house.

There is a wonderful production of *Hamlet* at Her Majesty's Theatre. You *must* go and see it. It is something you *mustn't* miss.

[1] See pages 341–2.

2. In another meaning *must* implies a logical conclusion, a strong likelihood, something that seems the only reasonable explanation, e.g.

If Fred left here at four o'clock he *must*[1] be home by now.
You have worked hard all day ; you *must* be tired.
George *must* be pleased that he has passed his examination.
Mr. Thompson was a grown man when I was a boy; he *must* be at least seventy now.
Mr. Green *mustn't*[2] have received my letter, otherwise he would have replied before now.
I can hear the Browns' 'phone bell ringing but no one is answering it; they *mustn't* be at home.

3. When the negative of *must* has the meaning 'it is not necessary', 'there is no obligation', *need not* (*needn't*) is used, e.g.

Must I be at the party by seven o'clock? No, you *needn't* be there by seven, but don't be much later.
You *needn't* do the work this evening; tomorrow will be soon enough.
Must I answer all the questions? No, you *needn't* answer them all; it will be sufficient if you do four of them.
You *needn't* go home yet, but I *must*.

4. When the meaning of *must* is 'logical conclusion', etc., the usual negative is *cannot* (*can't*), (see p. 198):

AFFIRMATIVE. If Fred left here at four o'clock he *must* be home by now.
NEGATIVE. If Fred didn't leave here until five o'clock he *can't* be home yet.
AFFIRMATIVE. If he said that, he *must* be mistaken.
NEGATIVE. If he said that, he *can't* be telling the truth.

MUST and HAVE TO

5. Instead of *must* the verb *have to* is often used, especially for past or future or conditional since *must* has no forms to express these concepts, e.g.

---

[1] See also *ought* and *should* (pp. 211, 204).
[2] These negatives can also be expressed by *cannot* (*can't*).

He *will have to* be told the truth.

We *shall have to* hurry if we are going to catch the twelve o'clock train.

I *have (got)*[1] *to go* to the dentist today about my bad tooth.

I *had to go* to the dentist yesterday about my bad tooth.

I *shall have to* go to the dentist soon about my bad tooth.

The dentist said that if my tooth got worse I *should have to* have it out.

But if *must* is used to suggest an inference (as in 2, p. 208) no synonym for *must* can be used.

With *must* the feeling of compulsion comes from the speaker; with *have to* the compulsion is generally from external circumstances, e.g.

You *must* do what I tell you.

I'm afraid you'll *have to* do this; it's a rule of the College.

Passengers *must* cross the line by the bridge. (Order by the Railway Authorities.)

Passengers *have to cross* the line by the bridge (there is no other way).

For further discussion of *have to* see p. 196.

Another form that can be used instead of *must* is *are (am, is, was, were)*, etc., *to* (see p. 193).

NEED

Something has already been said about the verb *need* in the section on *must*.

There are two verbs *need*. One of them, which we will call *need* **A**, is normal and quite regular. It has all the parts of a normal verb (*need, needs, needed, needing*) and makes its interrogative and negative with *do* (*does, did*). It means, 'to require'. *Examples:*

I *need* a new suit.

Your hair *needed* cutting; I am glad you had it cut.

You look tired; you *need* a rest.

Did you need all the food you took for your camp?

No, we *didn't need* it all.

[1] The use of *got* is common with the present tense of *have;* it is not so usual with other forms.

Need **A** is also used as an auxiliary verb. It is then followed by the infinitive with *to*, e.g.

He doesn't *need* to work so hard.

You *don't need* to answer that question.

The Past Tense of *need* **A** is *needed to;* its negative is *didn't need to*, e.g.

I *needed* to get new tyres for my car, the old ones were badly worn.

I *didn't need* to tell him the news, he already knew it.

The second *need*, (*need* **B**), is a special finite. It is defective, having only the one form. The third person Singular Present Tense does not take -*s*. Its meaning is similar to 'have to'. It forms its interrogative by inversion and its negative by adding *not* (this form is almost always shortened to *needn't*). It can make Question Phrases. When *need* **B** is followed by an infinitive, the infinitive is 'plain' (i.e. without *to*).

Examples:

Need he work so hard?

Need I answer that question?

Need you go so soon?

He *needn't* work so hard.

You *needn't* go yet, *need* you?

A peculiarity of this verb as a special finite is that it is not used in affirmative sentences, only in negative and interrogative ones.

In affirmative sentences it is replaced by *must* or equivalents like *have to, ought to, should*, e.g.

Need you go yet? Yes, I *must*.

You *needn't* see him, but I *must*.

It can, however, be used affirmatively with adverbs such as *never, hardly* and *scarcely*, which have negative implications, e.g.

I *hardly* (*scarcely*) need say how much I enjoyed the holiday.

The Past Tense of *need* **B** is *need . . . have*, e.g.

Need you *have* scolded him so severely for his bad work; he had done his best?

There is an idiomatic construction illustrating both the verbs *need* that ought to be noted:

He sent me the money he owed me, so I *didn't need* to write to him for it. (= I didn't write).

He sent me the money he owed me, so I *needn't have* written (= I did write).

We had plenty of bread, so I *didn't need* to buy a loaf (= I didn't buy one).

We had plenty of bread, so I *needn't have* bought a loaf (= I did buy one).

John went to the station with the car to meet Lucille, so *she didn't need* to walk to the house (= she didn't walk).

John went to the station with the car to meet Lucille, so she *needn't have walked* (= she did walk).

The form *needs* in such sentences as:

'*Needs* must when the devil drives.' (*Proverb* = We must follow some certain course when there is no alternative)

'We *needs* must love the highest when we see it.' (Tennyson)

is an adverb (= of necessity), not a verb.

OUGHT

Ought is a defective verb having only this one form. It is always a special finite. It is used to express the idea of moral obligation, duty, desirability. In most cases *ought to* can be replaced by *should;* of the two, *ought to* is the rather more emphatic. Note that *ought* is followed by the infinitive with *to; should* is followed by the infinitive without *to,* e.g.

They *ought to* (*should*) pay the money.

He *ought to* (*should*) be ashamed of himself.

You *ought to* (*should*) come for lessons at least three times a week.

I told him that he *ought to* (*should*) see you.

1. *Ought* is also used to express likelihood or strong probability, e.g.

If Alice left home at nine o'clock she *ought to* (*should*) be here any minute now.

There's a fine sunset; it *ought to (should)* be a fine day tomorrow.

Considering all the work you have done you *oughtn't to (shouldn't)* fail in your examination.

2. *Ought* does not use *shall* or *will* for its future tense. A future idea is indicated by a word or phrase denoting the future, e.g.

Henry's team *ought to (should)* win the match tomorrow.

Your new suit *ought to (should)* be ready on Tuesday.

You *ought to (should)* write to her as soon as you can.

3. To express a past obligation that was not fulfilled *ought (ought not) to have* or *should (shouldn't) have* + a past participle is used, e.g.

I *ought to (should)* have written that letter yesterday (= but I didn't).

You *ought to (should)* have told me about this earlier (= but you didn't).

4. *Ought not to have (should not have)* are used to express disapproval of something done in the past, e.g.

You *ought not to have (shouldn't have)* spent all that money on such a foolish thing.

What you heard was confidential. You *ought not to have (shouldn't have)* repeated it.

DARE

Dare can be a full, normal verb, or it can be a special finite. When *dare* is a special finite it forms its third person singular without *-s* and has all the other characteristics of the special finites except that:

(a) The constructions '. . . and so —— I', 'neither —— I' (see pp. 185–6) are not used with *dare*, and

(b) The 'adverbs or frequency' come *after* it, not before it.

1. *Examples* of *dare* as special finite:

Dare you climb that tree?

Dare he go and speak to her?

How *dare* you say such a thing?

'You *daren't* climb that tree, *dare* you?' 'Yes, I *dare*.'

2. But *dare* can be conjugated like a normal verb, e.g.

She *didn't dare* to say a word, *did* she?

He *doesn't dare* to answer my letter.

We *didn't dare* to ask if we could have a holiday.

3. When *dare* is a special finite it is followed by the infinitive without *to*. When *dare* is used as an ordinary verb, it is followed by *to* + infinitive.

4. There is another, slightly different, meaning of *dare*, viz. 'to challenge', e.g.

I *dared him* to ask the teacher to give us a holiday tomorrow.

He *dared me* to walk down Piccadilly in my pyjamas.

Do you dare me to swim to that rock and back again?

Here, *dare* has a personal object (*him*, *me*, etc.). It is conjugated with *do* and is followed by an infinitive with *to*.

5. Just one other expression should be noticed: *I daresay*, which simply means *perhaps*, *it is probable*, e.g.

He is not here yet, but *I daresay* he will come later.

They haven't widened this road yet, but I *daresay* they will some day.

'Do you think Alice will come and see us today?' 'Oh, I *daresay.*'

The expression is not generally used with any pronoun except *I*.

USED (TO)

Only one form, the preterite, exists. This verb is used to contrast past and present, to express something that existed or was done in the past (generally a repeated action), but no longer exists or is done now, e.g.

That is the house where we *used to* live (but we don't live there any longer).

He *used to* smoke fifty cigarettes a day (but he doesn't do so now).

People *used to* think that the earth was flat (but they, or at least most of them, don't think so now).

Used is a doubtful member of the special finites. It is a special finite in that it forms its interrogative by inversion, has a contracted *not* (*usedn't*) ['juːsnt] in the negative, and can form Question Phrases, e.g.

You *used* to live in London, *usedn't you?*

He *usedn't* to smoke as much as he does now.

'There used to be an old apple tree in the garden.' 'Oh, *used there?*'

Used you to climb the old apple tree in the garden?

You usedn't to make that mistake.

But the tendency is growing in spoken English to treat it as a normal finite and say:

He *didn't use* to smoke as much as he does now.

'There *used to* be an old apple tree in the garden.' 'Oh, *did there?*'

Did you use to climb the old apple tree in the garden?

You *didn't use* to make that mistake.

We still feel a little uneasy about using *do* and *did* in this way, and in negative sentences we often try to avoid the difficulty by using *never:*

You *never used* to make that mistake.

He *never used* to smoke as much, etc.

There is no present form of *used to*. A repeated action in the present is expressed by the Simple Present tense.

The verb *used to* ['juːstu] should not be confused with the verb *use* [juːz], or the past participle of this verb *used* [juːzd], e.g.

I *use* the same shaving brush that I have *used* for ten years.

I think you have *used* your time well while you have been in England.

Nor should it be confused with (*to be*) *used to* ['juːstu] meaning '(to be) accustomed to,' e.g.

Adam the gardener works better than I do in the garden; he's *used to* doing hard work. I'm not *used to hard work*, but I'll get *used to* it in time.

The cat comes only when I call her; she's *used to* me, she's not *used to* you.

This construction may be followed by the gerund (see pp. 246–8), e.g.

He is *used to getting* up early.

Would is sometimes used as a variant of *used to* to express a repeated action in the past (see p. 204), e.g.

The old man *would* go every day to the park to feed the birds.

But *would* differs from *used to* in that:

1. *Would* is generally used with a time phrase ('every day', etc.). This is not necessary with *used to*.

2. *Would* suggests willingness or voluntary action; so it would be inappropriate to substitute *would* for *used to* in such sentences as:

When he lived by the river, he *used to* suffer from rheumatism.

EXERCISES

I In what constructions is *do* used as a Special Finite? Make three sentences using *do* (*a*) as a full verb, (*b*) as a Special Finite.

To the following sentences add expressions with the verb 'do' indicating emphasis, agreement, or disagreement as you think the sentence demands. If two expressions can be used, give both.

(1) Do you like modern music? (2) He always works very hard. (3) May I borrow your dictionary? (4) I was afraid they would not catch their train. (5) Tom does not like getting up early.

II Complete the following sentences with one of the following words, as you may think is correct: *should, may, might*.

(1) There is no point in asking him for information; how —— he know? (2) Those bringing eggs to the harvest festival —— lay them in the font (*Church Notice*). (3) —— I borrow your ruler, please? (4) You —— go out for a short time, but come back soon. (5) Colonel, —— I speak to you after parade? (6) His account of what happened —— be true, but I doubt it. (7) Persons *in statu pupillari*[1] —— not play marbles on the Senate House steps (*Cambridge University Regulations*). (8) He —— get the prize if he is very lucky. (9) They —— have helped you if only you had told them all the facts. (10) You

---

[1] i.e. undergraduates.

——— at least have told me you were going to be married. (11) ——— all your Christmases be white (*Popular song*). (12) I hope they ——— find the sort of house they are looking for. (13) I'm doing this tonight so that I ——— have more time to spare in the morning. (14) You ——— at least show appreciation of his kindness. (15) What you propose ——— be useless but it's worth trying.

III (*a*) In the following sentences use the *have to* form instead of *must:*

(1) We must work hard to learn English. (2) I must go home now. (3) William must go to the dentist to-morrow.

(*b*) In the following use the *am to* form:

(1) I must see the Headmaster at three o'clock. (2) We must meet on Saturday. (3) Must I understand that you are not coming? (4) I told him he must not make that mistake again. (5) I said, 'You mustn't do that.'

IV Give the opposites of the following, (*a*) implying 'there is no necessity', (*b*) with negative prohibition:

(1) They must come to school tomorrow. (2) I must be home before ten o'clock. (3) You must pay him today. (4) You must answer every question on the paper. (5) He must go to Brighton next week.

V The verb *must* can be used to express various concepts, e.g. command, logical conclusion, compulsion. Construct sentences to illustrate all the possible forms, including negatives where they can be used, stating possible alternative forms wherever you know them, and explaining in each case the exact sense in which the verb is employed.

VI (*a*) Complete these sentences with 'Question Phrases':

(1) You needn't write to him, ——? (2) He needs a new overcoat, ——? (3) He needed all the help you could give him, ——? (4) You needn't answer every question, ——? (5) His hair needs cutting, ——?

(*b*) Give answers to these questions:

(1) Need you go so soon? Yes, ——. (2) Who needn't catch the early train? George ——. (3) Need we answer all the questions? Yes, you ——. (4) Need George go to London tomorrow? No, he ——. (5) Need George go to London tomorrow? Yes, he ——.

VII Rewrite the following sentences in such a way that *need* can take the place of the existing verb:

(1) Is it absolutely necessary for you to work late every night? (2) Surely we are not obliged to show our tickets again, are we? (3) It shouldn't be necessary for us to pass another medical examination, should it? (4) I found I had enough money after all so it was not necessary for me to cash a cheque. (5) Are you compelled to go to the station to see him off at three o'clock in the morning? (6) It can hardly be necessary for me to say that I am grateful for your kindness? (7) Is it imperative for me to apply in person? Yes, it is. (8) You are not compelled to answer all his questions. (9) He telephoned to me this morning, so it was unnecessary for me to go and see him. (10) You have no reason to be anxious about the time: it is quite early yet.

VIII In the following sentences explain how the meaning of (*a*) differs from the meaning of (*b*):

(1) (*a*) I didn't need to leave the door unlocked; John had a key.

    (*b*) I needn't have left the door unlocked; John had a key.

(2) (*a*) She didn't need to tell me the time of the train; I knew it already.

    (*b*) She needn't have told me the time of the train; I knew it already.

(3) (*a*) He didn't need to take a taxi; it is only five minutes' walk to the house.

    (*b*) He needn't have taken a taxi; it is only five minutes' walk to the house.

IX Rewrite the following so that they refer to *past* time:

(1) You ought to get here by nine o'clock. (2) I suppose I ought to pay the money. (3) How much time should I spend on this exercise? (4) The teacher ought to tell you about this before you do the exercise. (5) You shouldn't leave my book out in the rain. (6) He ought not to speak like that. (7) Why should I do all the work? (8) Ought I to write out this exercise? (9) How much ought I to give him? (10) The wireless shouldn't make that noise.

X Complete the following sentences with *ought* and describe the sense *ought* expresses in each case.

H

(1) If he is lucky he —— to pass his examination easily. (2) You —— to have told me about this before. (3) My father was very annoyed and said we —— not to have wasted our money like that. (4) If the plane arrives on time they —— to be here in time for dinner. (5) The strong —— to help the weak.

XI Add 'Question Phrases' to each of the following:

(1) You daren't do that, ——? (2) He didn't dare to do that, ——? (3) He won't dare to do that, ——? (4) He dared you to do that, ——? (5) You used to live there, ——? (6) He usedn't to work in London, ——? (7) He never used to spend so much money before he knew Lucille, ——? (8) You used to like dancing, ——? (9) He daren't say what he thinks, ——? (10) He didn't dare to say what he thought, ——?

XII Change the wording of the following sentences so that either *dare* or *used to* or its negative is employed as the verb:

(1) Have you the courage to dive from the top of the springboard? (2) How can you make such an impudent remark? (3) They weren't brave enough to tackle that fierce dog, were they? (4) We challenged them to côme and fight us. (5) Before they moved they came every day to play bridge. (6) It was his habit to ride in the Park every day. (7) At one time it was thought that the sun went round the earth. (8) Did you not visit my uncle's house frequently at one time? (9) They were not so rich in years gone by. (10) In their father's lifetime they were accustomed to drink wine with their meals.

XIII Explain the difference in meaning between:

(a) He dared to swim across the river; *and:*
(b) He dared me to swim across the river.

(a) She dared to ask the teacher for a holiday; *and:*
(b) She dared me to ask the teacher for a holiday.

CHAPTER FIFTEEN

VERBS: (4) VOICE

If the person or thing denoted by the subject of a sentence is the doer of the action, then that form of the verb is the ACTIVE VOICE, e.g.

The boy *kicked* the football (*Active Voice*).

If the person or thing denoted by the subject of a sentence is the receiver or sufferer of the action, then that form of the verb is the PASSIVE VOICE, e.g.

The football *was kicked* by the boy (*Passive Voice*).

The passive voice is formed by using the appropriate tense of the verb *to be* + the past participle of the verb, e.g. (See table on p. 220.)

Note that the passive may have the same form as *be* + past participle (used adjectivally), e.g.

The tree *was uprooted* by the wind. (*Passive Voice*)

The tree *was uprooted* when we saw it. (*be* + Past Participle)

The passive voice is not merely a formal variant of the active voice, able to replace it without any change of meaning; there is a difference of emphasis. Generally speaking, the subject of the sentence is the main point of interest; the passive voice is the grammatical device that gives the object of a transitive verb prominence by making it the subject. So, when we want to place the emphasis on the performer of the action, we generally use the active voice; when we want to place the emphasis on the action, or on the receiver of the action, we use the passive voice. Thus, in the sentence:

Albert is cleaning the car. (*Active Voice*)

our point of interest is primarily 'Albert'. The sentence is the answer to some question like: 'What is Albert doing?'

In the sentence:

The car is being cleaned by Albert. (*Passive Voice*)

the emphasis is now on 'the car' and the fact that it is being cleaned. This sentence is perhaps the answer to the question:

Tense	Active Voice	Passive Voice
Present Simple	Mr. Brown teaches this class.	This class is taught by Mr. Brown.
Present Continuous	Mr. Brown is teaching this class.	This class is being taught by Mr. Brown.
Present Perfect	Mr. Brown has taught this class.	This class has been taught by Mr. Brown.
Past Simple	Mr. Brown taught this class.	This class was taught by Mr. Brown.
Past Continuous	Mr. Brown was teaching this class.	This class was being taught by Mr. Brown.
Past Perfect	Mr. Brown had taught this class.	This class had been taught by Mr. Brown.
Future Simple	Mr. Brown will teach this class.	This class will be taught by Mr. Brown.
Future Continuous	Mr. Brown will be teaching this class.	This class will be being taught by Mr. Brown.
Future Perfect	Mr. Brown will have taught this class.	This class will have been taught by Mr. Brown.

NOTE: The Perfect Continuous Tenses are not used passively.

'What is happening to the car?' We are so little concerned with *who* is cleaning it that quite often we should omit all reference to the agent (i.e. the person or thing that performs the action) and simply say: 'The car is being cleaned.' This is particularly the case where the agent is vague or unimportant or unknown. So the passive voice is often used in English where, for example, *on* is used in French or *man* in German with the active voice. Thus:

'Ici on parle francais', *or:*

'Hier spricht man deutsch', would be in English:

'French ⎱
'German ⎰ (is) spoken here.'

In sentences like this, the agent with *by* is always omitted; and in many other cases, where the active construction is changed to the passive, it is better to omit the agent. For example, in turning the following sentence from active voice to passive voice:

People in Brazil speak Portuguese.

the answer should be:

Portuguese is spoken in Brazil. NOT:
Portuguese is spoken in Brazil by people.

The following examples will illustrate this point further:

Active	*Passive*
No one has used that door for twenty years.	That door hasn't been used for twenty years.
Readers must not take away books in the Reference Library.	Books in the Reference Library must not be taken away.
Someone stole my watch this morning.	My watch was stolen this morning.
We use pure butter in these cakes.	Pure butter is used in these cakes.
They make cotton goods in Lancashire.	Cotton goods are made in Lancashire.
Have you fed the chickens yet?	Have the chickens been fed yet?

Since, in the change from active to passive voice, the subject of the passive construction is formed by the object of the active one, only transitive verbs can be used in the passive voice. So verbs of Incomplete Predication, e.g. *seem, be, become*, etc., can never be used in the passive; e.g. *He became King* could never have a passive form such as *A king was become by him*. But certain intransitive verbs can be made into transitive ones by the addition of a preposition. These verbs can be used in the passive voice, e.g.

His plan *was laughed at* by everyone who heard it.

That is a famous bed; it *was slept in* by Queen Elizabeth I.

The children *will be cared for* while she is away.

I believe the house was deliberately *set fire to*.

Such success *was* never *dreamed of* when we first started.

Though all transitive verbs can, theoretically, be made passive, there are cases where, in practice, the passive would not be used; for example:

He had a good breakfast before he went to work

would not be used passively as:

A good breakfast was had by him . . .

Some verbs, such as *give, tell, show, lend, get, write, pay, sell, buy, bring, make, fetch, promise, teach*, take two objects, one usually standing for a person, the other for a thing.[1] The word for the person is the INDIRECT OBJECT and is the first of the two objects; the word for the thing is the DIRECT OBJECT, e.g. He sold *us* (indirect) *his house* (direct). Here, *us* means 'to us'. His mother made *Tom* (indirect) a cake. Here *Tom* = 'for Tom'. Further examples:

He told me a story. I showed him my new car. He gave me some good advice. You owe him ten shillings. She taught him French. They promised Henry a bicycle for his birthday.

If a sentence containing two objects is expressed in the passive voice, either of those objects may become the subject, though it is perhaps more usual to make the personal object the subject of the passive voice. *Examples:*

[1] The verb *give* may have an indirect object standing for a thing, e.g.
As the ball came to him he gave *it* a kick.
Give *this matter* your full attention.

Active	*Passive*
The Prime Minister offered him a post in the Cabinet.	(1) He was offered a post in the Cabinet.
	(2) A post in the Cabinet was offered him.
They awarded him the Nobel Peace Prize in 1951.	(1) He was awarded the Nobel Peace Prize in 1951.
	(2) The Nobel Peace Prize was awarded him in 1951.

Note in the above examples the omission of the agent with *by*. The construction *by* + agent would be unnatural and unnecessary in sentences like these, where the 'doer' is either clear from the meaning of the sentence, or is not of interest to us.

EXERCISES

I Turn the following sentences into the passive voice:

(*a*)

(1) The waitress brings the coffee. (2) The waitress is bringing the coffee. (3) The waitress brought the coffee. (4) The waitress has brought the coffee. (5) The waitress was bringing the coffee. (6) The waitress had brought the coffee. (7) The waitress will bring the coffee. (8) I shall bring the coffee. (9) The waitress will have brought the coffee. (10) I shall have brought the coffee.

(*b*)

(1) I finished my work at about five o'clock. (2) We use your books in our class. (3) They gave him a very handsome present when he retired. (4) We opened the boxes and took out the cigarettes. (5) Do people speak English all over the world? (6) Somebody built this house in 1585. (7) You must answer all the questions on the paper. (8) They blamed me for something that I hadn't done. (9) They are sending Mr. Brown abroad on business. (10) People will forget the whole incident after a few weeks. (11) He took them for a drive in the new car. (12) People are talking about him everywhere. (13) I told him to write to that address. (14) You must plan your work carefully. (15) Someone gave me a pair of gloves for Christmas. (16) They told me you had gone

to Paris. (17) It's time someone told him what is wrong. (18) They gave me a ticket for Newtown instead of for Newton. (19) They didn't tell me all the details of the case. (20) They took him to hospital in an ambulance.

II Turn the following sentences into the passive voice:

(1) The English people greatly love the Queen. (2) Did the Customs Officers search your luggage very carefully? (3) When the parade was over, the commanding officer dismissed the troops. (4) The police denied him entry to the country. (5) Somebody has taken all my books. (6) Scotland Yard officers are investigating the crime. (7) They cannot trace the criminal. (8) They shall not treat me as if I were a baby. (9) The council have approved the plans for the building but we haven't raised the money. (10) The garage mechanic has washed and greased your car.

III Indicate which word in each of the following sentences is the direct object and then write the sentences in the passive voice. In each sentence two forms are possible.

(1) The manager offered him the choice of two posts in the firm. (2) The school governors gave her a scholarship to the University. (3) We cannot award him good marks on the work he has done. (4) Their uncle left them all his property when he died. (5) They gave you the present that was intended for your father.

IV In the following sentences put all the finite verbs in the passive voice:

(1) He promised you that they would meet you at the station. (2) Certainly we shall count on you to devote yourself to the work we are giving you to do. (3) It astonished us to hear that you had not received our letter. (4) They had only lived in that house for three weeks when fire destroyed it. (5) His failure bitterly disappointed his parents, especially as they had been counting on his success.

CHAPTER SIXTEEN

VERBS: (5) MOOD

Mood is a grammatical term used to denote the forms that a verb takes to show what work it is doing (e.g. expressing a statement, a command, a wish, etc.), and the manner in which the action or state is thought of by the speaker.

There are three moods, INDICATIVE, IMPERATIVE, SUBJUNCTIVE. The one that is by far the most commonly used is the *Indicative*. This is the mood used to make statements and ask questions. All the tenses discussed in pages 157 to 180 are in the Indicative Mood.

THE IMPERATIVE MOOD

The Imperative mood has the same form, in the second Person singular and plural, as the infinitive without *to*. In the first and third persons it is preceded by *let* and an accusative, e.g. '*Let*'s[1] go the the cinema.' 'I can't see him just now; *let* him wait.' It is used to give orders or commands or to make requests, e.g. '*Open* your books.' '*Don't make* so much noise.' '*Pass* the salt, please.' The 'request' may be:

(1) An ENTREATY, e.g.

'*Spare* a penny, sir, for a starving man.'
'*Help! Help!* I'm drowning.'

(2) An INSTRUCTION:

'To get to the Shakespeare Theatre, *turn* to the right at the river and *keep* straight on.'

(3) An INVITATION:

'*Come* inside and meet my wife.'
'*Have* a cigarette.'

(4) A SUGGESTION:

'Where can I find Mr. Smith?' 'I'm not sure. *Try* his office or *ring* up his house.'

---

[1] = let us.

H*

(5) A CONDITION, e.g.

Do that again and I'll call a policeman![1]

Suppose you had a million pounds, how would you spend the money?

The subject (which is always in the second person) is not usually expressed with the imperative. If it is expressed (usually in negative sentences), it may be in order to add emphasis.

Don't you dare to say I am not telling the truth.

I've been answering questions all day. *Don't you start* now.

If the subject is put in an affirmative sentence it is usually to express contrast, e.g.

You take that piece and I'll take this.

You ask the first question and I'll ask the next one.

In conversation the imperative is often used to express a wish, e.g.

Have a good holiday! *Enjoy* yourself and *come* back quite well again.

THE SUBJUNCTIVE MOOD

There are three Subjunctive forms of the verb: the Present Subjunctive, the Past Subjunctive and the Past Perfect Subjunctive.

THE PRESENT SUBJUNCTIVE of all verbs other than the verb *to be* is identical with the Simple Present Tense Indicative, except that the third person singular form is the same as in all the other persons (i.e. without the -s ending). The Present Subjunctive form of *to be* is *be* for all persons.

THE PAST SUBJUNCTIVE is identical with the Simple Past Tense Indicative, except that the verb *to be* has *were* for all persons.

THE PAST PERFECT SUBJUNCTIVE is identical in form with the Past Perfect Indicative.

The subjunctive forms are used in a small number of constructions; the constructions with ·the Present Subjunctive tend to be rather literary.

---

[1] See also Conditional Clauses, pages 347–51.

USES OF THE PRESENT SUBJUNCTIVE

The Present Subjunctive is used:

(1) to express a wish or a prayer, e.g.

God *save* the Queen.
Heaven *forbid* that . . .
Heaven *help* us.
Be that as it may . . .
'Thy Kingdom *come*, Thy will *be* done . . .'

A wish can also be expressed by *may* (Past Tense *might*) + infinitive, e.g.

May you be happy all your life.
They prayed that he *might* soon be well again.

(2) after verbs expressing a will or wish for the future, and after verbs like *propose, suggest*, etc. This is chiefly in very formal English and especially in legal English. *Examples:*

It is our wish that he *do* what he pleases.
She urged that he *write* and *accept* the post.
I propose that the Secretary's resignation *be* accepted.
The King ordered that the man *be* released.

(3) occasionally in adverbial clauses of concession or condition, e.g.

Though the whole world *condemn* him, I will still believe in him.
This, if the news *be* true, is a very serious matter.
'Murder, though it *have* no tongue, will speak
With most miraculous organ.'[1]

In uses (2) and (3) the subjunctive, is often replaced by the SUBJUNCTIVE EQUIVALENT *should* + the infinitive, e.g.

It is our wish that he *should do* what he pleases.
Though the whole world *should condemn* him, I will still believe in him.
If we *should* fail in this, we are ruined.

---

[1] Shakespeare, *Hamlet.*

USES OF THE PAST SUBJUNCTIVE

The Past Subjunctive is used:

(1) In conditional clauses implying a negative, or in clauses in which the condition is combined with improbability or unreality, e.g.

If I *were* you, I should accept the offer.

If he *were* really interested in buying the property, he would have made an offer before now.

What would you say if I *asked* you to join us for a holiday?

(2) After such expressions as: 'I wish (that) . . .', 'Suppose (that) . . .', 'I had rather (that) . . .', 'as if . . .', 'It's (high) time (that)[1] . . .'. *Examples:*

I wish *I were* as handsome as he is.

I wish he *visited* us more often.

Suppose (that) the teacher *caught* us wasting time.

I had rather (that) you *told* him than (that) I *did*.

He ran as if his life *depended* on it.

It is (high) time I *went* home.

It will be noted that except in the case of *to be*, verbs in these expressions could be considered as being in the Simple Past Tense.

Notice that the PAST SUBJUNCTIVE is usually concerned with PRESENT time, e.g. It's a lovely day; I wish I *were* at the seaside (NOW).

To speak of PAST time the PAST PERFECT SUBJUNCTIVE is used, e.g. It was a lovely day yesterday; I wish I *had been* at the seaside then. (See also Conditional sentences, pp. 347–51.)

EXERCISES

I Name the moods of the verbs in the following sentences: (1) Keep straight on until you come to the theatre and then turn left. (2) We should have gone for a walk today if the weather had been fine. (3) Come and have a drink. (4) Heaven help the sailors on a night like this. (5) It is

---

[1] But after 'It's time that', *was* not *were* in the first and third person singular would be usual, e.g. It's time that I *was* going.

time we left for the airport. (6) Don't you touch that or you'll break it. (7) Did you enjoy his singing this evening? (8) Have a good time at the party. (9) If I were in his place, I should accept their offer. (10) I suggest that he be nominated as Chairman.

II Write five sentences in which the verbs are in the subjunctive mood.

III Name the moods of the verbs in the following sentences:

(1) Let us go to the theatre this evening, shall we?
(2) What shall we do, supposing there are no seats left?
(3) It was ordered that no smoking be allowed in the library. (4) If you did that, you would be very sorry afterwards. (5) Will you have a little more meat, Mr. X?

CHAPTER SEVENTEEN

VERBS: (6) THE NON-FINITES

The non-finites are the Infinitive, the Participles and the Gerund.

THE INFINITIVE

This is the 'dictionary form' of the verb, i.e. the form under which a verb appears in the dictionary. It expresses the notion of the verb in its general sense, not as it applies to any particular subject. It is called 'infinitive' because its form is not limited (Latin *finis* = limit), as a finite verb is, by the number and person of its subject. There are four forms of the Infinitive:

	Simple	*Perfect*
Active	(to) write	(to) have written
Passive	(to) be written	(to) have been written

The infinitive is usually, but not always, preceded by *to*, e.g.

He wants *to learn* English.
'*To err* is human, *to forgive* divine.' (*Alexander Pope*)
Let me *tell* you a story.
I saw him *take* the money.

The infinitive without *to* is sometimes called the 'plain' or 'bare' infinitive.

THE PLAIN INFINITIVE (WITHOUT -*to*) IS USED:

1. after the special finites *can* (*could*), *do* (*did*), *may* (*might*), *shall* (*should*), *will* (*would*), *must*, *need*, *dare*, e.g.

He can *speak* French. Did you *hear* a noise? I might *go*.
We shall *meet* him. I will *help* you. You must *come* with us.
You needn't *go* yet. I daren't *leave* him.

But THE INFINITIVE WITH *to* IS USED:

(*a*) after the special finites *ought* and *used*, e.g.

> You ought *to go.* I used *to live* there.

(*b*) with *do, need* and *dare* when they are used not as special finites but as full verbs, e.g.

> I did it *to please* you. You don't need *to go* yet.
>
> He won't dare *to disobey* his teacher.

(*c*) with *be* and *have* when they are used to express commands, compulsion, etc., e.g.

> You *are to go* to the Headmaster's room at once.
>
> I *have to be* in my office by 9 o'clock.

2. after the Verbs of Perception: *see, hear, feel,* etc. (see also p. 169), and after *make* and *let*, e.g.

> She saw him *take* the money.
>
> I heard her *play* the piano.
>
> He felt his blood *run* cold and his flesh *creep.*
>
> The teacher made him *write* out the exercise again.
>
> Don't make me *laugh.*
>
> I will let you *use* my bicycle.
>
> Let's all *go* to the cinema.

But if these verbs are used in the passive voice, the infinitive takes *to*, e.g.

> He was heard *to cry.*
>
> They had been made *to work.*
>
> He was seen *to take* the money.

The verb *help* sometimes, and generally in American English, is followed by the infinitive without *to*, e.g.

> He helped me (to) *compose* the letter.
>
> Will you help me (to) *clean* the car?

3. after *had better, had (would) rather, had (would) sooner, need hardly, cannot but,* e.g.

> You had better *tell* him the truth. I had (would) rather not *see* him. I'd sooner *take* a taxi than walk. I need hardly *tell* you how serious the matter is. I cannot but (= cannot do anything except) *agree* to his terms.

THE INFINITIVE WITH *to* IS USED in all other cases.

The Particle *to* without the Infinitive

There are occasions when the particle *to* is used without the infinitive verb. This construction (omission of the infinitive verb) occurs when the *to* refers to a verb that has previously been used and that, if expressed, would be an infinitive with *to*, e.g.

I shall go if I want *to* (go).

He won't work harder than he needs *to* (work).

He would like to come but he's afraid he won't be able *to* (come).

If you don't know the answer, you ought *to* (know it).

'Will you come to dinner with me?' 'I should love *to* (come).'

Functions of the Infinitive

1. The infinitive can act as a noun. Thus, it may be:

(*a*) The SUBJECT of a sentence, e.g.

To act like that is childish.

To know all about English is one thing; *to know* English is quite another.

(*b*) The COMPLEMENT of a verb, e.g.

They are *to be* married soon.

To live like this is *to enjoy* life.

This house is *to let*.

How do you think I am *to answer* the letter?

What I like is *to swim* in the sea and then *to lie* on the warm sand.

(*c*) The OBJECT of a verb, e.g.

I want *to know* the answer.

He must learn *to work* hard and *to save* money.

'Men fear death as children fear *to go* in the dark.' (*Francis Bacon*)

I should like *to have been told* the result earlier.

There is a construction in which the infinitive together with a noun or pronoun (in the objective case) makes a close group that forms the object of a verb. This is called the ACCUSATIVE INFINITIVE construction. *Examples:*

	Accusative	*Infinitive*	
He helped	me	to dig	my garden
I made	him	do	it
They let	us	go	
John asked	him	to write	to you
I watched	her	come	into the room
I have never known	him	to behave	so badly before
He couldn't bear	her	to be	unhappy

2. The infinitive may have an adverbial function, generally of purpose or result, e.g.

I went there *to see* him.

Mary has gone *to get* some fruit.

He is working late *to make up* for his absence yesterday.

I have come *to learn* English.

He was lucky enough *to win* the prize.

You should eat *to live*, not live *to eat*.

Help yourself to the cake; it is there *to be eaten*.

'And fools, who came *to scoff*, remained *to pray*.'

(Goldsmith, *Deserted Village*)

3. It may have an adjectival function and qualify a noun or an indefinite pronoun, e.g.

That is not the way *to speak* to your uncle. (qualifying *way*)

Look at the number of shops *to let*. (qualifying *shops*)

Alexander the Great wept because he had no more worlds *to conquer*. (qualifying *worlds*)

That was a silly thing *to do*.

He wore a pale blue shirt and a tie *to match*.

He gave me something *to eat*.

They have nothing *to do*.

Is there anyone *to take care* of these children?

The questions *to be answered* are on page 40.

4. It is used with adjectives expressing emotion or desire, e.g.

I was very glad *to see* you.

He is happy/delighted/content/*to be* with us.

George was anxious/eager/*to get* home.

I am very pleased *to have been* of help.

It is used also with some other adjectives, e.g. *fit, able* etc:

These shoes are not fit *to wear.*

Tom isn't able *to go* to the party.

Richard is sure *to come;* he'll be the first *to come* and last *to go* away.

Other adjectives that can take this construction are:

afraid, ready, worthy, easy, hard, certain, useless, possible, right, (un)able, wrong, etc.

Some adverbs also take this construction, e.g. *far, best:*

He knows how far *to go.*

She explained how best *to cook* the meat.

5. The infinitive can be used in 'absolute' constructions such as:

To tell you the truth, I don't know what the answer is.

To hear him talk, you would think he was a millionaire.

To cut a long story short . . .

To continue with what I was saying . . .

6. It is used after *know* and certain other verbs with interrogative words (see patterns on pages 396-7, 398), e.g.

I don't know how *to tell* you.

She knows where *to find* the key.

You will soon learn when *to use* that construction.

Show him how *to do* the exercise.

NOTE: The verb *know* must have one of the words *how, when* after it when a simple infinitive follows it. Such a sentence as:

'He knows to speak English' is wrong.

But *know* without one of these words is possible with *not,* e.g.

He knows *not to speak* (= that he must not speak) when the Headmaster is speaking.

7. It is sometimes used in exclamatory sentences, or in sentences expressing a wish unlikely to be realized, e.g.

To think he knew about it all the time!

Oh! *to be* young again.

'Oh! *to be* in England

Now that April's there.' (Browning, *Home Thoughts from Abroad*)

THE 'SPLIT INFINITIVE'

Some grammarians condemn the use of the 'split infinitive' i.e. the placing of a word or words between the *to* and the *verb*, e.g. 'to quickly agree', 'to really understand'. But the split infinitive dates back to the thirteenth century and can be found in the work of many famous authors.

Fowler says: 'A split infinitive, though not desirable in itself, is preferable to either of two things, to real ambiguity or to patent artificiality.'[1] He quotes with approval:

'Our object is *to further cement* trade relations.'

'This will tend *to firmly establish* good relations between Capital and Labour.'

Jespersen,[2] following Fowler, adds further examples of which he approves:

He likes *to half close* his eyes.

He was too ill *to really carry* out his duty.

The best guidance, perhaps, is: 'Don't use a split infinitive unless you have a good reason for doing so.'

EXERCISES

I Pick out the infinitives and describe the function of each in the following sentences:

(1) To complete that book in three months was a great achievement. (2) That seems hard to do but is less difficult than it looks. (3) Strain every nerve to succeed. (4) Why did you try to persuade him to come with us? (5) It is easy to criticize. (6) To climb Everest seemed an impossible task. (7) Will you teach me to play tennis? (8) I saw him run the mile in four minutes. (9) The dog wants something to eat. (10) We are to have a holiday

---

[1] *Modern English Usage.*   [2] *Essentials of English Grammar.*

tomorrow. (11) What do you think is the right thing to do? (12) I tremble to think what your father will say. (13) The men have come to take down the tree. (14) She must do as she is told. (15) He made me tell him the whole story.

II (*a*) Construct sentences each containing an infinitive and using one of the following as the finite verb in each sentence:

want, see, must, let, hope, ought, hear, intend, dare, like, had rather, do, help, need, need hardly.

(*b*) Give five sentences each containing a Perfect Infinitive.

III Complete the following so as to make complete sentences:

(1) —— if he wishes to.
(2) —— whether I shall be able to.
(3) —— faster than he needs to.
(4) —— I shall be glad to.
(5) —— you certainly ought to.

What characteristic of the infinitive do these sentences illustrate?

IV Construct five sentences, each one using one of the following adjectives plus the Infinitive of a verb:

difficult, impossible, correct, unfit, afraid, sure.

V Define the function of the infinitive in each of the following sentences after you have completed the sentences:

(1) To speak plainly ——.
(2) To be brief ——.
(3) —— just how fast to go.
(4) —— how to climb the stairs.
(5) Oh to be young ——.

VI Make a sentence, containing what you consider to be a permissible split infinitive.

THE PARTICIPLES

There are two participles, the Present Participle and the Past Participle.[1] The present participle ends in -*ing*, the past

---

[1] The terms 'present' and 'past' here may be misleading. The 'past' participles in such phrases as 'a *distinguished* scientist', 'a *crowded* train', '*spoken* English' do not refer necessarily to an action or state in the past; nor does the present participle in 'a *charming* woman', 'an *interesting* book' signify any time at all. It is, however, convenient —now that the reader has been warned—to retain the usual terminology.

participle in *-ed* in the case of regular verbs. For irregular verbs see pages 145–153.

The verbs *may, shall, can, will, must, ought, used* (to) have no participles.

The difference between the present participle construction and the past participle one is that the present participle construction generally has an active meaning, the past participle a passive one. Compare:

He found the fire *burning* brightly (= the fire was burning. *Active*)	He found the house *burned* down (= the house was burned. *Passive*)
I heard him *playing* the 'Moonlight Sonata' (= he was playing. *Active*)	I heard the 'Moonlight Sonata' *played* by Myra Hess (= it was played by. *Passive*)

But this is not invariably the case. The past participle is active in such examples as: a *retired* teacher (= a teacher who has retired); the *fallen* angels (= the angels who fell); a *withered* (*faded*) rose (= a rose that has withered (faded)); an *escaped* prisoner (= a prisoner who has escaped).

We have already seen one of the very important functions of the present participle; to form, with various parts of the verb *to be*, the Continuous Tenses (p. 168), e.g.

He is *working* in the garden. I shall be *writing* to you. They have been *visiting* their uncle.

We have noted also two functions of the past participle:

(1) To form, with various parts of the verb *to have*, the Perfect Tenses (p. 174), e.g.

He has *spent* all his money. She had *studied* English before she came to England. You should have *listened* to me.

(2) To form the passive voice (p. 219), e.g.

The window was *broken*. The cakes had been *eaten*.

THE ADJECTIVAL USES OF PARTICIPLES

But the participles have another function. Though they are partly verbs, they are also partly adjectives and can function as noun qualifiers. As such they can be used attributively, or predicatively, e.g.

PRESENT PARTICIPLES (used attributively):

> An *exciting* story, *disappointing* news, a *good-looking* man, an *unpromising*[1] start. 'Scrooge! a *squeezing, wrenching, grasping, scraping, clutching* old sinner.' (Dickens).

PRESENT PARTICIPLES (used predicatively):

> The story was *exciting*. He is very *good-looking*. The news is *disappointing*, etc.

PAST PARTICIPLES (used attributively):

> The *broken* bottles; *tired* workers; the *unknown*[1] hero; a *clean-shaven* man.

PAST PARTICIPLES (used predicatively):

> The bottles were *broken;* he is *clean-shaven;* she is *tired*.

The participles here are in fact exactly like adjectives; they admit of comparison (*most* charming, *more* tired) and can be modified by adverbs (*very* good-looking, *rather* disappointing, *completely* clean-shaven).

But many, in fact most, participles are not purely adjectival, as the following examples show:

> He stood there *watching* the men at work. I hope Henry didn't keep you *waiting*. George is busy *cleaning* the car. His objections, if *listened* to, would wreck the plan. He will come if *asked*.

THE POSITION OF PARTICIPLES

Like ordinary adjectives, participles, if they are adjuncts of a noun, usually precede it; but, when the participle forms part of a phrase or has more of a verbal than an adjectival quality, it follows the noun. Compare, for example:

The *spoken* language	The language *spoken* in England.
The *torn* sails of the ship.	The ship came into port, its sails *torn* by the gale.

[1] Note the negative form of the participle though there is no equivalent verb.

The knight still grasped his *broken* sword.	The knight stood at bay; his sword *broken* in the fight was useless.
I have his *written* promise.	Here is a letter *written* by Charles I.
Listen to the *singing* birds.	The birds *singing* in the trees filled the air with music.

Here are further examples:

Here is a leaflet *giving* full particulars of the plan.

Do you know the number of girls *coming* to the party?

Will you let me know the amount of the debts still *outstanding?*

Do you know the number of books *ordered?*

Participles with the Infinitive

There is a construction with the participle that is similar to the 'accusative infinitive' construction used with the infinitive (see p. 233). The construction is used after verbs like *see, hear, feel,*[1] *find, make, want, get, like.* Here are examples:

I saw him (*accusative*) *running* (*participle*) for the train.

I could hear the boys *playing* in the field.

He was glad to find the fire *burning* brightly.

When they came home they found the house *burnt* down.

He soon made his presence *felt* and his wishes *known.*

I should like this matter *settled* immediately.

He wanted his eggs *fried.*

PARTICIPLES AS ADJECTIVE CLAUSE EQUIVALENTS

The participle phrase is frequently the equivalent of an adjective clause or of an adverb clause, e.g.

There were a lot of boys in the field *playing football* (= who were playing football).

The woman *driving the car* (= who was driving the car) indicated that she was going left and then turned right.

[1] See also pages 169, 198.

The ship *battered* (= which had been battered) *by the storm* crept into the harbour.

The *escaped* convict (= who had escaped) has been captured.

The concert *given* (= which was given) *by the Philharmonic Orchestra* was a great success.

PARTICIPLES AS ADVERB CLAUSE EQUIVALENTS[1]

Being (= as/because he was) naturally cautious, he read the letter twice before saying anything.

Going (= as he went) cautiously into the dark room, he felt for the light switch.

Seeing (= because he saw) that it was raining, George put on his mackintosh.

Born and bred a countryman (= because he was born and bred a countryman), he was bewildered by London.

MIS-RELATED PARTICIPLES

Care should be taken in using this construction to make sure that the participles are correctly related. The word to which the participle relates should be the same as the subject of the verb. Thus in the following sentences the participles are correctly related:

Walking through the park *we* saw a lovely show of daffodils. (Since it was 'we' who were 'walking' the participle is correctly related.)

Standing on the church tower we could see the whole village below us. (It was 'we' who were 'standing')

Travel-stained and *tired*, the pilgrims rejoiced to see the inn. (It was the 'pilgrims' who were 'travel-stained and tired')

Compare those examples with the following, in which all the participles are wrongly related:

'*Walking* through the Park, the *daffodils* made a lovely sight.' (It was not the daffodils who were walking.)

Standing on the church tower, *the whole village* could be seen.

Entering the house, *the door* closed with a bang.

[1] This construction is literary rather than colloquial.

Travel-stained and tired, the sight of the inn was very welcome to the pilgrims.

Hated and persecuted by all, *the reader* feels sympathy for Shylock.

Securely pierced by a toasting-fork, *Elizabeth* held a piece of bread to the fire.

However, there are cases where a participle may be found unattached and not logically related to the subject of the verb. This occurs:

(1) in a number of expressions so frequently used that they are accepted as correct, e.g.

Generally speaking, a footballer of 20 is better than one of 40.

Talking of football, have you seen the Italian team play?

Considering the position as a whole, he is better off now than he was a year ago.

It has cost, *roughly speaking,* about £500.

Allowing for extras, the tour will cost £150.

Strictly speaking, you have no right to be here.

(2) in the NOMINATIVE ABSOLUTE construction, where the participle with a noun or pronoun preceding it and acting as its subject forms a phrase independent in construction of the rest of the sentence. The absolute phrase may be active, in which case the present participle is used, e.g.

Christmas Day being a holiday, the shops were all closed.

The last train having gone, we had to walk home.

We explored the caves, *Peter acting as guide.*

Weather permitting, the cricket match will be played on Wednesday.

Or it may be passive, in which case the past participle is used, e.g.

All things considered, I think we ought to award the job to Smith.

Granted that he is not brilliant, he is at least competent and works hard.

This done, they packed up their tools and went home.

The absolute construction is literary rather than colloquial.

In conversation the participle phrase is usually made into an Adverb Clause, e.g.

As Christmas Day was a holiday, the shops were closed.
When this was done, they packed up their tools and went home.

COMPOUND PARTICIPLES

In addition to the 'Simple' participles already noted, there are three 'Compound' ones. They are: (1) The Present Passive Participle (formed by *being* + a past participle) e.g. The essays *being written* will be sent to the Headmaster.

(2) The Perfect Participle Active (formed by *having* + a past participle) e.g. *Having written* the essay, the boy was allowed to go home.

(3) The Perfect Participle Passive (formed by *having been* + a past participle) e.g. All the essays *having been written* and collected, the teacher sent the class home.

Note that the perfect participle refers to an action that took place *before* the time expressed by the main verb.

EXERCISES

I Use appropriate participles as adjectives to complete the following sentences:

(1) I have just finished a very —— book. (2) Film stars are usually very —— men. (3) She is a most —— woman. (4) The weather during our holiday made a most —— start but grew better by degrees. (5) The play last night was very ——. (6) You must be very —— after such a long journey. (7) The writer of that book was hitherto quite ——. (8) He has no beard or moustache but is ——. (9) The first performance of his symphony was rather ——. (10) A —— bottle in the road punctured two of my tyres.

II Rewrite the following sentences so that the words in italics function as adjectives:

(1) There is a little difference between English as it is *written* and as it is *spoken*. (2) The child was *crying* because it had lost sixpence. (3) I like meat to be *well-cooked*. (4) The amount of his fortune is not yet *known*. (5) He gave me a contract he had *signed*.

III Rewrite the following sentences so that the participle is correctly related.

(1) Selecting Hyde Park Corner as a starting place, our route goes along Knightsbridge. (2) Stepping carelessly off the pavement, the bus knocked him down. (3) Climbing to the top of the tower, there is a magnificent view to be seen. (4) Going downstairs, the carpet tripped him. (5) Mocked at by everybody, I can't help feeling sorry for Malvolio. (6) Being Sunday, I shall have a quiet day at home. (7) Already worn out by illness, the bad news killed him. (8) Learning English, the pronunciation always caused me most trouble. (9) Eating his dinner, the telephone bell suddenly rang. (10) Driving a car on frozen roads the brakes should be applied gently.

IV Complete the following sentences with colloquial, accepted expressions containing unattached participles:

(1) Women are shorter than men. (2) The holiday cost less than I had expected. (3) It cost £35. (4) Only members are admitted. (5) We cannot hold him responsible for the accident.

THE GERUND

The gerund is indistinguishable in form from the present participle, but whereas the participle is a verbal adjective, the gerund is a verbal noun.

1. The gerund has most of the characteristics of a noun. Thus, it can be:

(*a*) The subject of a sentence, e.g.

Working in these conditions is a pleasure. The *reading* of the will took place in the lawyer's office.

(*b*) The complement of a sentence, e.g.

The only thing that interests her is *dancing*. Seeing is *believing*. To keep money that you have found is *stealing*.

(*c*) The object of a sentence, e.g.

I remember *seeing* him. She likes *dancing*. Your hair needs *cutting*. Have you finished *writing* your book?

(*d*) The object of a preposition, e.g.

He began by *explaining* the meaning of certain words. She is very fond of *dancing*. I don't like the idea of *spending* so much money. Thank you for *returning* the book that I lent you. He left without *saying* anything.

The only part of a verb that can be the object of a preposition is a gerund. (The *to* of the infinitive, though originally a preposition, no longer functions as one.)

2. But the gerund has some characteristics of a verb:

(*a*) It can take a direct object, e.g.

His hobby is *collecting* stamps. *Meeting* you has been a great pleasure. He left without *saying* anything.

(*b*) It can be modified by an adverb, e.g.

She likes *driving* fast. *Reading* poetry well needs a lot of practice.

3. The gerund can be a noun modifier, e.g.

A *walking*-stick, a *swimming*-pool, a *knitting*-needle, a *reading*-room, *sewing*-cotton, a *dancing*-teacher.

Note the difference in meaning between the participle as a modifier and the gerund as a modifier.

PARTICIPLE	GERUND
a *dancing* bear (= a bear which dances)	a *dancing*-teacher (= a teacher of dancing)
a *travelling* circus	a *travelling*-rug
a *sleeping* child	a *sleeping*-carriage
running water	a *running*-track

Points of distinction between the gerund and the participle are: (1) The participle, which is partly an adjective, can be expanded into an adjective clause. (2) Both the present participle and the noun it qualifies take a strong stress. In the gerund construction only the gerund takes stress. Note, too, the hyphen with the gerund.

4. The gerund is modified by a possessive adjective or by the possessive form of nouns that can take this form.

It's no use (good) *your*[1] *telling* me not to worry.
He was chosen because of *his being* a fully qualified engineer.
She was annoyed at *your saying* that.
Please excuse *my interrupting* you.
We are quite used to *William's grumbling*.
They are looking forward to *Mary's coming*.

This is, perhaps, particularly the case when the gerund is the subject of the sentence, e.g.

Your being right doesn't necessarily mean *my being* wrong.
I am sure *William's sitting* up so late is bad for his health.
Mary's grumbling annoyed her husband, but her *mother's coming* to stay with them was the last straw.

And it is almost always the case after the verbs, *delay, deny, postpone*, e.g.

The firm have *deferred my going* on holiday until next month.

Don't *delay your sending* in of the application form.

He doesn't *deny his breaking* of the agreement.

I had to *postpone my listening* to his plans to a later date.

This construction, however, is a literary one rather than a conversational one. In colloquial speech it is fairly common to hear a personal[2] pronoun instead of the possessive adjective, e.g. '. . . because of *him* being'; '. . . annoyed at *you* saying'; '. . . excuse *me* interrupting you'; '. . . used to *William* grumbling'; '. . . to *Mary* coming'.

---

[1] The possessive form of the pronoun (e.g. *your*) is used after *it's no use* (*no good*), but with a noun the possessive form would be very unusual, e.g. It's no good the *man*/Mr. *Smith*/my *brother*/telling me not to worry (NOT: the *man's*, Mr. *Smith's*, my *brother's*).

[2] C. C. Fries, Professor of English at the University of Michigan, made an investigation into the use of the genitive form of nouns and pronouns with gerunds in current Standard English (American), using as material certain files of informal correspondence in the possession of the U.S. Government. He writes: 'It is clear from the evidence . . . that the use of the inflected genitive form of nouns is not the normal practice before gerunds in Standard English. Only one example occurred in all our material. . . . In the case of pronouns, however, the situation appears to be different. Fifty-two per cent of the cases in Standard English have the genitive form of the pronoun before the verbal' (i.e. the gerund).   *American English Grammar*, page 84.

There are cases not only in colloquial but in literary English where the genitive form would never be used, e.g.

I don't like *strangers interfering* in my affairs.

I am surprised at *someone* so *rich having* difficulty in paying what he owes you.

He said he was in favour of *people working* shorter hours.

He laughed at my *brother and me liking* rice pudding.

The law was passed to prevent *people being* injured.

There is no need for *that being* done.

A shortage of steel would involve *men being* dismissed.

But it could be used in such a sentence as:

I cannot understand *their being* forbidden to go to the meeting.

VERBS FOLLOWED BY THE GERUND

It is not always easy to decide when the gerund should be used after a verb and when the infinitive, but this is the general usage:

1. The following verbs take a gerund after them:

advise, avoid, consider, delay, deny, detest, dislike, endure, enjoy, escape, excuse, fancy, finish, forbid,[1] *imagine, mind, miss, postpone, practise, risk, stop, suggest, understand.*

For example:

I couldn't *avoid meeting* him.

He *enjoys listening* to music.

I couldn't *risk missing* that train.

Do you *mind passing* the salt?

Mind, with the meaning 'object to' is generally used in interrogative and negative sentences, e.g.

Do you *mind* answering my question? I *don't mind* working overtime.

It can occasionally be used in affirmative sentences when it is in answer to a question, 'Do you mind . . .?' e.g.

Do you *mind* my smoking? Yes, I *mind* very much.

---

[1] This verb can be used also with the accusative infinite construction e.g. He forbade *me to drive* his car.

2. The gerund is also used after nearly all 'phrasal verbs', e.g.
You must *go on working*. He wants to *give up smoking*. She *burst out crying*. You must *keep on trying*.

3. It is used too, after the phrases: *it's no good, it's no use, is worth, to be fond of, capable of, sick of, look forward to*, e.g.

It's no use crying over spilt milk.
If a thing is *worth doing*, it's *worth doing* well.
I'm *tired of meeting* the same people day after day.

VERBS FOLLOWED BY THE INFINITIVE

The following verbs take the infinitive after them:
(*a*) all the special finites, (*b*) the following verbs:

dare, decide, desire, endeavour, expect, guarantee, hope, mean (= intend), *offer, pretend, promise, refuse, swear, undertake, want, wish*, e.g.

You *ought to go* there. He *has to see* the dentist tomorrow.
You must *endeavour to do* better.
I hope you *mean to do* better.
He *wants to pay* a visit to England.

VERBS FOLLOWED BY THE GERUND OR THE INFINITIVE

The following verbs may take the gerund or the infinitive, sometimes depending on the meaning to be expressed:

begin, can't bear, cease, continue, dread, forget, hate, intend, learn, like, love, omit, prefer, regret, remember, need, neglect, start, try, e.g.

The teacher said, 'You can *begin writing* now', and the children *began to write*.

I *hate lying* and *cheating*. I *hate to see* cruelty and injustice.

The buses have *ceased running* (or: The buses *ceased to run*).

The first sentence in the last example would probably mean 'They have ceased running for today, but they will start again tomorrow'; the second sentence would mean: 'They will not run again for a long time, perhaps never again.'

With *remember*, the infinitive is used for a *future* action, and means: 'not forget', e.g.

Please *remember to bring* your book tomorrow.

The gerund is used for a past event and means: 'call to mind', e.g.

I *remember hearing* Schnabel play the 'Emperor' Concerto.

With *forget*, the infinitive is used with the meaning 'fail to remember', e.g.

I'm afraid he will *forget to write* to me.

With the gerund it means 'lose the memory of', e.g.

I shall never *forget seeing* the Swiss Alps for the first time.

With *stop* and *try* also the meaning varies according to whether the infinitive or the gerund follows:

He stopped to eat means that he ceased doing something else in order to eat.

He stopped eating means that he discontinued eating.

Try with the infinitive has the meaning 'make an attempt', e.g.

You must *try to be* more careful. He will *try to meet* us at seven o'clock.

Try with the gerund means 'make an experiment', e.g.

Have you ever *tried cooking* meat in wine instead of water? He *tried gardening, keeping* pigs, *rearing* poultry, but didn't succeed in any of them.

After the Verbs of Perception, e.g. *hear, see, feel* (see pp. 169, 198, and 231), *watch, notice*, etc., either the infinitive or the -*ing* form can be used, e.g.

I heard him *come* in last night.

I heard him *coming* in last night.

I saw him *work* in the garden yesterday.

I saw him *working* in the garden yesterday.

With the infinitive we are more interested in the fact of the completion of the action. 'I heard him come in . . . so I know that he did come in.'

'I saw him work . . . so I know that he did work here yesterday.'

With the *-ing* form our interest was more in the continuity or the performing of the action. 'I heard him coming in . . . and what a lot of noise he made!'

'I saw him working in the garden . . . and noticed how interested he was in it.'

EXERCISES

I In the following sentences indicate whether the '-ing' form is used as (*a*) part of a Continuous Tense, (*b*) a participle used adjectivally (*c*) a gerund.

   (1) She was lying down because she was tired.
   Iago was a lying villain.
   Lying is a cowardly habit.

   (2) The moonlight was dancing on the water.
   The dancing waves glittered in the sun.
   Some people's greatest pleasure is dancing.

   (3) We shall have no money left; we are spending far too much.
   The spending habit is very easy to form.
   He is quite penniless after all his reckless spending.

II Construct two sentences each containing a gerund taking a direct object, and three sentences each containing a gerund modified by an adverb.

III In the following phrases insert hyphens where necessary, giving a reason in each case.

   (1) a motoring coat. (2) a wandering minstrel. (3) climbing boots. (4) marching feet. (5) a towering cliff. (6) a begging letter. (7) a climbing expedition. (8) a hunting horn. (9) a waiting room. (10) playing cards.

IV Construct sentences containing the gerund after any of the verbs in the following list which admit of this construction:

   enjoy, hope, believe, understand, advise, criticise, postpone, help, distinguish, propose.

V Complete the following, using a gerund or an infinitive in the part that you add:

   (1) It's hardly worth while . . . (2) I must remember . . . (3) They are quite incapable of . . . (4) I wouldn't dare . . . (5) Let me know if you decide . . . (6) We are sick and tired of . . . (7) I expect . . . (8) They keep

I

on . . . (9) She has a habit of . . . (10) He congratulated me on . . . (11) The company undertakes . . . (12) He promised . . . (13) You will never regret . . . (14) I don't feel equal to . . . (15) This thing is worth . . . (16) The firm guarantees . . . (17) I hope you don't mind . . . (18) I must try to stop . . . (19) Please excuse . . . (20) I wish . . . (21) They tried to keep on . . . (22) Reading English is easier than . . . (23) I know my work isn't good but I mean . . . (24) I apologise for . . . (25) It's no use . . . (26) My friend wants . . . (27) He has started . . . (28) He always avoids . . . (29) I am not used to . . . (30) I used to . . . (31) We always look forward to . . . (32) I prefer . . . to . . . (33) She does nothing but . . . (34) You had better . . . (35) He enjoys . . . (36) He kept on . . . (37) He can't help . . . (38) I dare not . . . (39) He can't bear . . . (40) They began . . . (41) He is very fond of . . . (42) He won't risk . . .

VI Explain the difference in meaning between:

'He stopped *talking*', and 'He stopped to *talk*'.

'I remember *paying* the milkman', and 'Remember to *pay* the milkman'.

CHAPTER EIGHTEEN

ADVERBS

Adverbs, like adjectives, are modifiers; generally they modify or add to the meaning of verbs, adjectives or other adverbs, e.g.

(Modifying a verb) He ran *quickly*. Come *here*. I went to the dentist *yesterday*.

(Modifying an adjective) It is *very* hot today. Are you *quite* comfortable? His work isn't good *enough* for a scholarship.

(Modifying an adverb) He plays *extremely* well. She drives *too* fast.

They may, occasionally, modify a noun or noun equivalent, e.g.

the *very*[1] thing I wanted; the *above* sentences; the *off*-side of the road; in *after* years; the *up* train; the *under*-secretary of the *then* Prime Minister; Is that car *really* yours?

Or a phrase, e.g.

I am *almost* through my work; they live *nearly* on top of the hill; his remarks were not *quite* to the point.

Or a whole sentence, e.g.

Fortunately, I remembered in time who he was.

Indeed, I won't do it.

Some adverbs are single, indivisible words (e.g. *yet*, *down*, *then*, *too*). Others are obviously formed from adjectives by the addition of a suffix (e.g. *quickly*, *clearly*, *splendidly*); others are formed from two words (e.g. *anywhere*, *sometimes*, *however*) but have become so fused together that the two parts have made a word whose meaning is different from the meanings of the individual parts. In some cases this fusion has not been complete and the two or three individual words, generally containing a preposition and a noun, are written separately, e.g.

[1] It might be better to consider that these words, though generally adverbs, are in these examples functioning as adjectives, just as in phrases like: The *ups* and *downs* of life; the *ins* and *outs* of business, the 'adverbs' are functioning as nouns.

next week, this morning, in front, at the side, with pleasure, at first, the day after tomorrow, on the outskirts of the city, not in the least, as a matter of fact. These are adverb phrases.[1]

THE CLASSIFICATION OF ADVERBS ACCORDING TO MEANING

Adverbs can be classified according to their meaning, i.e. according to the way in which they answer questions asking *when, where, how* an action was done.

1. Adverbs that express HOW an action was done, e.g.

The little boy behaved *badly*.

The birds sang *sweetly*.

Every soldier fought *bravely* and *well*.

are ADVERBS OF MANNER.

Adverbs of Manner commonly used are: *actively, anyhow, boldly, calmly, carefully, distinctly, easily, equally, fast, gladly, how, intentionally, late, promptly, quickly, quietly, simply, sincerely, still, suddenly, together, willingly, wisely, wrongly,* etc.

2. Adverbs that express WHEN an action is or was done are ADVERBS OF TIME, *Examples:*

The boy said, 'I will do the work *tomorrow*'.

The teacher said, 'You will do it *now*'.

Call me *early:* I want to see the sunrise.

What's going to happen *next*.

Adverbs of time commonly used are: *after(wards), already, before, immediately, late(ly), once, presently, shortly, soon, still, today (tomorrow, tonight), when, yesterday, yet.*

Included among adverbs of time are the 'Adverbs of Frequency', e.g. *always, often, frequently,* etc. These are words that answer the question 'How often'. They often differ from adverbs of time in the position they occupy in the sentence.[2] Here are examples:

He *always* does his work well.

She has *never* done that before.

I have not been to Paris very *often*.

You will *seldom*, in fact *hardly ever*, hear that said.

He is *sometimes* right.

[1] For Adverb Clauses see pages 337–51.   [2] See page 188.

Other adverbs of frequency are: *continually, frequently, generally, occasionally, rarely, regularly, scarcely, hardly ever*.

Note that *ever* is generally accompanied by a negative modifier like *hardly, scarcely* or *not*, e.g.

> We *hardly ever* see you now; you are *scarcely ever* at home. *Don't ever* say that again.

It is rarely used alone except in questions and conditional clauses,[1] e.g.

> Do you *ever* see George now that he has left London? (*Question*)
> If you *ever* see George, give him my kind regards. (*Conditional Clause*)

3. Adverbs that express WHERE an action is or was done are ADVERBS OF PLACE. *Examples:*

> I shall stand *here*.
> The child opened the door of the cage and the bird flew *out*.
> I've looked *everywhere* for my new pen.

The term 'adverb of place' covers the wider field of 'motion to', 'motion from', 'separation', etc., e.g.

> Come *nearer*. They walked slowly *past/by*. The sailors went *ashore*. He paced *to* and *fro* all night. She drew the curtains *apart*.

Adverbs of place commonly used are: *above, abroad, across, along, around, away, back, below, down, downstairs, in, nowhere, on, somewhere, there, through, together, under, up, upstairs, where*.

4. There are other adverbs that express 'TO WHAT EXTENT' or 'to what degree', e.g.

> This coffee is *very* bad.
> It has been a long journey but we are *nearly* there now.
> Are you *quite* sure we are on the right road?
> That's *all* right.
> He spoke French *too* quickly for me to follow him.

There is also the very colloquial: I'm *awfully/terribly/frightfully* sorry I'm late.

---

[1] For conditional clauses see page 343, 347–51.

These words are ADVERBS OF DEGREE. Adverbs of degree are not generally used with verbs; they are used with adjectives or other adverbs,[1] e.g.

very good; *quite* sure; *too* quickly; *nearly* there; *all* right

There are many degree adverbs. Some of the most commonly used are: *absolutely, completely, deeply* ('I'm *deeply* sorry'), *distinctly* ('This work is *distinctly* better'), *enormously, entirely, greatly, equally, exactly* ('*exactly* right'), *extremely, just* ('*just* right'), *much, partly, perfectly* ('*perfectly* correct'), *practically, rather, scarcely, slightly, thoroughly, utterly*.

5. The classes given are the most common types of adverbs, but there are also words which, in addition to expressing the idea of time or place, are also used in questions, e.g.

When are you going away? *Where* are you sending him?

These are INTERROGATIVE ADVERBS. The others are *how?* and *why?* e.g.

How did you come here?
Why did you say that?

6. The words *Yes, certainly, surely*, etc., are known as ADVERBS OF AFFIRMATION, the words *perhaps, maybe*, etc., as ADVERBS OF PROBABILITY and the words *no*[2] and *not, never* as ADVERBS OF NEGATION for obvious reasons. But these words are, especially in conversation, really abbreviated sentences, e.g.

'Do you know Mr. Smith?' '*Yes*.' (= Yes, I know him.)
'Is George there?' '*No*.' (= No, he isn't here.)
'Will you help me?' '*Certainly*.' (= Yes, I will help you.)
'Do you agree?' 'Oh, *quite*.' (= Oh yes, I agree.)
'Will you do what he wants?' '*Never!*' (= I shall never do what he wants.)

Note that both *Yes* and *No* may be used either to agree or to disagree with the previous speaker; but *Yes* can only accompany an affirmative statement and *No* a negative one.

---

[1] Some of them can be used with verbs, e.g.
　　The shock *nearly* killed him.
　　I *quite* like his pictures.

[2] *No* of course can also be a determinative (see pages 89–96).

Other adverbs of affirmation that are used as abbreviated sentences, are:

absolutely, certainly, decidedly, evidently, indeed, entirely, naturally, obviously, precisely, surely, willingly, and the adverb phrases *very well, of course.*

7. ADVERBS OF QUANTITY or ADVERBS OF AMOUNT AND NUMBER form another group. Here are examples:

Henry works very *little;* not nearly as *much* as George.

William has won the prize *twice;* no one else has won it more than *once.*

8. The adverbs *when* and *where,* which we have already noted, are sometimes used to introduce a clause.[1] They then take the place of a relative pronoun + a preposition, e.g.

I remember the day *when* (= on which) you told me you were going to America.

That is the room *where* (= in which) the Rembrandt picture is hung.

If *when* and *where* are used like this, they are RELATIVE ADVERBS.

THE FORMATION OF ADVERBS

1. Adverbs of manner are frequently formed by adding *-ly*[2] to an adjective, e.g.

Adjective	*Adverb*
She is a *quick* worker.	She works *quickly.*
He is a *careful* driver.	He drives *carefully.*
They are *noisy* children.	They play *noisily.*[3]
She gave a *merry* laugh.	She laughed *merrily.*[3]
He gave a *full* explanation.	He explained the whole thing *fully.*[3]

Adverbs are not usually formed from adjectives that end in *-ly,* that is from such adjectives as *manly, silly, fatherly, lively, brotherly,* etc. Instead of an adverb, an adverbial phrase is used, e.g. 'in a silly way', 'in a fatherly manner', etc.

[1] See page 328.
[2] The *-ly* developed from Old English *-lic* (= like).
[3] Note the usual change of *-y* to *-i,* and the omission of one *-l* when the adjective ends in *-ll.*

2. But there are other ways of forming the adverb; for example by using the same form as the adjective.

ADVERBS AND ADJECTIVES WITH THE SAME FORM

Adjective	*Adverb*
That is a very *fast* train.	It goes very *fast*.
He is a *hard* worker.	He works *hard*.

(The adverb *hardly*, e.g., 'He *hardly* ever works' gives a very different meaning.)

He has gone to the *Far* East.	We didn't walk very *far*.
It is a *straight* road.	It runs *straight* for miles.
He spoke in a *low* voice.	He spoke *low*[1] but clearly.
'The *early* bird catches the worm.'	Very *early* in his career Shakespeare wrote *Love's Labour's Lost*.
Take a *clean* sheet of paper.	The prisoner got *clean* away (= completely).
	The man was *clean*-shaven (= without beard or moustache).
I saw a *dead* bird in the garden.	'*Dead* Slow' (traffic notice).
	The wind is *dead* against us.
	The man was *dead* drunk.
Have you *enough* time to do the work?	He didn't try hard *enough*.
He went on a *long* journey.	I shan't be *long*.

ADVERBS WITH TWO FORMS

Frequently, both the adjective form and the 'adjective + -*ly*' form are used as Adverbs, sometimes, but not always, with different meanings, e.g.

Adjective	*Adverb*
There is a *bright* moon tonight.	The moon shines *bright* (or *brightly*).

[1] The word *lowly* is an adjective, not an adverb, e.g. 'Henry VIII's great Chancellor, Cardinal Wolsey, was of *lowly* (i.e. humble) parentage; his father was a butcher.'

Adjective	*Adverb*
The goods were very *cheap*.	I bought them *cheap* (or *cheaply*).
I went by a *direct* route.	The goods will be sent *direct* to you and not to our agent.

NOTE: In 'I will return *directly*', the adverb *directly* = 'at once'.

That is a very *high* building.	The birds are flying *high*. He was *highly* praised for his work.
James was *late* for his lesson.	He came *late*. I have not heard from him *lately*. (= for some time.)
He is not a very *near* relation.	The time is drawing *near* for my visit to France. I *nearly* missed my train.
She is a very *pretty* girl.	That is a *pretty* (= fairly) good picture. The little girl danced *prettily*.
There is a *short* way home through the woods.	The car stopped *short* only a few inches from where I stood. He will come *shortly*. (= in a short time.)
I didn't want to waken him; he was in a *sound* sleep.	He was sleeping *sound* (or *soundly*). In the football match Oxford were *soundly* (= decisively) beaten by Cambridge.
It was a *fair* fight.	You must play *fair* (or *fairly*). He was treated quite *fairly*. He did *fairly* (= moderately) well in his examination.
It was a *clear* sunny day.	Stand *clear* of the doors of the train. You must *clearly* understand that this is your last chance. 'I said it very loud and *clear;* I went and shouted in his ear.' [1]

[1] Lewis Carroll, *Alice Through the Looking-Glass*.

I*

Adjective	*Adverb*
It was a *close* (= airless) afternoon.	Keep *close* to me. The statement ran to twenty *closely*-written pages.
He is a *firm* friend of the family.	If we stand *firm*, I *firmly* believe we shall succeed.
I want a *sharp* pencil.	Turn *sharp* right at the cross-roads. The teacher spoke *sharply* to the boy.
He is a *slow* driver.	'Go *slow*' (traffic notice). The hours pass *slowly* when you can't sleep.
He was wearing very *tight* shoes.	Hold *tight;* the plane is going to dive. The passengers were *tightly* packed in the train.
This is a good, *wide* road.	The sleepwalker's eyes were *wide* open but he didn't seem to be seeing anything. The two people differed *widely* in their outlook.
I think we are on the *wrong* road.	It was at the cross-roads that we went *wrong*. He was *wrongly* accused of the crime.
Are we on the *right* road?	Turn *right* at the next cross-road. He was *rightly* blamed for the accident.

NOTE: With verbs like *taste, smell, feel*, etc. (in such sentences as: The milk *tastes sour*. The rose *smells sweet*. The fur *feels soft*) an adjective (*sour, sweet, soft*), not an adverb, is used. The verbs *taste, smell, feel*, as used here, are more or less equivalent to *is*, e.g.

The milk *is* sour. The fur *is* soft to the touch.

There are a few adverbs that have been formed from nouns by the addition of a suffix or a prefix, e.g.

(a) with suffix -*ly*:

He comes here *daily/weekly/monthly/hourly*,[1] etc.

The shed was lifted *bodily* (i.e. in one piece) and carried to another part of the garden.

[1] But these may be adjectives used as adverbs.

(b) with suffix *-ways, -wards, -wise:*[1]

The path was so narrow we had to walk *sideways.*
He went *backwards/forwards/homewards.*
He sat with his legs *crosswise.*

(c) with the prefix *a-*, e.g.:

ashore, aloft, abroad.

EXERCISES

I Pick out and classify the adverbs or adverb phrases in
the following passage:

We sometimes go to a football match (my wife,
however, rather reluctantly). Last Saturday we saw a
match that we greatly enjoyed. The play was fast and
skilful, the forwards manoeuvred rapidly and shot
hard and straight, the defence tackled resolutely and
the referee controlled the game firmly while, at the
same time, using his whistle with discretion. Frankly,
I much prefer rugby, but I could hardly take Janet to
a rugby match; she would never understand the
game. There, in that stadium on Saturday, she at least
knew when a goal had been scored, without having to
be told. She even knows some of the rules. At one
point I was about to tell her why a throw-in had to be
taken again when she told me she already knew: the
first throw had not been properly done.

II Mention six adverbs in each of the following classes:

Manner, Time, Frequency, Place, Degree.

Then choose one from each class and write a sentence
using it.

III Complete the following with an adverb or adverbial
phrase of the kind indicated in brackets at the end
of each sentence:

(1) He was —— anxious about the danger of fire.
(degree) (2) ——I don't agree with your opinions.
(time) (3) These two routes are —— hilly. (degree)
(4) We —— go to London to hear a concert. (frequency) (5) She has left her glasses ——. (place) (6)
——is the shop I was told to visit? (place) (7) ——
we shall go if the weather is fine. (probability) (8) We
shall —— submit to the enemy. (negation) (9) I'm

---

[1] Historically, these are genitive, dative or accusative cases of nouns;
in Old English these forms were often used adverbially.

—— determined to finish this exercise tonight. (degree) (10) He has —— attempted to pass that examination. (number)

IV Construct pairs of sentences in which the first of each pair uses one of the following words as an adjective and the second uses one as an adverb:

late, near, still, stiff, enough, wide, high, straight, far, direct.

V What are the adverbial forms of:

good, bad, little, side, back.

VI (*a*) Form adverbs or adverb equivalents from the following adjectives:

skilful, easy, fast, gay, friendly.

(*b*) Use all the following words in sentences as adverbs:

hard, hardly, dead, deathly, round, clean, stone, stonily, ice, icily, direct, directly, easy, foul, deep, low.

VII How many adverbs can you form with other words using *-ways, -wise* or *-wards* as a suffix? Use each in a sentence.

VIII Construct ten sentences, each containing one of the following adverb phrases and name the class to which each belongs:

on top of, at the far end, not in the slightest, hardly at all, all over the place, during the week, very late, round the corner, with pleasure, on the whole.

IX In which of the following sentences are the italicised words adverbs?

(1) One lies *soft* on a feather bed. (2) Incense smells *aromatic*. (3) Explorers often have to travel *rough*. (4) The climber fell *headlong* down the precipice. (5) '*Uneasy* lies the head that wears a crown.' (6) They struggled *hard* and *long* to win the match. (7) His unscrupulous rivals did him a grave *wrong*. (8) '*Fair* stood the wind for France.' (9) The door stood *half* open. (10) Though the current ran *fast* the bridge stood *fast* against it.

X Add adverbs to these sentences as indicated:

(1) I think it —— (*degree*) disgraceful. (2) You are an —— (*degree*) lucky boy. (3) That's —— (*degree*) useless. (4) This work is —— (*degree*) good, but not so good as what you —— (*frequency*) do. (5) Do you

—— (*frequency*) go to the pictures? ——, (*negation*) but I —— (*frequency*) go to the theatre. (6) Do you drink —— (*quantity*)? ——, (*negation*) only very —— (*frequency*). (7) Will you be —— (*place*) —— (*time*)? No, —— (*degree*) a few days. (8) I —— (*manner*) heard you tell him he need not do it. (9) 'Will you help me?' —— (*affirmation*) —— (*affirmation*). (10) The orator spoke so —— (*manner*) that he won his audience completely over. (11) I arrived at the moment —— (*relative*) the telephone bell rang. (12) Send him to a nursing home —— (*relative*), he will be taken care of. (13) John came home —— (*degree*) tired after his long day's work.

The Classification of Adverbs according to Position

There are three positions for adverbs in a sentence:

A. Front-Position, i.e. as the first word in a sentence.

B. Mid-Position, coming before the verb.

C. End-Position, i.e. as the last word in a sentence.

Front-Position Adverbs

1. The following can be used only in this position:

(*a*) INTERROGATIVE ADVERBS, *How? When? Where? Why?* e.g. *Where* are you going? *Why* did you say that? *When* shall I see you again?

(*b*) ADVERBS OF AFFIRMATION and ADVERBS OF NEGATION, e.g.
Yes, I know him quite well.
No, that is not correct.

2. Adverbs which are 'sentence modifiers'[1] are generally, but not quite always,[2] front-position adverbs, e.g.

Still, in spite of what you say, I don't think it is true.
Altogether, I don't think we have done too badly to get £400 for our old car.

Compare the following sentences. In those marked A the adverbs modify verbs or adjectives in the usual way. In those marked B, they modify a sentence. Note how the meaning of

---

[1] See page 251.　　　[2] See examples B 4, 5, 6 on next page.

the adverbs in the A sentences differs from that of their counterparts in the B sentences.

A	B
(1) I can't give you the answer *now*.	*Now*, this is what happened.
(2) I didn't think he would be *so* silly.	*So*, you don't believe what I told you?
(3) He asked for the money so I paid him *there* and *then*.	*There*, do you believe me now?
	Then let us get on with the work.
(4) The cat walked quite *surely* along the narrow wall.	You *surely* (*Surely*, you) won't pay that price.
(5) She spoke simply and *naturally*.	I couldn't, *naturally* (*Naturally*, I couldn't), agree to a proposal like that
(6) He is *fortunately* married.	He is, *fortunately* (*Fortunately*, he is), married.

3. In exclamatory sentences[1] the adverb used always has front position, e.g.

Away they went! *Here* he comes! *There* goes Helen! *How* well he speaks English! *How* quickly time has gone!

Note that in these exclamatory sentences with 'how', the other adverb (*well*, *quickly*) also has front position.

4. Some adverbs can be used at the beginning of a sentence but are not confined to that position, e.g.

Sometimes he sits and thinks, and *sometimes* he just sits.

Yesterday I went to a football match; *today* I am playing tennis; *tonight* I am going to the theatre and *tomorrow* I am going swimming.

This could equally well be written:

I went to a football match *yesterday;* I am playing tennis *today*, etc.

[1] See also page 316.

There are a considerable number of adverbs that may have front position. Some of them are:

afterwards, then, there, therefore, anyhow, now, so, soon, once, only, (un)fortunately, luckily, evidently, personally, possibly, suddenly, consequently, usually, naturally, certainly, really, perhaps, surely, indeed, next, occasionally, accordingly, however, first (secondly, thirdly, etc.*), originally, yet, eventually;*

and a large number of adverbial phrases, e.g.

by and by, up to now, before then, until then, just then, just now, by now, every day, of course, how far/long/much/often, at first/last/present/least; in future; later on; all at once; some day; sooner or later, etc.

INVERSION OF SUBJECT AND VERB WITH ADVERBS

(1) An adverb or adverb phrase which does not normally have front position may have it, usually for emphasis. In this case, inversion of subject and verb may occur. This usage is in many cases literary and emotional rather than colloquial, e.g.

Often *have I* heard it said that he is not to be trusted.
Twice within my lifetime *have world wars taken place.*
Many a time as a boy *have I climbed* that hill.
Near the church *was* an old ruined *cottage.*
By his side *sat his faithful dog.*
Here *is the book* that you wanted.
Such *was the tale* he told me.

(2) With a negative adverb or adverb equivalent in front position, inversion of subject and verb must occur, e.g.

In **no** circumstances *would I agree* to such a proposal.
Not until all attempts at negotiation had failed *did the men* decide to go on strike.
Nowhere else *will you find* so many happy, contented people.
Not only *has he* a first-class brain but he is also a tremendously hard worker.
No sooner *had they been granted* one increase of pay than they asked for another.

Seldom *is it wise* to disregard the advice that he gives.
'**Never** in the field of human conflict *has so much* been owed by so many to so few.'[1]

(3) Inversion must also occur when *only* is in front position, and not qualifying the subject, e.g.

Only when all attempts at negotiation had failed, *did the men* decide to go on strike.
Only with the full agreement of everyone *can we* hope to succeed.
Only in north-west Scotland *have I* seen such scenery as that.

(4) When unstressed *there* is in front position:

There *is no doubt* that the man is guilty.
There's *a letter* for you on your desk.
There *was a frost* last night, wasn't there?
There *is* still *a lot of work* to be done before the house will be ready for occupation.
There *are many people* still with too low a standard of living.

(5) In some exclamatory sentences introduced by *there* or *here* (see pp. 262, 316):

I heard a knock at the door and **there** *was George*.

Mid-Position Adverbs

An important group of mid-position adverbs are the adverbs of frequency. With them can be grouped such adverbs as *almost, nearly, quite, hardly, just*. Their usual position is immediately in front of the principal verb, e.g.

I	*always*	sleep	with my window open.
He	*never*	forgets	his wife's birthday.
We	*often*	wish	that you lived near us.
I	*almost*	forgot	to tell you this.
I	*hardly*	know	how to thank you.
He	*just*	picked	up his hat and walked away.

[1] Winston Churchill speaking about the R.A.F. in 1940.

But when a special finite is used with the verb, the adverb comes between the special finite and the main verb, e.g.

Henry's work	is	*always*	carefully done.
Richard	was	*never*	a very good footballer.
You	should	*never*	make that mistake again.
They	are	*just*	leaving the house.
The baby	can	*nearly*	walk.

If, however, the special finite is used emphatically the frequency adverbs precede it, e.g.

'Henry's work seems carefully done.' 'It *always* **is** carefully done.'

'Richard isn't a very good footballer now.' 'He *never* **was** a good footballer.'

This type of sentence usually becomes a 'Short Answer' in conversation, e.g.

'Henry's work seems carefully done to-day.' '*It always is.*'

'Richard isn't a good footballer.' '*He never was.*'

'Can you get a good lunch on the train?' '*You sometimes can.*'

Other examples of mid-position use of adverbs:

I *accidentally* upset the water jug. He *actually* told me it wasn't my business. They *anxiously* awaited the result. The soldiers *bravely* attacked the strong position. He *definitely* refused to do the job. I *deeply* regret having spoken. I *distinctly* heard him say that.[1] When the order was given they *immediately* sprang to their feet. I *almost* made that same mistake again. He *just* opened the door and walked in. He *then* told me what he wanted. That *indeed* surprised me very much. He *last* wrote to me a year ago. I *now* come to a very important matter. Having bought this land, he *next* proceeded to plant it with apple trees. They *perhaps* disliked what you said. I *rather* hoped that you would come to live near us. I *really* think that you are expecting too much. You

[1] Compare: 'I heard *distinctly* what he said', which has a different meaning.

once said that you had played football for England. He *already* knows what I think about him. I *nearly* missed my train this morning. He *quite* realizes that you can't help everyone.

All these adverbs can be used between the auxiliary and the main verb, e.g.

I have *accidentally* upset the water jug. They are *anxiously* awaiting the result. He will *definitely* refuse the job. I had *almost* made the same mistake again. I shall *now* come to an important matter. He has *already* heard what I think about him. He will *quite* realize that you can't help everyone.

End-Position Adverbs

1. The end position is the most natural one for adverbs, and the great majority are placed there. If there are several adverbs, the order is generally: manner, place, time, e.g.

Harry worked *well here yesterday*.

The fundamental structure of a sentence (statement) is SUBJECT + VERB + OBJECT + ADVERBIAL, and the general principle is that the object (or complement) should not be separated from its verb by having an adverb or adverb phrase interposed. So, if to the sentence: 'Mary sang that song.' we want to add 'beautifully', we must say: 'Mary sang that song *beautifully*.' NOT: 'Mary sang *beautifully* that song.'

The adverb should be put *after* the object or complement, e.g.

Henry does his work *well;* Richard generally does his work *badly*. George works *hard*. Robert drives *fast;* William drives *slowly*. Peggy played the accompaniment to Mary's song *perfectly*.[1] They flew to Paris *yesterday;* they hope to visit Lucille *tomorrow*. I like learning English *very much*.[2] Have you been learning English *long?*

---

[1] But in a passive construction the adverb may come after the auxiliary but before the main part of the verb, e.g.

Peggy's accompaniment was *perfectly* played.

[2] H. D. Streatfeild (*English Language Teaching*, Vol. III, No. 2) makes the point, very appositely, that there is a lot of difference between: 'I don't like wine very much' and 'I don't like very much

2. Almost the only adverbs that cannot be used in the end position are negative adverbs like *not, hardly, scarcely, never,* and degree adverbs like *very, too, quite, just, almost,* etc. Almost the only occasion when this is not the case is in such sentences as:

Turn *off* the gas. Help me to lift *up* the table.

which can be used as well as:

'Turn the gas *off*.' 'Help me to lift the table *up*.'

Note that if the object is a pronoun, the adverb must come at the end.

Turn it *off*. NOT: Turn off it.
Lift it *up*. NOT: Lift up it.

3. If a sentence has no direct object, the adverb generally comes immediately after the verb, e.g.

Mr. Owen died *yesterday* at the age of 85.
The boys have gone *there* to play tennis.

4. If the object is a clause, the adverb may be placed before it in order to avoid ambiguity, e.g.

'He told me *yesterday* what George said.'

which is not the same as:

'He told me what George said *yesterday*.'

5. We have noted that adverbs of definite time, e.g. *yesterday, today, tomorrow* and adverbials like *on Wednesday, next Christmas, in a few minutes,* etc., come at the end of the sentence. But if we wish to emphasize the time, the adverb is frequently put at the beginning, e.g.

Today I have worked indoors, but *tomorrow* I shall have a day in the garden.
Very soon we shall get the result of your examination.
Every now and then a little boat came into the harbour.

6. If there are two or more adverbs (or adverbials) of time, the more detailed expression comes before the more general, e.g.

The next meeting will be on *Thursday, March 26th,* 1960.

---

wine.' (In the first sentence *very much* is adverbial and means 'particularly', 'greatly'. In the second one it is adjectival and means 'a large quantity of'.)

7. An adverb of degree or manner is generally put before adjectives, participles and other adverbs, e.g.

He was *extremely* clever. You can't be *too* careful. He played *very* well. The glass was *badly* broken. The *dangerously* wounded soldier was *immediately* hurried to hospital. She is a *really* well-educated girl. You spoke *too* soon.

8. But the adverb *enough* comes after the adjective or participle.

That is good *enough* for me.

He ought to know the way to Oxford; he has gone there often *enough*.

9. Some adverbs, e.g. *only, sometimes, then, even, perhaps*, can occur in various positions in the sentence, sometimes expressing a difference of meaning, e.g.

Sometimes I am quite hopeful about the situation.

I am *sometimes* quite hopeful about the situation.

I am quite hopeful about the situation *sometimes*.

Then I went home. I *then* went home. I went home *then*.

Perhaps I was mistaken. I was, *perhaps*, mistaken. I was mistaken, *perhaps*.

Only goes immediately next to (usually before) the word it qualifies:

Only John admires his brother. John *only* admires his brother. John admires *only* his brother. John admires his *only* brother. (Here, of course, *only* is an adjective.) John admires his brother *only*.

This is particularly important in written English. In spoken English there is a tendency to put *only* before the verb and to make distinction of meaning by a varying stress and intonation. Other adverbs and adverbials that can be used in front, middle or end positions are: *(un)fortunately, especially, possibly, really, certainly, exactly, merely, mostly, simply, anyhow, about, however, indeed, altogether, not, no doubt, of course, at least, at once.*

EXERCISES

I Put the adverbs in the best position in the sentence, making any necessary changes in punctuation or word order:

(1) Charles is working; he has not retired. (yet; still)
(2) Joe works hard; he is too stupid to pass his examination. (however) (3) What Christopher said was wrong. (altogether; yesterday) (4) The whole family is going out. (tomorrow) (5) We have our dinner at seven o'clock. (generally) (6) We have had our dinner at seven o'clock. (always) (7) James has lots of porridge for breakfast. (sometimes) (8) James is hungry. (sometimes) (9) He went about in old clothes: he was very rich. (actually) (10) You don't need as much as that. (surely) (11) He goes about in old clothes as a rule, but I saw him with a brand-new coat on. (actually; yesterday) (12) She's a pretty girl. (rather) (13) It's a nice day. (quite) (14) We all went to town. (last week) (15) I will meet you. (at Victoria Station, under the clock, next Tuesday, at 3 p.m.) (16) He is becoming a chain-smoker. (fast) (17) When they left the field, the team looked beaten. (well) (18) Has he done the work? (well) (19) Has the work been done? (well) (20) He reads music. (easily) (21) I don't think we have spent too long on the journey. (altogether) (22) The train went! (away) (23) How the holidays have passed! (quickly) (24) I walk five miles every morning. (always) (25) We told them that the matter did not concern them. (actually)

II Construct sentences using the following words as 'front-position' adverbs:

down, however, along, yet, how.

III Read aloud and explain the difference in meaning between:

(1) I never did well; Well, I never did!
(2) My friend speaks English well; my friend speaks good English.
(3) Altogether, I consider it wrong; I consider it altogether wrong.
(4) Alice doesn't much like milk in her tea; She doesn't like much milk in her tea.
(5) Still, I believe him to be innocent; I still believe him to be innocent.
(6) She is always late; she always is late.

IV Compose sentences with each of the following adverbs in more than one position:

much; only; altogether; well; however; never; distinctly; afterwards; out; away; along.

V Correct the following sentences:

(1) Joseph speaks well Spanish. (2) Always I have trouble in December. (3) My parents often have told me this. (4) Let us tomorrow meet at two o'clock outside Madame Tussaud's. (5) You have enough said for the moment. (6) They perhaps will not after all go. (7) The meeting is indefinitely postponed. (8) I caught the sound of his voice distinctly. (9) He knows what already the punishment will be. (10) They will accept your offer tomorrow definitely. (11) When we lifted up it, we found underneath the money hidden. (12) He is hardly never late. (13) He generally always arrives on time. (14) They rather sometimes take too much to drink. (15) I always nearly go to London on Saturdays. (16) She quite never can act well. (17) Almost I had made the same mistake again. (18) They have to quite realise that they can't do as they like exactly. (19) The soloist played beautifully that concerto. (20) He needs badly a holiday. (21) A new contingent of visitors from time to time arrived. (22) We will today begin to study the use of Prepositions in English. (23) They every now and then come to stay with us. (23) We on Friday shall go away for the week-end. (25) The next concert in this series will take place in the Town Hall on 26th May, Friday. (26) I am quite really certain he has made a mistake. (27) Only once I have done that.

VI Construct a reply to each of the following remarks, using an auxiliary verb emphatically and an adverb of frequency.

(1) You're looking very cheerful this morning. (2) He should never go out till he has finished his homework. (3) You should drive carefully. (4) They will need warm clothing for winter days. (5) He should not spend his money so extravagantly.

COMPARISON OF ADVERBS

Comparison of adverbs is similar to comparison of adjectives.

(1) Adverbs of one syllable form their comparative in *-er* and their superlative in *-est*, e.g.

near — nearer — nearest; hard — harder — hardest; soon — sooner — soonest.

Early and *often*[1] also follow this pattern.

---

[1] *Often* also uses *more* and *most*.

(2) Adverbs of more than one syllable form their comparative by using *more,* their superlative by *most,* e.g.

brightly — more brightly — most brightly.

(3) A few are irregular, e.g.

well — better — best; little — less — least; much — more — most; badly — worse — worst.

Many adverbs do not have degrees of comparison, e.g.

here, there, now, then, once, very, etc.

The comparatives of *in, out, up* (*inner, outer, upper*) are used as adjectives, e.g.

The *outer* door was wide open but the *inner* one was locked. His room was on an *upper* floor of the house. The House of Lords is known as the *Upper* Chamber, the House of Commons as the *Lower* Chamber.

The superlative forms—also used as adjectives—are *inmost* (*innermost*), *outmost* (*outermost*), *uppermost.*

NOTES ON CERTAIN ADVERBS

QUITE

Quite has two practically opposite meanings:

(1) The football ground was *quite* (= completely) full: you couldn't get another person in it.

(2) As a pianist Peter is *quite* (= fairly) good. He is *quite* a good pianist but, of course, he is not in the same class as the great concert pianists.

In (1) there is a strong stress on *quite* and on the following adjective; in (2) there is a weaker stress on the adjective.

ALREADY, YET

Already means 'before now', 'up to now', 'by this time', 'so far', e.g.

I have *already* explained this.
Richard has *already* eaten six cakes and is starting on the seventh.

Yet has more or less the same meanings, 'up to now', 'at this moment', e.g.

He hasn't finished his work *yet*.
Has the postman come *yet?*
Have you heard from your brother *yet?*

The difference between them is that *already* is used in affirmative statements, *yet* is used in negative and interrogative sentences.

But *already* can be used in interrogative sentences if you expect an answer, 'Yes', e.g.

I didn't expect you till four o'clock. Is it four o'clock *already?*
'What! have you finished your work *already?*'

(Do not confuse *already* with *all ready*, e.g.

We are *all ready* now for the lesson.)

Both *already* and *yet* indicate periods of time that began in the past and extend to the present. They are therefore most frequently used with a Perfect Tense.

They can also be used with the Simple Present Tense of the verb *to be*, and with the Continuous Tenses.

Is Henry here *yet?* (meaning 'Has he come *yet?*')
You certainly haven't time to change your dress; we *are* late for the party *already*.
When I got there he *was already speaking*.

They can be used also with the Past Tense of those verbs that are not generally used in the Continuous forms, *know, understand, believe, think, feel*, etc. (See p. 170), e.g.

I already *knew* that.

STILL

Still has the meaning 'up to the present moment', e.g.

The money is *still* here if you want it.
Are you *still* living in Hampstead?
It is eleven o'clock but Henry is *still* hard at work.

With *still*, a Present Tense or Continuous Tense should generally be used, not a Past Tense or Perfect Tense.

In some cases *still* and *yet* may have the same meaning, e.g.

I have *still* a few more pages to read.

I've a few more pages to read *yet*.

'Isn't William here *yet?*'

'Is William *still* not here?'

(William is expected, and the speaker is rather surprised and perhaps annoyed that he hasn't arrived. The surprise and annoyance are rather stronger in the second sentence than in the first.)

But note the difference in meaning between:

'Is William *still* here?' and: 'Is William here *yet?*'

(In the first sentence William has been here, but the speaker doesn't know whether he has gone away or not. In the second sentence William is expected but the speaker doesn't know whether he has arrived or not.)

Note that *yet* almost always has an end-position; *still* generally, but not always, has a mid-position. Note the two positions, too, in the following constructions with comparatives:

You must work harder *yet*.

You must work *still* harder.

We have exported a lot of goods but we must export more *yet*.

We have exported a lot of goods but we must export *still* more.

When *still* is used in questions it frequently suggests feeling of some sort, e.g. surprise or annoyance:

What! are you *still* working? I thought you had gone home.

Is that fellow *still* here? I wish he'd go away.

AGO

The Adverb *ago* (originally *agone*, a past participle of an obsolete verb *ago* = go) is used for measuring a period of time from the present to some point in the past, e.g.

He was here a few minutes *ago*.

They came to London about three years *ago*.

Note that with *ago* a Simple Past Tense is always used.

TOO

Too has two meanings (1) = also, in addition, e.g.

> Fred is coming to the party; won't you come, *too?*
> If you are taking your suit to be cleaned, will you take mine, *too?*

With this use, *too* is always in end-position.

(2) (as a degree adverb) = 'excessive', 'more than necessary or desirable'. In this usage it has something of a negative implication, e.g.

> The coffee is *too* hot (. . . so I can't drink it). This exercise is *too* hard (. . . so I can't do it). He ran away *too* fast (. . . so I couldn't catch him).

This negative implication is frequently expressed as an infinitive:

> The coffee is too hot *to drink*. This exercise is too hard *to do*. He ran away too fast *to be caught*.

Too is not, therefore, a substitute for *very*.

BUT

But is an adverb (with the meaning of 'only') in constructions such as: He is *but* a child. There is *but* one chance left. We can *but* try. The adverb phrase *all but* has the meaning 'nearly', e.g. He was *all but* killed.

EXERCISES

I Give the comparative and superlative forms of:

quietly, badly, hard, little, well, low, backwards, beautifully, in a friendly manner.

II Give adverbs equivalent to the following phrases:

on board; in the direction of home; towards the shore; to the side; on the shore; on the water.

[*N.B.* The adverbs are not always interchangeable with these phrases.]

III Construct sentences, using one of the following adverbs or adverb phrases to modify the whole of each sentence:

happily, well, therefore, finally, first, of course, naturally, admittedly, certainly, seriously, still, on principle.

IV Complete each of the following sentences by adding one of the following adverbs in its correct position in the sentence:

quite, already, all ready, still, yet.

(1) I am not sure if they are coming this evening. (2) They are half an hour late. (3) But there is time to catch the train if we hurry. (4) Perhaps they have bought their tickets. (5) But I don't expect they will have done so. (6) 'Hurry up and put the kettle on.' 'I've —— done so; though it's not —— time for tea.' (7) 'Are you fellows coming?' 'Yes, we are ——.' (8) There's plenty of time ——. (9) There's —— plenty of time. (10) I was —— to come when the telephone rang. (11) You are not —— here, are you? I thought you went hours ago. (12) When she arrived I hadn't —— had breakfast.

V In each of the following sentences, say whether 'quite' has the meaning of 'completely' or of 'fairly' ('rather').

(1) This problem is quite difficult. (2) This problem is quite beyond me. (3) You have had quite enough pudding. (4) I can't quite make out this word. (5) The decorations are quite attractive, aren't they? (6) He's not a millionaire, but he's quite rich. (7) The work is not quite as good as I expected, though he's only ten.

VI Complete the following pairs of sentences with words that, though similar, are in one case an adjective and in the other an adverb.

(1) (*a*) He became very deaf in —— life.
    (*b*) Good-bye for the present. I'll see you ——.

(2) (*a*) The —— line was completely blocked by the derailment.
    (*b*) The path went —— and —— to the bottom of the cliff.

(3) (*a*) At —— we saw daylight again.
    (*b*) The —— occupant of the house was a rich and eccentric old lady.

(4) (*a*) There is no wind; the air is very ——.
    (*b*) I am —— hoping for better luck next year.

(5) (a) He was driving on the —— side of the road when the accident happened.

(b) The referee blew his whistle because one of the players was —— side.

VII (a) Correct the following sentences:

(1) I am here already half an hour. (2) John has not still been to London. (*Two* corrections possible. What is the difference in meaning?) (3) He yet doesn't know what to do. (4) This work is not still right. (5) Already I did that work.

(b) What is the difference between:

(1) 'I see him already', and 'I have seen him already'. (2) 'He still hasn't done the work', and 'He hasn't yet done the work'. (3) 'Is Henry here still?' (or 'still here'), and 'Is Henry here yet?'

VIII What feelings are expressed by the following sentences?

(1) Has he still not telephoned? (2) Don't you yet know which tense to use? (3) You can't have finished that exercise already. (4) They haven't done much work up to the present. (5) She must have got home by this time. (6) At this moment it's quite useless to ask him for money. (7) Couldn't you have got here earlier? (8) The teacher has already explained this four times. (9) Is that old bore still monopolizing the conversation at the club? (10) He doesn't know any better.

IX Construct five sentences in each of which an adverb which has no degrees of comparison is employed.

X Rewrite the following sentences, not using the word *too* but keeping their present meaning:

(1) This meat is too tough to eat. (2) The question is too difficult for me to answer. (3) The little boy was too excited to speak. (4) I am too tired to work any longer. (5) You have given me too much Christmas pudding. (6) That trunk is too heavy for you to lift. (7) This piece of chalk is too small for me to write with. (8) He is too sensible to believe a story like that. (9) 'It's never too late to mend.' (*Proverb*) (10) 'Too many cooks spoil the broth.' (*Proverb*.)

CHAPTER NINETEEN

PREPOSITIONS AND 'ADVERBIAL PARTICLES'

As English is an analytic language, prepositions play a large part in its structure and are the cause of many difficulties to the foreign student. Little guidance can be given in any grammar book as to which preposition is the right one to use, for there is no logical reason why one is right in certain contexts and another one is wrong. Idioms—in which prepositions are frequently concerned—are peculiarities of language whose 'rightness' or 'wrongness' is based on usage, not on logic or etymology.[1] A good dictionary will help, but wide reading with a sharp eye for idiom is the surest teacher. We have thought it best, therefore, to give here some general remarks on prepositions and then to add numerous examples of the principal ones in sentences, with notes on the usage of those that may cause difficulty.

PREPOSITIONS are words used with nouns (or noun equivalents) to show the relation in which these nouns stand to some other word in the sentence. Thus in the sentence:

The horse is *in* the stable.

the preposition *in* expresses the relation between *horse* and *stable*. The preposition and noun together make a 'case phrase' within the rest of the sentence. If case can be shown (as with some pronouns) the case is always objective, e.g.

He spoke *to* **me**. This came *from* **him**. He wrote *about* **them**.

Prepositions may be single words, e.g. *at, after, down, since, with*, etc., or they may be two or more words ('group prepositions'), e.g.

[1] Beware of the writer who says: '*in* the circumstances' is right and '*under* the circumstances' is wrong because *circum* in Latin meant 'around' and you are *in* things that are around you and not *under* them; or who says 'averse *from*' is more correct than 'averse *to*' because *averse* is derived from the Latin *vertere* (= to turn), and *averse* suggests 'turning from' not 'turning to'. The appeal to etymology is fallacious. Turkey was not the original home of *turkeys;* and a modern *candidate* is not a man who wears a white robe!

He will come *instead of* me.
The teacher stood *in front of* the class.
He said that *for the sake of* peace and quiet.
Henry sat *at the back* of the room.
What did he say *with regard to* my proposals?

It is almost impossible to give all the meanings that prepositions help to convey. Originally they denoted place or direction, e.g.

He works *at* the cotton factory.
The boys ran *to* school.

The principal prepositions used to express PLACE are:

about, above, across, against, along, among, at, by, before, behind, below, beneath, beside, between, beyond, down, from, in, inside, into, near, off, on, over, past, round, through, to, towards, under, underneath, up, and the 'group prepositions': *at the* back (front, side, top, bottom) *of, at the beginning of, at the end of, away from, far from, in front of, in the middle of, out of.*

Many of these are also used to express time relations, e.g.

I shall see him *at* four o'clock.

The principal prepositions used to help to express TIME are:

about, after, at, by, before, between, during, for, from, in, on, since, till, through, throughout, to, at the beginning (end) of, at the time of, in the middle (midst) of, down to, up to.

Generally speaking, *at, by, on* indicate a POINT of time, e.g. *at* six o'clock, *by* two o'clock, *on* Tuesday, *on* the 15th of March.

The prepositions *after, before, by, in, since, till (until)* indicate a PERIOD of time, e.g. *after* Easter, *before* Christmas, *in* the morning/afternoon/evening, *since* five o'clock, *until* seven o'clock.

The prepositions *for, during* indicate DURATION of time, e.g.

He has been working *for* three hours. He became ill *during* the night. (See also p. 290.)

The prepositions *to, in order to, so as to,* help to express PURPOSE; they are used with an Infinitive. Purpose is expressed by *for* with a gerund, e.g.

A hammer is used *for knocking* in nails.

One of the chief functions of the preposition is to make, with the noun or pronoun that follows it, a phrase. This phrase is usually an adverb equivalent, e.g.

I looked *through the window.* (*Place*)
I shall go there *on Friday.* (*Time*)
He worked on a farm *during the holidays.* (*Time*)
He spoke *in a loud voice.* (*Manner*)

or an adjective equivalent, qualifying the preceding noun, e.g.

The house *with the big garden* is Mr. Brown's.
That is the Tower *of London.*
I received a letter *from her.*
I don't like the sound *of a jet engine.*

There are also a number of words, having the form of participles, which act as prepositions, e.g.

She said nothing *concerning* him.
What did he say *regarding* my proposals?

PREPOSITIONS AND ADVERBS

As has been emphasized before in this book, it is a mistake to attempt to state what is the part of speech of any word in isolation. This is a matter that can be decided only by an examination of the work a word is doing. Consider, for example, the following:

(*a*) The boy came *down* the tree.
(*b*) The tree blew *down* in the wind.

(*a*) He put the book *on* the table.
(*b*) Put your coat *on.*

(*a*) Henry came *before* four o'clock.
(*b*) I have explained that point *before.*

(*a*) Mary is *in* the garden.
(*b*) I opened the door, and the cat walked *in.*

Obviously the words italicized in the sentences marked (*a*) are different in function from the corresponding words in those marked (*b*). In the first case they are prepositions; in the second they are adverbs and form ADVERB COMPLEMENTS.

PHRASAL VERBS

Note, too, how often words like these are attached to, and affect the meaning of, verbs. Consider, for example, the following:

I will *put out* the light.

This has *taken up* a lot of my time.

The boy accidentally *knocked over* the ornament.

Turn on the gas.

Take off your hat.

All these words (*out, up, over, off, on*) are used in front of nouns or noun equivalents, but they could go equally well elsewhere, e.g.

I will put the light *out*.

This has taken a lot of my time *up*.

The boy accidentally knocked the ornament *over*.

Turn the gas *on*.

Take your hat *off*.

They are not showing the relationship between the noun that follows them and any other word in the sentence; they belong much more closely to the verb. In fact most of these expressions could be replaced by a single verb of practically similar meaning, e.g.

put out — extinguish; take up — occupy; knock over — upset; take off — doff.[1]

There are a great many of these 'Phrasal Verbs' (i.e. verb + preposition or adverb) and a number of verbs (usually the commonest in the language) may have a dozen or more different meanings according to the adverbial particle which accompanies them, e.g.

put down, put back, put forward, put in, put into, put up, put off, put on, put upon, put up with, put about, put across, put away, put by, put forth, put out, put round, put through,

[1] *doff* is rather archaic. It is formed from *do off;* the opposite is *don* (= *do* (i.e. *put*) *on*).

put together. Make after, make at, make away with, make for, make from, make up, make off, make off with, make out, make out of, make over, make towards, make up for, make up to, etc.

Some of the meanings are literal and the meaning of the phrase may be gathered from the individual words that compose it, e.g.

Put the book *up* there.

The ice was *broken up* by the ice-plough.

But very frequently the meaning is figurative and can only be learned by treating the combination as one unit, e.g.

Can you *put* me *up* for the night? (= accommodate)

We have *broken up* for two weeks (= classes have finished for a two weeks' holiday).

In some cases the adverbial particle has become completely fused with the verb to become an inseparable particle. In that case it precedes it, e.g. *outnumber, overlook, upset, withstand.*

THE POSITION OF THE PREPOSITION

As we have noted, the preposition usually goes before the noun or noun equivalent which it governs, e.g.

He spoke *to* me. The football team is playing *at* Wembley.

He prevented me *from* speaking.[1]

(The adverbial particle, as we have seen, can be before the object or at the end of the sentence.)

But when the word governed by the preposition is an interrogative, which goes at the beginning of a sentence, the preposition is usually (in conversational English always) at the end of the sentence, e.g.

Who(m) did you write *to?*

What are you laughing *at?*

Which class are you *in?*

There is still a superstition among some English people that a sentence must not end with a preposition. They think it is more 'correct' to say:

---

[1] Note that if any part of the verb is used after a preposition it must be the gerund. (See also p. 244.)

'*At* what are you looking?' than:

'What are you looking *at?*' or:

'I have a book *in which* to write my notes' than:

'I have a book to write my notes *in.*'

John Dryden[1] went through his earlier writings changing the position of every preposition that came at the end of a sentence. And Fowler says: '. . . a reviewer condemned our book[2] out of hand on the ground that the first paragraph of its preface ended in a preposition.'

The truth is that, though in formal writing it is probably preferable to write:

He didn't say *to whom* he gave the money. OR:

That is the book *from which* he got his information.

this 'rule' is broken by every English-speaking person and has been ignored by almost every English writer within the last seven centuries.[3]

The preposition must have end position:

(1) In adjective clauses beginning with *that*, or in clauses beginning with *what*, e.g.

This is the kind of life that[4] he is used *to.*

It is a thing that I have dreamed *of* and worked *for.*

There is the book that I asked *about.*

This is what I was looking *for.*

That is not what he is used *to.*

But there are one or two phrases from which the preposition cannot be moved, e.g.

I don't know *on whose authority* you say that. (NOT: whose authority you say that *on.*)

He doesn't say *by what reasoning* he arrived at that conclusion. (NOT: what reasoning . . . *by.*)

---

[1] 1631–1700.

[2] The *King's English* by H. W. and F. G. Fowler.

[3] There is a story that Winston Churchill, furious at having some end-prepositions in a paper that he had written 'corrected' by an overzealous secretary, sent it back with the corrections marked in red and a note: 'This is the sort of English *up with which I will not put.*' (In English: 'which I will not put up with'.)

[4] Note that the *that* can be omitted also in all adjective clauses of this type. (See p. 327, Adjective Clauses.)

(2) In the passive construction, e.g.

Everything he said was laughed *at*.

He is a man whose word is relied *on*.

That is a subject that mustn't be spoken *about*.

ILLUSTRATIONS OF THE USAGE OF PREPOSITIONS, ADVERBS, AND ADVERBIAL PARTICLES

The following sentences illustrate all the principal meanings of the most commonly used prepositions and adverbial particles.

ABOUT

I want you to tell me *about* your work. Can you recommend a good book *about* life in the sixteenth century? I am thinking *about* you all the time you are away. You ought to be certain *about* a matter before you speak of it. I'll see you at *about* six o'clock. That is all right for you but what *about* me? What *about* that money you promised me? I've not had it yet. No matter what we discuss, he knows all *about* it. I wish I were as sure *about* any one thing as he is *about* every single thing. I go *about* the country a good deal and have seen many things. You will be warm enough if you move *about*. Don't rush *about*. Go slowly and quietly. This is not screwed down firmly; it moves *about* when you touch it. I don't know much Spanish; just enough to find my way *about* in Spain. There are a lot of men without work; they just stand *about* at street corners. You are very untidy; you leave all your books lying *about* instead of putting them away. Is Miss Smith anywhere *about*? He tried to order me *about*, but I soon told him he was not my master. There is *about* £20 difference between this car and that one. Richard plays *about* in school instead of working. The ship is *about* to leave.

ABOVE

We flew *above* the clouds. You can just see our house *above* the trees. Henry's work is well *above* the average. He was *above* George in the examination list. Brown's business is not doing well; he is finding it difficult to keep his head *above* water (= to remain solvent). William is *above* meanness (=he wouldn't ever be mean). There were *above* 100 people at the meeting. In the *above* examples (in the examples *above*) you can see the usage of 'above'. That car cost *above* £2,000. Think about what I have told you; but, *above all*, don't breathe a word of it to Henry.

ACROSS

The tree had fallen down *across* the railway line. Brown's house is just *across* the road from us. You cross a cheque by drawing two lines *across* it and writing /& Co./ like this. Unless there is a boat at the river edge you won't be able to get *across*. I ran *across* (= met unexpectedly) our friend Smith yesterday.

AFTER

I'll see you *after* dinner. I ran *after* the boy but couldn't catch him. They came to England *after* us (= later than we did). Life is just one trouble *after* another. He goes on day *after* day, week *after* week without any change. You see I was right *after* all (= despite what you said). I came here at six o'clock and George came shortly *after* that. I'll try to pay you the money the week *after* next. That's no use, I want it the day *after* tomorrow at the latest. If my wife goes away for a week, who's going to look *after* me and the children? Leave the work now; we can do it *after*. I came here at six o'clock and George came shortly *after*.

AGAINST

He who is not for us is *against* us. I am tempted to leave my work but I'm fighting *against* the temptation. It is *against* the law to leave your car there. He rested his bicycle *against* the wall. I'll do what you order me, but it is *against* my will.

AMONG (AMONGST)

You can see my house *among* the trees. I bought three hundred eggs and there was not a single bad one *among* them. Livingstone spent many years *among(st)* the peoples of Africa. Shelley is *among* (= one of) the world's greatest poets. The Browns' children are always quarrelling *among* themselves. Share these sweets *among* the five children and see that each one gets a fair share.

NOTE

Between is generally used for two, *among* for more than two, e.g. 'The sweets were divided *between* the two children'. But this distinction is not always strictly observed, e.g.

The tables in that restaurant are so close together that there's hardly room to move *between* them.

AT

I shall be *at* home tonight *at* any time you like to call. He lives *at* Torquay in Devon.[1] I'll see you *at* school tomorrow *at* nine o'clock.[2] Begin *at* the beginning of the story. Will he be *at* the meeting tonight? The boys threw a snowball *at* the old man.[3] The angry man shouted *at* the boys.[3] Henry's remarks were so witty that everyone laughed *at* them. Look *at* your books; don't look *at* me. You should knock *at* the door before entering the room. I was surprised *at* the progress he had made. He is very good *at* football. The country was *at* peace then; now it is *at* war. This was sold *at* 4d. a pound, but that was really *at* a loss not *at* a profit. I had my hair cut *at* the barber's and bought a writing-pad *at* the stationer's. *At* the very most he can't be more than eighteen years of age. He is always *at* his best/worst when fighting against difficulties. You might *at* least have sent me word that you were coming. The car went *at* full speed. I don't like to travel by car *at* night. *At* any rate we know the worst now. I will fight you one *at* a time, not two *at* a time. You ought to hear *at* the latest by Friday. *At* first sight I thought you were your brother. This train stops *at* all stations. Shakespeare died *at* the age of fifty-two. *At* first it seemed very easy but it soon got more difficult. He is *at* work on a new book. I shall see you again *at* Christmas/*at* Easter. Do what I tell you, *at* once! We arrived *at* his house the next day.

NOTES

1. *At* is generally used for small towns; *in* is used for large cities, regions and countries, e.g. He lives *in* London/Middlesex/England.

2. I shall see you *on* November 5th/*on* Sunday/*on* Christmas Day/*at* 3 o'clock, *in* the afternoon.

3. Compare: Throw the ball *to* John (but not to hit him).
   Shout *to* him (because he is far away).

BEFORE

Come and see me tomorrow any time *before* five o'clock. I met Smith yesterday, but I knew him long *before* that. *Before* long you will find this work quite simple. My appointment is not until 10.15; you go in *before* me. That happened in 400 B.C. (*before* Christ). I have been here *before*. My family are coming here for a holiday, so I came two days *before* to make all arrangements. The Headmaster congratulated the boy *before* the whole school. William went and stood *before* the fire.

BEHIND

The garage is *behind* the house. He put his hand *behind* his back so that I couldn't see what was in it. Never say anything *behind* a person's back that you wouldn't say to his face. He stood just *behind* me. This train is *behind* time (= is late). His ideas are all *behind* the times (= out of date). Two of the wounded soldiers couldn't keep up with the rest of the men and fell *behind*. Richard is a long way *behind* with his work. They are two months *behind* with the rent. He looked round the railway carriage before he got out to make sure he had not left anything *behind*.

WIFE (to husband trying, clumsily, to fasten her dress—the sort that fastens at the back). 'Hurry up; have you never hooked up a dress *behind before?*'

HUSBAND: 'No; you never had a dress *before* that hooked *behind.*'

BELOW

The temperature today is *below* freezing point. Sign your name *below* mine on this document. In boxing it is a foul to hit *below* the belt. The cost of the whole work was *below* £20. Write your name in the space *below*. From the Empire State Building we looked at New York *below*. The sea is very rough and breaking over the deck; I think I'll go *below*.

BENEATH

The daffodils were growing *beneath* the trees. He had two pillows *beneath* his head. We climbed the hill; the valley lay *beneath*.

NOTE

Beneath is often used figuratively, e.g.

What he said is *beneath* contempt. Richard is far *beneath* Henry in intelligence. She married rather *beneath* her. (= she married someone of inferior social position.)

BESIDE

Go and sit *beside* Richard. The man who spoke was standing just *beside* me. The church at Stratford is *beside* the river. He was *beside himself* with rage (= almost mad). What you have said is quite *beside the mark/point/question* (= irrelevant.)

BESIDES

There are many others *besides* me who disagree with what you say. He thinks there is no one *besides* himself to be considered.

NOTE

Beside = near by, at the side of. *besides* = in addition to.

BEYOND

The woods go for about two miles *beyond* (= further on than) the river. He lives in a small house, about four miles *beyond* Oxford. The explanation you give is quite *beyond* me (= I can't understand it). He is living *beyond* his means (= spending more than he earns).

BY

Let us have a walk *by* the seashore. Come and sit *by* me; there's plenty of room. You go and sit *by* the side of George. If you put those two books side *by* side you will see which is the bigger. I did this work all *by* myself. He often goes for long walks *by* himself. Although he knows me quite well he passed me *by* as if I were a complete stranger. These things are made *by* machinery,[1] not *by* hand. I go *by* his office every day. I know him *by* sight but not to speak to. *By* this time next year you ought to have a very good knowledge of English. This train is late; it ought to have been in *by* now (*by* this time). *By* next Friday[2] I ought to have finished the job. Multiply the amount *by* ten and then divide *by* three. He earns his living *by* selling matches. This little girl is afraid to cross the road; take her *by* the hand and see her across. Did you come *by* train or *by* car (*by* land, *by* sea or *by* air)? I like motoring *by* day but not particularly *by* night. What he said took me completely *by* surprise. *By* the way, don't forget our meeting next Wednesday. He is going to Brussels *by* way of Dover and Ostend. Don't judge a man *by* his clothes. You won't do this all at once; do it little *by* little. You must try to learn some of these things *by* heart. He landed the aeroplane all right, but it was more *by* good luck than good management. What do you mean *by* taking my hat? I'm sorry, I took it *by* mistake. He is *by* far the best teacher I have ever had. You must begin *by* learning a few simple rules—though you'll probably end *by* taking no notice of any of them. That music was composed *by* Beethoven. The book I read was 'David Copperfield', *by* Charles

Dickens. These cigarettes are sold *by* weight, 4s. 6d. an ounce. Sugar is sold *by* the pound, petrol *by* the gallon. He is paid *by* the hour, so if it rains and he can't work he gets no money. He won the race *by* about two yards. The pupils came into the classroom one *by* one. I want a piece of paper 3 inches *by* 5 inches. The house was struck *by* lightning. 'Give me the cup; let go; *by* heaven I'll have it.' (Shakespeare, *Hamlet*)

NOTES

1. *By* is generally used for the agent; *with* for the instrument, e.g.

The lock was opened *by* the thieves *with* a skeleton key. The drawing was done *by* the artist *with* a very fine pen.

2. *By* expresses the limit of time within which something is to be (done).

BUT (= except)

Who *but* Richard would have said such a thing. I could answer all the questions *but* one. There was nothing in the cupboard *but* a few biscuits. Isn't there anything *but* rolls and coffee for breakfast? I haven't told this secret to anyone *but* you. Mr. Brown lives in the next house *but* one to us.

DOWN

Let us walk *down* the hill together. The boy fell *down* the stairs and broke his arm. I like to walk *down* Regent Street and look at the shops there. The sun goes *down* in the west. The little girl has fallen *down*. Richard wasn't *down* for breakfast this morning until ten o'clock. Get *down* off that wall; you can jump *down*. The plane dropped *down* 5,000 feet into the sea. We all knelt *down* in church. I didn't feel very well so I went to lie *down*. I don't like to look *down* from a great height. Sit *down*, there is plenty of room for every one. I pushed the cork under the water but it wouldn't stay *down*. The arrangement for sending letters abroad seems to have

10

broken *down*. His house was burnt *down* last night. The picture was printed upside *down*. Write these notes *down* in your notebook. A good many trees were cut *down* to build ships. He insulted me so I knocked him *down*. The sleeve of my coat is too short ; I will ask the tailor to let it *down* an inch. Your coat collar is turned up at the back; shall I turn it *down?* The wind/fire/ has died *down*.

DURING

He was Prime Minister *during* the years 1910-15 and *during* that time he had to deal with many difficult problems.

NOTES

1. *During* means (i) 'throughout the duration or continuance of', e.g. The sun gives light *during* the day, the moon *during* the night.

(ii) 'in the course of'; 'at some point within', e.g.

I heard thunder several times *during* the night. He was in the army *during* the war. You will have to do a lot of work *during* the holidays.

2. *During* is not used when the idea of duration is expressed by the noun (or equivalent) that it governs. In that case *for* must be used, e.g.

He went to America *for* (not *during*) three years. *During* that time he studied American commercial practice.

Or, more simply, *during* answers the question, 'When?' *For* answers the question, 'How long?', e.g.

'When were you there?' '*During* the war.'

'How long were you there?' 'I was there *for* three years.'

EXCEPT

We have lessons every day *except* Saturday and Sunday. Everyone was present *except* Henry and me. This essay is good *except for* the careless mistakes. He is a good student *except that* he is occasionally careless.

FOR

That Company has 10,000 men working *for* it. It is time *for* our lesson to start. This fresh air is very good *for* you. This medicine is good *for* a cough. Don't wear that suit to work in the garden; it is too good *for* such dirty work. It's a good thing *for* you that you live in England; in some countries you would have been shot *for* saying that. I've no respect at all *for* him; he is a real good-*for*-nothing. He doesn't care *for* working at all. He repeated the conversation that he had heard word *for* word. The train *for* Liverpool leaves from No. 6 platform. I bought a car *for* £20; it was a real bargain. You were lucky; I had to pay £150 *for* mine. I don't like this book that I borrowed; will you please change it *for* another one. He is always looking *for* something *for* nothing. I wouldn't give away that ring *for* anything in the world, so once and *for* all don't ask me again. I think he is ill; send *for* the doctor. If you don't see what you want in our window, ask *for* it. He who is not *for* us is against us. I'm all *for* helping people who really need it. I have two cars, one *for* business and one *for* pleasure. He was sent to prison *for* stealing. John got a prize at school *for* English. The accident happened because I couldn't see *for* the fog. I'm doing this *for* your sake, not *for* my own. He didn't do that *for* fear of punishment or *for* hope of reward but because he thought it was right. William is big *for* his age. It is very warm *for* the time of the year (*for* October). I shall stay in London *for* about three weeks.[1] You can go *for* miles and miles in Scotland and see nothing but heather-covered hills. He has worked *for* hours at that essay. I think that is enough about this preposition *for* the present (*for* the time being).

NOTES

1. *For* is used when the duration of time is measured; *since* when the starting point is given. (See *since*, p. 299.)

2. In negative sentences looking towards the future *for* is used for a period of time, *before* for a point of time, e.g.

> He will not be here *for* an hour yet.
> He will not be here *before* seven o'clock.

FROM

This train starts *from* Plymouth and goes to London. What country do you come *from?* You can just see my house *from* here. They walked *from* one end of the island to the other in three hours. He read that book *from* beginning to end in an hour. He works *from* morning to night without resting. You must try to look at the matter *from* my point of view. I grew those plants *from* seed. The brothers are so alike I can't tell one *from* the other. Where did you get that idea *from?* I am going away *from* home for about three months. Are you going far *from* here? I want to save you *from* making the mistake that I made. They suffered terribly *from* cold and hunger. Stop that boy *from* spoiling the book. When I advise you to do this I am speaking *from* experience. He never makes any provision for the future; he just lives *from* hand to mouth. The plane rocked *from* side to side in the fierce wind. The man went *from* door to door trying to sell brushes. *From* time to time I will examine you on the work you have done.

IN, INTO

I have twenty students *in* my class *in* this room. Ottawa is *in* Canada. He carried a bag *in* his hand. I don't think there is anything *in* that idea. What news is there *in* the papers this morning? He came on Monday at ten o'clock *in* the morning.[1] I read that *in* a book. You will not easily find as good a workman as Brown; he is one *in* a thousand. I am *in* trouble with my teacher over some careless work. There were not many people at the meeting—about ten or twelve *in* number I should think. I want you to arrange these *in* order, putting the largest first, then the next, and so on. He spoke *in* a whisper. He is the best student *in* my class. She is the happiest woman *in* England. He lives *in* London:[2] I live at Watford. I began work here *in* January *in* the year 1940. The bird carried the worm *in* its beak. I was right *in* the middle of the crowd and could see nothing. Stand *in* front of me, you will see better then; there will be nothing *in* the way of your view. I can never talk easily with him; we seem to have nothing *in* common. Why are you *in* such a hurry? If I were *in* your place I should wait for a time; it is *in* your own interest to do so. Our preparations had to be made *in* secret but they were *in* time, and we are *in* readiness now for whatever happens. We shall do it *in* some way or other; I'm not quite sure how. To be *in* debt is to be *in* danger. I'll never see you *in* want of money while I have any. *In* time of war we have to agree to things we should refuse *in* time of peace. 'A stitch *in* time saves nine' and 'A bird *in* the hand is worth two *in* the bush.' (*Proverbs.*) I will give you a new hat *in* place of the one that I damaged. I am putting the matter *in* the hands of my lawyer. *In* case of fire ring up Watford 999. He is always *in* good health and is never *in* need of a doctor. You have never been *in* love or you wouldn't speak like that. We are *in* sight of land now and will soon be *in* port. You are *in* a bad temper this morning, aren't you? Tell me *in* one word (*in* short) what you want. The matter, *in* itself, is not important; *in* fact I was going to take no notice of it. *In* reply to your letter I beg to inform you that *in* addition to what he owes you he is also *in* debt to me, and *in* all he owes about £3,000. He walked *into*³ the room *in* which we were sitting. He wouldn't take advice, and now he has got *into* difficulties. The tree trunk was sawn *into* small logs for burning. Turn this from English *into* Spanish. He is always getting *into* trouble owing to his carelessness; he is *in* trouble with his teacher now. He felt *in* his pocket to see if he had any money *in* it. Has the nine o'clock train come *in* yet? Go *in*, don't wait outside. I want to, but I can't get *in*. I don't think I'll go to the cinema; I want to stay *in* and read. You must call *in* and see us sometime. Is Mr. Smith *in?* I've given you the lesson, but it will take some time for it to sink *in*. A party of us are going to the theatre; would you like to join *in?* The maid will take these plates away now and bring the pudding *in* (bring *in* the pudding). Who took the letters *in* this morning (took *in* the letters)? Here's a hammer; will you knock this nail *in* (knock *in* this nail)? I've put tea *in* the teapot; will you pour *in* the water (pour the water *in*)? I'm packing my bag, but I can't get all my clothes *in*. The conductor on the bus helped the old lady *in*. He opened the door and let the dog *in* and then locked him *in*. I've opened the bag; put your stuff *in*. If there is one thing I hate, it is filling *in* (or filling *up*) income-tax forms. The examination is over now; give *in* your papers to the examiner. The train arrives *in* London at 6 o'clock. We shall never give *in* (give in = surrender). I shall be ready *in* five minutes.[4]

NOTES

1. *On* for the day; *at* for a point of time; *in* for a portion of the day.

2. *At* for a place thought of as a point on the map; *in* for a place thought of as an area. Thus, *in* always for large cities.

3. *In* denotes position or rest; *into* denotes motion.

4. Where referring to time, *in* denotes the close of a period; *within* denotes a time less than the close of a period (see also p. 303).

LIKE

It was just *like* him to say that. I don't feel *like* dancing (= I don't want to dance). Don't look at me *like* that. I can't speak Spanish *like* you (= as you do). Your shoes are just *like* mine. There's nothing *like* exercise for making you warm. This stuff looks *like* gold; perhaps it is gold!

NEAR

Mr. Thompson lives *near* me; his house is *near* the station. We are *near* the end of the story. Don't go far away, stay somewhere *near*. Henry is sitting *near* the window, *next* to John.

NOTE

Near expresses proximity, *next* means 'immediately before or after'.

OF

This box is made *of* wood. My shoes are made *of* leather. His house was built *of* brick. He said he was going to make a singer *of* me, but I thought he was trying to make a fool *of* me as I knew I could never make a success *of* music. We can't get everything we want from life; we must just make the best *of* it. Go and get me a packet *of* cigarettes. That is a very good field *of* potatoes. Get me a piece *of* wood, a pound *of* nails and a pot *of* paint. I'll give you half *of* what I earn, but I don't get a lot *of* money. I wish I could give you the whole of it. Elizabeth is fond *of* going to dances. Three *of* them attacked me. The children *of* the poor were cared for. The writing *of* that book took him ten years. The doctor cured me *of* my illness. The ship was wrecked within a mile *of* the coast. That is a real work *of* art. He gave me a piece *of* good advice. Parliament consists *of* the House *of* Commons and the House *of* Lords. It was a story *of* adventure and romance. What is the advantage *of* doing this? What is the cause *of* your bad temper? He has travelled over the whole *of* England. The city *of* Edinburgh has seen some strange scenes in its history and so has the Tower *of* London. What did Mr. Brown die *of*? Have you heard anything *of* Smith lately? We often speak *of* him and think *of* him. What do you think *of* this sonata *of* Beethoven's? You are sure *of* a good welcome at my house; we are fond *of* visitors. I sat at the back *of* the room, the important people sat at the front *of* the room. His name was at the top *of* the honours list; mine was at the bottom *of* it. That was because I played instead *of* working. In spite *of* his ill-health Johnson did very well. It is very good *of* you to take so much trouble. He is a friend *of* mine (ours, yours, John's).

OFF

Water was streaming *off* the roof. Keep *off* the grass. I can't get this ring *off* my finger. Turn *off* the main road here and you will come to the lake. He took his hat and his coat *off*.

Is the gas on or *off*? I picked up the box and the top fell *off*. There is a little smell in the new cloth but it will soon wear *off*. I had a headache this morning but it soon passed *off*. He has a very good income. I wish I were as well *off*—though I must say I am not so badly *off* as some people. Lorenzo ran *off* with Shylock's daughter and his money. Shall we set *off* for our walk now? I've studied music on and *off* (i.e. at intervals) for about twenty years. That ship is two or three miles *off*; it won't see us. It's time the children were *off* to bed. I'll come to the station to see you *off*. His wealthy aunt disliked him so she cut him *off* with a shilling (i.e. left him only a shilling in her will). We finished *off* a very good dinner with coffee and cigarettes. The judge let the prisoner *off* with a warning. The gun went *off* unexpectedly. That fellow is always showing *off* (= he's always thinking of the effect he is making). I wish you would pay *off* this big debt. He helped his wife *off* with her coat. If you don't pay this electricity account the company will cut your supply *off*. Turn that tap *off* and switch the light *off*. I thought I could get the agreement signed, but the whole business is definitely *off* now.

ON

He put the book *on* the table and he sat *on* a chair. There were water colours *on* the walls of the room. Put the stamp *on* your letter in the right-hand corner. He came *on* Saturday.[1] I came *on* the 15th of May. He had a new hat *on* his head, a new coat *on* his back, new gloves *on* his hands and a ring *on* his finger. Vegetarians live *on* vegetables, fruit and nuts. The war was fought *on* land, *on* sea and in the air. Did you come here *on* foot? No, I came *on* horseback. The town is *on* the River Mersey, *on* the left bank. There are shops *on* both sides of the street. We live *on* the north side of the city; they live *on* the south side. I am planting the apple trees *on* the left and the pear trees *on* the right of the path. What are your ideas *on* the subject? Could you give us a little speech *on* this subject? They are at Blackpool *on* holiday; I went *on* business. The house is *on* fire. I think it was set *on* fire *on* purpose. There are goods *on* sale in all the shop windows. I thought I would sell my car but *on* second thoughts I changed my mind, and *on* the whole I think I was wise. *On* the contrary I think you were unwise; prices may go up, but, *on* the other hand, they are much more likely to go down. *On* getting his telegram I set off immediately for London. What I do will depend *on* the help you can give me. He shot the bird *on* the wing (i.e. while it was flying). *On* my honour, I did not do it. Have you got your coat *on* and your hat *on?* Did you leave the electric light *on* when you went out of the room? Is there anything good *on* at the cinema tonight? If I've nothing much *on* (= am not busy), I'll go. Time is getting *on;* it's getting *on* for eleven o'clock; we had better go home now. My father is getting *on* in years (= growing old); he's nearly seventy. How are you getting *on* (= progressing) with your English? I don't like Smith; I can't get *on* (= have friendly social relations) with him at all. No, he and I have never got *on* together. Come *on;* let's get *on* (= continue) with these prepositions: if you keep *on* trying, you'll master them. Lookers-*on* see most of the game. The rain came *on* at about five o'clock in the afternoon. Help me *on* with my coat. Switch the light *on*, please, and then turn the hot water *on* for my bath. I'll see you later *on;* I'm too busy now. You are further *on* with the work than I had expected. You carry *on* (= continue) with the work while I have a rest. I had lunch *on* the train.

NOTE

On is used for dates and for particular days or specified parts of days, e.g.

On May 1st; *on* Wednesday; *on* Christmas Day; *on* Saturday afternoon. (Compare *in* and *at*.)

OVER

The dog jumped *over* the table. Someone left a box in the garden and I fell *over* it in the dark. The aeroplane flew *over* the house. Give me a blue sky *over* my head and a green road under my feet and I am happy. An *over*coat is a garment that we wear *over* our other clothes. More people have laughed *over* and cried *over* the books of Dickens than of perhaps any other writer. English is being spoken all *over* the world. You don't need to pay back the money you borrowed, all at once; the repayment can be spread *over* a number of years. Will you look *over* this exercise (or look this exercise *over*) that I have done, and see if it is correct? I am sorry I *over*looked your letter (= did not notice it). There are *over* thirty people in this room. I don't want to make a decision at once; I will talk it *over* with my wife. You came too late; the football match is all *over* (= finished). I tried to waken the man but he just turned *over* and went off to sleep again. He said that he felt so strong he could push a house *over*. I know a visit to the dentist is unpleasant; but come along, let's get it *over*. If you will come to our factory I shall be very glad to show you *over* it. His work was done so badly that I told him to do it *over* again. I have told you *over* and *over* again not to make that mistake. I gave the children two apples each and I had three left *over*. You will get £50 a year *over and above* your usual salary. He is just getting *over* his severe illness.

NOTE

Over is used with a considerable number of verbs, as an Inseparable Particle, e.g.

*over*look, *over*turn, *over*flow, *over*eat, *over*load, *over*power, *over*take, etc.

PAST

He walked *past* the door. The door was open when I walked *past*. It is *past* three o'clock; it is nearly a quarter *past*. The situation is *past* (= beyond) hope/cure/control/belief.

ROUND (AROUND)

Drake sailed *round* the world in 1577–80. The earth moves *round* the sun. Would you like to walk *round* my garden? Come into the garden and walk *round*.

SINCE

He has lived in England *since*[1] 1949. He came to England in 1949 and has been here ever *since*. They had waited *since* four o'clock. Things have changed very much *since* the last time I wrote to you. The church was destroyed by the bombing in 1940 but has *since* been rebuilt (has been rebuilt *since*).

NOTE

Since is used when a STARTING POINT in time is given. Compare with *for* (page 291) which is used when the DURATION of time is measured. *Since* refers to the whole period from a point of time in the past up to the present moment or a given moment in the past, so it is almost always used with a Perfect tense.

THROUGH

The ball went *through* the window. The river flows *through* the town. We walked *through* the village. *Go through* (= examine) these papers carefully. I *saw through* (= was not deceived by) his trick. George has *got through* (= passed) his examination. He worked all *through* his holidays. It was *through* (= owing to) Fred's carelessness that the money was lost. The street is thronged with people; do you think we can get *through?* The soldiers were surrounded by the enemy but managed to break *through*. Your clothes are wet *through* with the rain. He got that job *through* (= by the help of) his uncle.

NOTE

Through suggests one more dimension than *across*, e.g. He walked *across* the fields and *through* the woods.

TO

I am going *to* America on Friday. I have already sent my luggage *to* the station. Come on, children; time *to* go *to* bed and go *to* sleep. Does this road go *to* Edinburgh? That coat is quite wet; hold it *to* the fire for a few minutes. He looks *to* me for help. It is now five minutes *to* six. He read the book from beginning *to* end. Will you lend your book *to* George, please? Did you send that letter *to* him? I prefer this book *to* that one. This one is superior *to* that. You can't compare this *to* that. He's a very wealthy man; a few hundred pounds is *nothing to* him. You must *set to work* on that job as soon as possible. I offered him money for the use of the bicycle, but *to my surprise* he refused it. Is that tea quite *to your taste* or do you need more sugar? No more sugar, thank you; it is exactly *to my liking*. I live quite *close to* the church; in fact *next door to* it. *According to* you there is nothing more to be done. Don't talk all round the question; come *to the point*. You will soon get *used to* his way of speaking. Let's *drink to* his success.

TOWARDS

A plane crossed the coast flying *towards* London. I'll pay you something *towards* what I owe you. He has never shown a really friendly spirit *towards* George. That is the first step *towards* getting the matter cleared up. It was somewhere *towards* five o'clock when he came.

NOTE

Towards expresses, 'in the direction of', but not 'arrival at' a place. Compare:

He went *to* London yesterday.
The aeroplane flew *towards* the sun.

UNDER

Don't stand *under* (underneath) a tree during a thunderstorm. He doesn't owe very much, it's *under* £10. It is raining heavily; come *under* my umbrella. I can't use my office at present; it is *under* repair. You can't sign that; you are *under age* (not twenty-one). I did that *under* orders. I came to Piccadilly Circus by *Underground*. I have *under*-lined all your mistakes. *Under* (in) the circumstances I will not give you any extra work. When Lord X goes abroad he travels *under the name* of Mr. Brown. Here is a tree that we can shelter *under*. The cost will be £2 or *under*. In the struggle for life the weakest go *under* (i.e. fail or die). I like beef *under*done rather than overdone. It was very late when I got to bed last night and I feel very much *under*slept this morning.

UNTIL, TILL

He waited *till* (*until*) all the students were quiet before he began the lesson. I shan't see you now *till* Friday.

NOTE

There is very little difference in use between *until* and *till*. To begin a sentence, *until* is more frequent than *till*. In short conversational phrases, *till* is perhaps more usual.

UP

He ran quickly *up* the ladder. They walked *up* the hill to their house. Is the lift going *up* or down? I was *up* at five o'clock this morning. *Wake up;* it's seven o'clock and time to *get up. Hang* your hat *up* here. My friend was very ill; I *sat up* all night with him; my brother will *stay up* tomorrow night with him. The soldiers blew *up* the bridge. *Hurry up* or you will be late. Will you break *up* this wood for the fire, please? You walk far too fast; I can't *keep up* with you. That stream never dries *up* even in the middle of summer. I've dropped my book; will you please *pick it up* for me? There are a lot of weeds in my garden; I'm going to *pull* them *up*. Put your hands *up* or I shoot! *Cover up* the food or the dust will get on it. You go on; I'll soon *catch you up. Cut up* the meat for little Margaret; she can't use a knife and fork very well yet. If you can't do the puzzle at first don't *give it up;* you will do it in time if you try. You have worked very well so far; *keep it up*. You could see there was someone at home, the house was all *lit up*. You ought to *lock up* these jewels in a strong room. Some girls take longer to *make up* their minds than to *make up* their face. I can't buy that car just yet but

I am *saving up* for it. He was very angry and *tore up* the letter. *Tie up* the dog; he might attack Smith's cat. After dinner Susan *washes up* (the dishes). John has *made up* a little song. Who has *used up* all my toothpaste? Harry's parents died when he was young and his aunt *brought him up*. *Ring me up* some time tomorrow. You have got the story all *mixed up*. He turned the box *upside down*. It's *up to you* (*Colloquial* = It is your duty) to do your best. What are you *up* to? (*Colloquial* = 'What are you doing?' Usually with the suggestion that it is something wrong.) I know you are *up* to no good. What's *up*? (*Colloquial* or *slang* = 'What's the matter?') Time's *up*. (= You have no more time now.)

WITH

Can you come and stay *with* me for a time, and bring your wife *with* you? Have you all brought your books *with* you? Leave your hats and coats *with* the attendant. He has been *with* that firm for a long time now. Compare this cheese *with* that and you will see the difference. The box of eggs was marked '*With* Care'. It is *with* great pleasure that I give you the prize. Orders for the new car came in *with* a rush. He went away *with* a smile and a song. The tide came in *with* great speed. *With* all his faults he was a kind-hearted fellow. I hope he hasn't met *with* an accident. A man *with* plenty of money has plenty of friends. He walked along *with* his hat on the back of his head. Sleep *with* your windows open but *with* your mouth shut. I've brought my brother along *with* me to help. *With regard* to that business we spoke about, if you are *going on with it* I can perhaps help you. I see *with* my eyes, hear *with* my ears and smell *with* my nose. Her eyes were filled *with* tears and she was trembling *with* cold. I am not at all satisfied *with* your work. The cushion is filled *with* feathers. Do you think this red tie *goes with* my blue suit? You are always *finding fault with* everything I do. I don't *agree with* you at all about that. Romeo was deeply *in love with* Juliet. He has *quarrelled with* George. I don't know why he *fell out* (= quarrelled) *with* him but I hope he will soon *make friends with* him again. I have no *patience with* you, you are so stupid. He went so fast I couldn't *keep up with* him. How is he *getting on with* the book that he is writing? What's the matter *with* you? You don't look very well. It's nothing to do *with* you what I say. I don't *get on very well with* George; you see, I have *nothing in common with* him. If you have any cabbage plants to spare I *could do with* (= could use) about fifty. I'm just using this spade, but you can have it when I've *done with it.* I'm not *arguing with* you, I'm telling you. He is content *with* very little. In 1066 the English fought a great battle *with* the Normans. In 1805 England was at war *with* France.

WITHIN

You must try to live *within* your income. He lives *within* five miles of London. Shout if you want me; I shall be *within* hearing. The house was painted green without and *within.* I shall be back again *within* a year.

WITHOUT

He always goes about *without* a hat on. That was done *without* my help, *without* my knowledge and *without* my consent. I will do this job for you *without* fail (= for certain) by tomorrow. You have been warned *times without number* about the danger and still you don't take any notice. He is, *without exception,* the best pupil I have ever had. I can say that *without fear* of contradiction. You haven't time to pack all those clothes; you will have to *go without* them. Can you get into the room *without* breaking the lock? 'You can't have omelettes *without* breaking eggs.' (*Proverbial saying*). I've gone *without* food for two days now. I've gone *without* eating for two days now. If we can't afford a new car, we shall have to *do without* it. But a car is something I can't *do without.* Of course I know you will work hard; that *goes without saying.* They left the party *without so much as* saying goodbye.

EXERCISES

I Use each of the following (*a*) as a preposition, (*b*) as an adverb:

on, in, up, about, after, before, behind, over, round, since, off, through.

II Put in the prepositions or adverbs that have been omitted:

(1) The man who spoke was standing —— me. (2) There are others —— me who believe that. (3) Put the two books side —— side. (4) Everyone was listening —— Richard. (5) He lived here —— the years 1940 and 1941. (6) Their plans have completely broken ——. (7) The soldiers came in two —— two. (8) That book was written —— Dickens. (9) That is a book —— Russia and the Russian people. (10) I ran —— the thief but couldn't catch him. (11) He who is not for us is —— us. (12) He has written ten books and there is not a single good one —— them. (13) The mother divided the apple —— the two boys. (14) Who is looking —— you? (15) Jan is very good —— English. (16) He did that —— my wishes. (17) I bought that —— the butcher's. (18) He put his hands —— his back. (19) That ought to cost sixpence or —— the very most ninepence. (20) I hoped it would be fine but it poured —— all afternoon. (21) My shoes are made —— leather; the box is made —— iron. (22) I can't get this ring —— my finger. (23) He put the book —— the table and sat —— a chair. (24) He has 10,000 men working —— him. (25) What country do you come ——? (26) He walked —— the room and sat —— his desk. (27) I shan't be away long; I'll be back —— a year. (28) The ship rocked —— side to side. (29) I don't like to be —— debt; that is to be —— danger. (30) It is cold —— this room now that the fire has gone ——. (31) You must make the best —— it. (32) The petrol is all running ——; turn the tap ——. (33) There are houses —— both sides —— the street. (34) I bought a bicycle —— £4. (35) You must try to look at it —— my point of view. (36) I shouldn't be —— such a hurry if I were —— your place. (37) A friend —— mine went with me to the Tower —— London. (38) Help me —— —— my coat. (39) I went there —— business; I have to work —— my living. (40) —— reply —— your letter —— the 15th of November, we wish to state that we are —— need —— a traveller —— the London district. If you will come

here —— Saturday the 12th —— April we can give you
our ideas —— the subject and it will then depend ——
you whether you accept and try to make a success ——
it or whether —— the contrary the whole matter must
be considered as definitely ——. (41) Someone left a box
—— the garden and I fell —— it —— the dark. (42) I
stood —— the corner —— the road and hundreds ——
cars went ——. (43) Walk —— the town —— me and
then we will come home and sit —— by the fire. (44) I
have been —— London —— the 25th —— July. (45) We
went —— France —— our way —— Spain. (45) This coat
is wet. Hold it —— the fire —— a few minutes. (47) That
is the first step —— getting the matter cleared ——.
(48) I can't use my office —— business —— present; it
is —— repair. (49) I had never had a lesson —— English
until I came —— London. (50) That stream never dries
—— even —— the middle —— summer. (51) Come and
stay —— us —— a few days —— Christmas and bring
your wife —— you. (52) I did not approve —— his
action and what he did was done —— my consent.
(53) You don't need to pay —— the money you borrowed
all —— once. The repayment can be spread —— a
number —— years. (54) Drake sailed —— the world ——
the reign —— Queen Elizabeth I. (55) I have been ——
England —— six months but have had lessons only ——
April. (56) The motor boat cut —— the water —— a
terrific speed. (57) I live quite close —— the church; in
fact next door —— it. (58) It was somewhere —— five
o'clock —— the afternoon when he called —— me.
(59) —— the circumstances, I will not give you any
extra work. (60) You could see —— a glance there was
someone —— home; the house was all lit ——. (61) I like
beef ——done rather than ——done. (62) They walked
—— the new road, then —— the hill —— my house.
(63) Orders —— the new car came —— —— a rush.
(64) He walked —— his hat —— the back —— his head.
(65) —— regard —— that business, I don't want to do
anything more —— it, but I'll keep —— touch —— you.

CHAPTER TWENTY

CONNECTIVES

1. We have noticed in the previous chapter that prepositions help to link a word with other parts of the sentence, but the most usual 'connective' is a CONJUNCTION. Conjunctions are used to join words, phrases or sentences together, e.g.

Time *and* tide wait for no man.
'To be *or* not to be, that is the question.'
You *or* I must tell him the truth.
She opened the door *and* let the cat in.
He tried hard *but* he was unsuccessful.
I don't think the price is too high, *nor* does Henry.

2. Some conjunctions are used in pairs, e.g.

You must *either* pay the price *or* do without the goods.
What he said was *neither* kind *nor* true.
It was *not only* unkind *but also* untrue.
He *both* reads Russian *and* speaks it well.

Conjunctions used in pairs are called CORRELATIVE CONJUNC-TIONS.

3. There are some words such as *nevertheless, however, meanwhile, indeed* which join sentences together perhaps rather more loosely,[1] e.g.

I don't know anything against the man; *nevertheless*, I don't trust him.
I don't see how he is going to pay back the money he has borrowed; *however/still*, that's his business not mine.
I'll buy a new suit when I get the cheque for the work I did; *meanwhile*, I'm afraid this old one will have to do a bit longer.
I can't buy a new suit till I get a cheque for the work; *so* this old one will have to do for a bit longer.
He'll never be a good violinist; *indeed*, the professor told him so.

[1] Sweet, *New English Grammar*, calls them 'half-conjunctions'.

These 'half-conjunctions' link the sentences logically rather than formally, and just before the half-conjunction there is a break in the flow of the sentence, indicated in the examples above by a semi-colon. The 'full conjunctions' join the two parts more tightly together so that the sentence flows on without interruption.

4. There are, however, other ways of linking together sentences or parts of sentences:

(*a*) In a few cases the use of the preposition is very similar to that of the conjunction. For example, there is practically no difference between these two sentences:

At the farm they gave us strawberries *and* lots of cream.
At the farm they gave us strawberries *with* lots of cream.

but a conjunction does not affect, as a preposition does, the pronoun that follows it.

(*b*) A prepositional phrase may be used as a conjunction, e.g.

He doesn't work hard; *in fact* he's incapable of hard work.
His behaviour hasn't improved; *on the contrary* it has become worse.

(*c*) It is possible to have sentences linked only by punctuation marks, commas, semi-colons or colons, e.g.

I looked round the room. Jan was working, Pedro was reading, Hob was sleeping. (*Commas*)
He doesn't work hard; he's incapable of hard work. (*Semicolon*)
He kicked open the door, revolver in hand: a dead man lay on the floor. (*Colon*)

5. Conjunctions which join together words, phrases or sentences of similar functional value (as in all the examples given so far) are called CO-ORDINATING CONJUNCTIONS. Those that join together sentences of differing functional value are called SUBORDINATING CONJUNCTIONS (see p. 320).

As regards meaning, co-ordinating conjunctions fall into four rough groups. (1) the 'and' group; (2) the 'but' group; (3) the 'or' group; (4) the 'so' group.

(1) *The 'and' Group*

The conjunctions in this group suggest addition, e.g.

On the table for tea there were cakes *and* biscuits *and* tarts *and* sandwiches.

Frequently in sentences of this type only the final *and* is used, the others being replaced by commas, e.g.

On the table for tea there were cakes, biscuits, tarts and sandwiches.

The addition introduced by *and* is generally something that would naturally be rather expected, e.g.

The fur coat was soft *and* warm.

The car is almost new *and* in excellent condition.

(We should expect a car that was almost new to be in good condition.)

Other connectives in this group are illustrated in the following examples:

The fur coat was *both* soft *and* warm.

The fur coat was soft *as well as* warm.

The fur coat was soft *and also* warm.

Not only was the coat soft; it was *also* warm.

The car was almost new; *furthermore,/besides,/ likewise,/ moreover,/again,* it was in excellent condition.

There is an idiomatic use of the conjunction *and* connecting two co-ordinate sentences (one of them an imperative) to express (*a*) condition, (*b*) purpose, e.g.

(*a*) Work hard *and* you'll get your reward (= if you work . . .)[1]

'Laugh, *and* the world laughs with you;
Weep, *and* you weep alone.'[2]

Utter one word, *and* you are a dead man!

(*b*) Go *and* ask him what he wants.
Come *and* help me to lift these boxes.
Write *and* ask him when he is coming.

---

[1] See page 343.   [2] Ella Wheeler Wilcox.

Note, also, the construction *'try and . . .'* instead of *'try to'* generally used in exhortations expressing encouragement, or in promises, e.g.

> *Try and do* this exercise. You must *try and visit* us in the spring. Do *try and stop* coughing. I shall *try and meet* you at the station. I will *try and have* the work finished by Wednesday.

Pedants discourage the use of this form and insist on substituting *try to . . .*, but it is good colloquial usage and is not without good literary justification. It is used only with the simple form *try*, not with any of the inflected forms.

(2) *The 'but' Group*

The connectives in this group suggest contrast; the addition introduced by them is generally something that would hardly be expected, e.g.

> The car was quite old *but* in excellent condition.

(We should expect the *new* car to be in excellent condition; we could hardly expect the same of a quite old one.)

> The coat was thin *but* warm.

Other connectives (conjunctions and prepositional phrases) of this type are illustrated in the following examples:

> The car was quite old; *yet/still/however/nevertheless* it was in excellent condition.
> *In spite of/despite/notwithstanding* its age, the car was in excellent condition.
> The car was quite old; *despite that* it was in excellent condition.

The subordinating conjunction *though* (*although*) can express this same meaning, e.g.

> *Though* the car was quite old, it was in excellent condition.

(3) *The 'or' Group*

The sense of *or* when joining words, phrases or sentences is:

(1) choice (one of two), e.g.

> Take this book *or* that one.
> You must work harder *or* go into another class.

(2) an approximation, e.g.

The work will cost £15 *or* £16.

The nearest big town is 20 *or* 30 miles from where they live.

But *or* is not used when the difference is big; we should not say, for example:

The work will cost £15 *or* £100.

The nearest big town is 5 *or* 40 miles from where they live.

Other connectives in this group are illustrated in the following examples:

Either my answer *or* yours is wrong.

You must *either* work harder *or* go into another class.

You must work harder, *or else* go into another class.

You must work harder; *otherwise* you will be put into another class.

Neither (. . . *nor*) has the meaning 'not one of two', e.g.

Your answer is not right, *neither* is mine.

Neither your answer *nor* mine is right.

Another pair of correlative conjunctions is *not only . . . but also*, e.g.

Not only is your answer wrong but mine is *also*.

He is *not only* the most intelligent student in the class *but also* the most hard-working.

Note that *either . . . or, neither . . . nor* take a singular verb, e.g.

Come and have lunch with me; *either* Tuesday *or* Wednesday **is** convenient for me.

I'm sorry, *neither* Tuesday *nor* Wednesday **is** convenient for me.

In these constructions the verb agrees in person with the nearest subject, e.g.

Either George or I *am* to blame.

Neither you nor he *is* to blame.

As this is felt to be rather awkward, the construction is sometimes changed to:

Either George *is* to blame or I *am*.

Either I *am* to blame or George *is*.

You *are* not to blame; neither *is* he.[1]
He *is* not to blame; neither *are* you.[1]

(4) *The 'so' Group*

So as a conjunction suggests consequence, e.g.

The rain began to fall, *so* we went home.

He didn't work hard, *so* he had to go to another class.

Other conjunctions in this group are *therefore, accordingly, thus, hence, consequently*, and the subordinating phrase *so that*. (See Clauses of Purpose, p. 340.) Note that when it introduces a clause of Purpose rather than of Consequence, *so that* is followed by *may, might, shall* or *should*.

Some adverbs function as conjunctions joining independent statements, e.g.

We worked until six; *then* we went home.

He broke the rules of the school; *therefore/so/consequently/ accordingly* he had to leave.

He is clever; *only* he can't be trusted.

Sometimes he is pleasant; *again*, he can be very unpleasant.

SUBORDINATING CONJUNCTIONS

Subordinating conjunctions are used to introduce (*a*) noun clauses and (*b*) adverb clauses of every kind. *Examples:*

He said *that* he would help us.

Ask him *when* he can come.

You will recognize him *when* you see him.

He came *because* he was interested in music.

I will come *if* you want me.

If you want me, I will come.

Though he wasn't interested in music, he came to the concert.

(For Adverb and Noun Clauses see pp. 333 to 343.)

The conjunction does not necessarily come between the sentences it joins.

---

[1] For the inversion of subject and verb in this construction, see p. 186.

The most commonly used subordinating conjunctions are: *that, when, where, while, before, until, if, after, since, because, (al)though, unless, as.*

In colloquial speech the conjunction *that* is often omitted; in fact, the conjunction would be unusual in such sentences as:

I wish you had told me.

I hope he passes his examinations.

It's high time those children were in bed.

I'd sooner/rather/you didn't ask me to speak.

There are other connectives, which are not conjunctions, that are used to introduce subordinate clauses. Thus adjective clauses are joined to other parts of a complex sentence by relative pronouns or relative adverbs, e.g.

That's the book *that/which* everybody is talking about.

He's the man *whom* I want to see.

That's the house *where* I was born. (See p. 328.)

In conversation these connectives are often omitted.

Again, all the interrogative words can be used as connectives in indirect questions, e.g.

Ask him
- *what* it is.
- *where* he went.
- *why* he did it.
- *how* he knows.
- *when* he saw me.
- *which* house it was.
- *whose* dog that is.

Note the changed word order when these interrogative sentences are made subordinate. The direct form: 'What *is it?*' has become 'Ask him what *it is*', etc.

THAN, AS . . . AS, SUCH . . . AS, BUT

It is not always easy to decide whether *than, as . . . as, such . . . as,* and *but* are prepositions (to be followed always by the objective case of the pronoun) or conjunctions (to be followed by either the nominative or the objective case according to the pronoun's logical status as subject or object of the verb). There would thus be hesitation in the following sentences:

You are a better player *than he/him.*

He is older *than I/me.*

One day you will be *as* old *as I/me.*

I never met *such* a man *as he/him* for hard work.

No one saw him *but I/me*.

There was no one in the house *but she/her*.

Some grammarians and a few, perhaps rather pedantic, speakers insist that *than, as*, etc., in the above sentences are conjunctions and that the sentences are elliptical for:

You are a better player *than* he (is).

One day you will be *as* old *as* I (am), etc.

But though examiners tend to frown on the use of these words as prepositions, the usage has not only the authority of the spoken word but of numerous standard authors including Shakespeare, Swift, Pope, Byron and many others. An interesting point, made by W. S. Allen,[1] is that if the pronoun is further qualified by *both* or *all*, the objective case is invariable used, e.g.

He is cleverer *than us all*.

'A stone is heavy and sand weighty; but a fool's wrath is heavier *than them both*.' (Bible)

Moreover, when a relative pronoun follows *than* (a literary rather than a colloquial usage) the relative is always in the objective case, e.g.

He is a man *than whom* no one has a better right to speak.

Belial came last; *than whom* a spirit more lewd

Fell not from Heaven.[2]

(Note, by the way, the ambiguity of: 'She loves him more than me', which could mean: 'She loves him more than I do' or 'She loves him more than she loves me'.)

BUT

But, when it has the meaning 'except', is now usually regarded as a preposition, e.g.

All of them *but me* had been there before.

There is, however, a well-known poem that begins:

The boy stood on the burning deck

Whence all *but he* had fled.[3]

---

[1] *Living English Structure* (p. 15).   [2] Milton, *Paradise Lost*.
[3] *Casabianca* by Felicia Hemans.

EXERCISES

I Construct ten sentences, five containing co-ordinating conjunctions and five containing subordinating conjunctions, using a different conjunction in each sentence.

II Complete the following sentences by filling the blank spaces with the connective words you consider appropriate.

(1) I don't agree with you, —— does my partner. (2) He drinks —— beer —— wine. (3) Their actions were—— —— risky —— positively suicidal. (4) I'm going out for a short time; —— you can get supper ready. (5) Those who are not prepared to study should —— change their ways —— make room for those who will work. (6) She can't hope to pass the exam. in December —— she'll have to wait till June. (7) He is very seriously ill; —— doctors have almost given up hope of his recovery. (8) They go to concerts of modern music —— they really like it. (9) ——I do not like him very much, I can appreciate his qualities. (10) Find out —— they are going this evening —— ask if we may join them.

III Construct four sentences, two illustrating the idiomatic use of 'and' to express condition and two to illustrate its use in expressing purpose.

IV Use each of the following connectives in a sentence:

(1) not only . . . but also. (2) both . . . and. (3) so. (4) still. (5) indeed. (6) therefore. (7) unless. (8) neither . . . nor. (9) as. (10) until.

V Explain, with examples, the difference in function between co-ordinating conjunctions and subordinating conjunctions.

CHAPTER TWENTY-ONE

INTERJECTIONS AND EXCLAMATIONS

The INTERJECTION is a word or sound used to express some sudden feeling or emotion. It thus belongs to the oldest form of the spoken language and represents the most primitive type of utterance. It does not enter into the grammatical construction of the sentence.

Among the most usual interjections are: *Oh!* (expressing pain or surprise), *Ah!* (surprise or satisfaction), *Hello!* (greeting or surprise), *Hey!* (to attract attention), *Alas!* (a 'literary' form expressing sorrow, disappointment). There are some interjections whose written form rather misrepresents their spoken sound, mainly because there are no conventional symbols which would represent it. There is, for example, *Tut, tut,* which stands for the sound made by clicking the tongue against the front teeth; and there is *Pshaw!* an expression of contempt, but it is difficult to say what exclamation in actual use the spelling is supposed to represent; certainly no one says [pʃoː] or [ʃoː] except when coming across *Pshaw!* in print.

The interjection *Oh!* is frequently written *O!* and either form is correct, but the form *O* (without an exclamation mark) should be used with the 'Nominative of Address' (the vocative case) occurring in oratorical speech, e.g.

'O all you host of heaven! O earth!' (*Hamlet*)
'O Julius Caesar, thou art mighty yet.' (*Julius Caesar*)

(The usual, modern form of the nominative of address occurs in such sentences as:

John, I want to speak to you.
Have you finished that work yet, *Smith?*

Here, *John* and *Smith* are not used as subject or object of a verb but merely to address or to attract the attention of these people.)

O can have occasionally, in rather rhetorical speech, something of a verbal force with a meaning something like 'I wish', e.g.

O that I had done what he told me.

'*O* that we now had here
But one ten thousand of those men in England
That do no work today.' (Shakespeare, *Henry V*.)

The dividing line is thin between interjections (reproductions of sounds or special words that we utter involuntarily under the stress of some emotion) and EXCLAMATIONS, in which an ordinary word or group of words are used as interjections. Examples of exclamations are: *Good! Bravo! Shame! Silence! Nonsense! Stop! I say! Hurrah! Well done! Just my luck!* and a variety of expletives ranging from the mild (and rather characteristically feminine) *Oh dear! Goodness! Gracious! Dear me!*[1] *Well I never! Oh bother!* to the more robust (and masculine) *Good Lord! Bless my soul! No fear!* and, less sociably acceptable, *Dash! Blast! Damn!*—and beyond.

Some of the exclamations just mentioned, e.g. *Silence! Well done! Stop!* etc., or *Goodbye! Farewell!* are perhaps elliptical sentences equivalent to something like: 'I want silence', 'You have done well', etc. *Goodbye* is an elliptical form of 'God be with ye'; *Farewell* an elliptical form of 'May you fare(= go) well'.

EXCLAMATORY SENTENCES

There are two types of exclamatory sentences whose sentence structure should be noted:

(1) Those beginning *How!* or *What!* e.g.

How well George writes! *How* nice of you to come and see us! *How* cold this room is! *What* lovely weather we are having! *What* a fool he is! *What* an awful noise! *What* rubbish he writes! *What* a shame that you can't come! *How* old he is!

(Note the difference between the exclamatory *How old he is!* and the interrogative *How old is he?*)

(2) Those beginning with an adverb like *There, Here, In,* etc., e.g.

There he is! Here it comes! Off they went! Away you go! In you get!

Sentences like the last two (in the second person) express a

---

[1] The accusative form of the pronoun is interesting.

kind of good humoured Imperative, less severe and commanding than *Go away. Get in.*

Note that if the subject is a personal pronoun (as in the examples above) it comes *before* the verb. If the subject is not a personal pronoun it comes *after* the verb, e.g.

There goes the train! Here comes George! There was a sudden gust of wind and *away went his hat!* The door burst open and *in rushed the crowd!*

EXERCISES

I From the following list of interjections and exclamations choose those you think most suitable as comments on the following sentences:

Goodness me! Bravo! Fancy that! Well played, Sir! Splendid!

(1) Do you know it's nearly midnight? (2) He's just won £1,000 in the football pools. (3) That's game and set, I think. (4) She's just begun to learn Russian—she'll be tackling Chinese next. (5) I managed to catch the post after all.

II Complete the following sentences with 'how', 'what', or suitable adverbs:

(1) He slipped on the ladder and —— he came. (2) —— went the thieves in the stolen car. (3) —— a pity she's so deaf. (4) There's no time to waste so —— you go at once. (5) —— beautiful the view is from your window.

CHAPTER TWENTY-TWO

SENTENCES AND CLAUSES

The traditional definition of a SIMPLE SENTENCE is: 'a group of words that contains a finite verb and makes complete sense.'

But this definition seems hardly adequate to cover such examples as the following, which 'make sense' to the person who hears them but which do not contain a finite verb:

'Stop!' 'Goodbye.' 'Thanks.' 'Of course.' 'Nonsense.' 'Waiter, another bottle of wine.' 'What a day!' 'Really?' 'This way, sir.' 'Oh! these exercises!' 'Hello!' 'Less noise there.' 'Fire!'

Consider, too, the replies to the following questions:

'What time is it?' *'Three o'clock.'*

'Who answered the question?' *'George.'*

'Did you know it?' *'Yes.'*

'How much butter do you want?' *'A pound and a half.'*

'Coffee, sir?' *'Yes, please.'*

'Black or white?' *'Black.'*

'I'll send you the books.' *'When?'*

Grammarians sometimes get over the difficulty by saying that these are 'elliptical' sentences, i.e. that a part is missed out but is 'understood' by the speaker and listener. Ellipsis is a common feature in English, e.g.

The work is done, the books put away (= are put away).

'To err is human, to forgive divine' (= is divine).

'Thank you' (= I thank you).

'First come, first served' (= *The* first *to* come *will be the* first *to be* served).

Your name and address, please (= Give me . . .).

What if I refuse to answer? (= What happens if . . . What will you do if . . .)

Any more fares, please? (*Are there* any more fares *still to be paid?*)

But in many sentences of this type it is not possible to state exactly what is 'left out'. In most of these examples, if the speaker and the hearer (both of whom understood exactly what was meant) were asked to supply the missing words, each would probably supply different ones.

Jesperson defines a sentence thus:

'A sentence is a (relatively) complete and independent human utterance—the completeness and independence being shown by its standing alone or its capability of standing alone, i.e. of being uttered by itself.'[1]

Other grammarians give these definitions:

'A sentence gives expression to a subject to which the speaker wishes to draw the hearer's attention, and also to something which he wishes him to think with reference to that subject; and this is equally true whether the sentence be examined from the psychological or the grammatical side.

Any utterance which calls up in the mind of the receiver these two linked things is a sentence (both psychological and grammatical), whether it consists of one syllable or fifty. And no utterance, however many words or syllables it contains, is a sentence, unless it does call up these two linked things.'[2]

'An oral or written communication is made up of one or more units, each of which contains a complete utterance formed according to a definite pattern. Such units are called sentences.'[3]

Sentences may be SIMPLE, COMPOUND or COMPLEX. For Simple sentences see Chapter Two.[4]

COMPOUND (DOUBLE OR MULTIPLE) SENTENCES

Two or more sentences may be joined by a conjunction (or conjunctions), e.g.

I am teaching you English *and* you are listening to me.

Do you understand that *or* is the point still not clear?

Bring your book here *and* open it at page 4; *but* don't begin reading.

Sentences like these are called COMPOUND or DOUBLE MULTIPLE sentences.

[1] *Philosophy of Grammar.*
[2] *Our Living Language*, Grattan & Gurrey.
[3] *A Handbook of English Grammar*, R. W. Zandvoort.
[4] Students who wish to examine the nature of a sentence more fully may be interested to read Chapter 2, 'What is a Sentence?' in *The Structure of English* by C. C. Fries (Longmans).

In compound sentences the subject or the auxiliary verb, or both, may be omitted in the second sentence if they are the same as those in the first sentence, e.g.

He is sitting and (he is) listening to me.

You must come tomorrow and (you must) bring your book with you.

COMPLEX SENTENCES

Each of the sentences in a compound sentence can stand independently. But there are some groups of words which, even though they contain a finite verb, are not 'complete and independent human utterances' and cannot stand alone, for example:

which I want; that he was tired; when he saw a policeman.

These groups of words, called SUBORDINATE CLAUSES, do the work of adjectives, adverbs or nouns (i.e. they can qualify nouns or verbs or be the subject or object of a verb) in a larger unit which is called a COMPLEX SENTENCE.

A clause is a group of words which include a finite verb, is grammatically complete and self-contained, forms part of a sentence, but does not by itself make complete sense.

A complex sentence consists of one or more of these subordinate clauses and a MAIN or PRINCIPAL clause.

A principal clause is usually defined as 'a clause that can stand alone and makes complete sense by itself'. But this is not always true (as, for example, in sentence 2 below). It might be better to say that the principal clause is what is left of a complex sentence when all the subordinate clauses have been taken away. *Examples:*

Principal Clause	Subordinate Clause
(1) That is the house	which I want.
(2) The man said	that he was tired.
(3) The thief ran away	when he saw the policeman.

In Sentence 1 the subordinate clause qualifies the noun *house* and is an ADJECTIVE CLAUSE.

In Sentence 2 it is the object of the verb *said* and is a NOUN CLAUSE.

In Sentence 3 it qualifies the verb *ran* and is an ADVERB CLAUSE.

When clauses of the same type are joined by *and* or *or*, the introductory conjunction, the subject and an auxiliary verb may be omitted if they are the same as those in the first clause, e.g.

If he had come and seen me *and* (if he had) discussed the matter with me, I should have given him my opinion.

If he will come and see me *or* (if he will) write to me . . .

After you have written your essay and after you have revised it, you may hand it in.

EXERCISES

I Construct examples of (1) a Simple Sentence:
   (*a*) statement, (*b*) question, (*c*) command.
   (2) a Compound Sentence. (3) a Complex Sentence.

II 'A Simple sentence is a group of words (including a subject and a verb) that makes complete sense.' Comment on this definition.

III Explain in what senses you could interpret the following expressions and supply the words necessary to express each idea fully.
   (1) Naturally (2) Keep left. (3) What a bore. (4) Murder! (5) Two whiskies, please. (6) Oh no! (7) Really? (8) Wait. (9) Oh, yes? (10) Just a moment. (11) Full-up. (12) No talking. (13) Seats on top. (14) Ridiculous. (15) Oh, my head!

IV Invent questions to which the following might be replies:
   (1) Half past two. (2) Three bottles. (3) Red, please. (4) On Monday next. (5) Yes. (6) First, please. (7) Upstairs. (8) Thick, please. (9) May 15th. (10) Of course.

V Pick out the different clauses (principal and subordinate) in the following sentences, and say which sort (Adverb, Adjective or Noun) each of the subordinate clauses is:
   (1) The coat that is hanging in the cupboard is mine. (2) This is the route I intend to take. (3) He slowed

L*

down the car as he approached the crossroads. (4) The house where he lives has just been repainted. (5) I don't know where they live. (6) The man I want to see is not here this morning. (7) When I went to his studio he showed me all the paintings he had done recently. (8) We shall go wherever he wishes to take us. (9) Wait while I get my overcoat. (10) The station closes immediately the last train has left. (11) Tell me where you are going for your holiday. (12) The place where we stayed for our holiday was right on the sea coast. (13) I don't know where we are going this year. (14) Come where we are going for our holiday. (15) Do you know where Shakespeare was born? (16) That is the house where Shakespeare was born. (17) I don't remember when Tom came to see me. (18) I think it was the day when we had that heavy thunderstorm. (19) If that was the day, it can't be a year ago. (20) I'll ask him if he remembers the visit. (21) Tell me who are coming to the party. (22) That's one of the boys who are coming to the party.

VI Form compound or complex sentences (as indicated) from the following groups of simple sentences. Omit a word or two where necessary:

(1) The boy closed the door. He walked away. (Compound)

(2) Richard works badly. He plays games well. (Compound)

(3) The children had finished their lessons. They went home. (Complex)

(4) We come to school on Friday. We have a holiday on Saturday. (Compound)

(5) Jack went up the hill. Jill went up the hill. They fetched a pail of water. (Compound)

(6) Jack fell down. He broke his crown. Jill came tumbling after. (Compound)

(7) We decided to remain at home. It was foggy. (Compound)

(8) We decided to remain at home. It was foggy. (Complex)

(9) You said something. I do not understand it. (Complex)

(10) A German is coming to see me. I made his acquaintance in Hamburg last year. (Complex)

(11) The students were trapped in a cave. One of them has already been brought out. (Complex)

(12) They could not decide what to do. They asked my advice. (Compound)
(13) She spoke French rapidly. He couldn't understand her. (Complex)
(14) Any of these problems can be solved by ordinary intelligence and hard work. None of them are too difficult for that. (Complex)

VII Complete the following sentences with main or subordinate clauses as may be necessary. Say what kind of a clause it is that you add.
(1) —— that I saw yesterday ——. (2) The concert —— was excellently performed. (3) —— can't be undone. (4) Do the work —— immediately. (5) Pupils should obey ——. (6) —— is quite obvious. (7) He didn't get the prize ——. (8) Because he didn't get up early enough ——. (9) —— where I lost my pen. (10) —— that he knew your sister.

CHAPTER TWENTY-THREE

SUBORDINATE CLAUSES

(i) ADJECTIVE CLAUSES

Adjective clauses (sometimes called 'Attributive' clauses or 'Relative' clauses) qualify nouns. The noun qualified is called the ANTECEDENT and the relative clause normally follows the antecedent, e.g.

That is the house *that I would like to buy*.

(Antecedent: *house*)

Sometimes the adjective clause divides the main clause, e.g.

The house *that I would like to buy* is not for sale.

An adjective clause is generally introduced by a relative pronoun (*that, which, who*, etc.). For relative pronouns see page 138.

DEFINING AND NON-DEFINING CLAUSES

(I) DEFINING CLAUSES

Adjective clauses are of two types. Consider the following examples:

The student *who* answered the question was John.
The book *which* you lent me was interesting.
He gave a tip to the porter *who* carried his luggage.
Thank you for the help *that* you have given me.
'This is the house *that* Jack built.'
The Duke of Marlborough was one of the greatest soldiers *that* England has ever had.

In all these sentences the adjective clause is a necessary part of the idea; if it is left out, the sentence does not make complete sense. All these clauses define the antecedent and give it its definite connotation; they indicate *which* student out of a number of students, *which* book out of thousands of books, *which* porter out of several porters, etc. So clauses of this type are called DEFINING clauses.

(2) NON-DEFINING CLAUSES

Now consider these sentences:

Bernard Shaw, *who* wrote *St. Joan*, died in 1950.

My father, *who* had been on a visit to America, arrived at Southampton yesterday.

That scientist, *whose* work is very important, has been made a knight.

Miss Smith, *whom* you met at our house, is going to marry Mr. Abbott.

The *Golden Hind*, in *which* Drake sailed round the world, was only a small ship.

In all these sentences the adjective clause could be omitted and the rest of the sentence would still make perfect sense. The adjective clauses here are a kind of parenthesis, a casual remark, an aside or an explanation. They could be written between brackets or dashes, e.g.

Bernard Shaw (who wrote *St. Joan*) died in 1950.

My father—who had been on a visit to America—arrived at Southampton yesterday.

They do not define the antecedent. They do not say *which* Bernard Shaw among a number of Bernard Shaws, *which* father among dozens of fathers. What they do is to give additional information about an antecedent which has already been sufficiently defined. They are therefore called NON-DEFIN-ING or AMPLIFYING CLAUSES. This parenthetical construction of non-defining clauses is shown by a comma in writing and by a pause in speaking at the beginning and end of the clause. Commas must not be put round a defining clause.

Compare the sentences:

(1) All the books, *which had pictures in them*, were sent to the little girl.
(She got *all* the books.) NON-DEFINING CLAUSE.

(2) All the books *which had pictures in them* were sent to the little girl.
(She got only those books which had pictures in them.) DEFINING CLAUSE.

(1) He has a brother, *who is an artist*.
(He has only one brother, and he is an artist.)

NON-DEFINING CLAUSE.

(2) He has a brother *who is an artist*.
(He may have several brothers, but one of them is an artist.) DEFINING CLAUSE.

Or compare:

(1) The work entailed a number of expenses, *which I had not allowed for*.
(I didn't expect there would be any expenses at all and so I hadn't allowed any money for expenses.) NON-DEFINING CLAUSE.

(2) The work entailed a number of expenses *which (that)[1] I had not allowed for*.
(I had expected a number of expenses. I had allowed money for these but then some unexpected ones had turned up.) DEFINING CLAUSE.

There is a type of non-defining clause which has for its antecedent a whole sentence. In this case the introductory relative pronoun is always *which. Examples:*

They have invited me to dinner, *which is very kind of them*.
He missed the train, *which annoyed him very much*.

There is a story of a clergyman, who, preferring not to wear the usual clerical dress, said:

'I will wear no clothes which will distinguish me from my fellow-men.'

But when his remark was reported in the newspapers, a comma was put in by mistake, and with its relative clause thus changed from a defining one to a non-defining one, the sentence then read:

'I will wear no clothes, which will distinguish me from my fellow-men.'

Non-defining clauses have also a 'continuative' or 'connective' use; that is, they are almost equivalent to a compound sentence, e.g.

[1] The relative pronoun *that* can be used with defining clauses; it cannot be used with non-defining clauses (see p. 140).

He put his proposal to George, who, after making full enquiries, decided to accept it.

In this example *who* could be replaced by *and he*, thus turning the non-defining clause into a co-ordinate sentence.

Except for the two types just mentioned (the 'continuative' and that in which a whole sentence is the antecedent), non-defining clauses are not common in conversational English. They are more usual in formal speech and writing.

OMISSION OF THE RELATIVE PRONOUN IN DEFINING CLAUSES

When the relative pronoun in a defining clause is in the objective case, it is often omitted, especially in spoken English, e.g.

The man (that) you spoke to was my brother.

The book (that) I want is on the table.

He is the kindest man (that) I know.

There's something (that) you don't know.

Clauses like these, in which the relative pronouns are omitted, are sometimes called CONTACT CLAUSES.

The relative pronoun can also be omitted in a defining clause introduced by *there is (was):*

The 9.15 is the fastest train (that) there is to Oxford.

I asked for the best book (that) there was on the subject.

In non-defining clauses, *who(m)*, *which* are never omitted, e.g.

My brother Alfred, *who* is eighteen years old, has bought a new bicycle.

My father, *whom* you met in Paris, is now back in London.

This poem, *which* almost everybody knows, is by Tennyson.

SUMMARY OF THE USAGE OF RELATIVE PRONOUNS IN ADJECTIVE CLAUSES

(1) DEFINING

	for people	*for things*
Subject	who, that	which, that
Object	whom, (that)	which, (that)
+ Preposition	to whom, (that) . . . to	to which, (that) . . . to
Possessive	whose	of which, whose

(2) NON-DEFINING

	People	Things
Subject	who	which
Object	whom	which
+ Preposition	to whom	to which
Possessive	whose	of which, whose

RELATIVE CLAUSES INTRODUCED BY OTHER WORDS

WHEN, WHERE, WHY

An adjective clause may be introduced by the words: *where, when, why* if these words have the meaning *in which, at which, for which*, etc., e.g.

The place *where* Macbeth met the witches was a desolate heath.

I remember the day *when* she first wore that pink dress.

I know the reason *why* he was so angry

In the above examples the adjective clause is a defining one; but *when* and *where* can also introduce non-defining clauses, e.g.

We will put off the picnic until next week, *when* the weather may be better.

They went to the Royal Theatre, *where* they saw Ibsen's 'Peer Gynt'.

BUT

A noun in a negative sentence is sometimes qualified by an adjective clause introduced by *but:*

There was not a single person there *but* thought you were in the right.

There's not a man here *but* would like to be in your place.

Here, 'but thought' = 'who did not think'; and 'but would like' = 'who would not like'. The *but* contradicts the negative. This construction is not common.

AS

After *same* and *such* an adjective clause is usually introduced by *as,* e.g.

I shall be surprised if he does this the *same* way *as* I do.

She wears the *same* kind of clothes *as* her sister wears.

I have never heard *such* stories *as* he tells.

'We are *such* stuff *as* dreams are made on.' (Shakespeare, *The Tempest.*)

But, occasionally, *that* can be used after *same,* e.g.

She wore the *same* dress *that* she wore at Mary's wedding.

ADJECTIVE CLAUSES WITH FORMAL SUBJECT[1] 'IT'

Sometimes a part of a sentence is given front position and is introduced by *it is* (or some other form of the verb *to be* singular number) and followed by an adjective clause, e.g.

It is work that we want, not charity.

It was Sir Rowland Hill who introduced the penny post in England.

It will not *be* you who will have to take the blame for this.

It was only John's hard work that made success possible.

EXERCISES

I Explain exactly, giving an example of each, what is meant by (1) antecedent. (2) contact clause. (3) defining clause. (4) non-defining clause.

II Pick out the adjective clause in each of the following sentences and give the antecedent:

(1) This is the bicycle that my uncle gave me. (2) Do you know anyone who wants to buy a motor-bike? (3) Here are the cakes which I bought. (4) The man was returning home with the money, which he had put in his pocket. (5) The bicycle which my uncle gave me was a birthday present. (6) A motor-bike that won't go is no use. (7) The cakes that I bought have all been eaten. (8) The money which the man had drawn from the bank was in his pocket book. (9) The house that you see over there is very old. (10) The thief who had robbed the man was caught by the policeman.

[1] See page 101.

III Combine the following pairs of sentences by using relative pronouns:

(1) This house is very modern. It has television and an electric washing-machine.

(2) That man seems very lonely. His wife and family are away.

(3) Dumas was a famous French novelist. He wrote *The Three Musketeers*.

(4) He is a reliable fellow. I can trust him with anything.

(5) That mountain is difficult to climb. It has many dangerous slopes.

(6) Those prize pigeons have been stolen. They were very valuable.

(7) Our dog Spot is seven years old. He is a great favourite with the family.

(8) The lecturer tonight was very interesting. He came from Cambridge.

(9) *Twelfth Night* is a famous comedy. It was written by Shakespeare.

(10) This summer has been very warm. That is very unusual in this country.

IV Punctuate the following complex sentences, according to whether the clauses are defining or non-defining:

(1) Many people were injured in the capital of Ruritania where 1,000 students took part in a demonstration. (2) I went to see their new house which I like very much. (3) The rubbish which John has collected must be burnt. (4) The river that flows through London is the Thames. (5) The Thames which flows through London is a beautiful river. (6) I do not know the town where he is going. (7) He is going to the golf course where he intends to put in some practice. (8) He is going to the golf course where he practised last week.

V Combine each of the following pairs of sentences into one sentence by means of a relative clause, using contact clauses where possible:

(1) He will have to get up early. He won't like it. (2) I've got to entertain my mother-in-law. I can't stand her. (3) He went to Oxford. He read Classics there. (4) The £30,000,000 issue was underwritten by X Y Z & Co. Lord A is Chairman of this company.

(5) The driver has driven a car for twenty years. His licence has just been endorsed. (6) The worries have aged him. He has had these worries. (7) Lewis Carroll was really a mathematician. He wrote *Alice in Wonderland*. (8) The firm have dispensed with his services. He has been employed there for thirty years. (9) The house has two spare bedrooms. We've bought it. (10) The rat is in the trap. It ate the cheese. Mary bought the cheese.

VI Express differently, by means of relative clauses:
(1) This is a book on zoology; there is none better. (2) The reason for his silence is not known. (3) I ended up by making a speech, and I hadn't wanted to. (4) My sister is quite mad to want to be an actress, for she has not the least talent. (5) Here is a girl with real talent and she really ought to have gone in for the theatre. (6) We are living in profoundly disturbing times.

VII Complete the following sentences by adding the appropriate relative pronoun and, where necessary, commas. If the relative pronoun can be omitted from any of the sentences, put it in the sentences but enclose it in brackets ( ). Say if any of the relative clauses are non-defining.

(1) The house —— you're looking for is at the other end of the street. (2) The bridge —— this photo was taken has since been rebuilt. (3) The child —— parents died in the air crash is living with his aunt. (4) The yacht —— you see moored in the harbour belongs to an American. (5) The place —— you are standing was the site of the old market cross. (6) You can telephone to the people —— you told me about yesterday. (7) What's the address of the firm —— advertisement we noticed the other day? (8) There's the bus —— I generally take to go to the office. (9) The family —— I stayed with in Rome are coming to England this year. (10) The umbrella —— you borrowed last night belongs to my brother. (11) Did you know that the actor —— you saw playing Hamlet is now doing King Lear? (12) William the Conqueror —— was Duke of Normandy invaded England in 1066. (13) King's College, Cambridge —— is a royal foundation has a beautiful chapel. (14) Tennis —— is the best summer game can be played by two or four players. (15) The 9th Symphony —— is Beethoven's greatest is very hard for the chorus.

VIII Construct three sentences containing adjective clauses in which *that* must be included and three from which it can be omitted.

IX Re-write the following sentences so that each contains a non-defining relative clause:

(1) Shakespeare was born at Stratford and wrote many plays. (2) Liverpool is a busy port containing miles of docks. (3) The Portuguese sailor, Magellan, gave his name to the famous straits. (4) The paintings by Vermeer in the Art Gallery are insured for a large amount. (5) This newly-published book was recently summarized in a Sunday paper.

X By introducing non-defining relatives combine each of the following pairs of sentences into one sentence:

(1) Toscanini was a world-famous conductor. He often visited London. (2) The Black Death was a terrible pestilence. It decimated the population of some parts of England. (3) Some fine stained glass can be seen in York Minster. It is in the North of England. (4) The Bill has been passed through Parliament. During the debate there were three all-night sittings. (5) The Fado is a popular form of song in Portugal. It is often nostalgic in character.

XI Construct sentences containing relative clauses introduced by the following:

There is (are, was, were), where, when, why.

XII Re-write the following sentences so that they contain clauses introduced by 'but':

(1) Nobody disagreed with your proposal. (2) There was no one there who didn't support the action taken by the Government. (3) There was hardly a year went by that did not bring him further honours. (4) There was no painter of that age who did not want to do for Siena what the Florentine artists had done for Florence.

XIII Complete these sentences by inserting the correct introductory words:

(1) He had a natural thoughtfulness such —— is rarely seen in one so young. (2) You may do ——ever you like, go ——ever you choose and with ——ever you please. (3) I remember the time —— you could buy a 2-oz. bar of chocolate for 2d. (4) 'What chapter have you reached?' 'The one —— the body disappears!'

(ii) NOUN CLAUSES

A noun clause is one which does the work of a noun. It may be:

1. THE OBJECT OF A VERB, e.g.

George said (*that*) *he was pleased to welcome our Italian friends.*
I know (*that*) *you must be tired after your long journey.*
William dreamed (*that*) *he was flying to the moon.*

This is the most usual function.

An object clause, i.e. a noun clause that is the object of a verb may be:

(*a*) a statement, direct or indirect, e.g.

He said, '*The car will be ready tomorrow.*'
He told me (*that*) *the debt had been paid.*

(*b*) a question, direct or indirect, e.g.

He said, '*Where do you live?*'
He asked me *where I lived.*
Can you tell me *what the time is?*

2. THE SUBJECT OF A VERB, e.g.

What you are doing seems very difficult.
That he will refuse the offer is unlikely.
How the prisoner escaped is a complete mystery.
'*How glad I am to see you*', were his first words.
'*Why are you so late?*' was his next remark.

A 'subject' noun clause always precedes its principal clause. The verbal predicate of subject clauses is almost always the verb *to be* or a verb with a similar meaning.

3. THE OBJECT OF A PREPOSITION, e.g.

He only laughed at *what*[1] *we said.*
They will be very thankful for *whatever you can give them.*
That student always pays attention to *whatever the teacher is saying.*
You can have this for *what I paid for it.*

[1] Note that *what* introduces noun clauses, not adjectival ones.

4. THE COMPLEMENT OF A VERB, e.g.

The fact *that he doesn't really try.*
It seems/appears *that he has never been paid the money.*
That is not *what I want.*
What surprised me was *that he spoke English so well.*

5. IN APPOSITION[1] TO A NOUN, e.g.

The fact *that the prisoner was guilty* was plain to everyone.
The news *that we are having a holiday tomorrow* is not true.
The idea *that you can do this work without thinking* is quite wrong.

6. USED WITH A NUMBER OF PREDICATIVE ADJECTIVES, like *certain, glad, sorry,* e.g.

I am certain *that I posted the letter.*
She is very glad *that you are able to come.*
I am afraid *that you are right.*
He is quite confident *that he will pass the examination.*
I am sorry *that your brother is ill.*
It is possible *that I may (might) not be able to come.*
It is impossible *that he should make (should have made) a mistake like that.*

In the last two sentences the noun clause is in apposition to *it.* In sentences like this, *it* is called the FORMAL SUBJECT; the real subject is the noun clause. In this construction the *that* clause is always in end-position. Note that the auxiliary after *it is possible* is *may* or *might;* after *it is impossible* it is *should.*

Noun clauses are usually introduced by *that* or an interrogative pronoun, adjective, or adverb, e.g.

STATEMENT: He said that he knew you.

QUESTIONS: He asked me
- what I wanted.
- where I was going.
- who I was.
- why I had come here.
- how often I had come.

---

[1] Another noun or noun clause that is added to a noun to explain it further is said to be in apposition to it, e.g. Mr. Priestley, *the teacher*, explained the work. Adam, *the gardener*, digs in the garden. Henry VIII, *King of England*, died in 1547.

The *that* may be omitted except when the noun clause precedes the main verb,[1] e.g.

He said (*that*) he would come.

I am afraid (*that*) you are right.

That he doesn't want to see us is quite obvious.

Noun clauses that express a hope or a suggestion often have the auxiliary verb *may, might* or *should*, e.g.

I hope we *may* have the pleasure of seeing you again.

He hoped that they *might* have the pleasure of seeing her again.

The teacher suggested that each student *should* tell a story.

A noun clause may occur in the exclamatory construction[2] with such words as *O* (meaning 'I wish'), *Alas* (meaning 'I am sorry'), e.g.

O that I could swim like you!

'*Alas*, that Spring should vanish with the Rose!'

(*Omar Khayyám*, translated by Fitzgerald)

In the chapter on Parts of Speech it was emphasized that words are classified into parts of speech according to the work they do and not according to their form. This stipulation applies to clauses also. The same clause may be a noun clause, an adjective clause or an adverb clause, e.g.

(1) Tell me *where you went*.

(2) I am going to the house *where you went*.

(3) I am going *where you went*.

In No. 1 the subordinate clause is a noun clause, object of the verb *tell*. In No. 2 it is an adjective clause qualifying the noun *house*. In No. 3 it is an adverb clause of place.

EXERCISES

I Pick out the noun clauses in the following, and describe the function of each:

(1) That it was done deliberately is quite clear. (2) We greatly regret that we were obliged to refuse your

---

[1] It is not omitted when the noun clause is used with a further subordinate clause that precedes it. Compare 'He said he would come for dinner' and 'He said *that*, if he could manage it, he would come for dinner.' [2] See page 315.

invitation. (3) Many people are wondering when inter-planetary travel will become possible. (4) Can you explain to me where he lives? (5) What you are attempting is really too difficult for you. (6) The hospital will greatly appreciate all you can do for the patients. (7) We were greatly amused by what you told us. (8) It seems that he is not coming to the party after all. (9) The notion that people can work less and earn more is contrary to reason. (10) I am delighted that you have succeeded in getting the job.

II Complete these sentences with noun clause objects. Use the interrogative pronoun or adjective indicated to introduce each clause.

(1) I do not know . . . (what). (2) I did not know . . . (how). (3) Nobody understands . . . (why). (4) Please tell me . . . (who). (5) He couldn't make out . . . (where). (6) Can you find out . . . (when).

III (a) Supply noun clause subjects to complete the following sentences:

(1) What . . . is none of my business.
(2) That . . . is clear to anyone with a grain of sense.
(3) How . . . is beyond my comprehension.
(4) When . . . depends on the time at her disposal.
(5) Whether . . . is for your husband to decide.
(6) Who . . . is more important than where it comes from.
(7) Why . . . beats me!
(8) Where . . . is immaterial, so long as it is done.

(b) Re-write the above sentences, using 'it' as the formal subject.

IV Form a noun clause:

(a) In apposition to the noun 'suggestion'.
(b) As object of the preposition 'on'.
(c) As complement of the verb 'was'.
(d) As complement of the adjective 'aware'.

V What kind of clauses are the ones in italics?

(a) Tell me the reason *why he did it*.
(b) You can do it *how you like*.
(c) We don't know *where we are going*.
(d) The place *where we are going* is a long way from any town.

VI Give a full description of the noun clauses in the following sentences:

(1) Tell me which of these patterns you prefer. (2) They want to know when we are going to take our holiday. (3) She enquired at the shop when her costume would be ready. (4) 'Why did you stay out so late?' was the mother's first question. (5) The rumour that prices will soon go down is unfortunately untrue. (6) The truth is he does not work hard enough. (7) 'What on earth,' he said, 'do you think you are doing?' (8) It is possible that I shall go away for the week-end. (9) That he should be deliberately dishonest is unthinkable. (10) As the day was fine I proposed that we should go for a picnic.

VII Turn the following sentences into indirect speech in such a way that each contains a noun clause:

(1) I have crossed the Channel about fifty times. (2) They have sold all their property in England. (3) How long have you been working in this office? (4) Smoking is strictly forbidden. (5) Don't wait for me after eight o'clock. (6) Notice: Ticket-holders are asked to be in their seats by 8.15. (7) Ought I to go to see him, I wondered? (8) Shall I ever master English pronunciation? (9) They hope to get away early this evening. (10) Will you join me in a drink? With great pleasure, thank you.

(iii) ADVERB CLAUSES

Adverb clauses do the work of adverbs. The chief types of adverb clauses are those of:

(1) MANNER, which indicate *how* an action is done, e.g.

Henry did the work *as it ought to be done.*

When I get the money I shall spend it *as I like.*

I shall do the exercises *as I have been taught.*

He ran *as if (though) his life depended on it.*

Adverb Clauses of manner are usually introduced by the conjunctions *as, as if, as though,*[1] followed by a past subjunctive, e.g.

You look as if (= as you would look if) you had seen a ghost.

---

[1] But the conjunction introducing a clause is no true guide to the kind of clause introduced. The same word may, as was shown earlier, introduce different kinds of clauses. The true guide is the work that the clause is doing.

(2) PLACE, which indicate *where* an action was done, e.g.

The house stood *where the London road meets the Brighton road.*

Stay *where you are!*

I will go *wherever you go.*

'Fools rush in *where angels fear to tread.*'[1]

Adverb clauses of place are introduced by *where*, or *wherever*.

(3) TIME, which indicate *when* an action was done. These clauses can be introduced by a number of conjunctions, e.g. *when, while, after, before, until, since, as, as soon as.*

Examples:

When it rains, I usually go to the office by bus.

I learned a lot of French *while I was in Paris.*

She learned English *before she came to England.*

He kept on with his work *until he had finished it.*

The thief was arrested *as he was leaving the bank.*[2]

TENSES USED IN ADVERB CLAUSES OF TIME AND PLACE

(a) *Time*

In adverb clauses of time, a Present Tense in the principal clause takes a Present Tense in the time clause; a Past Tense in the principal clause takes a Past Tense in the time clause.

Examples:

PRESENT: I *like* perfect quietness when I *am working.* As you *go* out, please *close* the door. As soon as it *is* dark, the lights of the town *go* on.

PAST: He *liked* perfect quietness when he *was working.* He *switched* off the radio as soon as the jazz music *started.* As he *went* out he *slammed* the door.

But a Future Tense in the principal clause generally takes a Present Tense in the time clause, e.g.

---

[1] Alexander Pope (1688–1724), *Essay on Criticism.*

[2] *As* is used when we are thinking of the course of an action. For that reason the verb in an adverb clause beginning with *as* is generally in the Continuous Tense.

I *shall wait* until you *come* back. (NOT: *shall come*)

He *will let you know* as soon as he *has* any news. (NOT: *will have*)

We *will send* the money as soon as the goods *are delivered*. (NOT: *will be* delivered)

I am *going to write* to John as soon as *I have* a spare moment.

By the time you *get* back, dinner *will be* ready.

(b) Place

The construction in place clauses is similar to that in time clauses. A Future Tense in the principal clause is generally accompanied by a Present Tense in the place clause.

I *will go* where you *tell* me.

'Where your treasure *is*, there *will* your heart *be* also.'

But other sequences of tense are possible according to the meaning, e.g.

I *shall meet* him where I first *met* you.

When a place clause is introduced by *wherever*, the subjunctive equivalent *may* is sometimes used, e.g.

I will find her wherever she *may* be.

Wherever you *may* go, he will not forget you.

(4) REASON (or CAUSE), which indicate *why* an action was done. These clauses are generally introduced by *because, since, as, seeing that, now that*, e.g.

He sold the car *because it was too small*.

Since/as/seeing that/now that/ you won't help me, I must do the job myself.

Clauses beginning with *as, since, seeing that*, usually precede the principal clause; those beginning with *because* usually come after it, e.g.

As my secretary is away at present, I have a great many extra letters to answer.

I have a great many extra letters to answer *because my secretary is away at present*.

In the former sentence the emphasis is thrown on to the principal clause; in the latter it is thrown on to the adverb clause.

Additional emphasis is given to the adverb clause of reason when it is preceded by *it is*, *it was*, etc., and followed by *that*, e.g.

It was (only) *because the car was so small* that he sold it.

In this construction *because* must always be used, never *as*, etc. If the sentence had read:

As the car was so small he sold it,

the emphasis on the reason for his selling it would not have been so strong.

(5) PURPOSE. These clauses are usually introduced by *so that*, *in order that*, and the somewhat archaic *lest* (modern: *for fear that*; *so that . . . not*).

Some people eat *so that they may live.*

Others seem to live *in order that they may eat.*

He worked hard *so that he might win the prize.*

He took his shoes off, *so that I shouldn't hear him.*

I am telling you this *lest you should make a mistake* (for fear that you should make a mistake/so that you should not make a mistake).

When affirmative clauses of purpose are introduced by *that*, *may* is generally used for present and future time and *might* for past time; in negative clauses, (including those introduced by *lest*), *shall* is used for present time and *should* for past time, e.g.

They are climbing higher so that they may[1] get a better view.

I will send him our proposals now so that he *may*[1] have time to consider them before our meeting.

He is working late so that he *may*[1] be free to go away tomorrow.

They climbed higher so that they *might*[2] get a better view.

I sent him the proposals last week so that he *might*[2] have time to consider them.

He worked late last night so that he *might*[2] be free to go away tomorrow.

[1] In these sentences *will* or *can* could be used instead of *may*.
[2] In these sentences *could* or *would* could be used instead of *might*.

I hid the book lest he *should* see it.

I hid the book so that he *should* not see it.

When the subject of the subordinate clause of purpose is the same person or thing as the subject of the principal clause, purpose is often expressed not by a clause but by the infinitive with *to*, *in order to*, or *so as to*, e.g.

They are climbing higher *to get* (*in order to get*, *so as to get*) a better view.

I will send him our proposals now *to give* (*in order to give*) him time to consider them.

'I come *to bury* Caesar not *to praise* him.'[1]

(6) CONCESSION (meaning 'I concede that . . .', 'I grant that . . .'). These clauses are introduced generally by *though*, *although*, *even though*, occasionally by *even if*, *wherever*, *whenever*, *however* (with an adjective), *whether . . . or not*, *no matter whether . . . or not*, e.g.

Though (*although*) *he tried hard*, he was not successful.

He did well in his examination, *even if he didn't get a prize*.

However hard he tries, he never seems able to do the work satisfactorily.

Whether he works or not, I don't think he will pass his examination.

Whatever you may say, I still think I did the right thing.

No matter whether you agree or not, I shall pay him the price he asks.

Quite often, especially in spoken English, the words, 'It doesn't matter' introduce a concession, e.g.

It doesn't matter what you say, I shall go to the dance.

In concessive clauses that imply a fact, the verb is in the indicative mood; but sometimes, in concessive clauses that refer to future or present time, the subjunctive mood or a subjunctive equivalent is used, e.g.

It would be worth while trying *even though it should not succeed at once*.

'*Though your sins be as scarlet*, they shall be white as snow.' (*Bible*)

[1] Shakespeare, *Julius Caesar*.

Other constructions with concessive clauses are:

Poor as he was (= though he was poor) he was honest.

Much as I admire him as a writer (= though I admire him a great deal) I do not like him as a man.

Try as he will (*try as he may*) (= though he tries hard), he never seems able to do the work satisfactorily.

For all that he seems so bad-tempered (= though he seems so bad-tempered), I still think he has a very kind nature.

There is also a construction—especially in conversation—in which *though* comes at the end of the sentence, e.g.

Henry looks stupid; he knows mathematics, *though*.

This is not a complex sentence so there is not a clause of concession in it, but *though* (= *nevertheless, all the same*) gives a concessive meaning to it.

When the subject of the clause of concession and the principal clause refer to the same person, a phrase with *though* may take the place of the concessive clause, e.g.

Though beaten, we were not disgraced.

Though no swimmer, Mary splashed about happily in the sea.

(7) COMPARISON. These clauses are introduced by *as* (preceded by *so, such, as* in the principal clause), *than* (preceded by a comparative in the principal clause), e.g.

This work is not so (as) easy *as you think*.

That question was not such an easy one *as I thought*.

That question is easier *than I thought*.

Another type of comparative clause has the construction '*The* . . . comparative . . . *the* . . . comparative', e.g.

The more you work, *the more* you earn.[1]

The more he has, *the more* he wants.

The sooner you finish your work, *the sooner* you will go home.

In some proverbial expressions this construction has become very elliptical, e.g.

The more, the merrier. The sooner the better.

[1] The meaning is, roughly, 'Your earnings will be proportionate to your work'.

When an adverb clause of comparison is introduced by 'than that', *should* is often used as an auxiliary, e.g.

I would rather lose the chance of getting this job *than that* you *should* ask your brother to recommend me.

Nothing would please me more *than that* my daughter *should* marry your son.

(8) CONDITION (or SUPPOSITION), which indicate on what condition a thing happens, happened or will happen. These clauses are introduced by the conjunctions *if, unless* (= if not), *whether, as long as,* or *that* (after *supposing, provided, on condition*) e.g.

I shall go *if he asks me.*

I shan't go *unless he asks me.*

I shall go, *whether he asks me or not.*

I shall go *as long as/provided that/on condition that/he asks me.*

Supposing that he asks you, will you go?

There is a type of conditional clause, used in sentences of a proverbial nature, where the condition is expressed in the form of a command, e.g.

Give (i.e. if you give) *him an inch* and he'll take a yard.[1]

Ask (= if you ask) *me no questions* and I will tell you no lies.

Spare the rod and spoil the child. (= if you spare the rod, you will spoil the child.)

For further treatment of adverbial clauses of condition, see Chapter Twenty-four.

(9) RESULT. A clause of simple result is usually introduced by *so that*, e.g.

I received my wages yesterday, *so that* I can now pay what I owe you.

He was speaking very quietly, *so that* it was difficult to hear what he said.

This construction differs from the similar construction introducing a clause of Purpose, in that it is not followed by *may, might* or *should*.

---

[1] The usual proverbial expression is '. . . and he'll take an *ell*'. (An *ell* was an old measure, in England 45 inches. Originally it was the length of an arm. Compare *elbow*, the 'bow' or bend in the arm.)

A clause of result associated with degree is introduced by *so . . . that, such . . . that* or *so . . . as to*, e.g.

He ran *so* fast *that* I could not catch him.

It was *such* a warm day *that* I took off my jacket.

Would you be *so* kind *as to* carry this?

EXERCISES

I Pick out the adverb clauses in the following sentences and say what type of adverb clause each one is:

(1) When we arrived at the football field the game had started. (2) Richard left dirty footmarks wherever he went. (3) Kick the ball hard, as Richard did. (4) Don't handle those cups and saucers as if they were made of iron. (5) I am standing where I can see the game. (6) You can't come into this room while we are having a lesson. (7) As soon as the boys came into the room the noise started. (8) Use the paint-brush as I showed you yesterday. (9) Everywhere I looked there were dirty footmarks. (10) Our friends had arrived when we got home. (11) I need a hammer and nails, because I am going to repair the shed. (12) We couldn't play the match, because the fog was too thick. (13) We shall come and see you, if we have a holiday. (14) Although it was rather foggy, we played the match. (15) We shall play the match, even though it is rather foggy. (16) We had to cancel the match, because it was so foggy. (17) Mrs. Brown locked the cupboard, so that Richard should not take the cakes. (18) I will tell you the secret, if you won't tell it to anyone else. (19) If you will tell me the secret, I won't tell it to anyone else. (20) They went swimming, although the sea was very rough. (21) He told me the secret, so that I should help him. (22) Mrs. Brown locked the cupboard, because she didn't want Richard to take the cakes.

II Complete the following sentences by putting conjunctions in the vacant spaces and, at the end of each sentence, say what kind of adverb clause is employed in it.

(1) He did his work —— he thoroughly enjoyed it. (2) —— I have finished my university studies I shall spend a year in travelling. (3) Put those books back immediately—— they belong. (4) We took a lot of photos —— we were in Switzerland. (5) The pianist waited for

silence —— he began to play. (6) They promised to wait —— the clock struck eight. (7) I gave up studying mathematics —— it was too difficult a subject. (8) It was only —— the train was late that I did not meet you. (9) He often worked late —— he could earn more money. (10) I am posting this letter tonight —— you will receive it in the morning. (11) —— she may have told you, I still think he is not to be trusted. (12) The expense may be justifiable —— it does seem excessive. (13) Much —— I enjoy his lectures his mannerisms irritate me. (14) —— we were very tired after the journey, we were in good spirits. (15) The oral examination was not so great an ordeal —— I had feared.. (16) —— that my expenses are paid I shall be willing to attend the conference. (17) You can count on him to do the job exactly —— you want it done. (18) —— the money does not arrive in time, how will you pay your landlady? (19) I shall use this money exactly —— I like. (20) Those books *must* be found —— they are.

III Add adverb clauses to the following main clauses, as indicated:

(1) He worked . . . (*Manner*)
(2) . . ., please come and call on me. (*Time*)
(3) . . ., you cannot afford to slack. (*Cause*)
(4) You don't want to go . . ., do you? (*Place*)
(5) He refused to have oil-stoves in his house . . . (*Cause*)
(6) . . ., it is better to have it, just in case. (*Concession*)
(7) . . ., your conscience will leave you no peace. (*Concession*)
(8) . . ., I shall write to him tomorrow. (*Purpose*)
(9) . . ., there is no need for rudeness. (*Concession*)
(10) . . ., you would not be so rude. (*Condition*)
(11) It's as broad . . . (*Comparison*)
(12) It's not so cold . . . (*Comparison*)
(13) There was a storm that night such . . . before nor . . . since. (*Comparison*)
(14) Mary is cleverer . . . (*Comparison*)
(15) The sooner he gets out of that habit, . . . (*Comparison*)
(16) I would rather come another day than that . . . (*Comparison*)
(17) . . ., he will go out tomorrow. (*Condition*)
(18) . . ., he would go out tomorrow. (*Condition*)
(19) . . ., he would have gone out yesterday. (*Condition*)
(20) You can do what you like . . . (*Condition*)

M

IV Pick out the adverb and adjective clauses in the following passage, and classify them:

D. was a tall boy who had outgrown his strength and had no brains. Whenever he was asked a question, he would say, 'Er . . .', as he never had the least idea what the answer was. One day, during a General Knowledge lesson, the master had a little joke with him. In order that he might give D. an opportunity to answer at least one question, he pointed to him and asked him to name Abraham's birthplace. Though D., as usual, hadn't the least idea, he replied quite correctly, 'Ur', which was no more than his usual 'Er . . .'.

Another habit by which D. will be remembered was his fondness for riding his bicycle up and down the High Street, where he could be seen by large numbers of the school. He would ride at fantastic speeds, as though his life were at stake; his sole object, however, was to see how many electric light bulbs he could break through an over-generation of electricity from the hub dynamo. The faster he rode, the more success he had in breaking bulbs. No boy I ever knew was quite so stupid, or, in his way, so memorable. If he were not so stupid, I'd say he must now be a racing-motorist—or an archaeologist!

V Construct ten sentences each containing an adverbial clause introduced by a word or expression from the following list, and at the end of each sentence name the kind of adverbial clause it contains:

as, though, as soon as, for fear that, however, seeing that, on condition that, in order to, no matter, the less . . . the less.

CHAPTER TWENTY-FOUR

CONDITIONAL CLAUSES

Conditional clauses are of two kinds, distinguished by the form and meaning of the principal clause. The difference between them is important.

Type I: OPEN CONDITIONS

Type I is represented by sentences like:

If John works hard he will pass his examination.
If the rain stops I shall go for a walk.
Unless the rain stops I shall not go for a walk.
If you are right, then I am wrong.

The positions of the clauses can be reversed. When the *if*-clause is placed first it is rather more emphatic.

I will help him *if he asks me.*
I won't help him *unless he asks me.*
He will do the work *if (provided that/on condition that) he has the time.*

All these sentences contain a condition that may or may not be fulfilled. Thus the rain may stop or it may not; John may work or he may not; you may be right or you may not. The sentences do not say that the condition will or will not be realized; they do not state that the rain will stop, that John will (or will not) work or that you are (or are not) wrong. The conditions in these sentences are 'open' conditions.

TENSES USED IN OPEN CONDITIONS

A great many combinations of tenses may be used in open conditions, e.g.

1.	*Present Tense in 'if' clause*	*Tense in Main clause*
	If you are right I am wrong.	Present
	If you help me I will help you.	Future

Present Tense in 'if' clause	*Tense in Main clause*
If I get this right, I shall have answered every question correctly.	Future Perfect
If what you say is right, then what I said was wrong.	Past
If you meet Henry, tell him I want to see him.	Imperative
If you should[1] meet Henry, tell him I want to see him.	Imperative
If the ground is very dry, don't forget to water those plants.	Imperative
If he should come, please give him this book.	Imperative
If you should be passing, do come and see us.	Imperative
If the train should be late, what will you do?	Future

The form with *should* (i.e. *should* + infinitive without *to*) is usually used when some course of action is to be envisaged in certain possible future circumstances. It is thus most frequently employed when the main clause is a command or a question.

2. *Past Tense in 'if'-clause*	*Tense in Main clause*
If I said that, I apologize.	Present
If I said that, I was mistaken.	Past
If I made a mistake, I will try to remedy it.	Future

3. *Present Perfect Tense in 'if'-clause*	*Tense in Main clause*
If I have made a mistake, I will try to remedy it.	Future
If you have done your work, you may go to the cinema.	Present

[1] This sentence (with *should*) suggests a rather more remote possibility than the previous one.

NOTE: The Future Tense cannot be used in the *if* clause even when the meaning is future, e.g.

I shall go for a walk if the rain *will* stop. (WRONG)
I shall go for a walk if the rain *stops*. (RIGHT)

Will is only possible in such cases if it is used to express not future time but willingness, e.g.

If you *will* sign this agreement, I *will* let you have the money at once.

This could be expressed rather more indirectly, diffidently or politely with *would:*

If you would (*would* be so kind as to/*would* be kind enough to) sign this agreement, I will let you have the money at once.

Type II. HYPOTHETICAL CONDITIONS, SUPPOSITIONS

The following are examples of Hypothetical Conditions:

If Henry were here, he would know the answer.
If I had the money, I would buy a new car.
'If wishes were horses, beggars would ride.'
If I were King, you should be Queen.

In this type of sentence, too, the clauses may be reversed, e.g.

I would buy a new car *if I had the money*.

Such sentences make a hypothesis which may be contrary to fact or just something not thought of as a fact. 'If Henry were here . . .' implies that he is *not* here: 'If I had the money' implies that I have not the money. Or they may imply a doubt; 'If John worked hard he would pass the Examination' suggests '. . . but I am doubtful whether he will work hard.'

In sentences of Type II (Hypothetical Conditions) the past subjunctive is used in the 'if' clause and *would* or *should* + the infinitive are used in the main clause. Sentences of this kind may refer to present time, past time or future time.

(*a*) PRESENT TIME

If Henry were here, he would know the answer.
If I had the money, I should buy a new car.

> *If the grass needed cutting,* I would cut it.
> *If the hat suited me,* I would buy it.

Despite the Modal Preterite forms *were, had, needed, suited,* these sentences express a PRESENT condition (see page 161). They mean: 'If Henry were here NOW . . .' 'If I had the money NOW . . .' 'If the grass needed cutting NOW . . .', etc.

(b) PAST TIME

Here are sentences expressing hypothetical conditions in the past time. You will note that in these there is usually an implied negative.

> 'If John *had worked* hard' (in the PAST) 'he would have passed the examination.' (*Implied Negative :* . . . but he didn't work hard).
> 'If you *had asked* me' (in the PAST) 'I *would have helped* you'. ('. . . but you didn't ask me').
> 'If I *had had* the money' (some years ago) 'I *would have bought* a bigger house' (. . . 'but I hadn't the money').
> 'If the hat *had suited* me' (when I saw it in the shop yesterday) '*I would have bought it.*'
> 'I *should never have done* that work, if you *had not helped* me.'
> 'If you *hadn't told* me about it, I *might* never *have gone* to see it.'

(c) FUTURE TIME

The idea of futurity in hypothetical conditions is often expressed by the same construction as is used for the present, sometimes with a time adverb or phrase, e.g.

> If Richard worked hard next term, he would pass the examination.
> If you went there, you would see what I mean.

But futurity in the 'if'-clause is frequently expressed by *were to* + infinitive, e.g.

> What would you say if I *were to tell* you that Mary is going to be married?
> If our train *were to arrive* punctually, we should have time to visit your sister.

We can summarize the verb forms in sentences of Hypothetical Condition like this:

	Verb in 'if' clause	*Verb in Main clause*
PRESENT TIME	Simple Past Tense (or Subjunctive)	*would (should)*[1] + bare infinitive.
PAST TIME	Past Perfect Tense	*would (should)*[1] *have* + past participle.
FUTURE TIME	As for Present Time (often with a time adverb or phrase) OR: *were to* + bare infinitive	*would (should)*[1] + bare infinitive.

CONDITIONS EXPRESSED BY INVERSION

When the *if* clause contains one of the auxiliary verbs *were*, *had* or *should*, it can be replaced by a clause without 'if' by inversion of verb and subject, e.g.

Were John here now (= if John were here now) he would explain the whole matter.

Were our train to arrive punctually at 12.45, we should have time to visit your sister.

Had you (= *if you had*) *asked me,* I would have told you the answer.

I will go, *should it be* (= *if it should be*) *necessary.*

---

[1] Normally *should* is used only in the 1st person singular and plural; but *should* may be used with other persons to express special ideas (promise, determination, etc.) for which *shall* is used (see pp. 163–5). Note the example on page 349—'If I were King, you *should* be Queen.' *Would* may be used in any person.

EXERCISES

I Complete the following sentences with the correct tense of the verb in brackets.

(1) If you are kind to me I ―― good to you (be). (2) If I ―― this time I shall have completed the examination. (succeed) (3) If your statement is correct what he ―― me is untrue. (tell) (4) If you ―― willing to go, so ―― I. (be) (5) I will pay him well if he ―― the work properly. (do) (6) If I really ―― that I am very sorry. (say) (7) If you ―― that you ―― the book by mistake I should have understood. (say, take) (8) If I did hurt his feelings I ―― to explain to him. (try) (9) If he has lost the key he ―― to buy another one. (have) (10) If you ―― your homework you may go out. (finish) (11) If you ―― me at the time I should have understood at once. (tell) (12) I should always have done that if they ―― it at the start. (explain) (13) We ―― much earlier if we had known the times of the trains. (go) (14) They would not have gone to that hotel if they ―― its prices. (know) (15) He ―― his children abroad for the summer if he ―― the money. (send, have) (Three forms possible.)

II Explain fully, with one example of each, the terms Open Condition and Hypothetical Condition.

III Add to each of the following what is necessary to make a complete sentence of each one, containing a clause of hypothetical condition:

(1) If I were Chancellor of the Exchequer. (2) If he had the choice of a career. (3) If I had more time to spare. (4) I should like to go to the theatre tonight. (5) If he took more trouble over his work.

IV Complete the following sentences by putting the bracketed infinitives in the correct tense.

(1) You can go wherever you (like). (2) When you (finish) your game, will you please have a word with grandma. (3) You had better prepare for failure, in order that you (not be disappointed) later. (4) Nothing is more conducive to unhappiness than that a man (fail) to realize himself completely. (5) If you (throw) a stone into a tank of water it (sink). (6) I am going into the country tomorrow if it (be) fine. (7) I should go

into the country tomorrow if I (be) you. (8) I should have gone into the country yesterday if it (be) fine.

V In all cases where it is *possible* to do so, re-write the following conditional sentences so that the conditions are 'hypothetical':

(1) Ice melts if you throw salt on to it. (2) This sheet of ice will melt if you throw salt on it. (3) If I finish this today, I shall have kept my promise. (4) If the taxi has arrived, we can go at once. (5) If that was so then, it is not so now. (6) If you found that he was not in his room, something was wrong. (7) Everything will be all right if you have done as you were told. (8) If he really *did* do it, I don't wish to have anything to do with him. (9) If James made a mistake, I am sure it was an unintentional one. (10) If James made a mistake when working out his problem, then the effects of his mistake will soon show themselves.

VI ⎰ *In the past*　　⎰ *now*　　⎰ *in the future*
　　⎱ Yesterday　　⎱ today　　⎱ tomorrow

Each of the following sentences could include, as it stands, one of the above adverbs of time. Write each sentence, including the time-adverb, and then re-write each one with the other two adverbs, *where possible*, making any changes necessary. To help you, the exercise has been partly done for the first sentence.

(1) If it is fine (today), I am going out (or 'shall be going out' or 'shall go out').

　　　If it had been fine yesterday, I ——.
　　　If it is fine tomorrow, I ——.

(2) It would not have been so bad if it hadn't been foggy.
(3) We should be very pleased if you would come.
(4) If he came, I should be very surprised.
(5) Tell me if you want to.
(6) If your behaviour does not improve, you will find yourself with no friends.

VII Express the following as conditions without using 'if' and add a main clause :

(1) If my parents were only here . . .
(2) If I had been warned . . .
(3) If it should be advisable . . .
(4) If it were not for the expense involved . . ,
(5) If it were to rain . . .

M*

VIII Express these sentences in another way without using *if:*

(1) If you haven't got time, don't worry. (2) If you asked him, he might consider it. (3) I'll help you if you haven't found it by the time I come back. (4) If James took up acting, I'm sure he would succeed at it. (5) If he were an honourable man, he could not behave thus. (6) If you see him, remember me to him, will you? (7) Neither of us would have gone if we had known how unwelcome we were.

IX Correct or improve the following sentences:

(1) If I should be rich, I would buy a Cadillac. (2) If it would be fine, I should go out. (3) I shall be glad if you kindly forward some samples. (4) Mother should be glad if you kindly closed the door. (5) Mother would be too hot if you would close the door. (6) Unless he doesn't put on his raincoat he will get wet. (7) I had done it, if my father had not begged me not to. (8) If you would have created a disturbance like the others, you, too, had been arrested.

CHAPTER TWENTY-FIVE

ANALYSIS OF SENTENCES

To analyse a complex sentence, that is to break it up into its component parts and to show the mutual relations of those parts, gives practice in the recognizing of the various types of clauses. The number of clauses in a passage for analysis can be ascertained by counting the number of finite verbs in it. Each clause contains one finite verb; so if we know the number of finite verbs we know the number of clauses.

It is often easier to recognize subordinate clauses than the principal clause. The student therefore may find it a help to pick out and draw a line through all the subordinate clauses: what is left will be the principal clause. The following examples will show the usual method of setting out a passage for analysis.

Analyse the following:

(1) The boy, who was crying as if his heart would break, said, when I spoke to him, that he was hungry because he had had nothing to eat for two days.

Clause	Kind of clause	Function
The boy said	Principal	makes a statement
who was crying	Adjective	qualifies *boy*
as if his heart would break	Adverb (Manner)	modifies *was crying*
when I asked him	Adverb (Time)	modifies *said*
that he was hungry	Noun	object of *said*
because he had had nothing to eat for two days	Adverb (Reason)	modifies *was hungry*

(2) If it were not for this perpetual imitation, we should be tempted to fancy that children despised us outright or only considered us in the light of creatures brutally strong and brutally silly, among whom they condescended to dwell in obedience, like a philosopher at a barbarous court.

Clause	Kind of clause	Function
we should be tempted to fancy	Principal	makes a statement
if it were not for this perpetual imitation	Adverb (Condition)	modifies *should be tempted*
that children despised us outright	Noun	object of *to fancy*
or only considered us in the light of creatures brutally strong and brutally silly	Noun	Object of *to fancy*
among whom they condescended to dwell in obedience, like a philosopher at a barbarous court	Adjective	qualifies *creatures*

If a 'full' analysis is required, the above two passages could be treated like this:

Clause	Kind	Function	Connecting Word	SUBJECT		PREDICATE				
				Subject Word	Subject Qualifier	Verb	Object	Object Qualifier	Complement	Adverb Adjuncts
The boy said	Princ.	makes a statement		boy	the	said				
who .. crying	Adj.	qualifies 'boy'		who		was crying				
as .. break	Adverb (manner)	modifies 'was crying'	as if	heart	his	would break				
when .. him	Adverb (Time)	modifies 'said'	when	I		asked	him			
that .. hungry	Noun	object of 'said'	that	he		was			hungry	
because .. days	Adverb (Reason)	modifies 'was hungry'	because	he		had had	nothing	to eat		for two days (Time)

Clause	Kind	Function	Connecting Word	SUBJECT		PREDICATE				
				Subject Word	Subject Qualifier	Verb	Object	Object Qualifier	Complement	Adverb Adjuncts
we . . . fancy	Princ.	makes a statement		we		should be tempted			to fancy	
if . . . imitation	Adverb (Cond.)	modifies 'should be tempted'	if	it		were			for . . . imitation	not (Negative)
that . . . outright	Noun	object of 'to fancy'	that	children		despised	us			outright (Degree)
or . . . silly	Noun	object of 'to fancy'	or (that)	(they)		considered	us			only (Degree) in . . . silly (Manner)
among . . . court	Adjective	qualifies 'creatures'	among whom	they		condescended			to dwell	in obedience (Manner) like . . . . . . court (Manner)

EXERCISES

I What do you understand by:

(1) a complement. (2) an adverbial adjunct. (3) function.
(4) a clause. (5) subject. (6) predicate. (7) object.

II Analyse the following passages indicating *only* the clauses, their kind and their function:

(1) The pirates, who had hidden the treasure on the island, went back again because they thought that they could now remove it with safety.

(2) Richard, though he had not previously answered any questions when the teacher asked him, now said that he knew the answer to this one because it was in the lesson that he had just read.

(3) When the teacher asked what part of speech a word was, John said, 'I can tell you the answer, if you will give me a sentence in which the word is used'.

(4) James controlled himself, for he did not want to betray his surprise, and his whole future depended on success at this interview.

(5) The bells, which had been silent for so long, pealed out to announce that an heir had at last been born.

(6) Nicholas and his wife, though they were bitterly cold, remained to cheer with the thousands that had gathered in front of the palace gates.

(7) As dawn approached, the sky grew red, the crowds became quieter, the cold was making itself felt somewhat less acutely, and an atmosphere of steady calm replaced the extremes of indifference on the one hand and uncontrolled abandon on the other.

(8) 'Though fond of many acquaintances, I desire an intimacy only with a few. The Man in Black, whom I have often mentioned, is one whose friendship I could wish to acquire, because he possesses my esteem.'—Oliver Goldsmith, *The Man in Black*.

(9) 'This authority of the Knight, though exerted in that odd manner which accompanies him in all the circumstances of life, has a very good effect upon the parish, who are not polite enough to see anything ridiculous in his behaviour.'—Joseph Addison, *Sunday in the Country*.

(10) Among the many tributes paid to him was one which said his services to the free world had been incalculable.

(11) 'In spite of this, however, most of us cannot help
believing that the philosophers were right—right
when they proclaimed, amid all their differences,
that most of the things we bother about are not
worth bothering about. It is easier to believe that
oneself is a fool than that Socrates was a fool, and
yet, if he was not right, he must have been the
greatest fool who ever lived. The truth is, that everybody is agreed that such men as Socrates and
Epictetus were right in their indifference to external
things.'

Robert Lynd, *On not being a philosopher.*

(12) Avenge, O Lord, thy slaughtered saints, whose bones
　　Lie scattered on the Alpine mountains cold;
　　Even them who kept thy truth so pure of old,
When all our fathers worshipped stocks and stones
Forget not: in thy book record their groans
　　Who were thy sheep, and in their ancient fold
　　Slain by the bloody Piedmontese, that rolled
Mother with infant down the rocks. Their moans
The vales redoubled to the hills, and they
　　To Heaven. Their martyred blood and ashes sow
O'er all the Italian fields, where still doth sway
　　The triple Tyrant: that from these may grow
A hundredfold, who, having learnt Thy way,
　　Early may fly the Babylonian woe.

Milton (1608–74), *On the late Massacre in Piedmont.*

CHAPTER TWENTY-SIX

DIRECT AND INDIRECT SPEECH

In direct speech we have the exact words of the speaker, e.g.
He said, 'I am learning English'. In indirect or reported speech
we give the same meaning but with a different form, so that
the words spoken are incorporated into the structure of the
main sentence, e.g.

Direct: 'I am learning English.'
Indirect: He said that he was learning English.

The difference between the two forms is shown by the tense
of the verb, together with changes in the person of the pronouns
and possessive adjectives and of certain words that denoted
'nearness' in the direct form. These latter may be replaced by
words suggesting 'remoteness' (in time and place). There are
also in some instances changes in word order.

The verb or verbs that were in the present tense in direct
speech are generally (but not always) replaced by corresponding verbs in the past tense. The changes are:

I. CHANGES IN VERBS

Tense		Tense
PRESENT SIMPLE PRESENT CONTINUOUS PRESENT PERFECT PAST SIMPLE FUTURE TENSE *shall* and *will* CONDITIONAL	becomes	PAST SIMPLE PAST CONTINUOUS PAST PERFECT PAST PERFECT FUTURE IN THE PAST *should* and *would* PERFECT CONDITIONAL

Examples:

DIRECT	INDIRECT
	He said that:
I *write* home every week.	he *wrote* home every week.
I *go* to *my* class every day.	he *went* to *his* class every day.
I *am learning* English.	he *was learning* English.
I *have learned* English.	he *had learned* English.
I *shall* see her in London.	he *would* see her in London.
I *have been playing* football.	he *had been playing* football.
I *wrote* a letter to my brother.	he *had written* a letter to his brother.
I *can* speak German.	he *could* speak German.
I *may* be able to go.	he *might* be able to go.
I *don't write* every week.	he *didn't write* every week.
I *don't go* to my class every day.	he *didn't go* to his class every day.
If I *had* my pen, I *could write* the answers.	If he *had had* his pen, he *could have written* the answers.

In short, in the examples so far considered, the reported verb goes one step into the past. If the verb in the principal clause is in the Present Tense, Present Continuous Tense, Present Perfect Tense or Future Tense, the verb in the reported sentence will not change, e.g.

DIRECT: 'This work is too difficult.'

INDIRECT: He *says*
He *is saying*
He *has said*   (that) this work *is* too difficult.
He *will say*

Note that 'inverted commas' (quotation marks) are not used in indirect speech.

When the sentence expresses a fact that is supposed to be universally true and not merely applicable to the time when the statement was made, the Present Tense may be used in reported speech, e.g.

DIRECT: 'Fools rush in where angels fear to tread.'

(Alexander Pope)

INDIRECT: Pope said that fools *rush* in where angels *fear* to tread.

DIRECT: The sun is 92 million miles away.

INDIRECT: He said that the sun is 92 million miles away.

The Present Tense may be used also with a statement expressing a repeated or habitual action, e.g.

DIRECT: I get up at seven o'clock every morning.

INDIRECT: He said that he *gets* up at seven o'clock every morning.

DIRECT: My wife always drinks coffee for breakfast.

INDIRECT: He said that his wife always *drinks* coffee for breakfast.

II. CHANGES IN PRONOUNS

The pronouns and possessive adjectives generally change as follows:

DIRECT		INDIRECT	
I, me	my, mine	he (she), him (her)	his (her), hers his
we, us	our, ours	they, them	their, theirs
you	your, yours	they, them	their, theirs

Examples:

DIRECT	INDIRECT
I bring *my* book every day; the book on the desk is *mine*.	*He* said that *he* brought *his* book every day; the book on the desk was *his*. *She* said that *she* brought *her* book every day; the book on the desk was *hers*.
We bring *our* books every day; the books on the desk are *ours*.	*They* said that *they* brought *their* books every day; the books on the desk were *theirs*.

But these pronouns and possessive adjectives may vary according to circumstance. Common sense will determine which pronouns should be used. For examples consider the following situations:

TEACHER: John, you must bring your book to the class.

WILLIAM (*reporting this to someone else*): The teacher told John that *he* must bring *his* book to the class.

WILLIAM (*reminding John of the teacher's orders*): The teacher said that *you* must bring *your* book to the class.

JOHN (*reporting what the teacher had said*): The teacher said that *I* must bring *my* book to the class.

III. OTHER CHANGES

Words denoting 'nearness' become the corresponding words denoting remoteness:

this		that
these		those
here		there
now	becomes	then
ago		before
today		that day
tomorrow		the next day
yesterday		the previous day: the day before

For example:

DIRECT	INDIRECT
I saw the boy *here* in *this* room *today*.	He said that he had seen the boy *there*, in *that* room *that day*.
I will see *these* boys *now*.	He said he would see *those* boys *then*. He had spoken to
I spoke to them *yesterday*.	them the *day before*.
I will teach the same lesson *tomorrow* that I taught two days *ago*.	He said that he would teach the same lesson *the next day* that he had taught two days *before*.

DIRECT	INDIRECT
I will do it *here* and *now*.	He said he would do it *there* and *then*.
George said, '*This* is the house where Shakespeare was born.'	George said that *that* was the house where Shakespeare had been born.

Note that if the principal clause governing the direct speech clause does not come at the beginning of a sentence, the verb generally comes before the subject. Compare the example given above and the following two versions:

'This,' *said George*, 'is the house where Shakespeare was born.'

'This is the house where Shakespeare was born,' *said George*.

INDIRECT QUESTIONS

All the examples given above are of statements; but the changes in tense, pronouns, etc., noted when direct speech becomes indirect speech apply also to questions and commands. But with these there are additional points to note. When a direct question is turned into an indirect question:

1. The interrogative construction of the direct question is replaced by the statement construction in the indirect question. So *do* (*does, did*) of the direct speech is not used in the indirect question.

2. The verb that introduces the indirect question is *asked* (or some similar verb, e.g. *enquired, wondered, wanted to know* according to the shade of meaning to be expressed).

3. The connective joining the indirect question to the principal clause is *if* or *whether*,[1] except when the direct question had been one beginning with an interrogative such as *who? what? why?* etc., in which case this interrogative is the connective. Some examples will make these points clear. Note particularly the change of word order from the interrogative construction to the statement construction.

[1] For *if* and *whether* see pages 368–9.

I. CHANGES WHEN THE VERB IS A SPECIAL FINITE

DIRECT QUESTION	INDIRECT QUESTION
Is Charles your brother?	He asked me if (whether) *Charles was* my brother.[1]
Has John many friends?	He asked me if (whether) *John had* many friends.
Can Henry speak Spanish?	He asked me if (whether) *Henry could speak* Spanish.
Will you help me?	He asked if (whether) *I would help* him.
Has Mary spent all the money?	He asked (enquired) if (whether) *Mary had spent* all the money.
Is Henry really working hard?	He asked (wondered) if *Henry was really working* hard.

II. CHANGES WHEN THE VERB IS NOT A SPECIAL FINITE

DIRECT QUESTION	INDIRECT QUESTION
Do you know Mr. Brown?	He asked if (whether) *I knew* Mr. Brown.
Does Pedro speak English?	He asked if (whether) *Pedro spoke* English.
Did you see George at the football match?	He asked if (whether) *I had seen* George at the football match.
Did they all do the exercise correctly?	He asked (wondered) if (whether) *they had all done* the exercise correctly.

[1] Note that in indirect questions the question mark is not used.

III. CHANGES WHEN THE DIRECT QUESTION BEGINS WITH AN INTERROGATIVE

DIRECT QUESTION	INDIRECT QUESTION
What *is her name?*	He asked me what *her name was.*
Where *are you going?*	He asked me where *I was going.*
How *will she* get there?	He wondered how *she would* get there.
Where *does she live?*	He asked where *she lived.*
Why *do they go* to Paris so often?	He asked me why *they went* to Paris so often.
What *did she say?*	He asked what *she had said.*
Why *did you come* here?	He asked me why I *had come* there.

Where there is a mixture of statements and questions the introducing verb will vary accordingly, e.g.

DIRECT: He said, 'I have left my watch at home. Can you tell me the time?'

INDIRECT: He *said* that he had left his watch at home and *asked* me if I could tell him the time.

INDIRECT COMMANDS

When a direct command is turned into an indirect one, the following will be noticed:

(*a*) The verb used is not *say*[1] (with *to*) but one like *order, command, tell,*[1] *ask, request,* according to the shade of meaning intended.

(*b*) A Direct Object, representing the person ordered, is introduced.

(*c*) The imperative form of the verb in the direct command becomes the corresponding infinitive.

[1] For *say* and *tell* see pages 369–72.

DIRECT COMMAND	INDIRECT COMMAND
Go away!	He *ordered* him *to go* away.
OFFICER (*to soldiers*): Fire!	The officer *commanded* the soldiers *to fire*.
Run quickly!	He *told* (*ordered, asked, requested, commanded*) me (him, her, us, you, them) *to run* quickly.
Play the piano, please.	He (she, etc.) *asked* me (him, her, etc.) *to play* the piano.
Do write to me as soon as you arrive.	He (she, etc.) *asked* (*begged, entreated*, etc.) me (him, her, etc.) *to write* to him (her, etc.) as soon as he (she, etc.) arrived.

An indirect negative command is expressed by *ask*, etc., and a negative infinitive, e.g.

DIRECT NEGATIVE COMMAND	INDIRECT NEGATIVE COMMAND
Don't shut the door.	He asked me (him, her, etc.) *not to shut* the door.
Don't all answer at once.	He told (ordered, etc.) them *not to answer* all at once.
Don't be late tomorrow.	He told them *not to be* late the next day.

'WHETHER' and 'IF'

In indirect questions there is not much difference in meaning between *whether* and *if;* usage generally favours *if* whenever the distinction in meaning is not important, e.g.

He asked me *if* (*whether*) I had seen the film.

Whether usually expresses a doubt and an alternative possibility or a choice between two alternatives, and so is often followed by the correlative *or*, e.g.

I don't know *whether* I should go away *or* stay here.
He asked me *whether* you would rather have tea *or* coffee for breakfast.

Whether is often followed by *or not*, e.g.

I don't know *whether* it is raining *or not*.

The alternative is frequently suppressed, e.g.

I am doubtful *whether* I can find time to see him (or not).
The question *whether* (or not) he should be invited is not for me to decide.
Ask him *whether* he's coming on Friday (or not).

Whether and not *if* is used:

(1) when the indirect question precedes the main clause, e.g.

Whether this is true or not, I cannot say.

(2) before an infinitive, e.g.

She hasn't decided *whether* to sail or fly to America.

(3) When the subordinate clause that it introduces is really a concessive one. (See CONCESSIVE CLAUSES (pp. 341–2) and CONDITIONAL CLAUSES (pp. 343 and 347–51).)

SAY and TELL

These two words often cause difficulty.

SAY

1. *Say* has the meaning 'to utter', 'to express in words', e.g.

He always *says* what he means. *Say* you are sorry for what you have done. What did you *say?* She *says* her prayers every night. Who *said* that? Shelley *said:*
'Life, like a dome of many-coloured glass,
Stains the white radiance of Eternity.'

2. *Say* is used with direct speech and indirect statements, e.g.

He *said*, 'The point is quite clear.'
He *said* that the point was quite clear.

3. With *say* it is not necessary to supply an indirect object, that is a word that represents the person addressed; but if an indirect object is given, *to* must be used, e.g.

He said *to* me that the point was quite clear.

4. In reported speech *say* is never followed by an infinitive. Compare:

I *told* the boy *to leave*.
I *said* to the boy *that he must leave*.

TELL

1. The original meaning was 'to count'. When Milton in *L'Allegro* says:

'And every shepherd *tells his tale*
Under the hawthorn in the dale.'

he means that the shepherd counts the numbers (*tale* originally meant 'number') of his flock. This meaning of *tell* still survives in a number of words and phrases; for example, officials who count votes in the House of Commons and bank officials who pay out money are called *tellers*. The phrase *all told* means 'all counted', e.g.

There were twenty of us, *all told*, who went on the excursion.

So, too:

His hard work is beginning *to tell*. (= to count, to have an effect)
That was a *telling* argument/a *telling* blow. (= one that counted)
A clock *tells* the time.

2. But the more usual meaning now is 'to narrate', 'to recount', 'to reveal', 'to explain', 'to order', e.g.

to *tell* a story; *Tell* me all you know; I can't *tell* you how sorry I am; 'She never *told* her love' (Shakespeare, *Twelfth Night*); to *tell* a secret; I can't *tell* how it was done; I *told* him to go away.

3. *Tell* is used with indirect speech, for statements and commands, e.g.

Olaf *told* Pedro that he had enjoyed his stay in England.
The teacher *told* the boy to leave the room at once.

In these cases *tell* must always have two objects: (1) the person addressed and (2) the noun clause or equivalent e.g. an infinitive. *Tell* is never used to introduce direct speech.

4. With commands *tell* is followed by an infinitive:

He told the boys *to leave.*

SAY and TELL

The difference between the meanings of *say* and *tell* can be seen in the following:

'Please *tell* me your name.' (= I do not know it.)

'Please *say* your name.' (= I want to hear how it is pronounced.)

IDIOMATIC USES OF 'SAY'

I am glad *to say* that he is better. I have nothing further *to say* on the matter. *It is said* that he is worth half a million pounds. He is *said* to be worth half a million pounds. You must go there because I *say* so. Suppose I were to lend him, *say*, five pounds. Mr. Brown is out; I can't *say* when he will be back. He *said* to himself (= thought) there was something wrong. What do you/What would you *say* to (= how would you like) a drink? What I *say* (= my opinion) is that women should be paid the same wages as men. Yes, I think that *goes without saying* (= it's so obvious that it doesn't need to be stated). I *say!* Look who's coming. (I say![1] is an exclamation expressing surprise, satisfaction, protest, etc.; also to attract attention). The concert takes place in a fortnight's time, *that is to say* on May 15th.

IDIOMATIC USES OF 'TELL'

Don't *tell* me it's four o'clock already (= surely it isn't . . .). The two children are so much alike that you can't *tell* (= distinguish) one from the other; you can't *tell* which is which. It's difficult to *tell* what this is made of. He may pass his examination; *you never can tell.* Nobody can *tell* what the consequences may be. You can't *tell* from his face what he

[1] In American English, *Say!* is preferred to *I say!*

is thinking. *There's no telling* what may happen. A gipsy *told* my fortune. I *tell you*, I'm sick of the whole business. George is very annoyed, *let me tell you* (these last two phrases express strong affirmation).

SENTENCE PATTERNS WITH 'SAY'

The sentence patterns with *say* are:

(1) *say* + object (or *so*), e.g.
He said nothing.
I say so.

(2) *say* + 'that' clause e.g.
He said that he was Mr. Brown.

(3) *say* + *to* + (pro)noun + 'that' clause, e.g.
He said to the porter that he was Mr. Brown.

SENTENCE PATTERNS WITH 'TELL'

(1) *tell* + indirect object + direct object, e.g.
He told me a story.

(2) *tell* + direct object + *to* + (pro)noun, e.g.
He told a story to his children.

(3) *tell* + (pro)noun + infinitive, e.g.
I told him to go away.

(4) *tell* + (pro)noun + noun clause, e.g.
He told the porter that he was Mr. Brown.
Tell me what is worrying you.

EXERCISES

I The following sentences are in indirect speech. Give the direct words of the speaker. Add the necessary punctuation.

(1) Henry said that he was going to London with his father. (2) Margaret said that their train would arrive in five minutes. (3) Lilian said that her sister spoke French well. (4) George said that he hoped it wouldn't rain. (5) Richard told Mary that he was playing

football on Saturday. (6) My father told me that I could go to England for a year. (7) Mary promised Ellen that she would write to her every week. (8) Timothy shouted that he would bring help. (9) Richard said that he was sorry he was late. (10) Mary said that she would be 18 on the 15th of May. (11) Mrs. Green asked Margaret if she was tired. (12) George asked if they had taken his dog Jock for a walk. (13) The hunter asked if they had heard the sound of wolves. (14) The little girl asked if the baby had a name yet. (15) The passenger inquired what time the train for London left. (16) Fred asked William if he had read *Treasure Island*. (17) The stranger asked the way to the railway station. (18) The lady asked George if he could swim. (19) Richard asked his mother if he might have another piece of cake. (20) John asked Henry if his exercise was correct. (*This is ambiguous. Give two answers.*) (21) The teacher ordered Richard to go away. (22) Mr. Brown asked his visitor to come in. (23) His mother told Richard not to eat all the cake. (24) The officer commanded the soldiers to fire. (25) The sergeant told the sentry to stay at his post until he was relieved. (26) The teacher told Timothy to do the exercise correctly or he would have to stay in. (27) The farmer asked the visitors not to leave the gate open. (28) Richard's father told him not to climb that tree in his new trousers. (29) The teacher told Henry to get his work done properly or he would punish him. (30) He told him to do some exercises every day if he wanted to pass his examination.

II When you change sentences from direct speech to indirect speech, what usually happens to (*a*) verbs in the Simple Present tense, (*b*) verbs in the Present Perfect tense, (*c*) pronouns and possessive adjectives in the 1st person?

III Change the following from direct speech to indirect speech. (Begin: *He (She, They, John, The teacher,* etc.) *said that.*)

(1) 'I like my dog Jock.' (2) 'I am going to the party with my brother.' (3) 'We have plenty of time to do our work.' (4) 'George has written me a long letter.' (5) 'We are very tired.' (6) 'You sing very nicely, Margaret.' (7) 'I am giving a prize for the best homework.' (8) 'I am French but I have learned English at school.' (9) 'I will take you to my house.' (10) 'You

can come with us if you like.' (11) 'I don't like English food very much.' (12) 'This time-table is too complicated for me.' (13) 'I have to go to the dentist tomorrow.' (14) 'This is the book we have been looking for,' (15) 'He has to catch an early train every morning.' (16) 'I caught sight of John this morning.' (17) 'I must go to the Post Office before it closes.' (18) 'I shall be doing exactly the same work next Monday as I am doing today.' (19) 'I wrote to them only last week.' (20) 'This book was lent to him weeks ago and he has only just returned it.'

IV Turn the following questions into indirect speech:

(1) Mary said, 'Are you hungry, Margaret?' (2) Lilian said, 'What do you want, Ellen?' (3) John said, 'Shall I close the window?' (4) TEACHER: 'Have you all understood me?' (5) MARGARET (to RICHARD): 'Where are you going for your holidays?' (6) RICHARD (to SHOPKEEPER): 'What is the price of that bicycle?' (7) George said, 'When will you get back from London, John?' (8) George said, 'How long does it take to get to London, John?' (9) Richard said, 'Can you swim, John?' (10) GEORGE (to TEACHER): 'Shall I finish my exercise at home?' (11) MARY: 'May I have another cake, please?' (12) LILIAN (to ELLEN): 'Do you like my new hat?' (13) MOTHER (to MARGARET): 'Have you finished your homework yet?' (14) GEORGE: 'Have you been using my tooth-paste, Richard?' (15) Mary said, 'Is your new baby a boy or a girl, Mrs. Thompson?' (16) Elizabeth said, 'Did Margaret feed the cat before she went out?' (17) RICHARD'S MOTHER: 'Did you brush your teeth properly, Richard?' (18) The hunter said, 'Do you hear the roar of a lion?' (19) The hunter said, 'Did you hear the roar of a lion?' (20) VISITOR (to boy): 'Do you go to school every day?' (21) GEORGE: 'May I borrow your bicycle, John?' (22) STRANGER to FRED: 'Can you tell me where Mr. Green lives?' (23) 'How are you going to do that?' (24) 'Which of the routes to London do you prefer?' (25) 'Can you tell me which is the road to Oxford?' (26) 'Is it true that Edward is getting married?' (27) 'Does he play the piano or the violin?' (28) 'I cannot find my purse. Can you lend me 10 shillings?' (29) 'How did they travel back home?' (30) 'Did they all attend the meeting last night?' (31) 'Where does Joe have his suits made?' (32) 'Which hotel in Edinburgh is considered the best?'

V Turn the following imperatives into indirect speech:

(1) TEACHER to RICHARD: 'Write that exercise out carefully.' (2) HUNTER to FRIEND: 'Shoot the wolf.' (3) OFFICER to SOLDIERS: 'Bring the gun into position.' (4) Mary said to John, 'Open the box for me, please.' (5) Mrs. Green said, 'Please sing at our party, Margaret.' (6) 'Release the prisoners,' said the officer to the sergeant. (7) The captain of the shipwrecked vessel said to the sailors, 'Lower the boats at once.' (8) TEACHER to GEORGE: 'Be careful; think before you answer.' (9) RICHARD: 'Read my exercise, John, and tell me if it is correct.' (10) TEACHER: 'Write your name at the top of your paper and answer four questions.' (11) TRAVELLER to TAXI DRIVER: 'Victoria station as fast as you can. I must catch the 12.50 boat-train.'

VI Re-write the following short story in indirect speech. Begin: The writer said that . . . (Call the ant *he* and the grasshopper *she*.)

The Ant and the Grasshopper

I will tell you the story of the ant and the grasshopper. It is a cold winter's day and an ant is bringing out some grains of corn that he gathered in the summer as he wants to dry them. A grasshopper who is very hungry sees him and says, 'Give me a few grains of corn; I am dying of hunger.'

'But,' says the ant, 'what did you do in the summer? Didn't you store up any corn?'

'No,' replies the grasshopper, 'I was too busy.'

'What did you do?' says the ant.

'I sang all day,' answers the grasshopper.

'If you sang all summer,' says the ant, 'you can dance all winter.'

VII Explain the uses of the verbs 'say' and 'tell' in indirect speech and illustrate your explanation with examples.

CHAPTER TWENTY-SEVEN

PUNCTUATION

Punctuation is simply a device for making it easy to read and understand written or printed matter. In speech we can make pauses between words or phrases, we can use gestures, give emphasis to a word and raise or lower the voice to help the listener to understand our meaning; in writing much of that work is done by punctuation.

Sentences are separated from one another, and the parts of a sentence are clearly distinguished, by means of the various kinds of stops. Whether you are reading aloud or silently, your voice and your eye require frequent rests. It is the function of punctuation to indicate where you can make these without injuring the sense of the passage.

The proper use of stops, too, gives clarity of meaning to a passage that might be misunderstood or even not understood at all. A sentence like the following, for example, would, without punctuation, be so ambiguous as to be practically meaningless:

> 'Among the people present at the theatre were the actress Elizabeth Dixon the wife of George Grey author of the play Harry Forster the son of the producer Sir Laurence Richardson Charles Hazlitt the dramatic critic of the *Daily News* and critics of other newspapers.'

But when it is punctuated the meaning becomes clear:

> 'Among the people present at the theatre were: the actress, Elizabeth Dixon, the wife of George Grey, author of the play; Harry Forster, the son of the producer; Sir Laurence Richardson; Charles Hazlitt, the dramatic critic of the *Daily News;* and critics of other newspapers.'

How a comma or two can change the meaning of a sentence may be illustrated by the charming (but probably fictitious) story of Mrs. Abington, the actress who played in the first performance of Sheridan's *School for Scandal.*[1] When she

[1] 1777.

returned to her dressing-room after the performance she found a note from a rival actress, Mary Robinson, which, very generously, said:

> Mary Robinson says Mrs. Abington is the greatest actress in London.

Mrs. Abington, equally generous, added two commas and sent the note back to Miss Robinson. It now read:

> Mary Robinson, says Mrs. Abington, is the greatest actress in London.

The principal stops are the full stop (.), the colon (:), the semicolon (;), the comma (,), the question mark (?), the exclamation mark (!), the dash (—), quotation marks (' '), and the apostrophe (').

It is virtually impossible to lay down exact rules for the use of stops, for punctuation is nearly as much a matter of the author's style as is his choice of words, and practically no two writers, given a fairly lengthy passage to punctuate, would use exactly the same punctuation.

But there are a number of *general* principles that can help, and we may briefly summarize them as follows:

THE FULL STOP

The full stop is used:

(1) At the end of all sentences except questions and exclamations, e.g.

> He needs your help. (*Statement*)
> Help him. (*Command*)
> Will you help him? (*Question*)
> He cried, 'Help! Help!' (*Exclamation*)

(2) After abbreviations such as M.A. (= Master of Arts), H.M.S. *Valiant* (= Her Majesty's ship *Valiant*), U.S.A. (= United States of America), e.g. (= Latin: *exempli gratia* = for example), etc. It is used after initials, e.g. C. H. Brown, and after contracted words, e.g. Nov. (= November), memo. (= memorandum).

But if the contraction includes the final letter of the word the full stop is often omitted, e.g. Dr, Mr, Ltd, Chas, etc.

N

THE COLON

(1) The colon is used to separate two sentences of which the second explains more fully the meaning of the first, i.e. it often means the same as 'that is to say', e.g.

Richard's work is unsatisfactory: his answers are thoughtless, his spelling is careless and his writing is bad.

It may also take the place of a conjunction introducing a clause of reason, e.g.

Thompson isn't going to join our firm: we couldn't offer him a big enough salary (= because we couldn't . . .)

(2) To introduce a number of items in a list, or to introduce a quotation, e.g.

He offered me the choice of any one of these for a wedding present: a set of fish knives, a pewter teapot, an electric toaster, a standard lamp.

Shakespeare said: 'Neither a borrower nor a lender be.'

THE SEMI-COLON

The semi-colon is useful when we need a longer pause than is indicated by a comma, but when we do not want to break the line of thought, as would happen if we used a full stop. It is used:

(1) To separate co-ordinate sentences when a conjunction is not used, e.g.

'Your appearance pleased my friend; it delighted me; I have watched your behaviour in strange circumstances; I have studied how you played and how you bore your losses; lastly, I have put you to the test of a staggering announcement, and you received it like an invitation to dinner.'—(R. L. Stevenson, *The Suicide Club*)

Note how, in this example, shorter pauses are shown by the commas.

(2) With words like *therefore, however, nevertheless, besides, also, otherwise,* and sometimes *so*. These words join sentences but are stronger than conjunctions like *and*, and so need a stronger punctuation mark. Here are some examples:

You have done the work well; therefore I will pay you well.
You must take more exercise; otherwise you will get too fat.
Richard didn't work hard; so he didn't pass his examination.

THE COMMA

The comma is the most frequently used punctuation mark and has many uses. Your common sense and the desire to make your meaning clear will often tell you where a pause is needed, but the following 'rules', though they do not cover all the uses, may be helpful. A comma is generally used:

(1) To record a list of things, etc., e.g.

At the party we had cakes, jellies, ices, biscuits, chocolate, and lemonade.

Notice that the comma is usually put before *and* and the last item. Some writers disagree with this.

(2) To mark off direct speech:

'Tell me,' I said, 'how you know all that.'
George replied, 'I heard it on the radio.'

(3) To mark off sentences or clauses where a pause is needed in reading. This is almost always the case when an adverb clause precedes a principal one.

Although it was foggy, we played the match.
I have explained this work to Richard, but he still doesn't understand it.
If you will help me, I will help you.

When an adverb clause follows the principal clause, the omission of the comma places more emphasis on the adverb clause, e.g.

'He came because I asked him to' (answering the question, 'Why did he come?')

(4) To mark off words used in addressing a person (the Nominative of Address), e.g.

George, I hope you and Mary can come to the party.
I should be very glad, Charles, if you would do this for me.

(5) To mark off words or phrases like *however*,[1] *therefore, of course, for instance*, etc.

You know, of course, the way to Lowton; I needn't, therefore, send you a route map.

(6) In descriptive titles such as:

Elizabeth II, Queen of Great Britain . . .
I saw Mr. Smith, your teacher, this morning.

(7) To mark off phrases containing a participle when a pause is required in reading:

George, seeing that his brother was hurt, ran to help him.

The comma is not used in English to separate a defining relative clause[2] or a noun clause from the rest of the sentence. It must be used before the relative pronoun in a non-defining clause.

Here is the book that you wanted. (*Defining Clause*)
He asked me where I was going. (*Noun Clause*)
George, who is in my class, has won a scholarship. (*Non-defining Clause*)

QUESTION MARK

A Question Mark is used after a direct question, but not after an indirect one, e.g.

Direct. I said to him, 'When are you going to Scotland?'
Indirect. I asked him when he was going to Scotland.

THE EXCLAMATION MARK

The Exclamation Mark is used after an interjection, an exclamatory sentence or an expression of great feeling.

'Hello! I didn't expect to see you.'
'There goes our train!'
'What a wonderful day that was!'

---

[1] The commas are not used when *however* has the meaning 'to what degree', e.g. However busy he may be, he always manages to answer letters promptly.
[2] See also page 325.

THE DASH

The dash is used to indicate (1) an afterthought—an emendation, or (2) an unexpected turn in a sentence, e.g.

I spoke to Mary—you know, Harry's wife—and told her what you said.

The information that Fred gives you on every subject under the sun is always very full and is given with an air of complete confidence. There is only one thing wrong with it—it is never correct.

QUOTATION MARKS

Quotation Marks are used to enclose direct speech.

I said, 'I have only spoken to him on one occasion.'

He shouted, 'What are you doing here?'

'I have spoken to him,' I said, 'on only one occasion.'

Note that the full stop, exclamation mark, the question mark and the comma come *inside* the quotation marks.

Quotation marks may be single (' ') or double (" ").

THE APOSTROPHE

The Apostrophe is used to show (1) the possessive case, e.g.

my brother's house, John's wife, the boy's cap (*singular*, one boy), the boys' school (*plural*, for a lot of boys).

(2) The omission of a letter or letters, e.g.

I've (= I have), *don't* (= do not), *it's*[1] (= it is), *o'clock* (= of the clock).

THE USE OF CAPITALS

A capital letter is used:

(1) For the beginning of a sentence.

(2) For proper nouns, e.g. John, November, London, etc., and for adjectives formed from proper nouns e.g.

Scotch whisky, the *French* language, *Elizabethan* poets.

---

[1] Compare this with the possessive adjective *its*, e.g.
That dog has hurt *its* foot.
There is no apostrophe in any of the possessive pronouns.

A capital letter is used for the name of *God*, *Christ*, *Trinity*, *Bible*, etc., and a pronoun or possessive adjective applying to God has a capital letter, e.g.

They trusted in *God* that *He* would save *His* people.

(3) For the chief words in titles of people, books, plays, etc., e.g.

Elizabeth the Second, Alfred the Great, A Midsummer Night's Dream, A Tale of Two Cities.

(4) For salutations and forms of address, e.g. on letters:

Dr, Mr, Miss, Mrs, and for the greeting and complimentary close, e.g. Dear Sir,

. . . . .
Yours faithfully,

(5) For the abbreviations of degrees, titles, etc.

M.P. (= Member of Parliament), Q.C. (= Queen's Counsel), B.Sc. (= Bachelor of Science).

(6) The opening word of direct speech, e.g.

He said, 'What do you want?'

The capital letter is not repeated in the second part of a broken quotation, e.g.

'I am working hard now', he said, 'in order to provide for my old age.'

(7) For the first word in each line of poetry:

She lived unknown, and few could know
When Lucy ceased to be;
But she is in her grave, and Oh,
The difference to me! (*Wordsworth*)

but some modern poets disregard this convention.

(8) For the first person singular *I* (but not for *me*, *my*, etc.)

(9) For personification (generally in poetry):

O wild West Wind, thou breath of Autumn's being.

. . . .
If Winter comes, can Spring be far behind? (*Shelley*)

The seasons, in ordinary writing, do not have a capital letter, nor do the points of the compass unless they refer to specific regions or are part of a name, e.g. He came from the West. They live in the Northern Territory.

EXERCISES

I Restore the capital letters and punctuation in the following passages:

(1)

The following was written on the gravestone of an army mule here lies maggie the mule who in her time kicked a general two colonels four majors ten captains twenty-four lieutenants forty sergeants two hundred and twenty privates and a bomb.

(2)

i cant understand it said mr williams oh what cant you understand said his friend well said mr williams just look at this suit im wearing the wool was grown in australia the cloth was woven in yorkshire the buttons were made in india the suit was made in london and i bought it in cairo whats so remarkable about that asked his friend isnt it wonderful said williams taking no notice of the interruption that so many people can make a living out of something i havent paid for.

(3)

a very agitated woman rang up her doctor and a servant answered the phone can i speak to dr russell she said its urgent im sorry madam the doctor is out will you leave a message oh dear oh dear my ten year old little boy has swallowed a fountain pen when will the doctor be in im afraid madam he wont be in for two hours perhaps three hours three hours cried the woman what shall i do in the meantime im afraid madam youll have to use a pencil.

II Our pursuer soon came up and joined us with all the familiarity of an old acquaintance my dear charles cried he shaking my friends hand where have you been hiding this half a century i had positively fancied you were gone down to cultivate matrimony and your estate in the country during the reply i had an opportunity of surveying the appearance of our new companion his hat was pinched up with peculiar smartness his looks were pale thin and sharp round his neck he wore a broad black ribbon and in his bosom a buckle studded with glass his coat was trimmed with tarnished twist he wore by his side a sword with a black hilt and his stockings of silk though newly washed were grown yellow by long service.

Oliver Goldsmith, *Beau Tibbs*. A book of English Essays. Pelican.

III youre a very small chap said mr toots yes sir im small enough returned paul thank you sir for toots had lifted him into the seat and done it kindly too whos your tailor inquired toots after looking at him for some moments its a woman that has made my clothes as yet said paul my sisters dressmaker my tailors burgess and co said toots fashionable but very dear paul had the wit to shake his head as if he would have said it was easy to see that and indeed he thought so your fathers very rich isnt he inquired mr toots yes sir said paul hes dombey and son and which demanded toots and son sir replied paul.

Dickens, *Dombey and Son*.

IV it is a little painful to picture our heroes at such moments it is disgraceful to visualize such vital and important beings submitting to the fingering and fussing of persons who if they will forgive my saying so evoke no very romantic image not merely is it unpleasant to envisage them as standing there turning round when told to raising their arms like zanies a little higher my lord if you please 49·3 mr burkinshaw 49·3 repeats the subservient mr burkinshaw scribbling in his notebook not merely is it humiliating to conceive of a mere tailor making chalk marks upon the backs of statesmen rounded with the weight of half the world nay the impression created is more profound than any pain evoked by the picture of the magnificent in humiliation it is an impression which derives its deep poignancy from the realization that even the most majestic among us wear two buttons on the back of a tail coat.

Harold Nicolson, *Men's Clothes*. A book of English Essays. Pelican.

CHAPTER TWENTY-EIGHT

SENTENCE PATTERNS

A student generally learns to use a language that he wants to acquire, not by the abstractions of grammar but mainly by practice in the patterns which are the living substance of the language. The most important of these are the *Verb patterns*, i.e. the combinations that the verb can make with complements, objects, gerunds, clauses, etc. So, when the student has learned one pattern, e.g. the pattern

(A)

Subject & Verb	+ Object	+ Plain Infinitive
I heard	the bird	sing

he can, by analogy, make a number of other sentences on the same pattern, e.g.

I saw	his hand	shake
He made	me	go
Watch	him	swim
I felt	his heart	beat rapidly
Did you see	him	turn pale?

Similarly from the pattern:

(B)

Subject & Verb	Infinitive	
I expect	to learn	English here
He likes	to do	his work well
Do you want	to come	to the concert?

he can, by analogy, make:

I intend	to work	hard
He decided	to go	to Paris for his holiday
He learned	to speak	English before he came here

385

N*

But, unless he recognizes which verbs can be used in which patterns, he may be tempted, on the analogy of pattern (A), to say:

| I | | listened | | the bird sing |

or on the analogy of (B) to say:

| I enjoy | to learn | English here |
| He can't help | to do | his work well |

all of which are incorrect.

In almost every case, the constructions illustrated in the patterns that follow have been noted and explained in earlier sections of this book; but it may be useful to list here the main verb patterns that occur in the language so that, as verbs are encountered in the student's general reading, he can note and record in which patterns they are used.

The following are the principal verb patterns:[1]

PATTERN I: **Subject + Verb**

Subject	Verb
Time	flies.
Birds	sing.
The lion	roared.
My tooth	is aching.
Who	is speaking?

Two variants of this pattern should be noted:

(1) When the formal subject *there* is used (see page 34). This occurs when the subject of the verb *to be* is indefinite. *There*, as used in this construction, is meaningless. The real subject comes after the verb, e.g.

---

[1] The order given here follows that listed by Dr. Palmer in his *Grammar of English Words* (Longmans, 1938). A fuller treatment is given in *A Guide to Patterns and Usage in English* by A. S. Hornby (O.U.P. 1954).

There & VERB	SUBJECT	
There is	nothing more	to do.
There were	five of us	in the room.
There will be	a good meal	for us at home.
There are	worse things	than hard work.
There were	a lot of people	there.[1]
'There needs	no ghost, my lord, come from the grave to tell us this.'	
		(Shakespeare, *Hamlet*)

(2) When the formal subject *it* is used. *It* in this construction is meaningless; the real subject follows the verb e.g.

It + VERB	SUBJECT
It seems	that both of you were wrong.
It pays	to give honest value for money.
It doesn't matter	what you think.
It (so) happened	that he was short of money at that time.

See pages 100–1

PATTERN 2: **Subject + Verb + Complement**

SUBJECT & VERB		COMPLEMENT
He	is	rich.
Nelson	was	a sailor.
This	is	my brother.
Seeing	is	believing.
Who	are	you?
That	is	what I want.

[1] Note the two uses of *there*. The first one is meaningless and unstressed; the second one is an adverb of place and is stressed.

SUBJECT & VERB		COMPLEMENT
What he asked for	was	out of the question.
Are these		the shoes that you were looking for?
I	am	in a hurry.
All I want	is	to help you.
The milk	tastes	sour.
These roses	smell	sweet.
The poet Chatterton	died	young.
The children are	running	wild.
Mr. Brown	is looking	old.
	Keep	calm!

The formal subject *it* is used also in this pattern. In this case the real subject of the verb is generally an infinitive phrase or a clause, but other subjects are possible.

FORMAL SUBJECT *it* + VERB	COMPLEMENT	SUBJECT
It is	silly	to talk like that.
It would be	better	to do as he says.
It's	obvious	that you are prejudiced.
It's	no use	your saying that you are sorry.
It was	a pity	that you didn't think of that earlier.
Is it	a fact	that the Robinsons are going to America?
It will be	very nice	when the good weather comes.
It is	easy	for someone as wealthy as you to talk about giving to charities.
It was	impossible	for two such people to work together happily.

See pages 11, 34, 101, 329, 334.

PATTERN 3: **Subject & Verb + Adverb Complement**

SUBJECT & VERB	ADVERB COMPLEMENT
They are	here.[1]
He went	to Manchester.
Go	away!
The glove must be	somewhere or other.
He tries	hard.
She cried	as if her heart would break.

The formal subject *there* can be used in this pattern.

FORMAL SUBJECT *there* + VERB + SUBJECT	ADVERB COMPLEMENT
There are fifteen students	in my class.
There's a lot of noise	outside.
Is there any cheese	in the larder?
Will there be a festival	at Edinburgh next year?

See pages 34, 183, 264.

PATTERN 4: **Subject & Verb + Direct Object**

SUBJECT & VERB		DIRECT OBJECT
He	did	the work.
The postman	delivers	letters.
Do you	know	the answer?
The little boy	can dress	himself.
He	said	that he was going to Germany tomorrow.

See pages 9, 22, 98, 114, 333.

[1] In exclamatory sentences the adverb comes before the subject. (For exclamatory sentences see p. 316.)

PATTERN 5: **Subject & Verb + Preposition + Prepositional Object**

SUBJECT & VERB	PREPOSITION	PREPOSITIONAL OBJECT
I will wait	for	you.
She depends	on	me.
He succeeded	in	opening the box.
Those tools belong	to	Fred.
Everyone was hoping	for	a fine day.
Don't worry	about	the result of your examination.
I was longing	for	him to invite me to the party.[1]
They waited	for	me to pay the bill.[1]
You can rely	on	him to do everything that is necessary.[1]

See pages 98, 277, 281.

PATTERN 6: **Subject & Verb + Direct Object + Adverb Complement**

SUBJECT & VERB	DIRECT OBJECT	ADVERB COMPLEMENT
I put	the shoes	in your cupboard.
He sent	the letter	by registered post.
Have you put	the cheese	in the larder?
You will want	this	tomorrow.
The dog chased	him	for half a mile.
Put	your coat	on.[2]
Turn	the gas	off.[2]

[1] The object here is the accusative infinitive (see p. 233).
[2] The direct object and adverb complement can be reversed in these sentences, e.g. Put on your coat. (See p. 280.)

SUBJECT & VERB	DIRECT OBJECT	ADVERB COMPLEMENT
He locked	the house	up.[1]
He gave	all his money	away.[1]
He engaged	a gardener	to do the hard work.[2]
He felled	the trees	to let in more light.[2]
He engaged	a gardener	because he wanted someone to do the hard work.[3]
He treated	his wife	as if she were a child.[3]

See pages 11, 280.

PATTERN 7: **Subject & Verb + Direct Object + Adjective**

SUBJECT & VERB	DIRECT OBJECT	ADJECTIVE
I will get	the dinner	ready.
He held	the door	open.
The dye turned	her hair	green.
You have made	the car	dirty.
Can you get	the window	open?
He drinks	his whisky	neat.

A considerable number of verbs can be used in this pattern; some of the commonest are:

bake, bend, boil, break, burst, cut, crush, fill, get, hold, keep, leave, make, pack, paint, pull, push, set, wash, wipe.

See page 12.

[1] The direct object and adverb complement can be reversed in these sentences, e.g. Put on your coat. (See pp. 267 and 280.)
[2] The adverb complement here is an infinitive of purpose. (See p. 233.)
[3] Here it is an adverb clause. (See p. 339.)

PATTERN 8: **Subject & Verb + Direct Object + *to be* + Adjective (or Complement)**

SUBJECT & VERB	DIRECT OBJECT	*to be*	ADJECTIVE *or* COMPLEMENT
They told	him	to be	careful.
I want	you	to be	happy.
He likes	his staff	to be	punctual.
This proves	me	(to be)	right.
We all thought	him	(to be)	a wealthy man.
I prefer	my coffee	(to be)	hot.

The commonest verbs with this pattern are:

believe, consider, declare, fancy, feel, find, guess, imagine, judge, know, like, prefer, prove, see, show, suppose, suspect, think, understand, want.

See pages 12, 233.

PATTERN 9: **Subject & Verb + Direct Object + Object Complement**

SUBJECT & VERB	DIRECT OBJECT	OBJECT COMPLEMENT
He called	his cat	Sally.
They have made	Richard	captain of the foot-ball team.
The Archbishop crowned	Henry	King of England.
Grandfather has made	William	his heir.
We shall name	this ship	*Princess Alice.*

There are not many verbs that are used with this pattern. The chief ones are:

appoint, baptize, call, choose, christen, crown, elect, entitle, name, nominate, proclaim.

See page 12.

PATTERN 10: **Subject & Verb + Direct Object
+ Preposition + Prepositional Object**

SUBJECT & VERB	DIRECT OBJECT	PREPOSITION	PREPOSITIONAL OBJECT
I gave	it	to[1]	him.
Please explain	this	to	me.
They offered	the house	to	us.
They welcomed	him	to	their home.
He owes	a lot of money	to	George.
I will do	the work	for[2]	you.
He bought	some gloves	for	Mary.
Please thank	him	for	me.
Save	some sweets	for	your brother.
Excuse	me	for	interrupting you.
I'll never forgive	him	for	that.
Tell	me	about[3]	your work.
I told	them	of[4]	you.
They accused	him	of	stealing.
He threw	a book	at[5]	me.
He spends	a lot of money	on[6]	cigarettes.
Compare	your work	with[7]	Henry's.
I supplied	him	with	money.

See pages 22, 98, 114.

[1] Some of the more common verbs with this pattern are:

(a) with *to: award, add, bring, carry, compare, deny, fasten, fetch, give, hand, join, move, offer, owe, pass, pay, promise, read, refuse, sell, send, show, take, teach, tell, tie, write.*

[2] (b) with *for: bring, buy, choose, cook, do, fetch, forgive, get, leave, make, order, play, praise, punish, reach, save, write.*

[3] (c) with *about: ask, consult, question, re-assure, remind, tell, trouble, warn, worry, write.*

[4] (d) with *of: accuse, inform, remind, tell.*

[5] (e) with *at: aim, hurl, point, shoot, throw.*

[6] (f) with *on: answer, make, read, spend, waste, write.*

[7] (g) with *with: compare, fill, mix, provide, supply.*

PATTERN 11:   **Subject & Verb + Indirect Object + Direct Object**

SUBJECT & VERB	INDIRECT OBJECT	DIRECT OBJECT
I gave	him	a lesson.
They sold	me	some bad apples.
He told	me	a lie.
Has he paid	you	what he owes you?
He wished	them	'A Merry Christmas'.
Did Richard leave	his brother	any sweets?
Your help has saved	me	a lot of work.
He did	me	a very good turn.

The most usual verbs with this pattern are:

ask, bring, buy, cause, deny, do, envy, find, get, give, hand, leave, lend, make, order, owe, pass, pay, read, sell, send, show, spare, tell, throw, wish, write.

See pages 22, 98, 114, 118, 222.

PATTERN 12:   **Subject & Verb + (for)[1] + Complement**

SUBJECT & VERB	(for)	COMPLEMENT
He walked	for	ten miles.
The Headmaster spoke	for	an hour.
They argued	for	hours.
We have come		a long way.
They waited	for	an hour before going away.
The river rose		ten feet in the night.
The house cost		£10,000.
That car will last (you)		a lifetime.

[1] *for* is used only in sentences expressing duration.

There are a great number of verbs with this pattern. Some of the most usual are:

climb, come, drive, drop, fall, fly, follow, grow, jump, march, move, ride, rise, run, sink, swim, walk, weigh, work.

See page 12.

PATTERN 13: **Subject & Verb + Infinitive (bare)**

SUBJECT & VERB	INFINITIVE (BARE)
He can	sing.
Shall we	join them?
I must	go now.
Need I	answer that question?
Dare you	refuse to go?
You had better	answer the question.
I would rather not	go.

The verbs following this pattern are the Special Finites *can* (could), *do* (does, did), *shall* (should), *will* (would), *may* (might), *must, need, dare* and the phrases: *had better, would rather.*

See pages 182–215.

PATTERN 14: **Subject & Verb + Direct Object + Bare Infinitive**

SUBJECT & VERB	DIRECT OBJECT	INFINITIVE (BARE)
I made	him	come.
Let	him	speak.
I heard	him	shout.
We saw	the boy	steal the money.
Watch	me	swim the river.
I have never known	him	come punctually.

The verbs with this pattern are chiefly:

bid, feel, have, hear, know, let, make, need **B,** *notice, see, watch.*

See pages 210, 225, 231.

PATTERN 15: **Subject & Verb + *to*- Infinitive**

SUBJECT & VERB	INFINITIVE
I want	to go away.
He ought[1]	to help you.
We have[1]	to be home by 10 o'clock.
You are[1]	to see the Headmaster at once.
We must try	to help him.
I don't like	to ask you.
Did you remember	to feed the cat?
I didn't dare	to ask for a rise in salary.

Some common verbs using this pattern are:

begin, cease, commence, continue, dare, decide, expect, forget, have, hope, intend, learn, like, love, mean, need (A), *offer, ought, prefer, pretend, promise, refuse, remember, start, swear, try, want, wish.*

See pages 210, 230, 341.

PATTERN 16: **Subject & Verb + Interrogative Word + *to*-Infinitive**

SUBJECT & VERB	INTERROGATIVE WORD	INFINITIVE
I will remember	how	to do this in future.
He will soon find out	how	to drive the car.
Do you know	how	to answer that question?
Go and ask	how	to get from the station to our hotel.

---

[1] *ought, have* (with the meaning illustrated above) and *be* (with the meaning illustrated above) are the only special finites that take the Infinitive with *to*. (See p. 231.)

SUBJECT & VERB	INTERRO-GATIVE WORD	INFINITIVE
I can't decide	where	to go for our holidays.
I've lost my pen-knife, and I can't think	where	to look for it.
He's very greedy and never knows	when	to stop eating.
I'm wondering	what	to do next.

The usual verbs taking this construction are:

ask, consider, decide, discover, enquire, explain, find out, forget, guess, know, learn, remember, see, settle, tell (= know), *understand, wonder.*

See page 234.

PATTERN 17: **Subject & Verb + Direct Object +** *to-***Infinitive**

SUBJECT & VERB	DIRECT OBJECT	*to-*INFINITIVE
I'll ask	him	to help us.
They want	me	to give them a lesson.
He taught	his cat	to open the door.
She likes	her guests	to feel at home.
I warned	him	not to be late.
He dared	me	to climb the tree.

Usual verbs:

advise, allow, ask, can't bear, beg, cause, choose, dare (= challenge), *encourage, expect, force, get, hate, help, intend, invite, leave, like, love, mean* (= intend), *order, permit, persuade, prefer, remind, teach, tell, tempt, urge, want, warn, wish.*

See pages 231, 233.

PATTERN 18: **Subject & Verb + Direct Object + Interrogative Word + *to*-Infinitive**

SUBJECT & VERB	DIRECT OBJECT	INTERROGATIVE WORD	*to*-INFINITIVE
Show	him	how	to do the exercise.
I had to tell	him	how	to make a telephone call.
You must teach	the children	how	to behave properly.
Can you advise	me	where	to go for a good meal?
Don't forget to tell	me	where	to turn off this main road.

Usual verbs:

advise, ask, inform, remind, show, teach, tell.

See page 234.

PATTERN 19: **Subject & Verb + Gerund**

SUBJECT & VERB	GERUND
He loves	skating.
Your hair needs	cutting.
Stop	wasting my time.
Would you mind	passing the sugar?
I can't bear	seeing performing animals.
Do you remember	seeing that film in London?

See pages 246–9 for verbs that are followed by the gerund, those that are followed by the infinitive and those followed by either gerund or infinitive.

PATTERN 20: **Subject & Verb + Direct Object + Present Participle**

SUBJECT & VERB	DIRECT OBJECT	PRESENT PARTICIPLE
He kept	me	waiting.
We saw	him	playing football.
I caught	them	stealing apples.
I can smell	something	burning.
Our fast car left	the others	standing.

Usual verbs:

catch, feel, find, hear, imagine, keep, leave, listen to, look at, notice, see, set, smell, start, watch.

See pages 237, 239.

PATTERN 21: **Subject & Verb + Direct Object + Past Participle**

SUBJECT & VERB	DIRECT OBJECT	PAST PARTICIPLE
I want	my fish	fried, not boiled.
You should get	those shoes	mended.
They have just had	their house	painted.
We heard	the music	played by the band.
When they opened the safe they found	the money	gone.
We saw	big trees	torn up by their roots.

Usual verbs:

feel, get, have, hear, like, make, prefer, see, want, wish.

See pages 195–6, 237, 239.

PATTERN 22: **Subject & Verb** + (*that*) + **Noun Clause**

SUBJECT & VERB	(*that*) + NOUN CLAUSE
He said	(that) they would come and see us.
He intended	that his son should inherit the business.
I hear	(that) you are going to America next week.
I expect	(that) you are surprised at the news.

Usual verbs:

acknowledge, admit, arrange, believe, can't bear, confess, don't care, declare, demand, deny, expect, explain, fear, hear, hope, imagine, intend, know, notice, propose, recommend, say, see, show, suggest, suppose, think, understand, wonder.

See pages 333–5.

PATTERN 23 (A): **Subject & Verb** + **Direct Object** + (*that*) + **Noun Clause**

SUBJECT & VERB	DIRECT OBJECT	(*that*) + NOUN CLAUSE
I told	him	(that) he must work harder.
He warned	us	(that) the road was a bad one.
That experience taught	him	(that) honesty is the best policy.
I finally convinced	him	(that) he had been mistaken.

PATTERN 23 (B): **Subject & Verb + Direct Object + Interrogative Word + Noun Clause**

SUBJECT & VERB	DIRECT OBJECT	INTERRO-GATIVE	NOUN CLAUSE
He told	James	why	he must work harder.
The teacher showed	him	how	he should answer the question.
I'll remind	you	what	I want you to do.
Can you tell	me	whose	statue that is?
Will you please inform	us	when	the goods we ordered will be despatched?

Usual verbs:

convince, inform, remind, satisfy, teach, tell, warn.

See pages 333, 334 and 369–71.

PATTERN 24 (A): **Subject & Verb + *so***

SUBJECT & VERB	*so*
I think	so
He hopes	so
I am afraid	so

Frequently the pattern is inverted, e.g.

so I believe;   *so I've heard,* etc.

PATTERN 24 (B): **Subject & Verb + *not***

The negative construction has *not* instead of *so:*

I hope *not*   He is afraid *not,* etc.

The verbs using these constructions are:

be afraid, believe, expect, hope, say, suppose, think. See page 102.

The verbs *hear, notice, see* can be used only with Pattern 24 (A) inverted (*So I hear,* etc.)

EXERCISES

I Complete the following sentences by adding the words you consider necessary and state the type of pattern used in each sentence:

(1) ——— may be snow this evening if the wind drops.
(2) ——— is cutting his lawn.
(3) ——— any matches in your pocket?
(4) ——— sent the parcel by registered post.
(5) We imagined ——— to be honest.

II With what types of Sentence Patterns do you associate the following verbs? How many of them can be used with more than one type of Sentence Pattern?

tell, leave, consider, suspect, choose, deny, rise, can, learn, expect.

Construct sentences to illustrate your answer.

III Construct three sentences with each of these patterns.

(1) SUBJECT AND VERB + DIRECT OBJECT + PREPOSITION + PREPOSITIONAL OBJECT.

(2) SUBJECT AND VERB + DIRECT OBJECT + BARE INFINITIVE. Give six verbs that can be used in this pattern.

(3) SUBJECT + VERB + DIRECT OBJECT + PRESENT PARTICIPLE. Mention six verbs which can be used in this pattern.

IV Name the Sentence Patterns mentioning all the constituent parts used in the following sentences:

(1) It seems that he did pass the examination after all. (2) Can't you keep quiet? (3) I can't tell when to telephone him. (4) She reminded her husband when she wanted to use the car. (5) I should like my hair cut short. (6) Keep plodding along steadily. (7) They challenged us to run a mile. (8) You must show your son how to dance smoothly. (9) He does not know when to speak and when to remain silent. (10) I offered to help them but they refused to accept my offer. (11) I would rather play tennis than watch it. (12) The frost lasted for six weeks. (13) This watch should last you all your life. (14) We envy you your good fortune. (15) He wastes a lot of time on propping up the bar at the Club.

CHAPTER TWENTY-NINE

THE PRONUNCIATION OF ENGLISH

There are innumerable different ways of pronouncing English. Canada, the United States, South Africa, Australia, New Zealand, Scotland, Ireland, Wales—all have their characteristic pronunciation of English and sometimes several varieties. In England itself there are many different town and country accents.

The type of pronunciation which is described in this chapter, and referred to in the book, is that which is sometimes known by the name 'Received Pronunciation' (R.P.). It is that used in the English 'Public Schools' and by B.B.C. announcers, and consequently by very many well-educated people in England, especially in the southern half of England. It is not associated with any particular town or region of England, and it is generally understood throughout the English-speaking world. For these reasons it is generally considered to be the most suitable pronunciation for foreign students of English to learn.

It will be appreciated that in a book it is not possible to describe sounds adequately—particularly the vowel sounds. The student should listen, if possible, to a good speaker of English or to gramophone records.[1]

The distribution of sounds in English is not shown consistently by the spelling, so that in writing about pronunciation it is necessary to use a phonetic alphabet. In this book a broad form of the International Phonetic Alphabet is used. In a phonetic transcription, the same letter always represents the same sound, or, more exactly, the same phoneme. Although the [l] at the beginning of a word, e.g. *leaf*, is a different *sound* from the [l] at the end of a word, e.g. *feel*, this difference is never used in English to distinguish words: both [l]s are members of the same *phoneme*, and we can use the same symbol for both, noting where each variety will occur. On the other hand, *sin* and *sing* are recognized as different words in English by the contrast between [n] and [ŋ]; these sounds therefore form separate phonemes.

[1] For example, *Essential English* gramophone records (Linguaphone).

THE SOUNDS OF ENGLISH

I. Vowels

The characteristic sound of a vowel is determined by the shape given to the interior of the mouth by the position of the lips and the tongue. Vowels may be classified as Front, Back or Central according to whether the front, back or central part of the tongue is raised. In English, the lips are generally spread wide for the front vowels—the higher the tongue is raised, the more the lips are spread; the lips are generally slightly rounded for the back vowels—the higher the tongue is raised, the more the lips are rounded. For the Central vowels, the lips are in a neutral position; they must not be rounded.

We distinguish twelve pure vowel sounds:

FRONT VOWELS

	Phonetic Symbol		*Examples*
High	(1)	i:	sea, sheep, eat, seat, leave.
	(2)	i	sit, live, city, sing, ink.
	(3)	e	set, bed, ten, egg, head.
Low	(4)	a	bad, sat, apple, man, cat.

BACK VOWELS

Low	(5)	a:	bath, cart, heart, father, far.
	(6)	o	hot, often, dog, long, wash.
	(7)	o:	saw, sort, caught, law, nor.
	(8)	u	good, put, book, full, wood.
High	(9)	u:	blue, soup, root, fool, boot.

CENTRAL VOWELS

	(10)	ʌ	cut, come, young, mother, gun.
	(11)	ə:	bird, word, earth, fur, hurt.
	(12)[1]	ə	*a*sleep, fath*er*, Sat*u*rday, lab*ou*r.

[1] This sound occurs only in unstressed syllables.

II. Diphthongs

A diphthong differs from a pure vowel in that the tongue and lips, instead of remaining in a fixed position, move while it is being pronounced. In practice it can be regarded as a combination of two vowel sounds; but a diphthong can form only one syllable or part of a syllable, and the transition from one element to the other is made not by an abrupt change but by a gradual glide. The phonetic symbols represent approximately the beginning and the end of each diphthong.

	Phonetic Symbol	*Examples*
(13)	ei	pay, cake, face, able, game.
(14)	ou	low, no, both, soap, own.
(15)	ai	lie, by, kind, five, ice.
(16)	au	cow, now, out, round, mouth.
(17)	oi	boy, toy, noise, oil, coin.
(18)	iə	beer, near, beard, here, ear.
(19)	eə	there, pear, chair, air, care.
(20)	oə	door, tore, roar, shore.
(21)	uə	tour, moor, curious ['kjuəriəs]

NOTE. Many speakers of R.P. do not use Diphthong No. 20. They use instead vowel No. 7 [o:], and pronounce [do:], [to:], etc.

III. Consonants

Consonants may be classified according to the way they are formed in the mouth. The following types are distinguished in English:

1. *Plosive.* The breath is stopped completely in the mouth and then released suddenly with an explosive sound.

2. *Fricative.* The breath is not completely stopped but the air-passage is narrowed in the mouth so that friction can be heard.

3. *Affricate.* Similar to a plosive consonant, but the release of the air is less sudden, so that it sounds like a plosive consonant followed by a fricative.

4. *Nasal.* The breath is completely stopped in the mouth (as for the plosive consonants) but is permitted to come through the nose.

5. *Semi-vowel.* Like vowel-sounds, but so short that they form only a glide to the following sound, and are treated as consonants.

In addition there are two English consonant sounds which cannot be placed in any of the above categories.

VOICED AND VOICELESS SOUNDS. Sounds may be produced with vibration of the vocal chords (voiced sounds) or without vibration (voiceless sounds). As a result there are many pairs of consonants which have the same formation in the mouth but are distinguished by being voiced in one case, voiceless in the other.

Voiceless	1. PLOSIVE CONSONANTS	*Voiced*
	Breath stopped by:	
p	Lower lip against upper lip.	b
t	Tongue against teeth-ridge.	d
k	Back of tongue against roof of mouth.	g
	2. FRICATIVE CONSONANTS *Air-passage narrowed between:*	
f	Lower lip and upper teeth.	v
θ	Tip of tongue and upper teeth.	ð
s	Tip of tongue and teeth ridge.	z
∫	Front of tongue and back of teeth-ridge, with wider opening than for [s, z].	ӡ
	3. AFFRICATE CONSONANTS	
t∫	Like [∫] and [ӡ] but tip of tongue touching teeth-ridge to make a complete stop at first.	dӡ
tr	Like [r] but tip of tongue touching teeth-ridge to make a complete stop at first. In [tr] the [r] also is voiceless; the [r] element has more friction than [r] alone.	dr

Voiceless	4. Nasal Consonants	*Voiced*
	Nasal passage open and	
	Mouth stopped as for [p], [b]	m
	Mouth stopped as for [t], [d]	n
	Mouth stopped as for [k], [g]	ŋ
	5. Semi-Vowels	
	Like very short [u]. Lips rounded.	w
	Like very short [i].	j
	Wider opening than for [ʃ] [ʒ]; tip of tongue curled back, but retracted from the teeth-ridge so that there is little or no friction. Body of tongue lowered.	r
	6. Other Consonants	
	Tip of tongue touching teeth or teeth-ridge, sides of tongue lowered. As the body of the tongue is free to take up many different positions in the mouth, it is possible to pronounce as many varieties of [l] as there are vowel sounds. In English we may distinguish two varieties—an [i]-like [l] that occurs at the beginning of a word or syllable (*leaf, laugh*) and a 'darker' [u]-like [l] that occurs finally or before a consonant (*feel, milk*).	l
h	Breath only, the mouth in position to articulate the following vowel.	

Note on [r]. By speakers of R.P., this sound is pronounced *only before a vowel sound*. It does therefore not occur in words like *card, worth, form* [kaːd, wəːθ, foːm], in words like *father, near, tore* pronounced in isolation ['faːðə, niə, toː], or in the sentences: 'He was near the door'; 'He tore the paper'. But [r] *is* pronounced in 'Fathe*r* ate them'; 'fa*r* away'; 'nea*r* and far'; 'fo*r* ever', since in these examples the words are pronounced without a break, and the sound immediately following the letter *r* is a vowel.

DOUBLE CONSONANTS

Double consonants rarely occur within English words. Even when two consonant letters are written (e.g. *bitter, banner, follow*), only a single consonant is pronounced. Double consonants may, however, occur in compound words or where a word ending with a consonant is followed by a word beginning with a similar consonant, e.g. *pen-knife* [pen-naif], *full load* [ful loud], *bad dream* [bad driːm]. In these circumstances a consonant of double length is pronounced. When two plosive consonants are brought together in this way, there is usually only one explosion, but the stop is held longer than for a single consonant, e.g. *bed time, big dog, sit down, what time?*

LENGTH OF SOUNDS

1. *Vowels and Diphthongs*

All the diphthongs, and the vowels containing the 'length mark' [ː] in their phonetic symbol[1] (iː, aː, oː, uː, əː) may be given greater length in certain positions. These are (*a*) when they are followed by a *voiced* consonant; (*b*) when they are in an open syllable at the end of the word. (Note that these are the *only* vowel sounds which can occur at the end of a word in a stressed syllable.)

Thus the vowel in:

bee [biː] and *bead* [biːd] is longer than the vowel in *beat* [biːt].
car [kaː], *card* [kaːd] is longer than the vowel in *cart* [kaːt].
saw [soː], *sword* [soːd] is longer than that in *sought* [soːt].
bow [bau], *bowed* [baud] is longer than that in *bout* [baut].
play [plei], *played* [pleid] is longer than that in *plate* [pleit].

[1] The vowel [a] may also be lengthened in the speech of many speakers.

When a voiceless consonant closes the syllable, these vowels and diphthongs are very little longer than other vowels in the same position. Thus there is little difference in the *length* of the vowels in the following pairs of words:

beat [biːt], *bit* [bit]; *foot* [fut], *boot* [buːt]; *short* [ʃɔːt], *shot* [ʃot]; *bite* [bait], *but* [bʌt]; *reach* [riːtʃ], *rich* [ritʃ].

2. *Consonants*

The consonants [l], [m], [n] and [ŋ] are similarly lengthened at the end of a word or before a final voiced consonant. Thus:

killed [kilːd][1]	kill [kilː]	kilt [kilt]
hummed [hʌmːd]	hum [hʌmː]	hump [hʌmp]
things [θiŋːz]	thing [θiŋː]	think [θiŋk]
wind [winːd]	win [winː]	wince [wins]

STRESS

Stress is the prominence given to certain syllables by variations in the pitch of the voice (intonation) and by the use of greater breath force. A syllable may have *main stress*, indicated in this section by the sign (ˈ) placed before the stressed syllable; or *secondary stress*, indicated by (ˈ) or (ˌ), depending on whether it is high-pitched or low-pitched; or it may be *unstressed*.[2]

When a syllable has main stress, it carries one of the rising or falling tones that characterize the intonation tunes described on pp. 412–415. When we quote monosyllabic words in isolation, we generally give them main stress and say them with a falling tone. When we quote words of two or more syllables in the same way, we give main stress (generally with a falling

---

[1] The [ː] is here a sign of extra length.

[2] In R. Kingdon's *The Groundwork of English Stress*, where the subject is fully treated, the term 'Kinetic stress' is used for main stress, and the terms 'Full Static stress' and 'Partial Static stress', are used respectively for the high-pitched and the low-pitched varieties of secondary stress.

O

tone) to one of the syllables. The main stress is on the first syllable in : 'orange, 'custom, 'picture, 'yellow. It is on the second syllable in : in'tend, for'get, ex'plain, a'gain.

When a syllable has secondary stress, it does not carry a rising or a falling tone (except when it forms part of certain complex tones) but it is said on a level pitch, which may be high or low depending on its place in the intonation tune that is being used. The following words have a main stress, a secondary stress, and one or more unstressed syllables: 'civili'zation, ex'ami'nation, 'photo₁graph, 'budgeri₁gar.

The principles governing the incidence of stress in English words are rather complex. The following points, however, may be of help:

1. In words of Germanic origin, the main stress is generally on the root. The prefixes *be-*, *for-*, *a-*, are unstressed. Thus: be'gin, be'low, for'get, for'lorn, a'sleep, a'cross, a'skew.

2. In words of Latin or Greek origin ending in *-sion, -tion, -ial, -ic(al), -ian, -ture*, the main stress is generally on the syllable preceding these endings. If this brings the main stress later than the second syllable a secondary stress is placed on one of the first two syllables. Thus: 'vision, pre-'cision, 'civili'zation, po'sition, 'bene'ficial, i'nitial, e'lectric(al), his'toric(al), 'photo'graphic, phy'sician, mu'sician, ad'venture, en'rapture, ex'ami'nation.

3. Two-syllable words which may serve as nouns or as verbs often have the main stress on the first syllable when nouns, and on the second when verbs, e.g.

Noun: 'produce, 'record, 'export, 'conduct.
Verb: pro'duce, re'cord, ex'port, con'duct.

Some two-syllable words have both syllables stressed (the second with main stress, the first with high secondary stress). When one of these syllables occurs next to another stressed syllable, it frequently loses its stress. Thus we say (in isolation): 'un'known, 'prin'cess, 'fif'teen; but (in context): 'Princess 'Margaret, the 'young prin'cess, the 'unknown 'soldier, 'two-fif'teen.

STRESS IN CONNECTED SPEECH
(SENTENCE STRESS)

In connected speech, words are not treated as separate units; they form themselves into intonation groups. In each intonation group generally only one syllable, belonging to the word to which the speaker is giving most prominence, will have main stress; the other words will have their normal main stresses weakened to secondary stresses or will be completely unstressed. The words which are frequently unstressed in speech [1] are the articles, the personal, possessive and relative pronouns, the parts of the verb "be", auxiliary verbs immediately preceding their main verbs, some conjunctions and some prepositions (except when final). So we say:

'What are you 'thinking a‚bout?

He should have 'finished it 'earlier.

He 'asked for his 'hat and 'coat.

RHYTHM

There is a strong tendency in English speech to make the stressed syllables occur at approximately regular intervals of time. · Thus the three sentences in each of the following groups, though differing from each other in number of syllables, take approximately the same time to say, because they have the same number of stressed syllables:

1. I 'saw the 'car 'last 'night.
   I in'spected the 'car 'yesterday 'evening.
   I should have in'spected the 'vehicle 'yesterday 'evening.

2. 'Please 'pass 'that 'book.
   'Kindly 'give me 'that 'book.
   'Kindly pre'sent him with the 'other 'book.

[1] Many of these words undergo changes in their sounds when unstressed. For the 'weak forms' see D. Jones, *English Pronouncing Dictionary*, and H. E. Palmer, *A Grammar of Spoken English*, sections 15 ff.

This characteristic of English may be compared to musical rhythm as represented by bar-lines. There may be any number of notes in a bar of music, but the accented notes (the first in each bar) will fall at regular intervals of time.

INTONATION

There is a close association, as we have seen, between stress and intonation [1]—the rise and fall in the pitch of the voice when speaking. In English, certain patterns or tunes of intonation tend to be associated with different types of sentence or utterance. The intonation may also indicate the speaker's *attitude* to what he is saying (e.g. degree of excitement, interest, surprise) or to his listener (e.g. apology, sympathy, impatience).

We can distinguish three basic intonation tunes:[2]

Falling Tune

(A) ˈGive it to me. ˈCome ˋhere. ˈPlease come ˈhere imˈmediately.

(B) ˈNo. He ˈwent aˈway ˈyesterday. He's   ˈremedying it.

(C) ˈWhy? ˈWhat do you ˋwant? ˈHow ˋare you?

ˈWhen did you ˈcome here?

---

[1] For fuller treatment of intonation see: R. Kingdon, *The Groundwork of English Intonation;* and for practice sentences, W. S. Allen, *Living English Speech*, and R. Kingdon, *English Intonation Practice.*

[2] The two horizontal lines represent the upper and lower limits of the speaking voice. A line is used for a stressed syllable, a dot for an unstressed syllable.

As will be seen from the examples, stressed syllables which precede the syllable with main stress (i.e. that on which the fall occurs) will be high-pitched at the beginning of the sentence, gradually descending as the main stress is approached. Unstressed syllables are generally said on a low tone if at the beginning of the sentence, and otherwise on the same pitch as the preceding stressed syllable; syllables following the main stress are low-pitched. The Falling Tune is used for: (A) commands; (B) simple statements of fact; (C) questions introduced by a "question-word" (i.e. When? Where? Why? What? Which? How? Who(m)? Whose?) In statements and commands it often suggests abruptness and finality.

Rising Tune

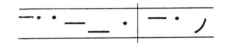

(D) 'As I had 'just ˌstarted . . . 'On the ˌwhole . . .

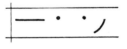

'When you arˌrive . . .

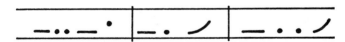

(E) . . . ˌif I reˌmember . . . ˌon the ˌwhole. . . . ˌwhen you arˌrive.

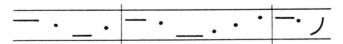

(F) 'Have you 'finished? 'Can you 'fix it for me?   'Is it 'true?

In this tune, the syllable with main stress—indicated by the sign (,) or (')—will, if it is the last syllable of the sentence or group, begin on a low pitch and rise sharply. If it is not the last syllable, it will be said on a low pitch, and the rise will be spread over the following syllables. Stressed and unstressed syllables preceding the main stress are treated as in the Falling Tune. The Rising Tune is used for: (D) subordinate clauses and phrases preceding the main clause and forming an intonation group separate from it; (E) similar clauses and phrases following the main clause; (F) questions that can be answered by 'Yes' or 'No'. In statements the tune frequently suggests incompleteness. In questions the rise is usually carried to a higher point than in statements.

Falling-Rising Tune

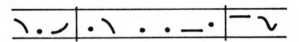

(G) 'Very ,well. I 'can't come to,morrow. 'Not ᵛnow.

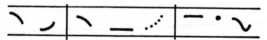

(H) 'Sit ,down. 'Come ,here, please. 'Wait for ᵛme.

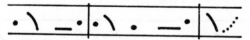

(I) I'm 'so ,sorry. I 'beg your ,pardon. ᵛSorry.

In this tune one word may take the fall, and a later one the rise, or the fall-rise may be concentrated on one word if it is the last word of the sentence; in this latter case it is shown by the sign (ᵛ). This tune is used: (G) for hesitant statements or those containing an implication, or where the Falling Tune would give the impression of abruptness; (H) for polite requests; (I) for apologies.

A variation of this tune is used to give special prominence to one word with the implication of contrast with some other word. Then the fall may be replaced by a rise-fall. If the prominent word is at end of the sentence, the resulting rise-fall-rise may occur on one word or even on one syllable; it is then shown by the sign (ᐱ).

(J) ᐱI don't ₍want it. It 'isn't the ᐱmoney that's im₍portant.

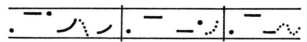

(K) I 'didn't ᐱmean ₍that. It's 'not ᐱdifficult. It's 'not ᐱhard.

EXERCISES

  I Which type of English pronunciation do you think it is best for you to learn?   Give reasons.

  II In each of the following groups of words, one has a different vowel (or diphthong) sound from the two others. Pick out this word and show the difference by using phonetic symbols:

    (1) bread, neck, snake. (2) live, leave, keep. (3) have, men, bad. (4) luck, come, put. (5) all, coal, law. (6) good, food, root. (7) cart, bath, bag. (8) cow, no, low. (9) hear, clear, bear. (10) caught, what, short.

  III Write the following passage, crossing out the letter 'r' each time that it is *not* pronounced as a consonant [r]:

    It occurred to me that I had never seen a pair of men more fitted for their chosen work. They were loyal to each other, and if they brought off a success for the College, they would each attribute it to the other. But most men considered that C. was the dominating spirit. He had a streak of fierceness, and the virility which attracts respect—and resentment—from other men.

IV Say in which of the following words the vowel (or diphthong) sound will be lengthened by the consonant which follows it:

Wheat, big, seed, cloud, clothes, rise, shoot.

V (a) Mark the main stress (and, where appropriate, secondary stress) in the following words:

operative, geographer, biographical, civilization, beginning, inclination, develop, eligibility, sympathetic.

(b) The following words can be stressed either on the first or on the second syllable. Show how the resulting pairs differ in meaning and pronunciation:

refuse, frequent, present, rebel, object.

VI (a) Mark the main stresses in the following sentences.

(b) Name, or show, the Intonation Tunes that would normally be used in speaking them.

(1) Can you remember the name of the manager?
(2) But where's the money that I left on the table?
(3) Don't be afraid. Come over here and sit down.
(4) I don't think you'll manage to cut it with *that* knife. Why don't you borrow mine?
(5) Although I should have liked to see her, it was impossible for me to go there.
(6) The big, brown book with the leather binding was written by a former Prime Minister.
(7) What I can never understand is why he comes here at all.
(8) He can certainly swim well, but he can't ride a bicycle.
(9) Wouldn't you like some more of these delicious chocolates?
(10) Get out of my sight and never dare to come near my house again!

CHAPTER THIRTY

A BRIEF HISTORY OF THE ENGLISH LANGUAGE

When the Romans came to Britain, first under Julius Caesar in 55 B.C. and later under Claudius in A.D. 42, they found a race of Celtic people, the Britons, in occupation. These Britons resisted the Romans fiercely on the shores of south-east England but they were finally conquered and driven back. The Romans were not the first invaders of the country. The Britons themselves had come as invaders and they had been preceded by others, but until the coming of the Romans no written record of these influxes had been made. Gradually the invader occupied the greater part of the country, but soon he came up against the obstacle that had no doubt held up earlier invaders and was to hold up later ones—the mountains of Wales and Scotland. Among the mountains the Britons took refuge and here the invader was forced to come to a stop.

During the next four hundred years, though England became a Roman colony, Wales and N.W. Scotland remained largely unconquered. The Romans made their magnificent roads into Wales (Watling Street went from London to Anglesey), they built camps at Caernarvon (Segontium) and at Caerleon, and great walls to keep back the Scots. But outside the camps and beyond the Wall, the Roman influence was hardly felt, the old Celtic language was spoken and Latin never became a spoken language there as it did in England, at any rate in the larger towns.

In A.D. 410 the Romans left Britain; their soldiers were needed to defend Rome itself against the Goths. It was then that the Angles and Saxons and Jutes came and seized the undefended Britain. And they came to stay. Once more the Britons of England were driven to the mountains of Wales and Scotland, W. Ireland and the Isle of Man, to Cornwall or Brittany.

THE CELTIC ELEMENT

The language spoken by those Britons has developed into Welsh, spoken by the people of Wales; Gaelic, spoken in

o*

parts of the Highlands of Scotland; Erse, spoken in Ireland; and Breton, spoken in Brittany in France. There is still some Manx spoken in the Isle of Man, but it is dying out; and there used to be a Cornish language, but this died out in the eighteenth century. Welsh and Erse, Gaelic, Breton and Manx, though they come from the same ancestor, are not of course the same language, but a Welshman would probably be understood (with difficulty) by a Breton, and a Manxman might make something of a speech in Gaelic or Erse. But if an Englishman heard a speech in any of these languages he would not understand a single word of it, for the English that he speaks comes, not from the Britons who withstood the Romans, but from the Angles who made Britain 'Angle-land'; and English took practically nothing from the old Celtic language. The words *ass*, *brock* (= a badger), *bannock* (= a loaf of home-made bread) and *bin* (= a manger) are probably survivals of British words, and there have been importations into English at a later date; from Welsh: *druid*, *flannel*, *gull*, *bard;* from Scotch Gaelic: *cairn*, *clan*, *plaid*, *whisky;* and from Irish: *brogue*, *shamrock*, *galore*.

But something of Celtic has been fossilized in numerous place names. Ten of our rivers still have the beautiful name of *Avon*, from the Celtic word for *river;* and *Esk*, *Ex*, *Usk*, *Ouse*, *Aire* are all from the word for 'water'. The *Don* and the *Doune* (like the *Danube*[1]) are from another old Celtic word for *water*. *Stour*, *Tees*, *Trent*, *Wye* and *Wey* are all Celtic names. The Celtic *dun* (= a protected place) can be seen in *Dun*dee, *Dun*bar and in the old name for Edinburgh, *Dun*edin; *Kill* (= a church) in *Kil*dare, *Kil*kenny; *-combe* (cwm) (= a hollow) in Ilfra*combe*, *Combe* Martin; *caer* (= a castle) in *Caer*leon, *Car*lisle, *Car*diff; and *-llan* (= holy) in *Llan*gollen, *Llan*dudno. The names *London*, *Dover*, *York*, *Glasgow* are British, and so is the first part of *Dor*chester, *Glou*cester, *Man*chester, *Win*chester, *Salis*bury, to which has been added the old English *ceaster* (from the Latin *castra* = a camp) or *-burgh* (= a fort).

THE ANGLO-SAXON ELEMENT

The story of English in England, therefore, begins in the first half of the fifth century when the invaders came, the Angles

---

[1] *German* Donau.

from Schleswig, the Saxons from Holstein, the Jutes from Jutland. The language they all spoke belonged to the Germanic speech family. This in turn was separated into three main families: EAST GERMANIC, which died out with Gothic about the eighth century;[1] NORTH GERMANIC, which developed into Swedish, Norwegian, Danish and Icelandic; and WEST GERMANIC, from which are descended Dutch, Flemish, Friesian and English. But the Germanic languages are merely one branch of another great family, the Indo-European, which comprises most of the languages of Europe and India. The parent Indo-European language began several thousands of years B.C., probably in South Europe near the Asian border. It spread West into Europe and East into India, splitting and modifying into various forms as it spread and came into contact with other languages of different origin. As a result of these divisions there are two main groups of languages in the Indo-European family: there is the Western group, containing Germanic, Celtic, Greek, Latin; and there is the Eastern group containing Balto-Slavonic, Indo-Iranian, Albanian and Armenian. The chart on page 421 will show the modern descendants of Indo-European and their relationship to each other.

The language that these invaders of England spoke was a west Germanic member of the Indo-European languages. We generally term it 'Anglo-Saxon'. The Jutes settled in Kent, Southern Hampshire and the Isle of Wight; the Saxons in the rest of Southern England south of the Thames; the Angles in the land north of the Thames. Each of the three tribes spoke a different form of their common language, and so in England ('Britain' had now become 'Englaland', 'the land of the Angles') three different dialects developed—or rather four dialects, for very soon two forms grew up in the North, one spoken north of the Humber (Northumbrian), the other south of the Humber (Mercian). The dialect of the Saxons was called West Saxon, that of the Jutes was called Kentish. At first it was the Northumbrian with its centre at York that developed the highest standard of culture. It was in Northumbria in the eighth century that Caedmon, the first great English poet,

---

[1] But the Gothic of the Crimea lasted until about 1500. Practically the only writings that we have of Gothic are fragments of a translation of the Bible made by Bishop Ulfilas (A.D. 311–81).

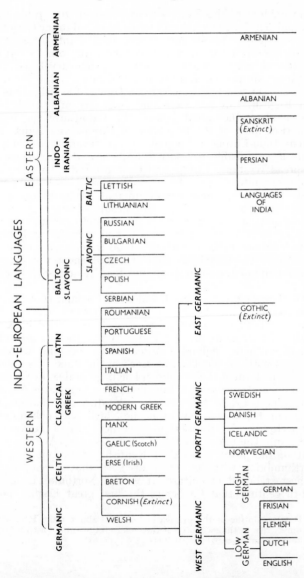

wrote his poetry, and it was into Northumbrian that the
Venerable Bede translated the gospel of St. John. Then for a
time under Alfred the Great (848–901), who had his capital in
Winchester and who encouraged learning in his kingdom and also
was himself a great writer, West Saxon became pre-eminent.
It remained pre-eminent until Edward the Confessor held his
court not in Winchester but in Westminster. Then London
became the capital of the country; and from Mercian, the
dialect spoken in London—and at Oxford and Cambridge—
came the standard English that we speak today. But the
language of England in the time of Alfred bears little resem-
blance to the language of today.

Anglo-Saxon or Old English[1] was an inflected language, but
not so highly inflected as Greek, Latin or Gothic. Thus there
were five cases of nouns (Nominative, Vocative, Accusative,
Genitive, Dative), 'strong' and 'weak' declensions for adjectives (each with five cases); there was a full conjugation of
verbs—complete with Subjunctive—and there was a system
of grammatical gender. So in Old English *hand* was feminine,
fot (= foot) was masculine, but *heafod* (= head) was neuter;
wif (= wife) was neuter, but *wifmann* (= woman) was
masculine; *dæg* (= day) was masculine but *niht* (= night)
was feminine.

Most of that has changed. In modern English, as you have
seen, grammatical gender of nouns has completely disappeared,
adjectives no longer 'agree' with their nouns in number, case
and gender, nouns have only two cases, verbs very few forms,
and the subjunctive has practically disappeared. Most of these
changes were caused, or at any rate hastened, by the two other
invasions of England.

THE DANISH ELEMENT

The first of these was by the 'Northmen' or Danes. Towards
the close of the eighth century they appeared, first as raiders,
then as conquerors and settlers. For a time they were held at
bay by Alfred and the country was divided, the northern half
or 'Danelaw' being ruled by the Danes, the southern half by

[1] The history of English is divided into three sections: *Old English*,
from the earliest written documents to the end of the seventh century;
Middle English, seventh century to 1500; *Modern English*, 1500 to
present day.

Alfred; but in 1016, after Alfred's death, a Danish King, Canute, became King of all England as well as of Denmark and Norway.

The language spoken by the Danes was not unlike the language of England—words like *mother* and *father*, *man* and *wife*, *summer* and *winter*, *house, town, tree, land, grass, come, ride, see, think, will* and a host of others, were common to both languages, and Saxon and Dane could more or less understand each other. But though the languages were similar, the endings were different; and, as the roots of the words were the same in both languages, Saxon and Dane found they could understand each other better if the inflectional endings tended to be levelled to the same form and ultimately to be dropped altogether.

There were, too, some positive gains in vocabulary and grammar. The word *law* is Danish, so are *leg, skin, skull, knife, sky* and *Thursday*. The Old English plural pronouns *hi, hiera, hem* were very like the singular forms *he, hiere, him*, so it was a great advantage when the Danish plural forms *they, their, them* ousted them.

Among adjectives from Danish there are *flat, happy, low, ugly, weak* and *wrong;* among verbs *want, call, cut, die, lift* and *take*. The Danish *are* replaced the Anglo-Saxon *sindon*, and *same* replaced *thilke*, and it is because of the Danes that today we say *eggs* instead of the Saxon *eyren* and speak of a *window* (old Norse *vindauga* = wind-eye) and not, as the Saxons did, of an *eye-thril* (= eye-hole), though we do say *nostril* ('nose-hole').

An interesting feature of the language is a number of Danish forms existing side by side with, and usually with a different meaning from, the English forms, e.g.

English	*Danish*	*English*	*Danish*
shirt	skirt	rear	raise
no	nay	from	fro
drop	drip	blossom	bloom
sit	seat		

THE NORMAN ELEMENT

There was still one other invasion which was to play a major part in the shaping of the English language, that of the

Normans. We generally date the Norman-French period in English history from the invasion by William the Conqueror in 1066, but Norman influence had appeared before then. The Saxon King Ethelred the Unready (reigned 978–1016) had married a Norman princess, and his son Edward the Confessor (1042–1066), who reigned after him, had been brought up in France, with the result that a number of French words had come into the language before William the Conqueror became King of England.

The Normans were descended from the same fierce warrior race of 'Norsemen' as had harried England a century before the coming of the Conqueror. In 912 Rollo the Rover was given Normandy by the French King Charles the Simple. With amazing vigour the Normans became one of the most highly organized states in the world. They adopted French as their language, embraced Christianity and became renowned for their learning, their military prowess and their organizing ability. After defeating the English king, Harold, at Hastings in 1066, William the Conqueror began to organize England on the Norman pattern. Many Frenchmen came to England bringing the rich learning and developed civilization of Normandy, and putting England into the full stream of European culture and thought. The Normans ruled with a hard hand, and the defeated Saxons suffered oppression and indignities. For the next three centuries all the Kings of England spoke French; all the power in Court and castle and Church was in the hands of the Normans, and the Normans organized from above the lives and activities of the common people. The language they spoke was French and they never dreamed of doing their organizing in any language except French or Latin. For about three hundred years two languages were spoken side by side in England. The 'official' language was French; English was spoken only by the 'common' people.

Robert of Gloucester, writing about 1300, says:

'So, England came into Normandy's hand; and the Normans spoke French just as they did at home, and had their children taught in the same manner so that people of rank in this country who came of their blood all stick to the same language; for if a man knows no French, people will think little of him. But the lower classes still stick to English as their own language. I imagine there is no country in the world that doesn't keep its own language except England. But it is well known that it is the best thing to know both languages, for the more a man knows the more he is worth.'

The language of Saxon times was being changed, but it was in no danger of dying out; and the changes were all to the good.

Ultimately Norman and Saxon united to form one nation, but it had taken more than three centuries. The turning point was perhaps marked in 1362 when for the first time Edward III opened Parliament in English. At the same time the Statute of Pleading enacted that proceedings in law courts should be in English because 'French has become much unknown in this realm'. In 1415 the English ambassadors who represented Henry V could not speak French, and the papers they had to sign were written in Latin. Henry himself said, according to Shakespeare, as he tried to woo Katherine: 'It is as easy for me, Kate, to conquer the Kingdom as to speak so much more French.'

When finally English emerged as the language of England, it had been greatly modified by the vicissitudes through which it had gone. The gradual dropping of inflectional endings and the general grammatical simplification which, we noticed, had begun in the time of the Danes, had gone on and had been greatly accelerated by the collision with French and by the fact that English had for three centuries been almost entirely a *spoken* language, no longer restrained and kept from change by literary models. The changes were striking and revolutionary. The language had now got rid of grammatical gender—a feat that so far as we can tell no other language in the world has achieved. Case endings of nouns had been reduced to one, the Genitive or Possessive; prepositions had taken the place of inflectional endings. Plural forms, though not made entirely regular, had been made much fewer, verb forms had been simplified, and the whole language had been made much more flexible and expressive.

All this was more or less the accidental or indirect result of the Norman Conquest. What was its more direct effect? There is no doubt that its greatest impact was on the vocabulary. The language emerged with its essential structure still Germanic. But an examination of the vocabulary of modern

English will show that approximately 50 per cent. of the words in it are of French or Latin origin, and half of these were adopted between 1250 and 1400. Nevertheless, despite this tremendous French element, English remains fundamentally Anglo-Saxon, for though it is easy enough to make sentences on ordinary subjects without using a single word of French or Latin origin, it is practically impossible to make even a short sentence without using Saxon words.

The borrowings throw an interesting light on the social history of the times.

> 'In it (the English language) as it were, there lies fossilized or still showing the signs of the freshness of the assimilation, the whole of English history, external and internal, political and social.'[1]

If all other sources of knowledge about the Normans were lost, we could almost re-construct the times from an examination of the language of today. We should know, for example, that the Normans were the ruling race, for almost all the words expressing government (including *government* itself) are of French origin. It is true that the Normans left the Saxon words *king* and *queen, earl, lord* and *lady;* but *prince, sovereign, throne, crown, royal, state, country, people, nation, parliament, duke, count, chancellor, minister, council* and many other such words are all Norman. So too are such words as *honour, glory, courteous, duty, polite, conscience, noble, pity, fine, cruel,* etc., words expressing the new ideas of chivalry and refinement (both, again, Norman words). From their activity in building (in the 'Norman style') and architecture came *arch, pillar, palace, castle, tower,* etc.; from their interest in warfare we got: *war, peace, battle, armour, officer, soldier, navy, captain, enemy, danger, march, company,* to mention but a few. The Normans were great law-givers, and though *law* itself is Scandinavian, the words *justice, judge, jury, court, cause, crime, traitor, assize, prison, tax, money, rent, property, injury* are all of French origin. By the thirteenth century there was a certain amount of translation of the Scriptures and of sermons from Latin into English by Norman monks. In making these translations it was often easier to adopt the Latin word, generally in French guise, than to hunt round for the Saxon equivalent. So a large number

---

[1] *The English Language,* C. L. Wrenn (Methuen).

of French words connected with religion came into the language: *religion, service, saviour, prophet, saint, sacrifice, miracle, preach, pray.*

The names of nearly all articles of luxury and pleasure are Norman; the simpler things are English. There was the Norman *castle* and *city;* but *town* and *hamlet, home* and *house* are English. The Norman had his *relations, ancestors* and *descendants;* but the English words are *father* and *mother, sister, brother, son* and *daughter.* The Norman had *pleasure, comfort, ease, delight;* the Englishman had *happiness* and *gladness* and *work.* The names of great things of Nature, if not of art, are English: the *sun,* the *moon,* the *stars, winds, morning* and *evening,* the *plough,* the *spade, wheat, oats, grass;* the Norman had *fruit* and *flowers, art, beauty, design, ornament.*

The lowly English worker was a *shoemaker, shepherd, miller, fisherman, smith* or *baker;* the men who came more in contact with the rulers were *tailors, barbers, painters, carpenters.* The Normans used *chairs, tables* and *furniture;* the Englishman had only the humble *stool.* The Norman ate the big *dinner, feast, supper,* at which food could be *boiled, fried, roasted;* the Englishman had the simpler *breakfast.* The whole situation is given in a very interesting passage in Scott's *Ivanhoe,* where Wamba points out to Gurth that the names of almost all the animals while they are alive are English, but when they are prepared for food they are Norman. In other words, the poor Saxon had all the work and trouble of looking after them while they were alive; but when there was the pleasure of eating them, the Englishman's *cow, bull* or *ox* became French *beef;* his *sheep* and *lamb* became French *mutton;* his *swine* or *pig* became *pork* or *bacon;* his *calf* turned to *veal,* and the *deer* (which he would be hanged for killing) went to Norman tables as *venison.*

The close relationship both for peace and war that England and France have always had from Norman times until the present has resulted in a constant influx of French words into the language. In the thirteenth century the University of Paris, the most renowned of its time, attracted English scholars and incidentally led to the founding of Oxford. It is interesting to note that at that time the pronunciation of the French of Paris was different from Anglo-Norman French. (Chaucer's Prioress, it will be remembered, spoke French 'after the scole of Stratford-atte-Bowe. For Frenssh of Paris was to hire unknowe'.)[1] So we have occasionally two English words, both derived from the same French word, but borrowed at different times, and, as a result, having different pronunciations and usually slightly different meanings. They are known as 'doublets'. Examples are: *warden, guardian;*[2] *warranty, guarantee; cattle, chattel; catch, chase.*

French words that came early into the language became fully anglicized both in accent and pronunciation. The later importations, say from the sixteenth century onwards, failed to achieve this complete incorporation into the language. A feature of Old English, and of the Germanic group generally, was that in words of more than one syllable the accent is on the first syllable. And we have that accentuation in early borrowings from French such as *virtue, nature, honour, favour, courage, reason, captain.* Words like *campaign, connoisseur, façade, ménage* have not yet acquired this accentuation. Again, words like *table, chair, castle, grocer, beauty* are so completely 'English' that it gives us almost a shock of surprise to realize that they have not always been native words. But with *amateur, soufflet, valet, chef* we do not have that feeling. The word *garage* is in a half-way stage. We are not quite sure whether it ought to be pronounced ['garaːʒ], [gəˈraːʒ] or whether, like *carriage* or *marriage*, it has reached anglicization as 'garidʒ]. Compare again the words of early borrowing, *chief, choiʻe, chapel, cherish, chimney, Charles* (where the 'ch' is pronounced [tʃ]) with the later ones *chef, chaperon, champagne, chauffeur, chandelier, Charlotte,* where the 'ch' is [ʃ]. Similarly, the 'g' pronounced [dʒ] in *rage, siege, age, judge,* dates these as old borrowings that have become anglicized, whereas the 'g' pronounced [ʒ], in *rouge, mirage, sabotage, camouflage* shows that these are more recent borrowings. Or compare the vowels in *suit* and *suite;*[3] *vine* and *ravine; duty* and *debut; beauty* and *beau; count* and *tour.*

In almost every century since Norman times French words

---

[1] *scole* = school, *hire* = her, *unknowe* = unknown.

Stratford atte Bowe. There was a nunnery, about 300 years old in Chaucer's time, at Bromley near Stratford-le-Bow (now called 'Bow' simply), London.

[2] The first word of each pair is Norman-French, the second is later French.

[3] The first of each pair of words is an early borrowing; the second a late one.

have entered the language. In the sixteenth we took, among many others: *pilot, rendez-vous, volley, vase, moustache, machine;* in the seventeenth: *reprimand, ballet, burlesque, champagne, naïve, muslin, soup, group, quart;* in the eighteenth: *emigré, guillotine, corps, espionage, depot, bureau, canteen, rouge, rissole, brunette, picnic, police;* in the nineteenth: *barrage, chassis, parquet, baton, rosette, profile, suede, cretonne, restaurant, menu, chauffeur, fiancée, prestige, débâcle;* and in this century we continue with *garage, camouflage, hangar, revue.*

An interesting effect of the French, particularly the Norman, element has been to give the language a sort of bilingual quality, with two words, one of Saxon origin and one of French origin, to express roughly the same meaning. Thus we have *foe* and *enemy;*[1] *friendship* and *amity; freedom* and *liberty; unlikely* and *improbable; homely* and *domesticated; happiness* and *felicity; fatherly* and *paternal; motherhood* and *maternity; bold* and *courageous; love* and *charity*, and a host of others. This duality has been turned to great use, for in practically no case are there any complete synonyms.[2] Quite often there is a difference of meaning, almost always there is a difference of association or emotional atmosphere; and the Saxon word has generally the deeper emotional content; it is nearer the nation's heart. *Brotherly love* is deeper than *fraternal affection; love* is stronger than *charity; help* expresses deeper need than *aid; a hearty welcome* is warmer than a *cordial reception.*

There is just one other rather interesting characteristic of Old English that largely died out with the coming of the Normans: that is its power and ingenuity in making compounds from its native words. Thus Old English had such words (replaced by the French word in brackets) as: *fore-elders*[3] (ancestors); *fair-hood* (beauty); *wanhope* (despair); *earth-tilth* (agriculture); *gold-hoard* (treasure); *book-hoard* (library); *star-craft* (astronomy); *learning-knight* (disciple); *leech-craft* (medicine); and the title of a moral treatise of about 1340 was *The Ayenbite of Inwit* (The 'again bite', i.e. 'remorse', of 'conscience').

---

[1] The first word in each pair is Saxon, the second French.

[2] A synonym is really a word that has the same meaning as another. It is probably true to say that no two words in English have exactly the same meaning or the same emotional connotation in all contexts. The term 'synonym' is often used for a word with *nearly* the same meaning as another one.

[3] The examples are given in modern spelling.

Since Norman times no other invader has come to England to impose an alien tongue on the country. But the stream of words has never ceased to flow in.

THE CLASSICAL ELEMENT

Both Latin and, to a lesser degree, Greek have been important contributors, though often Latin, and even oftener Greek, words have come in French form or via French or some other language. Some Latin words were taken into the language of the Angles and Saxons before these peoples came to England, e.g. *wine, cup, butter, cheese, silk, copper, street, pound, mile, plum*. A few came in during the Roman occupation and were learned by the English from Romanized Britons of the towns, chiefly place names like *ceaster* (Latin, *castra*). With the coming of Christian culture from Rome and Ireland in the sixth and seventh centuries numerous others came: *candle, monk, bishop* (Latin *episcopus*), *Mass*. In all about 400 Latin words became English before the Norman Conquest, but many of these are not commonly used.

In the Middle English period a number of technical or scientific terms were taken and given a wider application, e.g. *index, simile, pauper, equivalent, legitimate, diocese, tolerance*.

A great flood came with the Revival of Learning in the fifteenth and sixteenth centuries. For a time 'the whole Latin vocabulary became potentially English'. The English 'Grammar Schools' were schools where *Latin* grammar, not English grammar, was taught. Nor was it only a written language. It became a medium of international communication between scholars, and in the schools the boys spoke Latin—at least while their teacher was within earshot. Bacon and Newton wrote some of their books in Latin, writers like Milton and Sir Thomas Browne wrote magnificent but highly Latinized English; books to expound English grammar were written in Latin, and the English language was distorted to fit into the pattern of Latin grammar. Not all the words that were adopted then have lasted, but many of them have, for example in the sixteenth century: *specimen, focus, arena, album, minimum, lens, complex, pendulum;* in the eighteenth century: *nucleus, alibi, ultimatum, extra, insomnia, via, deficit;* in the nineteenth century: *ego, opus, referendum, bacillus*.

We have mentioned that many Latin words came through French. In the same way most Greek words came through Latin into French and English. Most of them were learned, technical or scientific words. At the time of the Revival of Learning many of the new ideas or branches of learning that the Renaissance brought were expressed by Greek words: *arithmetic, geometry, astronomy, grammar, logic, rhetoric, poetry, comedy, dialogue, prologue*. Of the more general terms that English had gained by the fifteenth century were: *Bible, academy, atom, tyrant, theatre*. In the sixteenth century came: *alphabet, drama, chorus, theory;* the seventeenth century contributed *orchestra, museum, hyphen, clinic*. Since then science, medicine, physics, chemistry and other sciences and arts have gone to Greek for their nomenclature, coining from Greek words that the Greeks never knew: *dynamo* and *psychology, zoology* and *telephone, photograph, bicycle, aeroplane, nitrogen, cosmetic* and *antiseptic*.

In addition there are a great number of words formed from Greek prefixes tacked on to words of English or other languages, like *anti* (= against): *anti*-British, *anti*podes; *hyper* (= beyond): *hyper*-critical, *hyper*bole; *arch* (= chief): *arch*bishop; *dia* (= through): *dia*meter, *dia*gonal; *hemi* (= half): *hemi*sphere; *homo* (= same): *homo*geneous; *homo*nym; *mono* (= single): *mono*plane, *mono*cle, *mono*tonous; *pan* (= all): *pan*tomime, *pan*theist; *poly* (= many): *poly*syllable, *poly*glot; *pro* (= before): *pro*phet, *pro*logue; *pseudo* (= false): *pseudo*nym; *syn* — *sym* (= with): *sym*pathy, *syn*thesis; *tele* (= at a distance): *tele*graph; *tri* (= three): *tri*pod, *tri*cycle. From suffixes, like *-ism*, we get Bolshev*ism*, vegetarian*ism;* from *-ology*, soci*ology*, radi*ology* and numerous others.

BORROWINGS FROM OTHER LANGUAGES

From almost every country in the world words have come into this language. Italy, for so long the centre of European culture, has given words to our vocabulary of music and architecture and poetry: *piano, piccolo, soprano, finale, solo, sonata, opera; palette, cameo, fresco, miniature, studio, model, vista; balcony, corridor, parapet, stucco; sonnet, stanza, canto*. But there have been more commonplace words, too, from Italy: *alarm, brigand, florin, pilgrim* (all before 1500), *umbrella, influenza, muslin, duel, milliner* and *monkey*.

From Spanish we have: *cargo, cigar, cigarette, cork.* English seamen clashed with Spanish ones in the sixteenth and seventeenth centuries and we see the evidence of this in *ambuscade, desperado, dispatch, grandee, renegade. Alligator* is really the Spanish *el lagarto* = 'the lizard'. *Sherry* gets its name from the Spanish port of Jerez. From the voyages of the Elizabethan seamen to the New World we have *potato, tobacco, canoe* and *toboggan.* From Mexico came *chocolate, cocoa* (a mistake for *cacao*), *tomato. Cannibal* is said to have been brought to Europe by Columbus, and *hammock, hurricane, maize* are Caribbean words.

Portugal gave us *port* (wine) from Oporto, *marmalade, tank, buffalo, verandah, parasol, caste* and *firm*[1] (a business Company) and, from Portuguese exploration in Africa, *banana,* and *negro.*

We are reminded of the fame of Holland as a maritime nation by *yacht, buoy, freight, hull, dock, skipper, cruise* and *smuggle,* and of the rich school of Dutch and Flemish painting by: *landscape, easel, sketch.*

From India we have *pyjamas, shampoo, bangle, chutney, khaki, teak, bungalow, curry, ginger* and *chintz.* From Persian we get *bazaar, caravan, divan, jackal, jasmine, lilac* and *checkmate* in chess (*shāh māt* = the King is dead). From Arabic comes *admiral, alkali, lemon, alcohol, algebra, coffee, cotton, crimson* and *assassin. Tea* is from the Chinese; *bamboo, bantam, gong* and *sago* from Malaya. From Polynesia and Australasia we have *taboo, cockatoo, boomerang, kangaroo.*

No language seems to be so ready as English to absorb foreign words, perhaps because there has never been any self-conscious worship of 'pure English' that opposed the 'debasing' of the language by the introduction of new words. So when, for example, the potato was brought to Europe, the English used the native American word; the French on the other hand gave it a French name, *pomme de terre.* Even though there is already a word in English similar in meaning to the foreign one, English still takes in the foreign word. Take for example the words *preface, foreword, prologue* where French, Anglo-Saxon and Greek have contributed to expressing the same idea; or *proverb, saying* (or *saw*), *aphorism, precept, motto* where, in addition, Latin and Italian have also been enrolled. In the course of time each word acquires a slightly or even markedly

---

[1] But it may be from Spanish or Italian.

different meaning from the others. Almost any group of synonyms in the language would illustrate this; but to take one at random, here are thirty-seven 'synonyms' for the general idea of 'thief': *robber, burglar, house-breaker, pick-pocket, cut-purse, shop-lifter, pilferer, stealer, filcher, plunderer, pillager, despoiler, highwayman, footpad, brigand, bandit, marauder, depredator, purloiner, peculator, swindler, embezzler, defrauder, gangster, pirate, buccaneer, sharper, harpy, cracksman, crook, poacher, kidnapper, abductor, plagiarist, rifler, thug, welsher.*

This borrowing has made English a rich language with a vocabulary of already about half a million words, and growing daily. It is this wealth of near-synonyms which gives to English its power to express exactly the most subtle shades of meaning.

EXERCISES

I Name in historical order the languages that have left the deepest mark on English, and illustrate by examples in what sections of the English vocabulary their influence can be most clearly seen.

II How can you show by examples that during one important period of history there were two languages in simultaneous use in England by two different social classes?

III What other languages have most influenced English in the following fields of human activity:

Government, religion, law, music, medicine?

Quote several examples of these influences for each of the above.

IV Describe the effect on the English language of the fact that English was, for a long period in the Middle Ages, almost exclusively a *spoken* language.

V Compare and contrast, so far as may be possible, the development of the English language with that of your own, noting especially any sections of vocabulary in which your own language and English have been subject to the same influences.

VI Express your opinion for or against the idea that English occupies a unique position among languages in respect of the contributions made to it by other languages and its consequent richness of vocabulary.

INDEX

Words discussed are in *italics;* the names of various concepts (Commands, Futurity, Obligation, etc.), the expression of which is dealt with in this book, are in SMALL CAPITALS.

433